GOR

We hope you enjoy this book. Please return or renew it by the due date.

You can renew it at www.norfolk.gov.uk/libraries or by using our free library app.

Otherwise you can phone 0344 800 8020 - please have your library card and PIN ready.

You can sign up for email reminders too.

NORFOLK ITEM

30129 083 104 456

NORFOLK COUNTY COUNCIL
LIBRARY AND INFORMATION SERVICE

D1342218

ALSO BY MARTIN AMIS

Fiction

The Rachel Papers
Dead Babies
Success
Other People
Money
Einstein's Monsters
London Fields
Time's Arrow
The Information
Night Train
Heavy Water
Yellow Dog
House of Meetings
The Pregnant Widow
Lionel Asbo
The Zone of Interest

Non-Fiction

Invasion of the Space Invaders
The Moronic Inferno
Visiting Mrs Nabokov
Experience
The War Against Cliché
Koba the Dread
The Second Plane

MARTIN AMIS

The Rub of Time

Bellow, Nabokov, Hitchens, Travolta, Trump and Other Pieces, 1994–2016

VINTAGE

1 3 5 7 9 10 8 6 4 2

Vintage
20 Vauxhall Bridge Road,
London SW1V 2SA

Vintage is part of the Penguin Random House group of companies
whose addresses can be found at global.penguinrandomhouse.com

 Penguin
Random House
UK

First published by Vintage in 2018
First published in hardback by Jonathan Cape in 2017

penguin.co.uk/vintage

A CIP catalogue record for this book is available from the British Library

ISBN 9780099488729

Printed and bound in Great Britain by Clays Ltd, Elcograf S.p.A.

Penguin Random House is committed to a sustainable future
for our business, our readers and our planet. This book is
made from Forest Stewardship Council® certified paper.

To Isaac
and Eleanor

Contents

CONTENTS

Author's Note and Acknowledgements

The Natural Sin of Language

In the process of its composition, a lyric poem or a very short short story can reach the point where it ceases to be capable of improvement. Anything longer than a couple of pages – as John Updike will later remind us, in a phrase of T.S. Eliot's – will soon succumb to 'the natural sin of language', and will demand much more concentrated work. By the natural 'sin' of language I take it that Eliot is referring a) to its indocility (how it constantly and writhingly resists even the most practised hands), and b) to its promiscuity: in nearly all of its dealings language is as indiscriminate as currency, and gathers many deposits of silt and grit and sweat.

Poets are familiar with the sudden surmise that their revisions had better be discontinued (and quickly too), that their so-called improvements are starting to do real harm. Even the novelist shares this fear: you are nervously tampering with an inspiration that is going dead on you. Northrop Frye, a literary philosopher-king to whom I owe fealty, said that the begetter of a poem or a novel is more like a midwife than a mother: the aim is to get the child into the world with as little damage as possible – and if the creature is alive it will scream to be liberated from 'the navel strings and feeding tubes of the ego'.

Discursive prose, on the other hand (essays and reportage of the kind represented between these covers), cannot be cleansed of the ego, and is in any case limitlessly improvable. So I have done some cutting, quite a bit of adding (footnotes, postscripts), a lot of elaborating, and a great deal of polishing. Very often I am simply trying to make myself clearer, less ambiguous, and more precise – but not more prescient (I haven't massaged my political prophecies, which tend, as is usual with such things, to be instantly dismayed by events). There are some repetitions and duplications; I have let them stand, because I assume that most readers will pick and choose along the way in accordance with their own enthusiasms (only the reviewer, the proofreader, and of course the author will ever be obliged to read the whole thing straight through). Also, rather to my surprise, I have done some bowdlerising, making war not against the 'improper or offensive' so much as against the over-colloquial: those turns of phrase that seem shop-soiled almost as soon as they are committed to paper. The natural sin of language is cumulative and unavoidable; but we can at least expel the frailties of mere transience.

And my thanks to ...

First, to my friend of forty-five years, Tina Brown, who edited me at the *New Yorker, Talk*, and *Newsweek* (at the *New Yorker* I also relied on Bill Buford, Deborah Treisman, and Giles Harvey). To Craig Raine, my pal and one-time tutor, at *Areté*. To Sam Tannenhaus and Pamela Paul at the *New York Times Book Review*. To Eric Chotiner at the *New Republic*, and to Giles Harvey, again, after he moved to *Harper's*. To Lisa Allardice and also Ian Katz at the *Guardian*. To David Horspool and Oliver Ready at the *TLS*. To Eben Shapiro and Lisa Kalis at the *Wall Street Journal*. To Aimee Bell and Walter Owen at *Vanity Fair*. I have always been very lucky in my editorial helpmates, including the fact-checkers, grammarians, spelling inspectors, redactors, and sub-redactors. Not reflexively impatient with advice, I have never been tempted to use Clive James's (in fact unspoken) rebuke: 'Listen. If I wrote like that, I'd be you'. And of course salutations to my hardback editor-publishers, Dan Franklin at Cape and Gary Fisketjon at Knopf. My thanks to you all.

I would like to pay special tribute to Bobby Baird, the freelance editor (currently at *Esquire*) who took a mass of clippings, typescripts, attachments, and cyber-litter and turned it into a book. I am as low-tech as it is possible to be, and Bobby loomed in my eyes like the Creator – like him who fashioned a world out of chaos. In the lines of Ted Hughes's *Tales from Ovid*, Bobby 'forbade the winds / To use the air as they pleased' and 'educated' the 'rivers / To observe their banks'.

Brooklyn, October 2016

By Way of an Introduction

He's Leaving Home

Once upon a time, in a kingdom called England, literary fiction was an obscure and blameless pursuit. It was more respectable than angelology, true, and more esteemed than the study of phosphorescent mould; but it was without question a minority-interest sphere.

In 1972, I submitted my first novel: I typed it out on a second-hand Olivetti and sent it in from the sub-editorial office I shared at the *Times Literary Supplement*. The print run was 1,000 (and the advance was £250). It was published, and reviewed, and that was that. There was no launch party and no book tour; there were no interviews, no profiles, no photo shoots, no signings, no readings, no panels, no on-stage conversations, no Woodstocks of the Mind in Hay-on-Wye, in Toledo, in Mantova, in Parati, in Cartagena, in Jaipur, in Dubai; and there was no radio and no television. The same went for my second novel (1975) and my third (1978). By the time of my fourth novel (1981), nearly all the collateral activities were in place, and writers, in effect, had been transferred from vanity press to Vanity Fair.

What happened in the interim? We can safely say that as the 1970s became the 1980s there was no spontaneous flowering of enthusiasm for the psychological nuance, the artful simile, and the curlicued sentence. The phenomenon, as I now see it, was entirely media-borne. To put it crudely, the newspapers had been getting fatter and fatter (first the Sundays, then the Saturdays, then all the days in between), and what filled these extra pages was not additional news but additional features. And the featurists were running out of people to write about – running out of alcoholic actors, ne'er-do-well royals, depressive comedians, jailed rock stars, defecting ballet dancers, reclusive film directors, hysterical fashion models, indigent marquises, adulterous golfers, wife-beating footballers, and rapist boxers. The dragnet went on widening until journalists, often to their patent dismay, were writing about writers: literary writers.

This modest and perhaps temporary change in status involved a number of costs and benefits. A storyteller is nothing without a listener, and the novelists started getting what they can't help but covet: not more sales necessarily, but more readers. And it was gratifying to find that many people were indeed quite intrigued by the business of creating fiction: to prove the point, one need only adduce the fact that every last acre of the planet is now the scene of a boisterous literary festival. With its interplay of the conscious and the unconscious, the novel involves a process that no writers, and no critics, really understand. Nor can they quite see why it arouses such curiosity. ('Do you write in longhand?' 'How hard do you press on the paper?') All the same, as J. G. Ballard once said, readers and listeners 'are your supporters – urging on this one-man team'. They release you from your habitual solitude, and they give you heart. So far, so good: these are the benefits. Now we come to the costs, which, I suppose, are the usual costs of conspicuousness.

Needless to say, the enlarging and emboldening of the mass-communications sector was not confined to the United Kingdom. And 'visibility', as Americans call it, was no doubt granted to writers in all the advanced democracies – with variations determined by national character. In my home country, the situation is, as always, paradoxical. Despite the existence of a literary tradition of unparalleled magnificence (presided over by the world's only obvious authorial divinity), writers are regarded with a studied scepticism – not by the English public, but by the English commentariat. It sometimes seems that a curious circularity is at work. If it is true that writers owe their ascendancy to the media, then the media has promoted the very people that irritate them most: a crowd of pretentious – and by now quite prosperous – egomaniacs. When writers complain about this, or about anything else, they are accused of self-pity ('celebrity whinge'). But the unspoken gravamen is not self-pity. It is ingratitude.

Nor should we neglect a profound peculiarity of fiction and the column inches that attend it: a fortuitous consanguinity. The appraisal of an exhibition does not involve the use of an easel and a palette; the appraisal of a ballet does not involve the use of a pair of slippers and a tutu. And the same goes for all but one of the written arts: you don't review poetry by writing verse (unless you're a jerk), and you don't review plays by writing dialogue (unless you're a jerk); novels, though, come in the form of prose narrative – and so does journalism. This odd affinity causes

4

no great tension in other countries, but it sits less well, perhaps, with certain traits of the Albionic Fourth Estate – emulousness, a kind of cruising belligerence, and an instinctive proprietoriality.

Conspicuous persons, in my motherland, are most seriously advised to lead a private life denuded of all colour and complication. They should also, if they are prudent, have as little as possible to do with America – seen as the world HQ of arrogance and glitz. When I and my wife, who is a New Yorker, entrained the epic project of moving house, from Camden Town in London to Cobble Hill in Brooklyn, I took every public opportunity to make it clear that our reasons for doing so were exclusively personal and familial, and had nothing to do with any supposed dissatisfaction with England or the English people (whom, as I truthfully stressed, I have always admired for their tolerance, generosity, and wit). Backed up by lavish misquotes together with satirical impersonations ('cod' interviews and the like), the impression given was that I was leaving because of a vicious hatred of my native land and because I could no longer endure the well-aimed barbs of patriotic journalists.

'I wish I weren't English': of all the fake tags affixed to my name, this is the one I greet with the deepest moan of inanition. I suggest that the remark – and its equivalent in any language or any alphabet – is unutterable by anyone whose IQ reaches double figures. 'I wish I weren't North Korean' might make a bit of sense, assuming the existence of a North Korean sufficiently well-informed and intrepid to give voice to it. Otherwise and elsewhere, the sentiment is inconceivably null. And for a writer to say it of England – the country of Dickens, George Eliot, Blake, Milton, and, yes, William Shakespeare – isn't even perverse. It is merely twee.

The term 'American exceptionalism' was coined in 1929 by none other than Josef Stalin, who condemned it as a 'heresy' (he meant that America, like everywhere else, was subject to the iron laws of Karl Marx). If that much-mocked notion still means anything, we should apply it to America's exceptionally hospitable attitude to outsiders (and America has certainly been exceptionally hospitable to me and my family). All friends of the stars and stripes are pained to see that this unique and noble tradition is now under threat, and from all sides; but America remains, definingly, an immigrant society, vast and formless; writers have always occupied an unresented place in it, because everyone subliminally understood that writers would play a part in construing its protean immensity.

Remarkably, the 'American Century' (to take another semi-wowserism) is due to last exactly that long – with China scheduled for prepotence in about 2045. The role of the writers, for the time being, is at least clear enough. They will be taking America's temperature, and tenderly checking its pulse, as the New World follows the old country down the long road of decline.

New Republic 2012

Twin Peaks – I

Nabokov and the Problem from Hell

The Original of Laura by Vladimir Nabokov

Language leads a double life – and so does the novelist. You chat with family and friends, you attend to your correspondence, you negotiate the public prints, you consult menus and shopping lists, you observe road signs (LOOK LEFT), and so on and so forth. Then you enter your study, where language exists in quite another form – as the stuff of patterned artifice. Most writers, I think, would want to go along with Vladimir Nabokov (1899–1977), when he reminisced in 1974:

> ... I regarded Paris, with its gray-toned days and charcoal nights, merely as the chance setting for the most authentic and faithful joys of my life: the coloured phrase in my mind under the drizzle, the white page under the desk lamp awaiting me ...

Well, the creative joy is authentic; and yet it isn't faithful (in common with pretty well the entire cast of Nabokov's fictional women, creative joy, in the end, is a ruthless flirt). Writing remains a very interesting job, but destiny, or 'fat Fate' as Humbert Humbert calls it, has arranged a very interesting retribution. Writers lead a double life. And they die doubly, too. This is modern literature's dirty little secret. Writers die twice: once when the body dies, and once when the language dies.*

*

*To confine ourselves to English literature: Dickens died at fifty-eight, Chaucer at fifty-seven, Shakespeare at fifty-four, Fielding at forty-seven, Jane Austen at forty-one, Charlotte Brontë at thirty-nine, Byron at thirty-six, Emily Brontë at thirty, Shelley at twenty-nine, Keats at twenty-five, and poor Thomas Chatterton at seventeen. Writers barely had time to assemble their powers, and had no time at all to mourn their passing.

Nabokov composed *The Original of Laura*, or what we have of it, against the clock of doom (a series of sickening falls, then hospital infections, then bronchial collapse). It is not 'A novel in fragments', as the cover states; it is immediately recognisable as a longish short story struggling to become a novella. In this palatial edition, every left-hand page is blank, and every right-hand page reproduces Nabokov's manuscript (with its robust handwriting and fragile spelling – 'bycycle', 'stomack', 'suprize'), plus the text in typed print (and infested with square brackets). It is nice, I dare say, to see those world-famous index cards up close; but in truth there is little in *Laura* that reverberates in the mind. 'Auroral rumbles and bangs had begun jolting the cold misty city': in this we hear an echo of the Nabokovian music. And in the following we glimpse the funny and fearless Nabokovian disdain for our 'abject physicality':

> I loathe my belly, that trunkful of bowels, which I have to carry around, and everything connected with it – the wrong food, heart-burn, constipation's leaden load, or else indigestion with a first install-ment of hot filth pouring out of me in a public toilet ...

Otherwise and in general *Laura* is somewhere between larva and pupa (to use a lepidopteral metaphor), and very far from the finished imago.

Apart from a welcome flurry of interest in the work, the only thing this relic will effect, I fear, is the slight exacerbation of what is already a problem from hell. It is infernal, for me, because I bow to no one in my love for this great and greatly inspiring genius. And yet Nabokov, in his decline, makes even the most well-attuned reader feel uncomfortable, seeming to impose authorial condemnation on you for being so vulgar, literal-minded, and prim. Nothing much, in *Laura*, qualifies as a theme (i.e., as a structural or at least a recurring motif). But we do notice the appearance of a certain Hubert H. Hubert (a reeking Englishman who slobbers over a pre-teen's bed), we do notice the twenty-four-year-old vamp with twelve-year-old breasts ('pale squinty nipples and firm form'), and we do notice the fevered dream about a juvenile love ('her little bottom, so smooth, so moonlit'). In other words, *Laura* joins *The Enchanter* (1939), *Lolita* (1955), *Ada* (1970), *Transparent Things* (1972), and *Look at the Harlequins!* (1974) in unignorably concerning itself with the sexual despoliation of very young girls.

Six fictions: six fictions, two or perhaps three of which are spectacular masterpieces. You will, I hope, admit that the hellish problem is at least Nabokovian in its complexity and ticklishness. For no human being in the history of the world has done more to vivify the cruelty, the violence, and the dismal squalor of this particular crime. The problem, which turns out to be an aesthetic problem, and not quite a moral one, has to do with the intimate malice of age.

★

The word we want is not the legalistic 'paedophilia', which in any case deceitfully translates as 'fondness for children'. The word we want is 'nympholepsy', which doesn't quite mean what you think it means. It means 'frenzy caused by desire for the unattainable', and is rightly labelled by my *COD* as 'literary'. Nympholepsy is therefore a legitimate, indeed an almost unavoidable subject for this very singular talent. 'Nabokov's is really an amorous style', John Updike lucidly observed: 'It yearns to clasp diaphonous exactitude into its hairy arms'. With the later Nabokov, though, nympholepsy crumbles into its etymology – 'from Gk *numpholeptos* "caught by nymphs", on the pattern of EPILEPSY'; 'from Gk *epilepsia*, from *epilambanein* "seize, attack"'.

Dreamed up in 1930s Berlin (with Hitler's voice spluttering out from the rooftop loudspeakers), and written in Paris (post-Kristallnacht, at the start of the Nabokovs' nerve-racking flight from Europe), *The Enchanter* is a vicious triumph, brilliantly and almost osmotically translated from the Russian by Dmitri Nabokov in 1987, ten years after his father's death. As a narrative it is logistically identical to the first half of *Lolita*: the rapist will marry – and perhaps murder – the mother, and then attend to the child. Unlike the redoubtable Charlotte Haze ('she of the noble nipple and massive thigh'), the nameless widow in *The Enchanter* is already promisingly frail, her large body warped out of symmetry by hospitalisations and surgeons' knives. And this is why her suitor reluctantly rejects the idea of poison: 'Besides, they'll inevitably open her up, out of sheer habit'.

The wedding takes place, and so does the wedding night: '… and it was perfectly clear that he (little Gulliver)' would be physically unable to tackle 'those multiple caverns' and 'the repulsively listing conformation of her ponderous pelvis'. But 'in the middle of his farewell speeches about his migraine', things take an unexpected turn, so that, after the fact, it was with astonishment that he discovered the corpse of the miraculously vanquished giantess and gazed at the moiré girdle that almost totally concealed her scar.

Soon the mother is dead for real, and the enchanter is alone with his twelve-year-old. 'The lone wolf was getting ready to don Granny's nightcap'.

In *Lolita*, Humbert has 'strenuous sexual intercourse' with his nymphet at least twice a day for two years. In *The Enchanter* there is a single delectation – non-invasive, voyeuristic, masturbatory. In the hotel room the drugged girl is asleep, and naked; 'he began passing his magic wand above her body', measuring her 'with an enchanted yardstick'. She awakes, she looks at 'his rearing nudity', and she screams. With his obsession now reduced to a cooling smear on the raincoat he throws on, our enchanter runs out into the street, seeking to rid himself, by any means, of a world 'already-looked-at' and 'no-longer-needed'. A tramcar grinds into sight, and under

this growing, grinning, megathundering mass, this instantaneous cinema of dismemberment – that's it, drag me under, tear at my frailty – I'm travelling flattened, on my smacked-down face ... don't rip me to pieces – you're shredding me, I've had enough ... Zigzag gymnastics of lightning, spectogram of a thunderbolt's split seconds – and the film of life had burst.

*

In moral terms *The Enchanter* is sulphurously direct. *Lolita*, by contrast, is delicately cumulative; but in its judgment of Humbert's abomination it is, if anything, the more severe. To establish this it is necessary to adduce only two key points. First, the fate of its tragic heroine. No unprepared reader could be expected to notice that Lolita meets a terrible end on page two of the novel that bears her name: 'Mrs "Richard F. Schiller" died in childbed', says the 'editor' in his Foreword, 'giving birth to a still-born girl ... in Gray Star, a settlement in the remotest Northwest'; and the novel is almost over by the time Mrs Richard F. Schiller (i.e., Lo) briefly appears. Thus we note, with a parenthetical gasp, the size of Nabokov's gamble on greatness. 'Curiously enough, one cannot read a book,' he had announced (at the lectern), 'one can only reread it.' Nabokov knew that *Lolita* would be reread, and re-reread. He knew that we would eventually absorb Lolita's fate – her stolen childhood, her stolen woman-hood. Gray Star, he wrote, is 'the capital town of the book'. The shifting qualification – gray star, silent lightning, torpid smoke, pale fire, and yes, even hot filth: this is the Nabokovian counter-tone.

The second fundamental point is the description of a recurring dream that shadows Humbert after Lolita has flown (she absconds with the cynically carnal Quilty). It is also proof of the fact that style, that prose itself, can control morality. Who would want to do something that gave them dreams like these?

> ... she did haunt my sleep but she appeared there in strange and ludicrous disguises as Valeria or Charlotte [his ex-wives], or a cross between them. That complex ghost would come to me, shedding shift after shift, in an atmosphere of great melancholy and disgust, and would recline in dull invitation on some narrow board or hard settee, with flesh ajar like the rubber valve of a soccer ball's bladder. I would find myself, dentures fractured or hopelessly misplaced, in horrible *chambres garnies*, where I would be entertained at tedious vivisecting parties that generally ended with Charlotte or Valeria weeping in my bleeding arms and being tenderly kissed by my brotherly lips in a dream disorder of auctioneered Viennese bric-a-brac, pity, impotence and the brown wigs of tragic old women who had just been gassed.

That final phrase, with its clear allusion, reminds us of the painful dif-fidence with which Nabokov wrote about the century's terminal crime. His father, the distinguished liberal statesman (whom Trotsky loathed), was shot dead by a fascist thug in Berlin; and Nabokov's homosexual brother, Sergey, was murdered in a Nazi concentration camp ('What a joy you are well, alive, in good spirits,' Nabokov wrote to his sister Elena, from the US to the USSR, in November 1945. 'Poor, poor Seryozha ...!'). Nabokov's wife, Véra, was Jewish, and so, therefore, was their son (born in 1934); and there is a strong likelihood that if the Nabokovs had failed to escape from France when they did (in May 1940, with the Wehrmacht seventy miles from Paris), they would have joined the scores of thousands of the racially impure delivered by Vichy to the Reich.

In his fiction, to my knowledge, Nabokov wrote about the Holocaust at paragraph length only once – in the incomparable *Pnin* (1957). Other references, as in *Lolita*, are glancing. Take, for example, this one-sentence demonstration of genius from the insanely inspired six-page short story of 1948, 'Signs and Symbols' (it is a description of a Jewish matriarch):

> Aunt Rosa, a fussy, angular, wild-eyed old lady, who had lived in a tremulous world of bad news, bankruptcies, train accidents, cancerous growths – until the Germans put her to death, together with all the people she had worried about.

Pnin goes further. At an émigré houseparty in rural America a Madam Shpolyanski mentions her cousin Mira, and asks Timofey Pnin if he has heard of her 'terrible end'. 'Indeed, I have', Pnin answers. Gentle Timofey sits on alone in the twilight. Then Nabokov gives us this:

> What chatty Madam Shpolyanski mentioned had conjured up Mira's image with unusual force. This was disturbing. Only in the detachment of an incurable complaint, in the sanity of near death, could one cope with this for a moment. In order to exist rationally, Pnin had taught himself ... never to remember Mira Belochkin – not because ... the evocation of a youthful love affair, banal and brief, threatened his peace of mind ... but because, if one were quite sincere with oneself, no conscience, and hence no consciousness, could be expected to subsist in a world where such things as Mira's death were possible. One had to forget – because one could not live with the thought that this graceful, fragile, tender young woman with those eyes, that smile, those gardens and snows in the background, had been brought in a cattle car and killed by an injection of phenol into the heart, into the gentle heart one had heard beating under one's lips in the dusk of the past.

How resonantly this passage chimes with Primo Levi's crucial observation that we cannot, we must not, 'understand what happened'. Because to 'understand' it would be to 'contain' it. 'What happened' was 'non-human', or 'counter-human', and remains incomprehensible to human beings.

By linking Humbert Humbert's crime to the Shoah, and to 'those whom the wind of death has scattered' (Paul Celan), Nabokov pushes out to the very limits of the moral universe. Like *The Enchanter*, *Lolita* is airtight, intact and entire. The frenzy of the unattainable desire is confronted, and framed, with stupendous courage and cunning. And so matters might have rested. But then came the meltdown of artistic self-possession – tumultuously announced, in 1970, by the arrival of *Ada*. When a writer starts to come off the rails, you expect skidmarks and broken glass; with Nabokov, naturally, the eruption is on the scale of a nuclear accident.

*

I have read at least half a dozen Nabokov novels at least half a dozen times. And at least half a dozen times I have tried, and promptly failed, to read *Ada* ('Or Ardor: A Family Chronicle'). My first attempt took place about three decades ago. I put it down after the first chapter, with a curious sensation, a kind of negative tingle. Every five years or so (this became the pattern), I picked it up again; and after a while I began to articulate the difficulty: 'But this is dead,' I said to myself. The curious sensation, the negative tingle, is of course miserably familiar to me now: it is the reader's response to what seems to happen to all writers as they overstep the biblical span. The radiance, the life-giving power, begins to fade. Last summer I went away with *Ada* and locked myself up with it. And I was right. At six hundred pages, two or three times Nabokov's usual fighting-weight, the novel is what homicide detectives call 'a burster'. It is a waterlogged corpse at the stage of maximal bloat.

When *Finnegans Wake* appeared, in 1939, it was greeted with wary respect – or with 'terror-stricken praise', in the words of Jorge Luis Borges. *Ada* garnered plenty of terror-stricken praise; and the similarities between the two magna opera are in fact profound. Nabokov nominated *Ulysses* as his novel of the century, but he described *Finnegans Wake* as, variously, 'formless and dull', 'a cold pudding of a book', 'a tragic failure', and 'a frightful bore'. Both novels seek to make a virtue of unbounded self-indulgence; they turn away, so to speak, and fold in on themselves. Literary talent has several ways of dying. With Joyce and Nabokov (and with others), we see a decisive loss of love for the reader – a loss of comity, of courtesy. The pleasures of writing, Nabokov said, 'correspond exactly to the pleasures of reading'; and the two activities are in some sense indivisible. In *Ada*, that bond loosens and frays.

There is a weakness in Nabokov for 'patricianism', as Saul Bellow called it (Nabokov the classic émigré, Bellow the classic immigrant). In the former's purely 'Russian' novels (I mean the novels written in

Russian that Nabokov did not himself translate), the male characters, in particular, have a self-magnifying quality: they are larger and louder than life. They don't walk – they 'march' or 'stride'; they don't eat and drink – they 'munch' and 'gulp'; they don't laugh – they 'roar'. They are very far from being the furtive, hesitant neurasthenics of mainstream anglophone fiction: they are brawny (and gifted) heart-throbs, who win all the fights and win all the girls. Pride, for them, is not a deadly sin but a cardinal virtue. Of course, we cannot do without this vein in Nabokov: it gives us, elsewhere, his magnificently comic hauteur. In *Lolita*, the superbity is meant to be funny; elsewhere, it is a trait that irony does not protect.

In *Ada* nabobism disastrously combines with a nympholepsy that is lavishly, monotonously, and frictionlessly gratified. Ada herself, at the outset, is twelve; and Van Veen, her cousin (and half-sibling) is fourteen. As Ada starts to age, in adolescence, her tiny sister Lucette is also on hand to enliven their 'strenuous trysts'. On top of this, there is a running quasi-fantasy about an international chain of elite bordellos where girls as young as eleven can be 'fondled and fouled'. And Van's sixty-year-old father (incidentally but typically) has a mistress who is barely out of single figures: she is ten. This interminable book is written in dense, erudite, alliterative, punsome, pore-clogging prose; and every character, without exception, sounds like late Henry James.

In common with *Finnegans Wake*, *Ada* probably does 'work out' and 'measure up' – the multilingual decoder, given enough time and nothing better to do, might eventually disentangle its toiling systems and symmetries, its lonely and comfortless labyrinths, and its glutinous nostalgies. What both novels signally lack, though, is any hint of narrative traction: they slip and they slide; they just can't hold the road. And then, too, with *Ada*, there is something altogether alien – a sense of monstrous entitlement, of unbridled, head-in-air seigneurism. Morally, this is the world for which the twisted Humbert thirsts: a world where 'nothing matters', and 'everything is allowed'.

*

This leaves us with *Transparent Things* (to which we will uneasily return) and *Look at the Harlequins!* – as well as the more or less negligible volume under review. 'LATH!', as the author called it, just as he called *The Original of Laura* 'TOOL', is the Nabokov swansong. It has some wonderful rumbles, and glimmers of unearthly colour, but it is hard-of-hearing and rheumy-eyed; and the little-girl theme is by now hardly more than a logo – part of the Nabokovian furniture, like mirrors, doubles, chess, butterflies. There is a visit to a motel called Lolita Lodge; there is a brief impersonation of Dumbert Dumbert. More centrally, the narrator, Vadim Vadimovich, suddenly finds himself in sole charge of his seldom-seen daughter, Bel, who, inexorably, is twelve years old (they are always twelve years old).

Now, where does this thread lead?

> ...I was still deliriously happy, still seeing nothing wrong or dangerous, or absurd or downright cretinous, in the relationship between my daughter and me. Save for a few insignificant lapses – a few hot drops of overflowing tenderness, a gasp masked by a cough and that sort of stuff – my relations with her remained essentially innocent.

Well, the dismaying answer is that this thread leads nowhere. The only repercussion, thematic or otherwise, is that Vadim ends up marrying one of Bel's classmates, who is forty-three years his junior. And that is all.

Between the hysterical *Ada* and the doddery *Look at the Harlequins!* comes the mysterious, sinister, and beautifully melancholic novella, *Transparent Things*: Nabokov's remission. Our hero, Hugh Person, a middle-grade American publisher, is an endearing misfit and sexual loser, like Timofey Pnin (Pnin regularly dines at a shabby little restaurant called The Egg and We, which he frequents out of 'sheer sympathy with failure'). Four visits to Switzerland provide the cornerstones of this expert little piece, as Hugh shyly courts the exasperating flirt, Armande, and also monitors an aged, portly, decadent, and forbiddingly highbrow novelist called 'Mr. R.'.

Mr R. is said to have debauched his stepdaughter (a friend of Armande's) when she was a child or at any rate a minor. The nympholeptic theme thus hovers over the story, and is reinforced, in one extraordinary scene, by the disclosure of Hugh's latent yearnings. A pitiful bumbler, with a treacherous libido (wiltings and premature ejaculations mark his 'mediocre potency'), Hugh calls on Armande's villa, and her mother diverts him, while he waits, with some family snapshots. He comes across a photo of a naked Armande, aged ten:

> The visitor constructed a pile of albums to screen the flame of his interest ... and returned several times to the pictures of little Armande

in her bath, pressing a proboscidate rubber toy to her shiny stomach or standing up, dimple-bottomed, to be lathered. Another revelation of impuberal softness (its middle line just distinguishable from the less vertical grass-blade next to it) was afforded by a photo of her in which she sat in the buff on the grass, combing her sun-shot hair and spreading wide, in false perspective, the lovely legs of a giantess.

He heard a toilet flush upstairs and with a guilty wince slapped the thick book shut. His retractile heart moodily withdrew, its throbs quietened ...

At first this passage seems shockingly anomalous. But then we reflect that Hugh's unconscious thoughts, his dreams, his insomnias ('night is always a giant'), are saturated with inarticulate dreads:

He could not believe that decent people had the sort of obscene and absurd nightmares which shattered his night and continued to tingle throughout the day. Neither the incidental accounts of bad dreams reported by friends nor the case histories in Freudian dream books, with their hilarious elucidations, presented anything like the complicated vileness of his almost nightly experience.

Hugh marries Armande and then, years later, strangles her *in his sleep*. So it may be that Nabokov identifies the paedophiliac prompting as an urge towards violence and self-obliteration. Hugh Person's subliminal churning extracts a terrible revenge, in pathos and isolation (prison, madhouse), and demands the ultimate purgation: he is burnt to death in one of the most ravishing conflagrations in all literature. The torched hotel:

Now flames were mounting the stairs, in pairs, in trios, in redskin file, hand in hand, tongue after tongue, conversing and humming happily. It was not, though, the heat of their flicker, but the acrid dark smoke that caused Person to retreat back into the room; excuse me, said a polite flamelet holding open the door he was vainly trying to close. The window banged with such force that its panes broke into a torrent of rubies ... At last suffocation made him try to get out by climbing out and down, but there were no ledges or balconies on that side of the roaring house. As he reached the window a long lavender-tipped flame danced up to stop him with a graceful gesture of its gloved hand.

Crumbling partitions of plaster and wood allowed human cries to reach him, and one of his last wrong ideas was that those were the shouts of people anxious to help him, and not the howls of fellow men.

★

Left to themselves, *The Enchanter, Lolita*, and *Transparent Things* might have formed a lustrous and utterly unnerving trilogy. But they are not left to themselves; by sheer weight of numbers, by sheer iteration, the nympholepsy novels begin to infect one another – they cross-contaminate. We gratefully take all we can from them; and yet … Where else in the canon do we find such wayward fixity? In the awful itch of Lawrence, maybe, or in the murky sexual transpositions of Proust? No: you would need to venture to the very fringes of literature – Lewis Carroll, William Burroughs, the Marquis de Sade – to find an equivalent emphasis: an emphasis on activities we rightly and eternally hold to be unforgivable.

In fiction, of course, nobody ever gets hurt; the flaw, as I said, is not moral but aesthetic. And I intend no innuendo by pointing out that Nabokov's obsession with nymphets has a parallel: the ponderous intrusiveness of his obsession with Freud – 'the vulgar, shabby, fundamentally medieval world' of 'the Viennese quack', with 'its bitter little embryos, spying, from their natural nooks, upon the love life of their parents'. Nabokov cherished the anarchy of the inner mind, and Freud is excoriated because he sought to systematise it. Is there something rivalrous in this hatred? Well, in the end it is Nabokov, and not Freud, who emerges as our supreme poet of dreams (with Kafka), and our supreme poet of madness.

One commonsensical caveat persists, for all our literary-critical impartiality: writers like to write about the things they like to think about. And, to put it at its sternest, Nabokov's mind, during his last period, insufficiently honoured the innocence – insufficiently honoured the honour – of twelve-year-old girls. In the three novels described above he prepotently defends the emphasis; in *Ada* (that incontinent splurge), in *Look at the Harlequins!*, and now in *The Original of Laura*, he does not defend it. This leaves a faint but visible scar on the leviathan of his corpus.

'Now, *soyons raisonnable*,' says Quilty, staring down the barrel of Humbert's revolver. 'You will only wound me hideously and then rot in jail while I recuperate in a tropical setting.' All right, let us be reasonable. In his book about Updike, Nicholson Baker refers to an order of literary achievement that he calls 'Prousto-Nabokovian'. Yes, Prousto-Nabokovian, or Joyceo-Borgesian, or, for the Americans, Jameso-Bellovian. And it is at the highest table that Vladimir Nabokov coolly takes his place.

Lolita, Pnin, and *Despair* (1936; translated by the author in 1966), and four or five short stories are immortal. *King, Queen, Knave* (1928, 1968), *Laughter in the Dark* (1932, 1936), *The Enchanter, The Eye* (1930), *Bend Sinister* (1947), *Pale Fire* (1962), and *Transparent Things* are ferociously accomplished; and little *Mary* (1925), his first novel, is a little beauty. *Lectures on Literature* (1980), *Lectures on Russian Literature* (1981), and *Lectures on Don Quixote* (1983), together with *Strong Opinions* (1973), constitute the shining record of a pre-eminent artist-critic. And the *Selected Letters (*1989), the *Nabokov – Wilson Letters* (1979), and that marshlight of an autobiography, *Speak, Memory* (1967), give us a four-dimensional portrait of a delightful and honourable man. The vice Nabokov most frequently reviled was 'cruelty'. And his gentleness of nature is most clearly seen in the loving attentiveness with which, in his fiction, he writes about animals. A minute's thought gives me the cat in *King, Queen, Knave* (washing itself with one hindleg raised 'like a shouldered club'), the charming dogs and monkeys in *Lolita*, the shadow-tailed squirrel and the unforgettable ant in *Pnin*, and the sick bat in *Pale Fire* – creeping past 'like a cripple with a broken umbrella'.

They call it a 'shimmer' – a glint, a glitter, a glisten. The Nabokovian essence is a miraculously fertile instability, where without warning the words detach themselves from the everyday and streak off like flares in a night sky, illuminating hidden versts of longing and terror. From *Lolita*, as the fateful cohabitation begins (*nous connûmes*, a Flaubertian intonation, means 'we came to know'):

> *Nous connûmes* the various types of motor court operators, the reformed criminal, the retired teacher, and the business flop, among the males; and the motherly, pseudoladylike and madamic variants among the females. And sometimes trains would cry in the monstrously hot and humid night with heartrending and ominous plangency, mingling power and hysteria in one desperate scream.

Guardian 2009

Saul Bellow, As Opposed
to Henry James

Whereas English poetry 'fears no one', E.M. Forster wrote in 1927, English fiction 'is less triumphant': there remained the little matter of the Russians and the French. Forster published his last novel, *A Passage to India*, in 1924, but he lived on until 1970 – long enough to witness a profound rearrangement in the balance of power. Russian fiction, as dementedly robust as ever in the early years of the century (Bulgakov, Zamyatin, Bely, Bunin), had been wiped off the face of the earth; French fiction seemed to have strayed into philosophical and essayistic peripheries; and English fiction (which still awaited the crucial infusion from the 'colonials') felt, well, hopelessly English – hopelessly inert and inbred. Meanwhile, and as if in obedience to the political reality, American fiction was assuming its manifest destiny.

The American novel, having become dominant, was in turn dominated by the Jewish-American novel, and everybody knows who dominated that: Saul Bellow. His was and is a pre-eminence that rests not on sales figures and honorary degrees, not on rosettes and sashes, but on incontestable legitimacy. To hold otherwise is to waste your breath. Bellow sees more than we see – sees, hears, smells, tastes, touches. Compared to him, the rest of us are only fitfully sentient; and intellectually, too, his sentences simply weigh more than anybody else's. John Updike and Philip Roth, the two writers in perhaps the strongest position to rival Bellow, or to succeed him, have both acknowledged that his seniority is not merely a question of Anno Domini. Egomania is an ingredient of literary talent, and a burdensome one: the egomaniacal reverie is not, as many suppose, a stupor of self-satisfaction; it is more like a state of red alert. Yet American writers, in particular, are surprisingly level-headed about hierarchy. John Berryman claimed he was 'comfortable' playing second fiddle to Robert Lowell; and when that old flagship Robert Frost sank to the bottom, in 1963, he said impulsively (and unsentimentally), 'It's scary. Who's number one?' But that was just a rush of blood. Berryman knew his proper place.

Rather impertinently, perhaps, you could summarise the preoccupations of the Jewish-American novel in one word: 'shiksas' (literally, 'detested things'). It transpired that there was something uniquely riveting about the conflict between the Jewish sensibility and the temptations – the inevitabilities – of materialist America. As one Bellow narrator puts it, 'At home, inside the house, an archaic rule; outside, the facts of life'. The archaic rule is sombre, blood-bound, guilt-torn, renunciatory, and transcendental; the facts of life are atomised, unreflecting, and unclean. Of course, the Jewish-American novel subsumes the experience of the immigrant, with an 'old country' at one remove; and the emphasis is on the anxiety of entitlement (marked in Roth, too, and in Malamud). It is not an anxiety about succeeding, about making good; it is an anxiety about the right to pronounce, the right to judge – about the right to write. And the consequence would seem to be that these novelists brought a new intensity to the act of authorial commitment, offering up the self entire, holding nothing back. Although Jewish-American fiction is often comic and deflationary, concerning itself with what Herzog called 'high-minded mistakes', something world-historically dismal lies behind it – a terminal standard of human brutality. The dimensions of this brutality were barely graspable in 1944, the year that saw the beginning of Bellow's serial epic. And America would subsequently be seen as 'the land of historical redress,' a place where (as Bellow wrote with cold simplicity) 'the Jews could not be put to death'.

Universalisingly, the Jewish-American novel poses a mind-body problem – and then goes ahead and solves it on the page. 'When some new thought gripped his heart he went to the kitchen, his headquarters, to write it down,' says Bellow on page one of *Herzog* (1964). 'When some new thought gripped his heart': the voice is undisassociated; it responds to the world with passionate sensuality, and at a pitch of cerebration no less prodigious and unflagging. Bellow has presided over an efflorescence that clearly owes much to historical circumstances, and we must now elegiacally conclude that the phase is coming to an end. No replacements stand in line. Did 'assimilation' do it, or was the process something flabbier and more diffuse? 'Your history, too, became one of your options,' the narrator of *The Bellarosa Connection* (1989) notes drily.

'Whether or not having a history was a "consideration" was entirely up to you'. Recalling Philip Rahv's famous essay of 1939, we may say that the Palefaces have prevailed over the Redskins. Roth will maintain the tradition, for a while. Yet he is Uncas – last of the Mohicans.

Praise and dispraise play their part in the quality control of literary journalism, but when the value judgement is applied to the past its essential irrationality is sharply exposed. The practice of rearranging the canon on aesthetic or moralistic grounds (today such grounds would be political – that is, egalitarian) was unanswerably ridiculed by Northrop Frye in his *Anatomy of Criticism* (1957). To imagine a literary 'stock exchange' in which reputations 'boom and crash', he argued, is to reduce literary criticism to the sphere of 'leisure-class gossip'. You can go on about it, you can labour the point, but you cannot demonstrate that Milton is a better poet than Macaulay – or, indeed, that Milton is a better poet than McGonagall. It is evident, it is obvious, but it cannot be proved.

Still, I propose to make an educated guess about literary futures, and I hereby trumpet the prediction that Bellow will emerge as the supreme American novelist. There is, hereabouts, no shortage of narrative genius, and it tends, as Bellow tends, towards the visionary – a quality needed for the interpretation of a New World. But when we look to the verbal surface, to the instrument, to the prose, Bellow is sui generis. What should he fear? The melodramatic formularies of Hawthorne? The multitudinous facetiousness of Melville? The murkily iterative menace of Faulkner? No. The only American who gives Bellow any serious trouble is Henry James.

*

All writers enter into a platonic marriage with their readers, and in this respect James's fiction follows a peculiar arc: courtship, honeymoon, vigorous cohabitation, and then growing disaffection and estrangement; separate beds, and then separate rooms. As with any marriage, the relationship is measured by the quality of its daily intercourse – by the quality of its language. And even at its most equable and beguiling (the androgynous delicacy, the wonderfully alien eye), James's prose suffers from an acute behavioural flaw.

Students of usage have identified the habit as 'elegant variation'. The phrase is intended ironically, because the elegance aspired to is really pseudo-elegance, anti-elegance. For example: 'She proceeded to the left, towards the Ponte Vecchio, and stopped in front of one of the hotels which overlook that delightful structure.' I can think of another variation on the Ponte Vecchio: how about that vulgar little pronoun 'it'? Similarly, 'breakfast,' later in its appointed sentence, becomes 'this repast', and 'tea-pot' becomes 'this receptacle'; 'Lord Warburton' becomes 'that nobleman' (or 'the master of Lockleigh'); 'letters' become 'epistles'; 'his arms' become 'these members'; and so on.

Apart from causing the reader to groan out loud as often as three times in a single sentence, James's variations suggest broader deficiencies: gentility, fastidiousness, and a lack of warmth, a lack of candour and engagement. All the instances quoted above come from *The Portrait of a Lady* (1881), from the generous and hospitable early-middle period. When we enter the arctic labyrinth known as Late James, the retreat from the reader, the embrace of introversion, is as emphatic as that of Joyce, and far more fiendishly prolonged.

The phantom marriage with the reader is the basis of the novelist's creative equilibrium. Such a relationship needs to be unconscious, silent, tacit; and, naturally, it needs to be informed by love. Bellow's love for the reader has always been at once safely subliminal and thrillingly ardent. And it combines with another kind of love, to produce what may be the Bellovian quiddity. Looking again at the late short story 'By the St Lawrence', I found I had marked a passage and written in the margin, 'So is this it?' The passage runs:

> She was not a lovable woman, but the boy loved her and she was aware of it. He loved them all. He even loved Albert. When he visited Lachine he shared Albert's bed, and in the morning he would sometimes stroke Albert's head, and not even when Albert fiercely threw off his hand did he stop loving him. The hair grew in close rows, row after row.
>
> These observations, Rexler was to learn, were his whole life – his being – and love was what produced them. For each physical trait there was a corresponding feeling. Paired, pair by pair, they walked back and forth, in and out of his soul.

And this *is* it, I think. Love has always been celebrated for, among other things, its transformative powers; and it is with love, in concert with his overpowering need to commemorate and preserve ('I am the nemesis of the would-be forgotten'), that Bellow transforms the world:

> Napoleon Street, rotten, toylike, crazy and filthy, riddled, flogged with harsh weather – the bootlegger's boys reciting ancient prayers. To this Moses' heart was attached with great power. Here was a wider range of human feelings than he had ever again been able to find. The children of the race, by a never-failing miracle, opened their eyes on one strange world after another, age after age, and uttered the same prayer in each, eagerly loving what they found. What was wrong with Napoleon Street? thought Herzog. All he ever wanted was there.

*

'I am an American, Chicago born,' Augie March says, at the outset. It could have gone, 'I am a Russian, Quebec born – and moved to Chicago at the age of nine.' And Bellow is a Russian, a Tolstoy, in his purity and amplitude. Which brings us to another ghost from Saint Petersburg: Vladimir Nabokov. An earnest admirer of *Pnin* (1957) and *Lolita* (1955), Bellow has nonetheless always felt that Nabokov was artistically weakened by entitlement (the Jamesian flaw); and it is a sense of social otherness, certainly, that isolates *Ada* (1969), a novel in which all common ground with the reader simply disappears. Nabokov was not an immigrant ('Don't carry on like a goddamn immigrant,' says an older brother as Herzog weeps at their father's funeral): Nabokov remained an émigré. He couldn't become an American; he was – however delightfully – slumming it over there. Bellow as a child, to his immense advantage, knew what slums really were: they presented the widest range of human feelings, but also directed the gaze upward, to the transcendent.

Some years ago I had a curious conversation with a notably prolific novelist who had just finished re-reading *The Adventures of Augie March* (1953). We talked about the book; then he thought he was changing the subject when he said, 'I went into my study today – and there was nothing. Not a phrase, not a word. I thought, "It's all gone"'. I said, 'Don't worry, it's not you. It's *Augie March*.' Because the same thing had happened to me. That's what Bellow can do to you, with his burning, streaming prose: he can make you feel that all the phrases, all the words, are exclusively his. At the same time, we share Augie's utopian elation when, reduced almost to non-entity in Mexico (c. 1940), he glimpses none other than Leon Trotsky.

> I believe what it was about him that stirred me up was the instant impression he gave – no matter about the old heap he rode in or the peculiarity of his retinue – of navigation by the great stars, of the highest considerations, of being fit to speak the most important human words and universal terms. When you are as reduced to a different kind of navigation from this high starry kind as I was and are only sculling on the shallow bay, crawling from one clam-rake to the next, it's stirring to have a glimpse of deep-water greatness. And, even more than an established, an exiled greatness, because the exile was a sign to me of persistence at the highest things.

Atlantic Monthly 2003

Postscript. 'Multitudinous facetiousness', as a characterisation of the prose of Herman Melville, is not perhaps gravely misleading; but it is gravely inadequate. After an interval of almost half a century I took another look at *Moby-Dick*, and spent a month of last summer slowly shaking my head in gratitude and awe. Technically it is a unique achievement, because about four-fifths of it is padding (it even out-pads *Don Quixote*). In Melville, though, the padding is necessary ballast. *Moby-Dick* would be a strong contender for the Great American Novel; but there isn't much America in it, and there are no women (even the hunted whales are, without exception, bulls) – and who can give us a national panorama without America and without women? At the same time this novel is almost disconcertingly full of love: if *Augie March* captures the American soul, then *Moby-Dick* captures the American heart. The warmth of Melville's generosity flows into the reader, and the reader responds and reciprocates. This lends yet more sadness to the contemplation of his literary arc. His dates are 1819–91; *Moby-Dick* appeared, and then disappeared, in 1851; he was more or less out of print by the age of forty (and reduced to working at the New York Customs House). Thereafter he drew back into poetry (like Thomas Hardy); the Melville Revival began exactly a century after his birth ... Incidentally, the 'notably prolific novelist' who was rendered wordless by *Augie March* was Salman Rushdie, who soon recovered.

Politics – I

The Republican Party
in 2011: Iowa

'Oops' sounds even worse – even more sheepish and abject – if you say it with a Texan accent: something like 'Ewps'. It was certainly an arresting moment, and not just for Governor Rick Perry and his numerous handlers, sponsors, investors, and depositors. When was the last time a would-be emperor denuded himself in the space of a single syllable? Yet it also pointed to more general confusions.

Over the course of about a generation, it has come to seem that while the Democratic Party represents the American mind, the Republican Party represents, not its heart, and not its soul, but its gut. The question is as old as democracy: should the highest office go to the most intellectually able candidate, or to the most temperamentally 'normative' (other words for normative include 'unexceptional' and 'mediocre')? In the rest of the developed world, the contest between brain and bowel was long ago resolved in favour of brain. In America the dispute still splits the nation. Things are slightly different, and more visceral, in periods of crisis. Eight years ago, if you remember, the populace looked on in compliant silence as the president avowedly 'went with his gut' into Iraq.

Until very recently it looked as though the Grand Old Party had been blessed with the most intensely average candidate of all time. Rick 'Crotch' Perry (the nickname derived from his habit of readjusting his blue jeans) was a shoeless farm boy from an old Rebel family, a straight-C student and Aggie yell leader, a devout Air Force pilot who rose to become the potent governor of a major state.

All right, he speaks like a drunkard or a stroke victim (for example, his attempt to say 'Joe Arpaio' came out as 'Joe Aroppehyeh') – but so did George W. Bush. All right, he used to hunt deer at a game reserve called Niggerhead – but he carefully avoided that other Texan beauty spot, Dead Nigger Draw. All right, he may be prone to errors of fact – but don't we feel that it's somehow quite manly to make mistakes? Here was a gut candidate with a barrel chest. What on earth could go wrong?

But now it is time to meet the people. This, we're still told, is what presidential campaigns are all about. So on a cold and frosty morning the car trundles east out of Des Moines, across the North Skunk River, and into the great tray of the Iowan plain. The destination is Marshalltown. You go past Casey's General Store and the GitnGo gas station, past signs saying 'Snowblower Sale' and 'Masonic Temple', past the fuming hulks of vague industrial shapes in the misty distance, till you reach the modest community centre tucked in behind the railway tracks and the rusted-over rolling stock.

I took my seat among about a hundred windbreakers and woolly hats, in an atmosphere of friendly inclusiveness, and passed the time with the complimentary pamphlet *The Ron Paul Family Cookbook* – twenty-eight pages of recipes 'to warm your kitchen and your heart'. Why, here we have the Razzle Bo-Dazzle Tenderloin and Mama's Peanut Butter Cookies. As ten o'clock neared, I turned to the biblical tags, and then to Carol Paul's family newsletter, where I caught up with the huge Paul dynasty and the doings of Rand, John David, Collin, Caylee Joy, Kelly, Lori, Valori ...

Glowingly introduced, the candidate takes the stage: Mr Ron Paul, seventy-six, lean-faced and thin-lipped under a silvery comb-over, and with that endearingly excitable crack in his voice and his laugh. Fiscally responsible, Ron is an isolationist and a constitutional fundamentalist; he is also 'a pro-life libertarian' – which means that he favours minimal state intervention except when it comes to pregnant women.

All this has its eccentric side, but you could reasonably claim that the community centre, that day, showed us American democracy at something close to its best: an uncynical candidate affably bonding with his base. Paul told the constituents that their votes, in the coming caucuses, would be 'magnified a thousandfold', which is true in the anomalous case of Iowa. Yet there's an inescapable sense that the back-and-forth of the parish pump ('We have time for one last question') is becoming a sideshow.

'Meeting people is bullshit,' said a prominent politician who, unsurprisingly, wishes to remain anonymous – and he said it twenty years ago. Similarly, it now seems that the community centre is bullshit too; swinging by the coffee shop or the diner is bullshit; pressing the flesh is bullshit. An old friend of mine, a veteran of polls and primaries whom I will call the Insider, assures me that ads, too, are bullshit. 'They haven't mattered at all,' he says. 'Perry has spent – what? – $5 million, Huntsman $3 million, to no visible effect. Ads only make a difference if you go late and nasty.'

So what isn't bullshit? The debates matter, the media matter – but mainly as they relate to the 'narrative' associated with each particular candidate. And, as in other walks of public life, the narrative is often only one word long.

Take Mitt Romney. The narrative on Mitt is 'flip-flopper'. He has a murky past, what with his health-care plan (anti-individualist), his environmental vigilance (anti-job creation), and above all his laxity on abortion (anti-life). The stigma of Mormonism – the temple underpants, the recruitment and 'praying in' of the dead, among other inanities – costs him surprisingly and perhaps scandalously little (no more than two or three points). He is an outstandingly proficient technocrat; he has electability; he alone has presidentiality. So why does he keep bumping into his 25 per cent glass ceiling?

There is something strangely semi-human about Mitt. To enlarge on a metaphor first articulated by the great Clive James, Romney looks as though he went to the dentist one afternoon, and came out with his head capped. With Mitt, we run up against what is known as the 'dog food' problem. 'The dog just won't eat the dog food' – and nobody knows why. But make no mistake, the Insider warns: 'Gingrich is ahead in the polls. Romney is still the frontrunner. The White House thinks it's Romney – though of course they're hoping for Gingrich. Obama is *crushing* Gingrich in Florida.'

Who else is hoping for Gingrich? And what are people of even moderate good taste supposed to make of Newt and Newt's surge? He is hoping to change the Gingrich narrative to 'redemption', but for now he is stuck on 'insider' (or 'provenly corrupt insider', if you prefer). Newt has been around the Capitol so long that you could see him in some old sandal movie, like *Quo Vadis* (1951), limply reclining in his toga between Peter Ustinov and Deborah Kerr.

A couple of weeks ago we learned that Gingrich was doing book-store signing sessions on the campaign trail – alongside Callista, who was pushing *Sweet Land of Liberty*, a story about Ellis the Elephant. Well, said a source in the *New York Times,* he 'monetized' his years as speaker (as a consultant 'historian' for Freddie Mac, and so on), why wouldn't he monetise his jump in the numbers? 'I believe in free enterprise,' Newt explained (at least he didn't say he 'happened' to believe in it), 'and I think it's O.K. to make money'. Yes, but making money cost him a $300,000 fine, and a scathing reprimand, just fifteen years ago. Gingrich is not just an abysmal vulgarian; he is also a serial adulterer who, while having an affair with a staffer, persecuted Bill Clinton for the identical offence.

'Before you can win,' says the Insider, 'you have to be humiliated. Right now, Romney is being humiliated. Then things will change. Remember, Newt's negatives are an all-you-can-eat buffet.'

On, then, to the debate, at the Drake campus in Des Moines. The six candidates stand at lecterns ribbed with bars of white light, as if in the control bay of the Trekkie starship, and ready to beam down to the planet Earth. Taken together, they are quite a crew. In two weeks' time, the Iowa Caucus, like a death panel, will give its verdict. Only three will live.

The narrative on the absent Jon Huntsman is 'absent'. So apart from the two likely finalists, chameleonic Romney and avaricious Gingrich, we were left with Rick Santorum ('work in progress'), Ron Paul ('shame he's so elderly'), the gorgeous corpse of Rick Perry ('can only count up to two'), and the equally decorative, and equally discredited, Michele Bachmann ('very creepy husband'). Much as expected, the debate was a dismal anticlimax. In the only high point, Newt showed his dialectical skills, turning a painful question about marital fidelity – by way of spousal oaths and oaths of office – into a disquisition on the Federal Reserve.

There was a spectre at the feast. Our Banquo was of course the sorely missed Herman Cain – Cain, who hoped to apply the lessons he absorbed at Burger King and Godfather's Pizza to the management of the free world. And we recall, with some incredulity, that the flamboyantly ridiculous Herman was once leader of the pack. How much clearer does it need to be? The flip-flopper in chief, the most hopeless ditherer and button-puncher of them all, is the Republican electorate.

And this is perfectly understandable. To see how far the GOP has travelled in recent years, it is necessary only to turn to the much-saluted figure of Ronald Reagan. As governor of California, Reagan raised taxes, expanded the number of state employees, defended gay rights, and passed a conspicuously liberal law on abortion; as president, he closed corporate loopholes and amnestied illegal aliens. In short, Reagan would these days be considered a pariah.

'All the "isms" are "wasms",' said Tony Blair, quite a while ago, affirming the end of the age of ideology. With its Taxpayer Protection Pledge, the patriarchal, philoprogenitive, science-averse, fact-averse, anti-governance government-in-waiting has imprisoned itself in dogma. The gut party is all tangled up, both within and without. What we are now hearing is little more than the sullen grumble of its stomach, and the fitful rattle of its chains.

Newsweek 2011

The Republican Party
in 2012: Tampa, Florida

'How much', Josef Stalin once asked, 'does the Soviet Union weigh?'
He was hoping to instil in his terrified advisers a sense of their country's
rightful place in the world: i.e., number one. For those who come to
the US to live as opposed to visit (me, for instance), it's the first thing
that strikes you: the astronomical mass of America. You ask yourself,
how much does America weigh? And soon you are wondering about
its place in the world (number one), and about the durability of its
predominance.

And what is the tonnage of its political machinery? Arriving in Tampa,
and making your way to the hub of the Republican National Committee,
you initially confront the great humourless grid of American 'security'.
The roped-off streets, the menacingly geo-stationary helicopters, the
(false) rumours of drones in the stratosphere, the National Guardsmen, the
three thousand cops from all over Florida, the men with SHERIFF or SECRET
SERVICE stamped on their bulletproof aprons, and the operatives who are
even more secret than that: they wear (i) a twirly plastic tube in the ear,
and (ii) an adamantine scowl. That's what security people are, 99.9 per cent
of the time: professional scowlers. And soon there will be X-rays and pat-
downs, and the sort of lines that would make you groan at LAX or JFK.

First, the colossal edifice of the Convention Center. In the Google
Media Lounge I found myself transfixed by a valiant multi-tasker who
was power-walking on an exercise machine while apparently shooting
a film about his own computer. And in the gaping atrium everyone
who wasn't yelling out greetings stood hunched in tense communion
with their BlackBerrys or their iPads. On the second floor the networks
were carving the hangar-like space into exclusive nooks and crannies.
The scale was gargantuan, like a De Quinceyan opium vision of infinity.

Thence, by shuttle bus, to the Tampa Bay *Times* Forum, the stadium-sized amphitheatre soon to be graced by the stars of the GOP, their innumerable delegates, and fifteen thousand representatives of the media. Up on stage long-haired middle-aged men twanged out the kind of patriotic folk music we might call jingobilly. Filling the giant screens, typically, were clips of soldiers on airfields moving in heroic slow motion, as in an agonising dream of effort and retardation. And the platforms were scattered with the impedimenta of the television crews, arc lights, gantries, metal trunks, and beyond, ankle-deep in a snake pit of cables, hovered vaguely familiar figures, wearing slightly sickly smiles – household faces, under a light coating of Skippy.

That TV anchors strongly resemble politicians – the otherworldly glow, the dense hairdos, the makeup – is, as Marxists say, no accident. They are *communicators*, above all. And what exactly was communicated, down on the Gulf of Mexico, among the megatons of tackle and clobber, the silly hats, the glut of money (thanks to the super PACs 'there is no airtime left to buy'), the sweating, sneezing journos (alternately drenched by the cloudbursts, steamed by the humidity, and frozen by the arctic AC), and the succession of tub-thumpers and cue-card readers on the podium – what ideas were voiced, what policies adumbrated, what philosophies explored?

The Republican dialectic, in 2012, can be summarised as follows. Obama might or might not have inherited a difficult situation (and Democrats, at least, will remember George W. Bush's historic warning in 2008: 'This sucker could go down'); but he hasn't fixed it, so let's try Romney, who's a businessman, not a socialist. This lone notion was pressed home with repetition, tautology, platitude, redundancy – and then more repetition.

Madamic good ole girls in scarlet ensembles, peanut-faced glozers in ambassadorial suits and ties, puns, rhymes, tinkertoy wordplay ('Give me *liberty – not* gimme, gimme, gimme'), alliteration, iteration, my mom said to me, started a small business, almighty God is the truth of all we have, inherit our hopes and dreams, my daddy said to me, started a small business – and all of this seconded by the brain-dead, couch-potato tweets that looped the hall in illuminated script: 'I'm so proud to be a Republican', 'The Bush family is so awesome', 'Look at all the Olympians on stage for Romney. SO COOL!' And the Party was partying, all bounce and yelp and whoop. By the second day I felt as sour as Bill

Murray, mingling for the thousandth time with the capering revellers ('Pick out your partner and join in the fun') on Gobbler's Knob.

Once a night, on average, the grim torpor briefly lifted. With Ann Romney, the interest was human interest. Here was a woman who had submitted, no doubt with qualms, to the inevitable falsity of political display; and you warmed to her warmth, even as you realised that much of her speech, with its emphasis on 'working moms', 'the couple who want another child' but can't afford it, and so on, was plainly disingenuous. The strugglers she claimed to champion (and it was allegedly tough for the basement-dwelling Romneys, back in the day) are the very people that her husband, if elected, will do nothing for. You realised, too, that Ann won't help the GOP's desperate quest for diversity: she looks like the worthy winner of Miss Dairy Queen 1970. 'Tonight I want to talk to you about love', Ann had said. And then Governor Christie waddled on. Chris wanted to talk about Chris, though he did what he could for the cause: his mom told him, apparently, that love was bull and what you needed was respect.

That was on Tuesday. On Wednesday we gathered to heed the words of Romney's VP pick, Paul Ron. Now I know that should really be Paul Ryan, but it's easy to mix him up with Ron Paul: both are anti-abortion libertarians who have managed to distil a few predatory slogans from Ayn Rand's unreadable novel, *Atlas Shrugged* (and if young Paul is blessed with another daughter, he will surely christen her Ayn Ryan – to match Ron's Rand Paul). Many of us thought that Romney would want someone splashier and more populist on the ticket, Christine O'Donnell, say, or Joe the Plumber. But he went instead for a hard-nut wonk who actually 'stands for something'.

Intriguingly, part of what Ryan stands for will mean electoral defeat in Florida. The whole point of holding the RNC in Tampa was to secure Hillsborough County, a district seen as vital for prevailing in the Sunshine State. But this is also the Seniors' State. And we know how much the elderly relish the challenge of something new, especially when it concerns their physical survival. They will embrace the chance to redeem those 'vouchers' with this or that health-and-pelf consortium – a professional stratum now so frankly gangsterish that it disguises debt collectors as doctors, and fans them out over the A & E units of America's hospitals.

We will return to Ryan. But first we have to get through Romney. This was the best thing about the Clint Eastwood warm-up: he ignored the red light and mumbled on for an extra seven minutes, sowing panic, as well as excruciation, in the control tower. All we lacked was a live feed to Romney – to Romney's characteristic smile of pain (that of a man with a very sore shoulder who has just eased his way into a tight tuxedo). Perhaps this partly explains why the nominee remained so opaque and unrelaxed. He never came close to settling the question that all Americans must ask: is Mitt the kind of guy you'd like to have a glass of water with? At this late stage it's time to remind ourselves of a salient fact. There is only one principle on which Romney has never wavered, and that is his religion.

He is a crystallised and not an accidental believer. You can see it in his lineless face. Awareness of mortality is in itself ageing – it creases the orbits of the eyes, it torments the brow; and Romney has the look of someone who seriously thinks that he will live for ever (curiously enough, he also resembles a long-serving pornstar). Mitt is a Mormon – though he doesn't like talking about it. And if I were a Mormon, I wouldn't like talking about it either. Whatever you may feel about their doctrines, the great monotheisms are sanctioned by the continuities of time: Islam has fifteen centuries behind it, Christianity has twenty, Judaism at least forty. One of the dozens of quackeries that sprang up during the Great Revival, Mormonism was founded on April 6, 1830. The vulgarity and venality – the tar and feathers – of its origins are typical of the era. But there are aspects of its history that might still give us pause.

The first Prophet of Mormonism, Joseph Smith, had eighty-seven wives, of whom the youngest was fourteen. Brigham Young, the second Prophet, was husband to seventy; he also incited a series of murders (to quell intra-church rivalries). Mormons suffered persecution, and they retaliated – in 1857, for example, they killed a hundred and twenty men, women, and children (the Mountain Meadows massacre). During the Civil War, the Mormons' sympathies lay with the South, and unavoidably so, for they too dealt in human chattels; as one historian, Hugh Brogan, puts it, 'Lincoln might as well have said of polygamy what he said of slavery, that if it was not wrong, nothing was wrong'. Not until 1890 did the church renounce the practice (though it persisted well into living memory); not until 1978 did a further 'revelation' disclose that black people were the equals of whites – by which time Mitt Romney was thirty-one years old.

It may be that the heaviest item in the Mormon baggage is not its moral murk or even its intellectual nullity so much as its hopeless parochialism. 'A man with a big heart from a small town,' they called him in Tampa. We don't question the big heart; but we gravely doubt the big mind. The truth is that Romney, who aspires to lead the free world, looks ridiculous when he's not in America. How can he bestride the oceans – the Latter-Day Saint with the time-proof face, who believes that the Garden of Eden was located in Missouri?

At the RNC it was Ryan's oratory, not Romney's, that inspired the rawest gust of triumphalism. And that rapture, we were told, would remain undiluted by the discovery, the next morning, that the speech was very largely a pack of lies. According to the campaign managers, there is 'no penalty', these days, for political deceit. When planning this race the Republicans envisaged a classic 'pincer' strategy: they would buy the election with super-PAC millions, while also stealing it with gerrymandering and voter suppression (an effort that seems to be faltering in the courts). No penalty? Don't you believe it. Who will perpetually submit to being lied to with a sneer? The effects of dishonesty are cumulative. Undetectable by focus groups or robocalls, they build in the unconscious mind, creating just the kind of unease that will sway the undecided in November.

It has to be admitted, meanwhile, that Uncle Sam is highly distinctive, even exotic, in his superstitious reverence for money. In every other country on earth, the Republicans' one idea so far this century would never be mentioned, let alone tabled, passed, and given a second term. Tax *cuts* ... for the *rich*? And this plainly indecent policy is already an established failure. According to the Pew Research Center, only 8 per cent of ordinary Americans – and only 10 per cent of the 'upper class' – think the rich are taxed too much. The GOP, moreover, is doomed by demographics. It is simply running out of the white people who form its electoral base; as one of Romney's strategists conceded, 'This is the last time anyone will try to do this.' We know that Republicans refuse to compromise with Democrats. For how long can they refuse to compromise with reality?

Now compare Tampa to the decisively more attractive words and mentalities coming out of Charlotte, N.C. It has not been pleasant, during this last term, to watch the desacralising, the chastening, and some might say the attritional coarsening of the young president. And the populace has not liked watching it either: the approval rating of Congress is 9 per cent (whereas the first lady stands at a Colin Powell-like 66). The violence of Republican rejectionism was vestigially supremacist, just as the love inspired by the Obamas was vestigially abolitionist: the passions that gave rise to 650,000 fratricides do not soon evaporate. Seeming to confirm this, the audience in Tampa looked practically antebellum, while the audience in Charlotte looked just like the future.

Henry James once said that America is more like a world than a country. And for the last seventy years, the world, the globe, has been shaped by the example, and the gravitational force, of the American idea. It is an epic responsibility. Obama's least-touted virtue is his astonishing self-possession in the face of the planet's highest office. Think back to the primaries, in which Mitt Romney, at various stages, managed to trail to the likes of Michele Bachmann, Newt Gingrich, Rick Perry, Rick Santorum, and Herman Cain. Whenever he did notch up a win, Romney reminded me of Dan Quayle in 1988, tapped for the vice presidency in New Orleans: in the words of Stuart Stevens (now Romney's chief strategist), 'he looked like he just did a gram of coke'. In common with George W. Bush, Romney shows little resistance to what Maxim Gorky (onetime friend of Lenin) called 'the filthy venom of power'. Now think back to Obama in Chicago in November 2008: the calmest man in America. Perhaps the calmest man in the world.

Newsweek 2012

The Republican Party
in 2016: Trump*

Not many facets of the Trump apparition have so far gone unexamined, but I can think of a significant loose end. I mean his mental health. What is its present condition, and how will it adapt to the challenges that lie ahead? We should bear in mind, I think, that the phrase 'power corrupts' isn't just a metaphor.

There have been one or two speculative attempts to get Donald to hold still on the couch. Both Ted Cruz and Bernie Sanders have called him a 'pathological liar', but so have many less partial observers. They then go on to ask: Is his lying merely compulsive, or is he an outright mythomaniac, constitutionally unable to distinguish non-truth from truth – rather like those 'horrible human beings', journalists (or at least spiteful, low-echelon journalists), who, Trump claims, 'have no concept of the difference between "fact" and "opinion"'. PolitiFact has ascertained that Donald's mendacity rate is over 90 per cent; so the man who is forever saying that he 'tells it like it is' turns out to be nearly always telling it like it isn't.

With greater resonance, and with more technical garnish (lists of symptoms and giveaways), Trump has been identified as a 'pathological narcissist', a victim, in fact, of Narcissistic Personality Disorder (or NPD). Certainly Trump's self-approbation goes well beyond everyday

* This piece was delivered on May 23, not long after the two remaining candidates, Ted Cruz and John Kasich, dropped out of the primaries (May 3), and just before Trump questioned Judge Gonzalo Curiel's fitness to preside over the civil fraud lawsuits brought against Trump University. The piece was published on July 15, at which point Trump was girding himself for the Republican Convention (July 18–21)

egocentricity or solipsism. 'My fingers,' he recently explained, 'are long and beautiful, as – it has been well documented – are various other parts of my anatomy.' He really does remind you of the original Narcissus, the frigid prettyboy of Greek myth who was mortally smitten by his own reflection. Narcissus is auto-erotic; he is self-aroused.

Cynics will already be saying that these two 'diseases', chronic dishonesty and acute vaingloriousness, are simply par for the course. In recent years the GOP has more or less adopted the quasi-slogan *there is no downside to lying* (itself a clear and indeed 'performative' tall story: how can you devalue truth, and devalue language, without cost?). And such voices would also argue that a laughably bloated sense of self is a prerequisite, a *sine qua non*, for anyone aspiring to public office. Well, we'll see. President Trump won't get away with too much pathological lying in the Oval Office and the Situation Room. But we may be sure that his pathological narcissism, his poor old NPD, will become unrecognisably florid and fulminant, as he nears the 'ultimate aphrodisiac' (H. Kissinger) – namely power.

Our psychological exam cries out for hard evidence. Now, the written word is always hard evidence; and I have before me 'two books by Donald Trump'. That phrase is offered advisedly, particularly the preposition 'by'. But we can be confident that Trump had *something* to do with their compilation: it very quickly emerges that he is one of nature's reluctant micromanagers, having discovered (oh, long, long ago) that every single decision will hugely profit from his superintendence. 'By' is provisional, and even the epithet 'books' is moot, because Trump always calls his books his 'bestsellers'. Anyway, almost three decades separate *The Art of the Deal* (1987) and *Crippled America* (2015). I suppose a careful study of the intervening bestsellers – among them *Surviving at the Top* (1990), *How to Get Rich* (2004), *Think Like a Billionaire* (2004), *The Best Golf Advice I Ever Received* (2005), and *Think Big and Kick Ass in Business and Life* (2007) – might have softened the blow. As it is, I can report that in the last thirty years Trump, both cognitively and humanly, has undergone an atrocious decline.

*

Insofar as it is a memoir, *The Art of the Deal* resembles a rags-to-riches story from which the rags have been tastefully excised. Donald's dad,

Fred C. Trump, did the rags bit, becoming the man of the house at the age of eleven (Donald's grandfather was 'a hard liver and a hard drinker'); so it was Fred who shined shoes, delivered fruit, and hauled lumber. Even at sixteen, though, Trump Sr. was starting to get ahead, 'building prefabricated garages for fifty dollars apiece'.

By the time Donald appeared, Trump Sr. was a grandmaster of what we would now call 'affordable housing'; and little Donald was his father's sidekick as together they toured the sites, checking up on builders, suppliers, and contractors, and intimidating penniless tenants when they fell behind on the rent. But 'I had loftier dreams and visions,' Trump writes. Not for him the little redbrick boxes, nor yet 'the three-story Colonials, Tudors, and Victorians' that Fred went on to erect. In the early 1970s, fortified by that 'small loan' from his father ($1m), Donald strode across the Brooklyn Bridge and started to traffic in unaffordable housing: skyscrapers.

If you have ever wondered what it's like, being a young and avaricious teetotal German-American philistine on the make in Manhattan, then your curiosity will be quenched by *The Art of the Deal*. One of the drawbacks of phenomenal success, Trump ruefully notes, 'is that jealousy and envy inevitably follow' ('I categorize [such people] as life's losers'); but the present reader, at least, felt a gorgeous serenity when contemplating Trump's average day. Nonnavigable permits, Floor Area Ratios, zoning approvals, *re*zoning approvals ('involving a dozen city and state agencies, as well as local community groups'), land-rights and air-rights purchases, tax concessions ('property tax abatements'), handouts to politicians ('very standard and accepted'), and, if push came to shove ('I'm not looking to be a bad guy when it isn't absolutely necessary'), coerced evictions.

On the other hand, think of all the exceptional human beings he is working with. Alan 'Ace' Green Greenberg, CEO of Bear Stearns; Ivan Boesky, crooked arbitrageur; Arthur Sonnenblick, 'one of the city's leading brokers'; Steve Wynn, Vegas hotelier; Adnan Khashoggi, 'Saudi billionaire' (and arms dealer); and Paul Patay, 'the number-one food-and-beverage man in Atlantic City'. And on top of all this there's Barron Hilton, 'born wealthy and bred to be an aristocrat', and 'a member of what I call the Lucky Sperm Club'. (An ugly formulation, that: I respectfully advise Mr Trump to settle on a more demotic synonym – the Lucky Scum Club, say.)

Then you have the social life. A sustaining can of tomato juice for lunch ('I rarely go out, because mostly, it's a waste of time'); a minimum of parties ('frankly, I'm not too big on parties, because I can't stand small talk'); and an absolute minimum of hanging about in cocktail bars ('I don't drink, and I'm not very big on sitting around'). But of course there are treats and sprees. Take the dinners. A dinner in St Patrick's Cathedral with John Cardinal O'Connor and his 'top bishops and priests'. A dinner, chaired by Trump, for the Police Athletic League. A visit to Trenton 'to attend a retirement dinner for a member of the New Jersey Casino Control Commission'.

It is thus exhaustively established that Trump has a superhuman tolerance for boredom. What are his other commercial strengths? Nerve, tenacity, patience, an unembarrassable pushiness ('simply' cold-calling the top guy), a shrewd aversion to staking his own money, the aforementioned readiness, at a pinch, to play the villain, the ability to be 'a screamer when I need to be' (but *not* when he feels that 'screaming would only scare them off'), and the determination 'to fight when I feel I'm being screwed'. Above all, perhaps, his antennae are very sensitive to weakness.

Looking to buy an old hotel in midtown, Trump rejects the Biltmore, the Barclay, and the Roosevelt as being 'at least moderately successful', and goes instead for 'the only one in real trouble', the Commodore, which he can pitch as 'a loser hotel in a decaying neighborhood' and so flatten the price. Similarly, his long and apparently hopeless campaign to get Bonwit Teller, store and building, suddenly takes fire when he learns that its parent company has started 'to experience very serious financial problems'. And he gets Bonwit Teller. Perhaps that's the defining asset: a crocodilian nose for inert and preferably moribund prey.

Trump can sense when an entity is no longer strong enough or lithe enough to evade predation. He did it with that white elephant the Grand Old Party, whose salaried air-sniffers never saw him coming even when he was there, and whose ruins he now bestrides. The question is, Can he do it with American democracy?

*

We now turn to *Crippled America: How to Make America Great Again*, a bestseller so recent that it includes a dig at Megyn Kelly. But first a word about the cover.

'Some readers', writes Trump sternly in his opening sentence, 'may be wondering why the picture we used on the cover of this book is so angry and so mean looking.' Quite recently he 'had some beautiful pictures taken' – pictures like the one that bedizens *The Art of the Deal* – in which he 'looked like a very nice person'; and Trump's family implored him to pick one of those. But no. He wanted to look like a very nasty person to reflect 'the anger and unhappiness that I feel'. And there he is in HD colour, hammily scowling out from under an omelette of makeup and tanning cream (and from under the little woodland creature that sleeps on his head).

Harper's readers will now have to adjust themselves to a peculiar experiment with the declarative English sentence. Trump's written sentences are not like his spoken sentences, nearly all of which have eight or nine things wrong with them. His written or dictated sentences try something subtler: very often indeed, they lack the ingredient known as content. In this company, 'I am what I am' and 'what I say is what I say' seem relatively rich. At first, you marvel at a mind that considers it worth saying – that what was said was what was said. But at least an *attitude* is being communicated, a subtext that reads, Take me for all in all. Incidentally, this attitude is exclusively male. You have heard Chris Christie say it; but can you hear a woman say, in confident self-extenuation, that she is what she is?

Fascinating. And perhaps there's some legible sedimentary interest in 'Donald Trump is for real.' Or perhaps not. As well as being for real, Trump has 'no problem telling it like it is'. Or, to put it slightly differently, 'I don't think many people would disagree that I tell it like it is.' He has already claimed that he *looks* like a very nice guy, on page ix, but on page xiv he elaborates with 'I'm a really nice guy,' and on page 89 he doubles down with 'I'm a nice guy. I really am.' 'I'm not afraid to say exactly what I believe.' 'We need someone who understands greatness.' 'The fact is that I give people what they need and deserve to hear – and that is The Truth.' See if you can find anything other than baseless assertion in this extract from the chapter 'Our Infrastructure Is Crumbling':

> In Washington, DC, I'm converting the Old Post Office Building on Pennsylvania Avenue into one of the world's greatest hotels. I got the building from the General Services Administration (GSA). Many people wanted to buy it, but the GSA wanted to make sure whoever

they sold it to had the ability to turn it into something special, so they sold it to me. I got it for four reasons. Number one – we're really good. Number two – we had a really great plan. Number three – we had a great financial statement. Number four – we're EXCELLENT, not just very good, at fulfilling or even exceeding our agreements. The GSA, who are true professionals, saw that from the beginning. That's the way the country should be run.

Before we turn to the naked manifestations of advanced paranoia (defined as delusions not only of 'persecution' but also of 'self-importance'), we had better tick off the ascertainable planks in Trump's national platform; they are not policies, quite, more a jumble of positions and intentions. On climate change: he would instantly desist from any preventive action, which is 'just an expensive way of making tree-huggers feel good'. On healthcare: he would stoke up interstate competition among insurers, and let the market sort it all out. On governmental style: he would 'restore a sense of dignity to the White House', bringing back all 'the pomp and circumstance'. On religion: 'In business, I don't actively make decisions based on my religious beliefs,' he writes, almost comatose with insincerity, 'but those beliefs are there – big-time.' On gun control: here, Trump simply quotes the Second Amendment with its famously controversial line about the necessity of 'well regulated militias', and then appends the one-word paragraph, 'Period.'

But by now the one-word paragraph has taken up long-term residence in Trump's prose:

> ... people say I don't provide specific policies ... I know it's not the way the professional politicians do it ... But there's nobody like me.
> Nobody.

Or:

> I have proven everybody wrong.
> EVERYBODY!

If we agree that referring to yourself in the third person is not usually a sign of psychological well-being, how do we assess the following?

Donald Trump builds buildings.

Donald Trump develops magnificent golf courses.

Donald Trump makes investments that create jobs.

And Donald Trump creates jobs for legal immigrants and all Americans.

Well, Martin Amis thinks, for a start, that the author of *Crippled America* is a lot crazier than the author of *The Art of the Deal*.

Martin Amis has taken it on board that *Crippled America* was published on November 3, 2015, at which point only a couple of blatant no-hopers had quit that crowded field:

Martin Amis is sure that *Crippled America* would be even crazier if Trump updated it now, with the nomination under his belt.

And Martin Amis concludes that after a couple of days of pomp and circumstance in the White House, Trump's brain would be nothing more than a bog of testosterone.

Emotionally primitive and intellectually barbaric, the Trump manifesto would be a reasonably good sick joke – if it weren't for one deeply disturbing observation, which occurs on page 163. Every now and again Americans feel the need to heroise an ignoramus. After Joe the Plumber, here is Don the Realtor – a 'very successful' realtor, who, it is superstitiously hoped, can apply the shark-and-vulture practices of big business to the sphere of world statesmanship. I will italicize Trump's key sentence: after he announced his candidacy, 'A lot of people tried very hard to paint a bleak picture of what would happen.' New paragraph: '*Then the American people spoke*.' Remember the old witticism about democracy? 'The people have spoken. The bastards.'

Who are they? Trump's base, we are told, is drawn from the members of the proletariat who feel 'left behind'; white, heterosexual, and male, they have discovered that the prestige of being white, heterosexual, and male has been inexplicably sapped. At the same time they imagine that their redemption lies with Trump Inc., which has the obvious credentials ('We manage ice-skating rinks, we produce TV shows, we make leather goods, we create fragrances, and we own beautiful restaurants') to turn it around for the non-rich and the non-educated – as well as for the non-coloured, the non-gay and the non-female.

Telling it like it is? Yes, but telling *what* like *what* is? Throwing off the shackles of political correctness, Trump is telling us that he, like every other honest Republican, is a xenophobe, and proud of it. That is worth knowing. And what he is additionally telling us is that roughly 50 per cent of Americans hanker for a political contender who a) knows nothing at all about politics, and b) won't need to learn – because the old 'politics' will be rendered defunct on his first day in office. In 2012, Joe the Plumber, Joe Wurzelbacher, failed to win his race for the Ninth Congressional District in Ohio. In 2016, as I write, Donald Trump has odds of 9/4 (and shortening) for the US presidency.

★

In valediction, two characterological footnotes.

First, Trump and violence. As we know, he has championed mass deportations, torture, and murderous collective punishment; and then there are the bullying incitements at his Nuremberglike rallies … When did Trump become an admirer of the kinetic? There is nothing substantial on this question, or on any other, in *Crippled America*. In *The Art of the Deal* he describes one of his rare interventions in the fine arts: he gave his music teacher a black eye ('because,' Trump bafflingly clarifies, 'I didn't think he knew anything about music'). But otherwise he comes across as someone naturally averse to the wet stuff of brutality; the chapter-long reminiscence entitled 'Growing Up' quite convincingly suggests that it was the father's rough way of doing things (rent collecting in assault conditions) that made the son decide to quit the outer boroughs. I think the taste for violence has come with the taste of real power. It is something new in him – a recent corruption.

Second, the connected topic – Trump and women. This isn't new. This is something old that has recrudesced, an atavism that has 'become raw again'. This is a wound with the scab off. And now he just can't hold it in, can he, he just can't stop himself – out they come, these smoke signals of aggression. And he is being empirically *stupid*. The question you want to ask Trump is clearly not 'If you're so smart, how come you aren't rich?'; it is 'If you're so rich, how come you aren't smart?' Has something very grave happened to Trump's IQ? He's been worrying about it too, it seems. Responding on the air to David Cameron's opinion of his ban on Muslims ('stupid, divisive, and wrong') Trump touchily (and ploddingly) shot back: 'Number one, I'm not stupid, okay? I can tell you that right now. Just the opposite'. Don't you blush for the lavishness of his insecurity? But Trump is insecurity incarnate – his cornily neon-lit vulgarity

47

(reminding you of the pin-ups on *Lolita*'s bedroom wall: 'Goons in luxurious cars, maroon morons near blued pools'); his desperate garnering of praise (*Crippled America* quotes encomia from *Travel and Leisure, Condé Nast Traveler, Businessweek*, and *Golf Digest*, among many other outlets); his penile pride.

To Democrats at least, 'Crossing the Line: How Donald Trump Behaved With Women in Private', the detailed analysis in the *New York Times* (fifty interviews with 'dozens of women'), was a sore disappointment. All we got from it was Miss Utah's 'Wow, that's inappropriate' (Donald's introductory kiss on the lips, which might not have bothered Miss California or Miss New York). Trump was born in 1946. Almost every reasonably energetic baby boomer I know, women included, would be utterly destroyed by an equivalent investigation; we behaved far more deplorably than Trump, and managed it without the wealth, the planes and penthouses, the ownership of modelling agencies and beauty pageants. The *Times* piece, in effect, 'flipped' the narrative: the story, now, is one of exceptional diffidence – and fastidiousness (obsessive self-cleansing is a trait he twice owns up to in *The Art of the Deal*). A gawker, a groper, and a gloater; but not a lecher.* In Trump's eros one detects a strong element of vicariousness. As with the Greek anti-hero: 'What you hope / To lay hold of has no existence. / Look away [from your own reflection] and what you love is nowhere' (Ted Hughes, *Tales from Ovid*).

Trump's sexual yellow streak is, in itself, an interesting surprise. Where, then, does it come from – the rancour, the contempt, the disgust? In 1997 he agreed with Howard Stern's proposition that 'every vagina is a potential landmine' (and therein, perhaps, lies a tale). Yet Donald remains an indifferent student, and needs more tuition in biology. As a man of the world he has (we know) faced up to the fact that women menstruate. But it is as if he has never been told a) that women go to the bathroom ('disgusting,' he said of a Clinton toilet break), and b) that

---

* This last word was ill-chosen, I thought, even at the time. No, Trump is not a lecher, but only in the sense that lechers (those who show 'excessive or offensive sexual desire') want to get on with it and mean what they insinuate. Trump isn't like that. Why does he keep making passes at female strangers in public, at gala luncheons, in crowded parking lots? Because he can throw his weight around while feeling free of any pressure to get on with it ... So 'lecher' is no good, and 'stud' and 'swordsman' are no good for the same reason. Perhaps 'ladies' man' was all I meant. Trump is not a ladies' man.

women lactate ('disgusting,' he said of a lawyer who had to go and pump milk for her newborn). Has no one told him c) that women vote? And I hope he finds that disgusting too, in November. Because this race will be the mother of a battle of the sexes, Donald against Hillary – and against her innumerable sisters in the ballot box.

Any visitor to the US in an election year will be touched by how seriously Americans take their national responsibility, how they vacillate and agonise. And yet they very seldom acknowledge that their responsibility is also global. At an early stage in Trump's rise, his altogether exemplary campaign staff decided that any attempt to normalise their candidate would be futile: better, they shruggingly felt (as they deployed the tautologous house style), 'to let Trump be Trump'. As a lover of America (and as an admirer of the planet), I offer this advice: Don't shrug. Don't stand by and let President Trump be President Trump.

Harper's 2016

Literature – 1

Philip Larkin: His Work
and Life*

In the mid-1970s I edited the Weekend Competition in the literary pages of the *New Statesman* (with the judicious assistance of Julian Barnes). One week we threw down the following challenge: contestants were asked to reimagine Marvell's 'To His Coy Mistress' in the style of any modern poet. It was a corpulent postbag: many Gunns, Hugheses, Hills, Porters, Lowells, Bishops, Plaths; and many, many Larkins. First place went to our most trusted star – a reclusive gentleman named Martin Fagg. At the Comp we gave out small cash prizes (Fagg got the maximal fiver), but no prizes are now on offer for guessing which poet he had in mind. This was his opening stanza:

> You mean you *like* that poncy crap
> Where some sex-besotted chap
> Makes love a kind of shopping list?
> Item: two juicy tits. Get pissed!

The lines have a pleasantly hysterical tone (as do many of the best parodies). They also have the virtue of being rich in allusion: allusion to Marvell (the octosyllabic couplets, the poet's fantasised vow to spend two hundred years adoring 'each breast'); and allusion, also, to Larkin. The 'crap' / 'chap' rhyme inverts the 'chap' / 'crap' rhyme in 'A Study of Reading Habits' (whose anti-literary sullenness Fagg noisily endorses); that poem ends, 'Don't read much now ... Get stewed: / Books are a load of crap.' Now, to transform 'Get stewed' – where '[I]' is torpidly or indeed drunkenly understood – into an emphatic imperative ('Get pissed!') surely veers close

*This was the introduction to my selection of Larkin's *Poems* (Faber, 2011).

to genius. More than this, though, Fagg manages to imitate what is surely inimitable. I read his lines twice, thirty-five years ago, and yet I summoned them without the slightest strain. This is the key to Larkin: his frictionless memorability. To use one of Nabokov's prettiest coinages, he is *mnemogenic*.

Literary criticism, throughout its long history (starting with Aristotle), has restlessly searched for the Holy Grail of a value system – a way of separating the excellent from the less excellent. But it turns out that this is a fool's errand. Northrop Frye has great fun with the 'evaluative' style in his classic *Anatomy of Criticism* (1957); he takes three poets, Shakespeare, Milton, and Shelley, and 'promotes' and 'demotes' them in all possible permutations, which include:

4. Promoting Shakespeare, on the ground that he preserves an integrity of poetic vision which in the others is obfuscated by didacticism.

5. Promoting Milton, on the ground that his penetration of the highest mysteries of faith raises him above Shakespeare's unvarying worldliness and Shelley's callowness.

6. Promoting Shelley, on the ground that his love of freedom speaks to the heart of modern man more immediately than poets who accepted outworn ...

Etc., etc. (there are eight permutations in all). The 'value' words here, both positive and negative, are in effect mere synonyms for individual preferences. Evaluative criticism is rhetorical criticism: it adds nothing to knowledge; it simply adds to the history of taste. After all, when we say 'Shakespeare is a genius' we are joining a vast concurrence; but we are not quite stating a fact.

How good / great / important / major is Philip Larkin? Instinctively and not illogically we do bow, in these matters, to the verdict of Judge Time. Larkin died twenty-five years ago, and his reputation (after the wild fluctuation in the mid-1990s, to which we will return) looks increasingly secure. And we also feel, do we not, that originality is at least a symptom of creative worth. Larkin certainly felt so. In a letter of 1974 he quotes a remark by Clive James – 'originality is not an ingredient of poetry, it is poetry' – and adds, 'I've been feeling that for years'. Larkin's originality is palpable. Many poets make us smile; how many poets make us laugh – or, in that curious phrase, 'laugh out loud' (as if there's any other way of doing it)? Who else uses an essentially conversational idiom to achieve such a variety of emotional effects? Who else takes us, and takes us so often, from sunlit levity to mellifluous gloom? And let it be emphasised that Larkin is never 'depressing'. Achieved art is quite incapable of lowering the spirits. If this were not so, each performance of *King Lear* would end in a Jonestown.

★

I said earlier that Larkin is easily memorised. Like originality, memorability is of course impossible to quantify. Yet in Larkin these two traits combine with a force that I have not seen duplicated elsewhere. His greatest stanzas, for all their unexpectedness, make you feel that a part of your mind was already prepared to receive them – was anxiously awaiting them. They seem ineluctable, or predestined. Larkin, often, is more than memorable. He is instantly unforgettable.

Let us now consider the diversity and scope of Larkin's registers and moods. From 'Self's the Man', militant anti-romanticism:

> He married a woman to stop her getting away
> Now she's there all day,
>
> And the money he gets for wasting his life on work
> She takes as her perk
> To pay for the kiddies' clobber and the drier
> And the electric fire …

From 'Aubade', epigrammatic brilliance and truth:

> This is a special way of being afraid
> No trick dispels. Religion used to try,
> That vast moth-eaten musical brocade
> Created to pretend we never die …

From 'The Trees', an onomatopoeic prayer for renewal:

> Yet still the unresting castles thresh
> In fullgrown thickness every May.
> Last year is dead, they seem to say,
> Begin afresh, afresh, afresh.

From 'Toads Revisited' ('toad' being Larkin's metaphor for salaried employment), the grimmest and most plangent stoicism:

> What else can I answer,
>
> When the lights come on at four
> At the end of another year?
> Give me your arm, old toad;
> Help me down Cemetery Road.

From 'A Study of Reading Habits', callow dreams of power and predation:

> Later, with inch-thick specs,
> Evil was just my lark:
> Me and my cloak and fangs
> Had ripping times in the dark.
> The women I clubbed with sex!
> I broke them up like meringues.

From 'Livings, II', an unusually modernist description – spondee-laden, with almost every syllable stressed – of a nightscape as seen by a lighthouse-keeper:

> By night, snow swerves
> (O loose moth world)
> Through the stare travelling
> Leather-black waters...
> Lit shelved liners
> Grope like mad worlds westward.

From 'The Whitsun Weddings', a feeling of epiphanic arrest, as the promise of young lives (or so the poet sees it) goes down the long slide to drudgery:

> [...] We slowed again,
> And as the tightened brakes took hold, there swelled
> A sense of falling, like an arrow-shower
> Sent out of sight, somewhere becoming rain.

Then, too, there are the lines that everyone knows and everyone automatically gets by heart. 'They fuck you up, your mum and dad,' 'Sexual intercourse began / In nineteen sixty-three', 'Never such innocence again', 'And age, and then the only end of age', 'What will survive of us is love'. This is a voice that is part of our language.

*

It is important to understand that Philip Larkin is very far from being a poet's poet: he is something much rarer than that. True, Auden was a known admirer of Larkin's technique; and Eliot, early on, genially conceded, 'Yes – he often makes words do what he wants.' But the strong impression lingers that the poets, in general, 'demote' Larkin on a number of grounds: provinciality, lack of ambition, a corpus both crabbed and cramped. Seamus Heaney's misgivings are probably representative: Larkin is 'daunted' by both life and death; he is 'anti-poetic' in spirit; he 'demoralises the affirmative impulse'. Well, these preference-synonyms are more resonant than most, perhaps; but preference-synonyms they remain (still, Heaney is getting somewhere in 'The Journey Back', where the imagined Larkin describes himself as a 'nine-to-five man who had seen poetry'). No: Larkin is not a poet's poet. He is of course a people's poet, which is what he would have wanted. But he is also, definingly, a novelist's poet. It is the novelists who revere him.

Particularly in his longer poems, which resemble Victorian narrative paintings, Larkin is a scene-setting phrasemaker of the first echelon. What novelist, reading 'Show Saturday', could fail to covet 'mugfaced middleaged wives / Glaring at jellies' and 'husbands on leave from the garden / Watchful as weasels' and 'car-tuning curt-haired sons'? In 'The Whitsun Weddings' the fathers of the brides 'had never known / Success so huge and wholly farcical'; in 'To the Sea,' immersed in the 'miniature gaiety' of the English littoral, we hear 'The distant bathers' weak protesting trebles' and 'The small hushed waves' repeated fresh collapse ...'

Many poems, many individual stanzas, read like distilled short stories, as if quickened by the pressure of a larger story, a larger life. The funny and terrrifying 'Mr Bleaney' (a twenty-eight-line poem about the veteran inhabitant of a bedsit) has the amplitude of a novella. And Larkin's gift for encapsulation is phenomenal. Admire this evocation, in 'Livings, III', of the erudite triviality of high-table talk in, as it might be, All Souls, Oxford – and Larkin does it *in rhyme*:

> Which advowson looks the fairest,
> What the wood from Snape will fetch,
> Names for *pudendum mulieris*,
> Why is Judas like Jack Ketch?

'Livings, I' begins: 'I deal with farmers, things like dips and feed.' And after a single pentameter the reader is lucidly present in another life.

Larkin began his career as an exceptionally precocious writer of fiction: he had two pale, promising (and actually very constricted) novels behind him, *Jill* and *A Girl in Winter*, by the age of twenty-five. Twenty-five, and two novels. The reason he gave for abandoning his third (to be called *A New World Symphony*) is, in my view, dumbfoundingly alien. Which brings us to the more fugitive and subliminal component of the fascination Larkin excites in all novelists and in all students of human nature. The poems are transparent (they need no mediation), yet they tantalise the reader with glimpses of an impenetrable self: so much yearning, so much debility; an eros that self-thwarts and self-finesses. This is what rivets us: the mystery story of Larkin's soul.

*

Every serious devotee will have read, not only the *Collected Poems* (1988), but also Anthony Thwaite's edition of the *Selected Letters* (1992) and Andrew Motion's *A Writer's Life* (1993). Thus, in our response to Larkin the man, there is a Before and there is an After.

The transition, if you recall, was prodigiously ugly and violent. It began with an attack by the poet Tom Paulin (in the correspondence columns of the *Times Literary Supplement*):

> race hatred ... racism, misogyny and quasi-fascist views ... For the present, this selection [the *Letters*] stands as a distressing and in many ways revolting compilation which imperfectly reveals and conceals the sewer under the national monument Larkin became.

Here we see, up close, the fierce joys of self-righteousness. You will also notice how quaintly commissarial Paulin's words now sound. For this there is a historical explanation. The *Letters*, and Motion's disaffected *Life*, appeared during the high noon, the manly pomp, of the social ideology we call P.C. (a.k.a. Westernism, Relativism, and – best – Levellism). All ideologies are essentially bovine; and Paulin was simply the leader of the herd, which then duly stampeded.

Next, like a toiling enactment of the domino effect, came the business of 'demotion.' 'Essentially a minor poet,' decided one literary weathervane. 'He seems to me more and more minor,' decided another. Yet another, in a piece nobly entitled 'Larkin: the old friend I never liked', suddenly spoke for many when he said that Larkin's poems 'are good – yes – but not that good, for Christ's sake'. And so the *trahison* continued, slowly winding down as the ideology lost stamina. Its efforts were of course quite futile. Today, long After, Larkin is back to being what he was Before: Britain's best-loved poet since World War II.

> But if he stood and watched the frigid wind
> Tousling the clouds, lay on the fusty bed
> Telling himself that this was home, and grinned,
> And shivered, without shaking off the dread
>
> That how we live measures our own nature,
> And at his age having no more to show
> Than one hired box should make him pretty sure
> He warranted no better, I don't know.
>
> 'Mr Bleaney'

Larkin's life: he was wifeless and childless; he was a nine-to-five librarian, who lived for thirty years in a northern city that smelled of fish (Hull – the sister town of Grimsby). There were in all five lovers: the frail, bespectacled teenager, Ruth; the neurotic 'poetess', Patsy; the religious virgin, Maeve; the 'loaf-haired secretary', Betty (buoyant, matter-of-fact); and overspanning them all, the redoubtable Monica Jones. There were, after a while, no close friends: penpals, colleagues, acquaintances, but no close friends.

What follows is a personal assessment of Larkin's character, and one that reflects a preoccupation that can fairly be described as lifelong. It began in the 1950s, when Larkin was an occasional houseguest at Glanmore Road, Uplands, Swansea. As I now see it, my parents teasingly mythologised Larkin as a paedophobe and skinflint: 'Ooh, don't go near *him*,' my mother used to say, semi-seriously. 'He doesn't like children. And he *hates* giving you your tip.' My 'tip' consisted of three big black pennies; my older brother Philip – Larkin's namesake and godson – got four. The poet unenergetically played his part (the doling out of the pennies was always a grim and priestly ritual). These rare visits continued; he came to Cambridge, London, Hertfordshire. Thinking back, I sense a large, grave, cumbrous yet mannerly figure – and someone distinctively solitary: unattached, unconnected.

I started to read him in my early twenties; we had some professional dealings (he reviewed the odd book for the *Statesman*, and I badgered him for poems); now and then we corresponded; and I spent about half a dozen evenings with him (and others). The closest we came to any kind of intimate exchange was at a drinks party in the late 1970s. We talked about his poem 'Money' (see below). Then I praised him for his courage in learning to drive and buying a car (no other poet I knew would ever go near a steering wheel). Then it went like this:

> 'You should spend more, Philip. No, really. You've bought the car,
> and that's good. Now you – '
> 'I just wish they wouldn't keep on sending me all these *bills*.'
> 'Well it costs a bit to run a car.'
> 'I just wish they wouldn't keep sending me all these *bills*.'

If given the slightest encouragement, I might have gone on to suggest, with juvenile impertinence, that he move to London and ... and what? Well, start to live, I suppose. 'He didn't listen,' I said to my father as I drove him home. 'He just went on and on about his bills.'

Larkin died in 1985. And when the *Letters* and the *Life* appeared, almost a decade later, I wrote a long piece in his defence. I should say that I too was struck by Larkin's reflexive, stock-response 'racism', and by his peculiarly tightfisted 'misogyny'. But I bore in mind the simple truth that writers' private lives *don't matter*; only the work matters. A better understanding of the Larkin puzzle would come later. But I felt a premonitory twinge about this, in 1992, when I construed the nature of Larkin's feelings about my father – supposedly his closest friend.

It was always clear to everyone that Kingsley loved Philip with a near-physical passion. Philip probably felt the same, at first (and Kingsley remained his most rousing correspondent). But in his letters to others he seldom mentions my father without sourness. We could adduce envy (sexual and material). Yet there is also a social distaste that feels wholly unworthy: the fastidious suspicion with which the bourgeois regards the bohemian. Kingsley was effectively spurned in the *Letters*; but he never spoke ill of Philip (and continued to read two or three of his poems every night, all the way to his own death in 1995). Still, I remember my father defeatedly saying, on his return from Larkin's funeral, 'It sounds odd, but I sometimes wonder if I ever really knew him.'

No conceivable disclosure could make me demote Larkin's work. But I have come to find his life ever more estranging, and this involves a re-evaluation of his character. The long process of assimilating Philip Larkin has been complicated by a process of my own: the ageing process, and what it means.

*

Nikolai Gogol, who deliberately starved himself to death at the age of forty-two, had this to say, in *Dead Souls* (1842), about the river of time:

> [A]s you pass from the tender years of youth into harsh and embittered manhood, make sure you take with you on your journey all the human emotions! Don't leave them on the road, for you will not pick them up afterwards! Old age ... is terrible and menacing, for it never gives anything back, it returns nothing!

Implicit here, though, is the suggestion that old age does or can give something back: all the human emotions, in the form of memory. The past goes on being present, especially the erotic and romantic past (and a sense of youth remains, vicariously refreshed by one's children). This is an indispensable and, I believe, a near-universal resource.

Now consider the abysmal capitulation of Larkin's letter to Monica Jones in 1956:

> Hum. Ha. Ah, don't talk about our lives and the dreadful passing of time. *Nothing* will be good enough to look back on, I know that for certain: there will be nothing but remorse & regret for opportunities missed ...

This is near-nihilistic: he was thirty-four. And, sure enough, in a letter of 1973 to a fellow poet, Larkin wrote: 'Middle age is depressing anyway. The things one tries to forget get bigger and bigger.' This is a psyche trapped in neutral gear: he was fifty-one.

Why did Larkin abandon his third novel? I quote from a letter of July 6, 1953, to the poetess Patsy (described by Kingsley, in a letter to Philip, as 'the most uninterestingly unstable character' he had ever met; she went on to die of alcohol poisoning at the age of forty-nine):

> You know, I can't write this book: if it is to be written at all it should be largely an attack on Monica, & I *can't* do that, not while we are still on friendly terms, and I'm not sure it even interests me sufficiently to go on.

The novel 'should' be an attack on Monica? Well of course. What else is there to write about?

The attack on Monica was published six months later. But its author was Kingsley Amis and its title was *Lucky Jim* – where Monica is remade as the unendurable anti-heroine, with her barndancer clothes, her mannerisms and affectations, her paraded sensitivity, and her docile-hostile adhesiveness. And *Lucky Jim* was *mentored* by Larkin. In his one concession to gallantry, Philip made Kingsley change the girl's name – from Margaret Beale to Margaret Peel. The real-life Monica's full name was Monica Margaret Beale Jones.

In 1982 I had dinner with Philip and Monica (and with my brother, father, mother, and stepfather). At the time I found the occasion only mildly bizarre, and wrote about it cheerfully enough in a memoir published in 2000 (though I see that I did describe Monica as 'virile'. This understates the case). Ten years on, I look back at that evening with something close to horror. In Monica's presence, Larkin behaved like the long-suffering nephew of an uncontrollably eccentric aunt. And she was the love of his life.

But that was the kind of life it was. Larkin cleaved to a Yeatsian principle: seek 'perfection of the work rather than perfection of the life' (this is what he means, in 'Poetry of Departures,' by 'a life / Reprehensibly perfect'). All the same, there must *be* a life. And it isn't fanciful to surmise that the gauntness of Larkin's personal history (with no emotions, no vital essences, worth looking back on) contributed to the early decline of his inspiration – and, indeed, of his physical instrument. Self-starved, like Gogol, he died at sixty-three.

Larkin is the novelist's poet. He is most definitely *this* novelist's poet. And it is symmetrical, at least, that my final attempt to parse him will be in the form of prose fiction. If I do get anywhere with a (cautiously) novelised Larkin, I may rest assured that I won't be telling his shade anything it doesn't know. Larkin's self-awareness, his internal candour, was without blindspots. Here are the first and last stanzas of the sixteen-line 'Money.' It shows, as clearly as any poem can, that Larkin siphoned all his energy, and all his love, out of the life and into the work. That he succeeded in this is a tragic miracle; but it is still a miracle.

> Quarterly, is it, money reproaches me:
> 'Why do you let me lie here wastefully?
> I am all you never had of goods and sex.
> You could get them still by writing a few cheques.'
> [...]
> I listen to money singing. It's like looking down
> From long french windows at a provincial town,
> The slums, the canal, the churches ornate and mad
> In the evening sun. It is intensely sad.

★

In quality, Larkin's four volumes of verse are logarithmic, like the Richter scale: they get stronger and stronger by a factor of ten. My selection reflects this. From *The North Ship* (1945), one poem out of thirty-two; from *The Less Deceived* (1955), eleven out of twenty-nine; from *The Whitsun Weddings* (1964), twenty-four out of thirty-two; from *High Windows* (1974), twenty-two out of twenty-four. There are four uncollected poems (among them 'Aubade'); I also include two unpublished poems, 'Letter to a Friend about Girls' and (after much hesitation) 'Love Again'.

'Love Again' is there because it is the only poem in which Larkin tries to account for what he called his 'neutered' nature. The attempt fails, partly for technical reasons. As he remarked to an ex-colleague, 'It broke off at a point at which I was silly enough to ask myself a question, with three lines in which to answer it.' 'Love Again' concludes:

> ... but why put it into words?
> Isolate rather this element

That spreads through other lives like a tree
And sways them on in a sort of sense
And say why it never worked for me.
Something to do with violence
A long way back, and wrong rewards,
And arrogant eternity.

'Well, of course,' Larkin continued, 'anyone who asks a question by definition doesn't know the answer, and I am no exception. So there we are.'

Postscript. Some years after Larkin's death I had a half-hour chat with Kingsley about 'Love Again'. The poem begins, 'Love again: wanking at half past three.' And I relayed an anecdote of Anthony Thwaite's: while editing the *Collected Poems* a proofreader asked him if the 'n' in 'wanking' was a misprint. Well, 'waking,' certainly, would be more romantic (and it would also tend to obscure the fact that the poem is set in mid-afternoon). Anyway, Larkin, true to 'the Movement' he led, was always Against Romanticism. If we were to submit to the 'biographical fallacy', and wondered about the identity of the poem's 'her' ('Someone else feeling her breasts and cunt, / Someone else drowned in that lash-wide stare'), then we would conclude that she is the virginal and religious Maeve (his one self-confessed 'romance'), for whom the word 'wanking' was in any case a mystery ...

Kingsley and I, between the two of us, managed to recite the poem's closing lines (quoted above). And my father said, almost with vexation, '*Violence?*' What violence?' Nobody has ever suggested that there was any physical violence (even 'a long way back') in the Larkin household. But ponder this. Sydney Larkin, a pompous male-supremacist and a reflexive sexual harasser in the workplace, was a notoriously passionate admirer of the German Nazi Party. And isn't it fair to say that the N.S.D.A.P. was the most destructive cult of violence known to history? Sydney took Philip to Nazi rallies in Germany in the mid-1930s; and he continued to root for Hitlerism even after September 1939, and even after the historic blitzing of his hometown Coventry (November 1940), and even after V.E. Day, and beyond. Now the funny thing is that Philip loved and honoured his father. On post-cremation day in early 1948, Larkin wrote to an old friend: 'I felt very proud of him: as my sister remarked afterwards, "We're nobody now: he did it all."'

Larkin's *Letters to Monica*

The age of the literary correspondence is dying, slowly but surely electrocuted by the superconductors of high modernity. This expiration was locked into a certainty about twenty years ago; and although Edna O'Brien and V.S. Naipaul, say, may yet reward us, it already sounds fogeyish to iterate that, no, we won't be seeing, and we won't be wanting to see, the selected faxes and emails, the selected texts and tweets of their successors. The present book covers the period 1945–70, and passively evokes it: digs and lodgings ('I have *put in for a flatlet*!!!'), pre-decimal currency ('I owe you 21/1d I think – 24/11 plus 1/2 minus 5/-'), *The Archers*, Pickford's Movers, and myxomatosis; its settings are remorselessly provincial, mainly Leicester and Hull (and Belfast, true), with so-called holidays in York, Sark, Lincoln, Poolewe, and Bournemouth ('I hope you got my card from Pocklington'). *Letters to Monica* will be of vital interest to all admirers of Larkin's work, and to all students of the profound mystery of Larkin's life, with its singularly crippled eros. Much of the time, though, readers will be thinking that the 'literary correspondence' is something we're well shot of – a postwar embarrassment, like child labour, bread rationing, and outdoor toilets.

Sexual intercourse, as everyone knows, began in 1963 (which 'was rather late for me'). But what preceded it?

> Up till then there'd only been
> A sort of bargaining,
> A wrangle for a ring,
> A shame that started at sixteen
> And spread to everything.

Larkin got to know Monica Jones in the late 1940s, at which stage he was wrangling over a ring with Ruth Bowman, who was a sixteen-year-old sixth-former when they met. The wrangle with Ruth lasted eight years; the wrangle with Monica would last for thirty-five, and had the same outcome. Ruth's frail yet defiant homeliness can only be described as quite extraordinarily *dated*. Monica was a robust and comparatively worldly blonde, with well-shaped bones (but ogreish teeth). A lecturer in English at Leicester, she was a small-community 'character': she wore tartan when she taught *Macbeth*, and in general favoured dirndl skirts, low-cut tops, and markedly cumbrous jewellery. Yet her defining characteristic was her voice – or, rather, her overpowering idiolect.

This is an extract from the most memorable letter in the book (October 1952):

> Dear, I must sound very pompous & huffy … It's simply that in my view you would do much better to revise, drastically, the amount you say and the intensity with which you say it … I *do* want to urge you, with all love & kindness, to *think* about *how much* you say & *how* you say it. I'd even go so far as to make 3 rules:
>
> One, *Never* say more than two sentences, or *very rarely* three, without waiting for an answer or comment from whoever you're talking to; Two, abandon *altogether* your harsh didactic voice, & use *only* the soft musical one (except in special cases); & Three, don't do more than *glance* at your interlocutor (wrong word?) once or twice while speaking. You're getting a habit of *boring* your face up or round into the features of your listener – don't do it! It's most trying.

Larkin's tone, as we see, is wholly unmalicious; it is affectionately, even pleadingly protective. And he at once retreats, explaining that those '3 rules' are merely 'simple points of technique'. We may take it as significant that the word *boring* is used here in an unexpected application – as a verb rather than a naked adjective. The person this letter describes is not just an individual but a familiar and fearsome type: the juggernaut gasbag.

The present collection qualifies as inside information; so it is not indecorous, I hope, to add some inside information of my own. Although the trajectory of Larkin's relationship with Kingsley Amis was already evident in the *Selected Letters* (Thwaite, 1992), *Letters to Monica* adds substance and detail: undergraduate infatuation, measured disaffection, growing irritation, unregulated envy (envy being best understood as empathy gone wrong), a genteel distaste for bohemianism ('Patsy says [so-and-so's] house is *filthy*. I pressed her: "As filthy as Kingsley's?"'), and finally a settled ill will, occasionally tempered by nostalgia. Kingsley's feelings were more constant. But there was a Larkinian peculiarity that filled him with almost lifelong incredulity and dismay: Philip and the women. And, most especially, Philip and Monica.

In 1948 or 1949 Kingsley spoke slightingly of – or quite possibly to – Ruth Bowman. What followed was an alarming froideur ('Kingsley was *petrified*,' my mother later told me. 'He thought he'd never see Philip again'). But Larkin extended no such chivalric shielding to Monica Jones. This is from an Amis-to-Larkin letter of the same period:

> It doesn't surprise me in the *least* that Monica is [studying George Crabbe, 1754–1832, poet and parson]; he's *exactly* the sort of *priggish, boring, featureless* (especially *that*; there isn't *anything* about him, is there?), *long-winded, inessential* man she'd go for; if she can see beauty in a derelict shit-house, she must have more [sensibility] than you. Talking of [SHIT-HOUSES] ...

In addition, as is well-known, Larkin acquiesced and indeed connived in Amis's merciless portrait of Monica (as Margaret Peel) in *Lucky Jim* (1954). And 'Margaret' is not only plain, theatrical, garrulous, and of course boring; she is also a lying manipulator bent on entrapment. And Larkin would continue to regale Kingsley with grimly jovial asides about Monica's affectations – and, for instance, about her facial resemblance to Stan Laurel (an improvement, one supposes, on Oliver Hardy).

Ruth and Monica shared a certain trait: a restless self-importance unaccompanied by the slightest distinction (Monica, for all her strong opinions, published not a single word in her entire career). Two of the other three women in Larkin's life were similarly 'superior': the rowdily 'permissive' Patsy Strang (who drank herself to death at the age of forty-nine); and the virginal, religious, and implausibly naïve Maeve Brennan (who claimed, in her maturity, not to know the meaning of the word *wank*). Only Betty Mackereth, Larkin's 'loaf-haired secretary', seemed cheerfully content in her being. When it comes to women, as Kingsley wrote (in a style not to everyone's taste), 'I fucking give you up'. My mother, who revered Larkin, used to say, 'Well, don't forget he went bald in his twenties. And he had a stutter. I think women frightened him.' Then why, one wonders, were the women he chose so frightening?

And why was it Monica he always ended up with – Monica, the most frightening of them all? To describe Larkin's half of it as 'love-hate' is perhaps too bold. On the positive side we register an urgent warmth, a snug intimacy of jokes and whimsies, and Monica's courageous accept-ance of Larkin's intense melancholia – melancholia not as a mood or a susceptibility, but as a besetting Jonsonian *humour* ('black bile'). Larkin could be frightening too (and without much provocation):

> No, I really can't do anything *at all* – it really is *disgusting*, I feel tearful with rage – why must [the landlady] leave her door open so that her filthy radio *floods the whole house*? ... It really affects me strongly: a kind of spiritual claustrophobia – I can't get out, & can't get away, there's no way out, I can't stand it! Oh *hell*. How long will this go on, wasted time, wasted wasted wasted ...

All this Monica shouldered and palliated. Still, on the negative side, we register Larkin's solemn exasperation, and his suppressed hostility and contempt. As early as 1953 Larkin told Patsy Strang why he was aban-doning *A New World Symphony* (his third novel and his last attempt at fiction):

> You know, I *can't* write this book: if it is to be written at all it should largely be an attack on Monica, & I *can't* do that, not while we are still on friendly terms, and I'm not sure it even interests me sufficiently to go on.

It is hard to construe this singular blend of animus and apathy. Even the 'attack' on her bores him. So why did he cleave to Monica for another thirty-two years – till death did them part? He knew why. The reasons he gives Monica for not marrying her (often-rehearsed) are the same reasons he surely gave himself for not leaving her. Failures of energy and courage, and a vast inertia.

Well, there was sex, too. Or was there? No indication is given, in the early letters, of the transition from friendship to romance. Turning to Andrew Motion's biography, we learn that Larkin 'had come to me', as Monica quaintly put it, by the summer of 1950. (What would be the male equivalent of this phrase? 'It was in August that I first took her'?) But such brooding cadences seem inapposite. 'If it were announced that all sex would cease on 31 December,' writes the hot thirty-two-year-old on December 15 (1954), 'my way of life wouldn't change at all.' Evidently, though, they fumbled along. '[O]ften I'm quite uncertain whether you are feeling anything ... you rarely *seem* to like anything more than anything else.' 'I'm sorry our lovemaking fizzled out ... I'm sorry to have failed you!' Larkin seeks a kind of safety in portraying himself as the omega male. Anyway, 'taking care of business' (to paraphrase Aretha Franklin) was definitely *not* this man's game.

But these are turbid waters, thick with suspended matter, and go far deeper than Larkin's admittedly preternatural indolence. I defy any man – even the most self-sufficient poodlefaker and stud-muffin – to read the following without a twinge:

> I think ... someone might do a little research on some of the *inherent qualities* of sex – its *cruelty*, its *bullyingness*, for instance. It seems to me that *bending someone else to your will* is the very stuff of sex, by force or neglect if you are male, by spitefulness or nagging or scenes if you are female. And what's more, both sides *would sooner have it that way than not at all*. I wouldn't. And I suspect that means not that I can enjoy sex in my own quiet way but that I can't enjoy it at all. It's like rugby football: either you like kicking & being kicked, or your soul cringes away from the whole affair. There's no way of *quietly* enjoying rugby football.

'In bed,' the poet Ian Hamilton once told me, 'you don't want to be *too* clear-headed about what you're doing.' Larkin's clarity, his almost clinical over-sensitivity (naturally vital to his genius), could not be muted or muffled. This was his curse.

Or one of them. In Dostoevsky's *Demons* (1871) Varvara Petrovna accuses a portly valetudinarian bachelor of being 'an old woman' – a verdict she promptly refines to 'an old bag'. Larkin, in his daily dealings (haircut, train ticket, utilities bill, new pullover, salaried employment), had a fair bit of the old bag in him ('I think there's a lot of infection about these days,' he typically quavers, 'upsetting one's insides: with all these foreigners about [in Hull, in 1966], one is never completely well, as when abroad'). There was, of course, a prominent old woman in his life – his mother, whose solitary widowhood lasted thirty years:

For her the daily round is hideous with traps, and dangerous with hidden ambush, and calamity: it is all she can do to creep through it unscathed. She ... spends the time thinking about next summer's thunder-storms, gas taps, electricity switches, dark clouds, and I don't know what.

Eva Larkin, then, in combination with the long-deceased Sydney (clever, cynical, despotic, and pro-Nazi even after the outbreak of World War II), might be expected to leave her son a heavy legacy.

'[M]y mother seems to be resuming her normal whining panicky grumbling maddening manner,' he writes, perhaps self-revealingly. On the whole, though, Larkin tries to resist Freudian entendres and psychological determinisms:

[I]f one starts blaming one's parents, well, one would never stop! Butler said that anyone who was still worrying about his parents at 35 was a fool, but he certainly didn't forget them himself, and I think the influence they exert is enormous ... I never remember my parents making a single spontaneous gesture of affection towards each other, for instance.

And the instance certainly hurts and connects. In an unpublished memoir (quoted in Motion's Life), Larkin wrote: 'When I try to tune into my childhood, the dominant emotions I pick up are, overwhelmingly, fear and boredom ... I never left the house without the sense of walking into a cooler, cleaner, saner and pleasanter atmosphere.' Feelings of guilt, and possibly a desire for utter self-immolation, subjected Larkin to a recurrent temptation: that of setting up house with Eva. On this question Monica was impressively firm: 'don't be robbed! don't be robbed of your soul!'

Monica Jones had many other virtues, chief among them her kindness and gentleness; she was stoical and unshockable, and could stand her ground under the awful searchlight of Larkin's candour and truthfulness. Anthony Thwaite, the editor, quotes sparingly but tellingly from her letters (some of which were two or three times the length of this review), where she also emerges as a tenacious literary critic, and an exceptionally close reader of Larkin's works in progress: it is startling to see how hard and how gingerly he struggled with poems that we now regard as etched in flint ('Church Going', say, or 'The Whitsun Weddings'). From Larkin's viewpoint, of course, her main strength was her toleration of meagre rewards: 'I accept, don't I, & *without* private reservation or grudge,' she wrote in 1962, 'that you don't like me enough to marry me.' She accepted much else: his emotional sluggishness, and his morbid dread of effort in any sphere except poetry.

The fact that Larkin made little effort with Monica is everywhere apparent in these pages. His *Selected Letters* constitutes a literary event of the first order (alongside, for example, the imminent *Saul Bellow: Letters*). But the present book will remain a literary curiosity. Here, Larkin's prose is habitually perfunctory and pressureless: 'Sun still shining here, but "not for long" I fear'; 'Of course, I might have been peevish anyway. More than likely!'; 'Sheldon [the new Sub-Librarian] has started: seems all right, but nothing to write home about'; 'Oh dear. I don't seem to be able to write you the interesting sort of letter I should like to ...' 'Aren't I writing badly,' he writes – and quite rightly. 'The day didn't get off to a very good start by my reading some stories by "Flannery O'Connor" in the bath – horribly depressing American South things.' American South 'things'? Larkin would never have written so exhaustedly to Amis, or to Thwaite, or to Barbara Pym, or to Robert Conquest (the world-famous historian whom he monotonously defames: 'a cheerful idiot', 'the feeblewit', 'what an old bore Bob is'). An old bore is what Larkin becomes, all too often, when he writes to Monica. But this too was no doubt salutary: a regular collapse into the unadorned everyday.

'It seems to me that what we have is a kind of homosexual relationship, disguised ... Don't you think yourself there's something fishy about it?' What I take this to mean is that Larkin wasn't very masculine and that Monica wasn't very feminine. They lived, or subsisted, in middle-sex. The process was far advanced, if not complete, by 1982, when I spent a long evening in their company. Larkin was demurely diffident (though he retained his 'impeccable attentive courtesy: grave, but at the same time sunlit', as Kingsley would say in his funeral address, four years later). As for Monica, well, despite her clothes (brown trousers of crushed velvet, wifebeater blouse, plus earrings the size of hula hoops), she resembled an all-in wrestler renowned for his indifference to the norms of fair play. She also dominated the evening, despite the presence of my father, as host. Larkin had clearly ceased to urge her to revise, drastically, the amount she said and the intensity with which she said it.

Still, one way or another, Monica enabled Larkin to cherish his crucial essences – and to turn them into immortal poetry. 'I am sure you are the one of this generation!' she wrote in 1955.

I like your poetry better than any that I ever see – oh, I am sure
you will make yr name! yr mark, do I mean – really be a real poet,
I feel more sure of it than ever before, it is *you* who are the one ...

Many a muse, no doubt, has murmured these words to many a poet. But Monica happened to be right. Larkin's life was a pitiful mess of evasion and poltroonery; his work was a triumph. That's the one to choose if (as he believed) you can't have both. The life rests in peace; the work lives on.

Guardian 2010

Iris Murdoch (1919–1999):
Age Will Win

'Like being chained to a corpse, isn't it?' This remark was offered to John Bayley by a fellow-sufferer in an Alzheimer marriage. He found himself 'repelled' by the simile, and didn't care to give it the demolition it deserved. A corpse, we may reflect, has several modest virtues: it is silent, stationary, and, above all, utterly predictable. A corpse, so to speak, has done its worst. In addition, a corpse is not loved, and a corpse will not die.

Moreover, the corpse John Bayley was allegedly chained to was Iris Murdoch: the pre-eminent female English novelist of her generation, and some would say (Updike is one of them) the pre-eminent English novelist of her generation, period. There can be no argument about the depth, the complexity, and indeed the beauty of Murdoch's mind: the novels attest to this on every page. And so the terror and pity evoked by Alzheimer's are in her case much sharpened. Bayley gave us that tragedy in three leisurely acts, namely *Iris, Iris and the Friends*, and the more tangential and novelistic *Widower's House*. The recent movie, Richard Eyre's *Iris*, unfolds the story before our eyes in one hundred minutes.

Very broadly, literature concerns itself with the internal, cinema with the external. In Bayley's meditative trilogy, the agony is partly eased by the consolations of philosophy, by the elegant and entirely natural detours into Proust, Hardy, Tolstoy, James. Eyre's version, on the other hand, for all its subtlety and tenderness, is excruciatingly raw. As you collect yourself while the credits roll, you find you have developed a lively admiration for cancer.

The Bayleys were eccentric – 'out of centre' – in their complementary brilliance (he is a novelist, a quondam poet, a literary critic of effortless fluidity). But they were also famously weird in their temperament and habits; and if you're an American, you don't know the type. They're the

73

kind of people who like being ill and like getting old, who prefer winter to summer and autumn to spring (yearning for 'grey days without sun'). They want rain, gloom, isolation, silence. 'We had no TV of course,' writes Bayley, commalessly; and the reluctant acquisition of a radio feels like a surrender to the brashest promiscuity. The Bayleys were further cocooned and united, it has to be said, by their commitment to extreme squalor.

At their place, even the soap is filthy. 'Single shoes [and single socks] lie about the house as if deposited by a flash flood ... Dried-out capless plastic pens crunch underfoot.' An infestation of rats is found to be 'congenial, even stimulating'. Everywhere they go, they have to hurdle great heaps of books, unwashed clothes, old newspapers, dusty wine bottles. The plates are stained, the glasses 'smeary'. The bath, so seldom used, is now unusable; the mattress is 'soggy'; the sheets are never changed. And we shall draw a veil over their underwear. On one occasion a large, recently purchased meat pie 'disappeared' in their kitchen. It was never found. The kitchen ate it.

One of the unforeseen benefits of having children is that it delivers you from your own childishness: there's no going back. John and Iris, naturally, did not toy long with the idea of becoming parents; it was themselves they wished to nurture ('two quaint children' and 'co-child' are typical Bayleyisms). This is intimately connected to their embrace of dirt and clutter, a clear example of *nostalgie de la boue* – literally, home-sickness for the mud, for the stickiness and ooziness of childhood, baby-hood, wombhood. The plan seems to work. Professor Bayley and Dame Iris are crustily cruising into a triumphant old age. And then a three year old comes to stay, to live, to die. It is Iris Murdoch.

Richard Eyre's movie is devotedly faithful to the main lines of Bayley's narrative. Yet there is also an undertow of creative defiance. The director has taken a highly unusual story about two very singular people – a story saturated with oddity, quiddity, exceptionality – and he has imbued it with the universal. How?

In the Iris books, Bayley glides around in time and space, indulging his 'intellectual being', in Milton's phrase, 'the thoughts that wander through eternity.' Eyre, characteristically, is direct and rigorous, almost geometrical in his approach. He constructs a double time-scheme of present and past, and lays down a reciprocal rhythm of back and forth, ebb and flow. Throughout, the film tremulously oscillates between the 1950s, when the two principals are just entering each other's force fields, and the 1990s, and the protracted visit from 'the dark doctor': Doctor A.

Thus, in the opening scenes, we watch the young Iris riding her bicycle (comfortably outspeeding the more timorous John), her head thrown back in exhilaration, appetite, dynamism; she is rushing forward to meet the fabulous profusion of her talent. Then we fade to the elderly Iris, in the chaos of her study, working on what will be her final fiction. In the margin she writes out, again and again, the word 'puzzled'. 'Puzzled' puzzles her; she is puzzled by 'puzzled.' 'All words do that when you take them by surprise', says her husband, comfortingly. Iris puzzles on; and in her eyes we see an infinity of fear. 'It will win' is the pathologist's prognosis. It will win: age will win. Eyre's emphasis is very marked. *Iris* becomes a tale of everyman and everywoman; it is about the tragedy of time.

What scenarists would call the 'back story' is a comedy of courtship. A vital symmetry establishes itself here, because young John is younger than young Iris (thirty-one to her thirty-seven) and most decidedly the junior partner. He is a lovestruck provincial virgin with a bad stammer. She is a robust bohemian and free spirit; and he soon learns 'how fearfully, how almost diabolically attractive' she is to all men (and most women). Her numerous lovers are artists and scholars, big brains, dominators. And her greatest resource is the private universe of her imagination. This, though, turns out to be John's entrée. In at least two senses, Iris settles for him, however lovingly. She intuits that domesticity – and the scruffier the better – will liberate her art.

The 'front story', the age story, begins with the onset of the disease, and spans the five years between diagnosis and death. Soon, 'the most intelligent woman in England' (Bayley's plausible evaluation) is watching the Teletubbies with a look of awed concentration on her face. This is now Iris at her best. A clinging, smothering dependence is punctuated by spells of terrifying agitation; she rattles the latch; she bolts, she flees. Alzheimer's is symmetrical, too, in its way: each new impoverishment reduces the awareness of loss. It is John's sufferings that multiply; and we are not spared his surges of rage, bitterness, and contempt. He had always wanted to possess her mind and its secrets. Now, as total master, he does possess it. And there's nothing there. Murdoch-readers won't mind (because they already know), but the movie never quite gives a sense of the intellectual height from which she fell.

Certain cerebrovascular disasters are called 'insults to the brain'. As already noted, the more prodigious the brain, the more studious (and in this case protracted) the insult. Iris's brain was indeed prodigious.

Returning to her novels, with hindsight, we get a disquieting sense of their wild generosity, their extreme innocence and skittishness, their worrying unpredictability. Her world is ignited by belief. She believes in everything: true love, veridical visions, magic, monsters, pagan spirits. She doesn't tell you how the household cat is looking, or even feeling: she tells you what it is thinking. Her novels constitute an extraordinarily vigorous imperium. But beneath their painterly opulence runs the light fever of fragility, like an omen.

Eyre's film is built on the cornerstones of four performances. As the young Iris, Kate Winslet is slightly hampered by the conventionality of her good looks; but the seriousness and steadiness of her gaze effectively suggest the dawning amplitude of the Murdoch imagination. Hugh Bonneville and Jim Broadbent play Bayley quite seamlessly (their stutters must have been calibrated by stopwatch); much more is asked of Broadbent, of course, and it is duly given. As for Judi Dench, as the mature Iris: she is transcendent. I knew Iris; I have respectfully kissed that cunning, bashful, secretive smile. It is as if Dame Judi and Dame Iris were always on a metaphysical collision course. Her performance has the rarest quality known to any art – that of apparent inevitability.

Maritimers talk of a turn in the tide as the moment when the waves 'reconsider'. Over and above its piercing juxtapositions of youth and age, *Iris* has an oceanic feel, and this provides a further symmetry. Although she never cared for George Eliot (or, relevantly, for bathwater), as Bayley notes, Iris's 'wholly different plots and beings remind me of Maggie Tulliver in *The Mill on the Floss*-saying, "I am in love with moistness."' And *Against Dryness* was one of the more famous of her philosophical essays. The imagery of Eyre's film is against dryness: the lakes and rivers in which John and Iris habitually immersed themselves; the sea, of course (Iris's key novel was *The Sea, the Sea*); and the rain, the rain, that seemed to hide them from the world. Hold yourself in readiness, too, for the floods of your tears.

Talk 2001

Postscript. In the row behind me at the screening of *Iris* sat John: Professor Bayley. When I staggered up to him, afterwards, it seemed to me that, of the dozen of us in the theatre, John was easily the most composed. He wasn't undone by *Iris*, as we were. He had already lived it. He alone was perfectly prepared.

The House of Windsor

Princess Diana: A Mirror, Not a Lamp

The strapline on the news channel was saying PRINCESS DIANA IN PARIS CAR CRASH; then it was saying PRINCESS DIANA SERIOUSLY INJURED; then it was saying PRINCESS DIANA DEAD. And for just an hour or so it felt like November 1963. 'This will be a fixing moment in your lives,' I intoned to my two sons, Louis and Jacob (I was thinking, naturally, about their two contemporaries, William and Harry). 'You will always remember where you were and who you were with when you heard this news.' Princess Diana dead: it seemed brutally inordinate. Because Diana had never been hard news, until then; Diana, in every sense, had always been soft. For once I found myself longing for a euphemism: 'passed away', perhaps, or 'succumbed'.

A sense of proportion would soon return. Or at least it would in my house. The true comparison, of course, is not with Kennedy but with Kennedy's wife, who was only fortuitously revered. (And consider the passive figure of Mr Zapruder, his shutter innocently open on the grassy knoll, as opposed to the darting figure of the crack paparazzo.) But in the immediate aftermath, one experienced some of the emotions associated with a major loss. You felt stunned from nowhere, as if something had veered in out of your blind spot.

That fatal ride has the quality of a dreadful dream. What was it like, being driven by a vainglorious drunk at appalling speed in an urban tunnel? With rising claustrophobia, the passenger will sense that the driver's mind is disorganised – that 'control' is in the process of being relinquished. And so it was. It makes your shins shudder to imagine the atrocious physics of the impact, as the Mercedes transformed itself into a weapon of blunt force. Next, the swat team of photographers and the final photo shoot. Whether or not the paparazzi helped cause Diana's death, they undoubtedly defiled its setting. They took pictures of the dying woman. How could they? But they did. And now the two sons, the princes, face not only the loss of a loving and lovable mother but also a bereavement uniquely contaminated by the market forces of fame.

Let us for a moment examine the nature of Diana's fame. One might call it a collateral celebrity, because it relied on no discernible contribution – except to the gaiety, and now the grief, of nations. Lady Diana Spencer awakened the love of the introverted heir to the English throne. And that was all. Brightness of eye, whiteness of tooth, a colluding smile, a certain transparency, a vividness, an exposed vulnerability: it was enough for him, and it was enough for us. Madonna sings. Grace Kelly acted. Diana simply breathed. She was a social-page figure who became a cover girl. One can soberly assert that the Diana story, in itself, was a non-story, remorselessly and fanatically annotated by our own projections and desires. Rather, *we* are the story. Equipped with no talent, Diana evolved into the most celebrated woman alive. What does that tell us about the planet Earth?

She certainly believed she had a talent: a talent for love. She felt she could inspire it, transmit it, increase its general sum. It has been said about her (what hasn't been said about her?) that she adopted various charities as 'accessories'. But the causes Diana was most strongly identified with – Aids, hospices, land mines – demanded more than an unreflecting commitment. There is no question that she made a difference to the gay community, in England and perhaps elsewhere; her support came at a crucial time, in defiance of tabloid opinion as well as royal prudence. Yet the fact remains that Diana was far less dedicated than, for instance, her onetime sister-in-law, Princess Anne, whose Hanoverian homeliness consigned her to near-total obscurity. Through no fault of her own, Diana was the heiress of the tyranny of appearances and the snobbery of looks.

She could touch and soothe; perhaps she believed she could heal. Watching her on television, jolting with tears as she listened to a speech praising and defending her work, one saw signs of an almost delusional inner drama. If power corrupts the self, then absolute fame must surely distort it. Her enthusiasms were crankish, hypochondriac, self-obsessive: aromatherapy, colonic irrigation, the fool's gold of astrology. Diana, I repeat, was 'soft' news. She caused sensations by wearing a strapless party dress or by gaining a kilo of weight.

Here was a woman who made headlines with every wave of her hand, every twitch of her eyebrow. This is why her death – her meta-morphosis into hard news – feels so savage. Death has enshrined her and frozen her in time. It has also fulfilled her own prophecy. She did have a gift for love: look at the people, in their millions, weeping on the streets of London. Diana was a mirror, not a lamp. You looked at her and saw your own ordinary humanity, written in lights. After all, everyone is a star, everyone is a prima donna, in the karaoke age.

On the larger scale, Diana's contribution to history is both paradox-ical and inadvertent. She will go down as the chief saboteur of the mon-archy. It wasn't just the divorce, the tell-all boyfriend, the married rugby star. She introduced an informality, a candid modernity, into a system that could offer no resistance to it; and she had a daily beauty in her life that made the Windsors ugly.

Above all she will be remembered as a phenomenon of pure star-dom. Her death was a terrible symbol of that condition. She takes her place, among the broken glass and crushed metal, in the iconography of the car crash, alongside James Dean, Albert Camus, Jayne Mansfield, and Princess Grace. These other victims died unpursued. They weren't fleeing the pointed end of their own renown: men on motorcycles with computerized cameras and satellite-linked mobile phones. The paparazzi are the high-tech dogs of fame. But it must be admitted that we sent them into that tunnel, to nourish our own mysterious needs.

Time 1997

The Queen's Speech, the Queen's Heart

Word of the accident reached Balmoral Castle, in Scotland, at one o'clock in the morning of August 31, 1997. Word of the death came through at four. Prince Charles was in residence, with his sons; the Queen advised him not to wake them (they would be needing their strength), and added, 'We must get the radios out of their rooms.' Charles broke the news just after seven. Prince Harry, then twelve, couldn't quite take it in. Was everyone sure? he wondered; would somebody check? The boys were asked if they would like to accompany the family to church (it was Sunday). Prince William, then fifteen, wanted to attend – so he could 'talk to Mummy'.

'The world's going to go completely mad,' Charles said, presciently, when he heard. By the following Thursday, the Royal Family was facing the strangest crisis in its history. Certainly, King Egbert (802–39) would not have known what to make of it; and neither did Queen Elizabeth II (1952–). 'We don't have protocol here,' an eminent equerry once drawled, 'just bloody good manners.' But national cohesion, and indeed public order, now depended on a preposterous punctilio: the people wanted a flag flying at half-mast above Buckingham Palace, and the Queen wasn't having it. Flags were flying at half-mast at other royal seats; the flag at the palace flies only when the Queen is staying there (and she was still tarrying in Scotland: a further scandal). The flag at the palace doesn't go halfway down for anybody's death, even the monarch's. Within the inner circle, the dispute was unprecedentedly fierce ('A lot of people,' said an aide, 'were heavily scarred by it'). The desperate courtiers were unanimous: the flag must go (halfway) up. But the Windsors hadn't yet sensed which way the wind was blowing.

As in all matters royal, we are dealing here not with pros and cons, with arguments and counter-arguments; we are dealing with signs and symbols, with fever and magic. To the Queen, the flag (or its absence) was an emblem of her non-negotiable inheritance. To her subjects, the flag was an emblem – a display – of grief; and a display of grief was what they were demanding. Prime Minister Tony Blair was on to 'the mood' so quickly that you feel he must have partaken of it. Before noon on that same Sunday, he huskily addressed the nation: 'We are to-day a nation, in Britain, in a state of shock, in mourning, in grief that is so deeply painful for us … She was the People's Princess, and that's how she will stay, how she will remain in our hearts and in our memories for ever.' Now the British newspapers, having cheerfully savaged Diana for years (right up to and including that weekend), were cheerfully at work on her black-bordered canonization. 'WHERE IS OUR QUEEN? WHERE IS HER FLAG?' 'SHOW US YOU CARE.' 'YOUR PEOPLE ARE SUFFERING. SPEAK TO US, MA'AM.'

Diana's funeral was set for Saturday. The Queen had intended to process south, in the royal train, on Friday night. But by now she had adapted to the new reality – had remembered that she was a servant as well as a potentate. She flew down on Friday afternoon; she would speak, she would show us she cared; the flag, which had not been lowered for her father, George VI, would be lowered for Diana. There were heightened fears for the safety of the Queen and Prince Philip when they arrived at Buckingham Palace. Obligingly they climbed out of their limousine and inspected the shoulder-high heaps of flowers and tributes ('Diana, Queen of Heaven', 'Regina Coeli', and so on). It was felt that, at the very least, there might be a repetition of Queen Victoria's experience in her Golden Jubilee year (1887), when she was greeted in the East End by what she called 'a horrid noise' she had never heard before: booing. It didn't happen. Here is Robert Lacey's account in his exemplary book *Monarch: The Life and Reign of Elizabeth II*:

> As Elizabeth II, dressed in black, walked down the line of mourners, an eleven-year-old girl handed her five red roses.
>
> 'Would you like me to place them for you?' asked the queen.
>
> 'No, Your Majesty,' replied the girl. 'They are for you.'
>
> 'You could hear the crowd begin to clap,' recalls an aide. 'I remember thinking, "Gosh, it's all right."'

Well, not yet. There was also the speech. The Queen would have to come as close as she could bring herself to pretending that she loved Princess Diana.

★

Lacey is very good on the Queen's feelings about feelings, the 'curious knotting in the impulses' that complicates her attempts to exercise emotion. She could write a passionate four-page letter to a friend in response to a brief commiseration about the violent death of a favourite corgi. This was heartache of a manageable and articulate order. But when, in 1966, a hill of slag collapsed on a village in South Wales, Aberfan, killing a hundred and sixteen children (and twenty-eight adults), the Queen, against all advice and family precedent, delayed her visit for more than a week. Her husband and her brother-in-law went (and so did the PM, Harold Wilson); but she felt she would be an immodest distraction from the continuing rescue and relief.

When she did go (and she has maintained her links with Aberfan), she involuntarily revealed why she had stayed away. In the photographs, you can see the terror as well as the pity in her eyes, and the doubt. She was the Queen. What did Aberfan tell her about the state of Great Britain? And what did it tell her about her habitual (and sincere) worship of a beneficent deity? One of her titles is Defender of the Faith, a mission close to her (Protestant) heart; and that faith was rattled at Aberfan. Monarchical emotion is emotion hugely magnified. It asks for a detachment that Queen Elizabeth only imperfectly commands.

She respects sincerity, and cannot fake it. This is one of Lacey's typically pertinent anecdotes:

Early in her reign, Elizabeth II was due to visit the Yorkshire town of Kingston upon Hull and asked one of her private secretaries to prepare a first draft of her speech.

'I am very pleased to be in Kingston today,' the draft confidently started.

The young queen crossed out the word 'very'.

'I will be *pleased* to be in Kingston,' she explained. 'But I will not be *very* pleased.'

One duly notes that she was, nonetheless, 'pleased' to mingle with various humdrum worthies in the dour surrounds of Kingston upon Hull. The woman is adamantine. How could she emote, to order, for the definitively brittle Diana?

It was to be, in effect, her first live televised speech – in two senses. The Queen addressed the people in real time; and she also had to show them the live being, the creature of glands and membranes. She spoke from the Chinese Dining Room in Buckingham Palace. The windows were open, and you could hear the crowd, ten thousand or more, milling and murmuring in the background. An aide asked the Queen, 'Do you think you can do it?' And she answered, 'If that's what I've got to do.' The countdown began; the floor manager mouthed 'Go.'

She was being asked to confront an intense need that she didn't understand. No one understood it. Deborah Hart Strober and Gerald S. Strober's *The Monarchy: An Oral Biography of Elizabeth II* (Broadway) contains, at this point, entry after entry from assorted insiders expressing blunt incomprehension of the public mood: 'absolutely amazed ... really amazing ... beyond my capacity to understand ... inexplicable ... astonished ... staggered,' and so on. And we still don't understand it. My best guess is that the phenomenon was millennial. Human beings have always behaved strangely when the calendric zeros loom. And Diana-mania bore several clear affinities to the excesses described in (for example) Norman Cohn's classic *The Pursuit of the Millennium*: it involved mass emotion; it exalted a personage of low cultural level; it was self-flagellatory in tendency; and it was very close to violence. The phenomenon was, then, part of mankind's cyclical festival of irrationality. In the Middle Ages and beyond, Cohn shows, something like this – the exaltation of an illiterate ploughboy – happened without fail not every thousand years but every hundred, and every fifty.

'So what I say to you now,' Elizabeth II made clear, 'as your Queen and as a grandmother, I say from my heart.' It was an extraordinary act of balance: she gave a near-pathological populace what it wanted, while remaining true to her own being. Of the two words they most needed to hear, she allowed them one ('grief'), but not the other (see below). She didn't sell her integrity to the delusive yearnings of the many. Nor did she attempt the solace of aphoristic eloquence. Curiously enough, she saved that for the events of September 11: 'Grief is the price we pay for love.' And there is the word that England thirsted to hear. One final, mangled irony: Diana's boyfriend, Dodi Fayed, was an Egyptian Muslim. 'To Diana and Dodi,' read the inscription on one floral tribute, 'together in heaven'. But which heaven?

And it was not yet over. With the Windsors, a familial drama inevitably becomes a national drama; but the drama had now become global. At dinner on Friday, it was still uncertain whether the two young princes would walk behind the gun carriage that held their mother's coffin; and 'their composure', as Lacey notes, 'would be the pivot on which the whole occasion turned'. The struggle, once again, was not to divulge emotion but to master it. This was a heavy call on their courage, and, of the two, Prince William was the more uncertain. The royal, the kingly thing, plainly, was to walk. Prince Philip, who had not intended to join the cortège, finally asked his grandson, 'If I walk, will you walk with me?' And William walked.

If we are to venture into the psyches of the royals, we must first understand that they were all world-famous *babies*. Driven out of the Royal Mews in an open carriage for her regular airings, the diapered Elizabeth drew large crowds of cheering, waving admirers; one of her earliest skills was to wave back. She made the cover of *Time* at the age of three. The first biography, *The Story of Princess Elizabeth*, appeared when she was four. 'She has an air of authority & reflectiveness astonishing in an infant,' wrote Winston Churchill, who would be the first of her ten Prime Ministers. As the Queen celebrates her seventy-sixth birthday, she can reflect that the only time she misbehaved in public was at her christening. She cried throughout, and had to be dosed with dill water.

And Princess Elizabeth was, at this stage, a minor royal. She was the granddaughter of George V (whom she called Grandpa England), and the niece of the heir apparent, Edward, Prince of Wales. The King died in January 1936, when Elizabeth was nine. On December 10, Edward VIII signed the 'Instrument of Abdication' (in order to marry the twice-divorced Wallis Simpson), and, in his later wanderings, became a living example of royal futility. The ten year old now became the heir presumptive. While her father, who was suddenly George VI, went off to the Accession Council on December 12, Princess Elizabeth and her sister, Princess Margaret, were given a refresher course on their curtsy by their governess, Marion Crawford; on his return they greeted him with this formality, and it jolted him. 'He stood for a moment touched and taken aback. Then he stooped and kissed them both warmly,' Crawford wrote.

'Does that mean you're going to be Queen?' was a question Margaret put to her sister. 'Yes, I suppose it does,' said Elizabeth. 'Poor you,' said Margaret. Their grandmother Lady Strathmore noticed that Elizabeth had started 'ardently praying for a brother'.

Prince Philip of Greece was her third cousin, and she had known him, slightly, since childhood. The *coup de foudre* seems to have come when she was thirteen and he was an eighteen-year-old cadet – and the Second World War was six weeks away. Although penniless and homeless, and a nomad all his life, Philip could boast a sensational pedigree (he had a great-great-grandmother in common with Elizabeth: Queen Victoria). His penurious father moped in Monte Carlo. His deaf mother fancied that she was the mistress of both Jesus Christ and Buddha; Freud himself advised radiation of the ovaries 'to accelerate the menopause'. The mental frailty of Diana Spencer has sometimes been attributed to her unhappy childhood. Much more graphic insecurity had the opposite effect on Philip, investing him with a brisk, and sometimes brusque, self-sufficiency. Elizabeth knew what she would be needing in a husband – a source of strength. And this was the strength that Philip was still able to offer his grandsons, nearly sixty years later, on that Saturday in 1997.

Philip and Elizabeth both had a 'good' war, Philip distinguishing himself on the battleship *Valiant*, Elizabeth forming part of the royal *tableau vivant* of national solidarity (Hitler called her mother 'the most dangerous woman in Europe'). The two of them corresponded, and there were visits to Windsor and elsewhere when Philip was on leave. Early in 1947, Elizabeth went abroad for the first time, to South Africa; the idea was to train her up for royal responsibilities but also to test the constancy of her feelings for Philip, to whom she was now unofficially engaged. On April 21, her twenty-first birthday, she addressed the Empire and the Commonwealth, and the speech was to be broadcast from Cape Town. 'It has made me cry,' she admitted, after reviewing the final draft. Elizabeth was talking to her people, but one suspects that she was also talking to her future husband:

> It is very simple. I declare before you all that my whole life whether
> it be long or short shall be devoted to your service and the service
> of our great imperial family to which we all belong. But I shall not
> have strength to carry out this resolution alone unless you join in it
> with me, as I now invite you to do: I know that your support will

be unfailingly given. God help me to make good my vow, and God
bless all of you who are willing to share in it.

It is not *very* simple, is it – to agree to become a metaphor? At this time,
Philip told a friend, 'This is my destiny – to support my wife in what lies
ahead for her.'

They married later that year – a flash of luxury in the postwar mono-
chrome. Within three months, Elizabeth was carrying Charles III. Philip
was posted to Malta, and for a while she experienced the unrelieved
exoticism of ordinary life. They were in Kenya when word of the King's
death reached the royal party. An old friend passed the news on to Philip,
and later said, 'I never felt so sorry for anyone in all my life.' George VI
was fifty-six. The total claim on the young couple's freedom was now
formally submitted. 'He took her up to the garden,' the friend went on.
'And they walked slowly up and down the lawn while he talked and
talked and talked to her.'

In addition to their innumerable duties, almost all of them excruciating, the Royal Family has one main function: to go on being a family.
In *The Royals*, Kitty Kelley's louche but lively blockbuster of 1997, the
most capacious subsection in the index for Prince Philip is 'and women'
('76, 152, 154–55, 159–60, 192, 196, 265, 422, 423–27, 510–11'). Lacey's
emphasis falls the other way ('rumours of infidelities, 166-168, 212').
And there is certainly a moral persuasiveness in Philip's confidence to a
relative, 'How could I be unfaithful to the Queen? There is no way that
she could possibly retaliate.' The skittish Diana could not dissimulate her
exasperation with married life; but neither could the duteous Charles.
The demeanour of his father and mother, at least to this distant observer,
is eloquent of mutual ease and admiration. Anyway, there they are, still,
in 2002.

Divorce is modern, and monarchs must fear modernity. Now
modernity came to the Windsors in the form of their children. When
Princess Margaret broke up with Antony Armstrong-Jones, it was the
first royal divorce in centuries. It used to be the case that the Lord
Chamberlain personally excluded the divorced from the Queen's
presence. 'In later years the Lord Chamberlain's duties were modified,'
Kelley writes, her acerbity finding its mark, 'so the Queen could visit
her divorced cousins, her divorced sister, her divorced daughter, and
her two divorced sons, including the heir to the throne.' Meanwhile,

her third son, Edward (recently married), was somehow acquiring the nickname of Dockyard Doris.

So we come to 1992, the 'annus horribilis'. Princess Anne divorced in April. In August, the Duchess of York – Fergie – was photographed topless with a 'financial adviser' (who was administering the famous 'toe-job'). At this juncture, another tabloid released the 'Squidgygate' tapes, in which Diana pillow-talked on the phone with a young car salesman. And that November it was revealed that Charles had been recorded while having a similarly intimate chat with Camilla Parker Bowles. Long intrigued by the idea of the transmigration of souls, Charles saw himself reborn as, 'God forbid, a Tampax', so that he could 'just live inside your trousers'. The Camillagate and Squidgygate tapes were both available on phone lines provided by the newspapers. You could listen to Charles saying, 'I want to feel my way along you, all over you and up and down you and in and out ... particularly in and out.' Then you could listen to Diana saying, 'Bloody hell, after all I've done for this fucking family.' Then came the great fire at Windsor. The monarchy was burning.

Or so it seemed. In fact, only Diana had the power to bring it all down; and this was her semi-subliminal intention. George Orwell, in his long essay 'The English People', described the placards in the streets during the Silver Jubilee celebrations for George V, in 1935: 'Some of the London slum streets bore ... the rather servile slogan "Poor but Loyal."' Other slogans, though, 'coupled loyalty to the King with hostility to the landlord, such as "Long Live the King. Down with the Landlord", or more often, "No Landlords Wanted" or "Landlords Keep Away."' Orwell elaborates:

> The affection shown for George V ... was obviously genuine, and it was even possible to see in it the survival, or recrudescence, of an idea almost as old as history, the idea of the King and the common people being in a sort of alliance against the upper classes.

What Diana tried to bring about was an alliance between herself and the common people against the Royal Family. 'The People's Princess' was an entirely sophistical notion – and it worked. Despite the 'pattern of deceit and narcissism' (Lacey), the schemes and manipulations, and the near-Sicilian taste for revenge, Diana, of course, had a genius for love – for indiscriminate love. Her besetting humour was self-pity;

and temporary relief from its corrosiveness, I think, lay behind the undoubted force of her presence among the suffering. This connects again to the dangerous emotions that attended her death. Self-pity is a natural component of grief, of a roused sense of mortality, but in Dianamania it sourly predominated. 'Bloody hell, after all I've done for this fucking family': in the end, horribly, what she did for the family was to die. It was a little Restoration.

This project of Diana's was doubly radical, because the monarchy is maintained by love. If you are English, then your patriotism is unconscious (Orwell again); when it becomes conscious, and focused, it surprises you with a sense of hunger awakened and allayed. The feeling is unmistakably familial. 'A princely marriage is the brilliant edition of a universal fact,' Bagehot wrote, 'and as such, it rivets mankind.' The same could be said of a princely funeral – or, nowadays, of a princely divorce. The Royal Family is just a family, writ inordinately large. They are the glory, not the power; and it would clearly be far more grownup to do without them. But riveted mankind is hopelessly addicted to the irrational, with reliably disastrous results, planetwide. The monarchy allows us to take the occasional holiday from reason; and on that holiday we do no harm.

New Yorker 2002

More Personal – I

You Ask the Questions (1)*

How is John Self (from Money*) doing in 2001? What about Keith Talent* (London Fields)*?*
Chris O'Hare, Belfast

John still works in advertising. He no longer toys with the prospect of a career in Hollywood. He has traded in his Fiasco for a second-hand Culprit. He has gained yet more weight, and his girlfriends are not getting any younger. But sometimes I think he is reading a little bit more than he used to.

Keith goes away every winter: to prison. In the temperate months, he lives semi-rough way up Ladbroke Grove. He never sees his wife and daughter (who are both fine). He still hopes for fame in the world of professional darts, though less ardently, believing that all this clean-look rubbish has destroyed the sport's historical links with the pub.

But these are just guesses. Curiously, the moment you type that last full stop, your characters gain, or regain, free will. At the end of *Night Train*, I make it look as if the narrator-heroine's suicide is inevitable and imminent. Every now and then, though, I think she came through and survived.

In memory and thought your minor characters are perhaps static, but the main ones continue to have their world (not very often visited) where they strive and age.

Have you read Zadie Smith's White Teeth *or Dave Eggers's* A Heartbreaking Work of Staggering Genius*? If not, why not?*
Katie Bowden, by email

---

* 'You', in this case, referred to readers of the *Independent* (in 2001). The questions and answers were written, not spoken – hence their inclusion here. For the vital difference between spoken and written, please turn to the first paragraph of the piece on Christopher Hitchens (page 317).

I have read Zadie Smith, and with a constant smile of admiration. I haven't read Dave Eggers's book, but I have read the title, and that took quite a while. The Nabokov novel we know as *Invitation to a Beheading* was for a while called 'Invitation to an Execution', but the 'repeated suffix' was of course avoided. *A Heartbreaking Work of Staggering Genius* has two-ings in it. But I'm embarrassed to say that my immersion in Eggers is only title deep. I did an event with him once, and found him very likable and articulate.

You have attacked the brutality of journalists, yet when young, you could be a savage reviewer of older writers. Do you regret that now?
Joseph Dartford, Hertfordshire

Insulting people in print is a vice of youth and a minor corruption of power. You ought to stop doing it as you get older, or else you look like mutton dressed as lamb. Insulting people in your middle-age is undignified, and looks more and more demented as you head towards the twilight. The increasingly twitchy and uncertain figure of Tom Paulin, still insulting away, springs to mind. I think I did write a couple of career-ending reviews in my youth, and, yes, I do regret that.

Do you believe that you have evolved into the 'New Man', as you describe yourself in your latest work, The War Against Cliché?
Jazz Kilburn-Toppin, by email

I said that the 'New Man' (an idealistic figure of the 1970s) was in danger of becoming an old man prematurely, what with all the housework he's done. I had (and have) a hand in raising four children. I got through that without becoming a New Man, but not without becoming an old one.

Why are the classics of modern US fiction superior to their British equivalents?
Peter Miley, Plymouth

Perhaps because America is the centre of the world – just as we were in the nineteenth century, and had all those epic novels to prove it. But the days of American centrality are numbered, and I think British fiction is in very good health, now that it includes Indian fiction, Australian fiction, and all the rest.

*Are you less worried about nuclear war / ecological crisis than a decade ago? If so,
were those anxieties more to do with you rather than the planet?*
Liam Knights, Winchester

The nuclear situation has changed radically, and so have my concerns
about it. We are no longer in the age of Mutual Assured Destruction; we
are in the age of Uncontrolled Proliferation. It's still a mess, but the species has made a great evolutionary advance, and has clawed its way clear
of the most obvious firebreak: arsenal-clearing thermonuclear exchange.

Ecology will soon be a universal obsession: just wait. More generally, it's natural for us to identify with the planet now, because the
planet seems to be ageing at the same rate we are. That the planet is
getting older would not have occurred to a native of the eighteenth
century, any more than it would have occurred to the dog sleeping at
his feet.

Do you ever worry about turning into your father, Kingsley?
Jonathan Connolly, Bristol

This question cannot but sound sinisterly comic to me. If the Kingsley
we are referring to is the Kingsley of his last years, then I could naturally
do without the physical metamorphosis for at least the time being. Probably the suggestion is: am I worried about inheriting his political curve,
worried about waking up one morning as the apoplectic reactionary he
would sometimes (morosely but playfully) impersonate? No. Our political histories are antithetical. I have always been pallidly left-of-centre.
In our more vituperative disagreements (about nuclear weapons, for
example), I used to counter-attack by saying that *he* was the politically
excitable creature, not me (my father served as an active Communist
from the late 1930s to 1956). In other ways, I wouldn't mind turning into
Kingsley. I would like to maintain such lifelong affections with all my
children. And I wouldn't mind writing a novel as good as *The Old Devils*,
when I'm sixty-four.

I saw A High Wind in Jamaica *[the film in which Amis appeared aged thir-
teen] and thought you died quite movingly. Why did your acting career pack up
at such an early age?*
Chloe Sinclair, Norwich

My acting career was not a career but a blip and a fluke. I was spectacularly talentless. They had to shoot my final scene ten or twelve times, because I kept falling to my death (in fact a three-foot drop on to a mattress) with a look of glee on my face.

Why have you persistently smoked roll-ups over the years? They're messy and fiddly, they're always going out, they hurt your throat, and they must drive you nuts while you're writing.
Claire George, Gloucestershire

I didn't just happen upon roll-ups. I tried every other smoke on the planet (and had long cohabitations with Marlboro and Disque Bleu) before crystallising into Golden Virginia and Rizla Greens. It's simply the best burn available. Also, on long plane journeys, during epic movies, etc., you can stick your nose into the pouch and snort up some aromatic nicotine: it postpones the craving, and feels genuinely and impressively detrimental to your health.

One of the websites about your work (http: / /martinamis.albion.edu) had a poll a while ago on which was your best novel. Money *(1984) won by quite a way. Do you agree with the verdict, or at least understand the reasons for it? And is there an emotional impulse not to agree, as it implies that you haven't written anything better in seventeen years?*
Stephen Pepper, Kingston upon Thames

In *Money*, I dispensed with form and trusted entirely to voice, and this released a great deal of energy. I'm glad that gamble worked, but I have not felt the urge to repeat it. If the urge resurfaces, I will obey it. Anyway, it doesn't mean much to say that *Money* is a 'better' novel than, say, *Time's Arrow. Money* is just more fun. Nowadays I look back less and less. Even to check the proofs of a completed work feels like a chore and a distraction. I think about the next one, and the one after that, and the one after that.

Is writing novels regulated by the law of diminishing returns, or do you still get the same surge of adrenalin that must have come during the creation of Success, Money, *etc.?*
Tom De Castella, Brixton, London

Well, it's not the same surge. And, on the page, I suppose your musical energy can expect to proceed diminuendo. But put it this way. A decade ago, when I wrote, I used to say to myself, 'I'm too busy to shit.' Now I say to myself, 'I'm too busy to pee.' And 'busy' is shorthand: I do not face a blizzard of engagements, I sit alone in my study all the working day. 'Busy' means fascinated to the point of being incapable of doing anything else.

Which of your books do you think will be most valued in 100 years' time?
Linda Grayburn, by email

Your books are like your children: you try not to have favourites. When asked to name his favourite novel, Anthony Burgess always said, 'The next one.'

Do you feel you have ever successfully portrayed a female character? Does the heroine of Night Train *count?*
Linda Grayburn, by email

An early novel, *Other People*, was written entirely from the heroine's point of view, as were about 200 pages of *London Fields*. The heroine of *Night Train*, Mike Hoolihan, is about as butch as a woman can get, but she certainly 'counts'. She's my only first-person heroine, and going from the 'she' to the 'I' is like a slow zoom inside you. It felt natural, all the same.

State your preferences, Martin: Coke or Pepsi? Regular or Ruffles? Tom Jones or Engelbert Humperdinck? Oreos or Hydrox? Tolstoy or Dostoyevsky? Sean Connery or Roger Moore? Budweiser or Miller or Coors? Levi's or Wrangler? Cheez-Its or Cheese Nips? Hemingway or Fitzgerald? Ford or Chevy? Beatles or Rolling Stones? Domino's or Pizza Hut? Gielgud or Richardson? New York or L.A.? Twinkies or Ding Dongs? Kingsley Amis or Martin Amis?
Gooch McCracken, by email

Coke. No opinion. Tom Jones. Oreos. Tolstoy. Sean Connery (are you kidding?). None: Corona or Becks. Levi's (said quietly). No opinion. Fitzgerald. Chevy. Both. Pizza Hut (and Pizza Express). Gielgud. New York. No opinion. No strong opinion.

What inspires you to write?
Nick Flach, by email

The inspiration for a particular novel can be a phrase, a sentence, an image, a situation. But novelists aren't poets. They are grinders. What sends me up to my study is a feeling in the back of the throat – like the desire for my first cigarette. Writing is a far more physical process than is generally believed. Half the time you seem to be mutely and helplessly obeying your body.

When you write about your own emotions – as when discussing the deaths of your father and Lucy Partington [Amis's cousin, murdered by Fred West] – how hard is it not to lie?
Laura Cartwright, Cambridge

It was my intention in *Experience* [a memoir published in 2000] to show all my nearest and dearest in the most generous possible light. There are no lies in my book, though there are lapses of memory, chronological snarl-ups, and so on. Some of these surprised me, startled me, but did not distress me. I suppose it's integrity of memory that's important. In writing a memoir you also find out how screwed-up you are – how many beefs and grudges you harbour. 'When a writer is born into a family', said Philip Roth, 'that's the end of that family.' It hasn't been the end of mine, because I had no familial scores to settle.

What's the one question you've never been asked? And the answer?
Janet Spence, by email

There are millions of questions I've never been asked. These do not include the one that goes: 'Do you set yourself a time to write each day or do you just do it when you feel like it?' Answer: both. The related question I've never been asked is the one that goes: 'When you write, how hard do you press on the paper?' I suppose my imaginary answer would be: 'quite' or 'fairly' or 'reasonably'.

Independent 2001

The Fourth Estate and the Question of Heredity*

I was born in Clapham in 1922. My literary career kicked off in 1956 when, as a resident of Swansea, South Wales, I published my first novel, *Lucky Jim*. This was followed by *That Uncertain Feeling* and *Take a Girl Like You*, among others; but my really productive period began in 1973, when I published both *The Riverside Villas Murder* and *The Rachel Papers*. The year 1978 saw the appearance of *Jake's Thing* and *Success*; in 1984 it was the turn of *Stanley and the Women* and *Money*; in 1991 it was *The Russian Girl* and *Time's Arrow*. This last was shortlisted for the Booker Prize; but I had already won the Booker Prize with *The Old Devils* in 1986. I am, incidentally, the only writer to have received the Somerset Maugham Award twice – the first time for my first first novel, the second time for my second first novel.

That period, alas, came to an end in 1995. Since then, though, I have been far from sluggardly. This year, at the age of eighty-eight, I publish my thirty-seventh work of fiction, *The Pregnant Widow*, and next year will see another novel, *Lionel Asbo: State of England* – my sixty-seventh book, which nicely sets the scene for my ninetieth birthday. I am responsible

---

*This piece (of 2010) was satirical in intent, and satire tends to need a bit of commentary, or in this case a bit of cladding (hence the introductory footnote and the appended last paragraph, which is technically a postscript). There had been a flurry in the British press, supposedly in answer to some (approving) comments of mine about euthanasia. In my opinion the hostility of the response boiled down, as so often, to the fact that I was the writer child of a writer parent. Such an alignment is for some reason extremely rare – writer siblings are by comparison ten a penny (the Brontës, the Jameses, the Manns, the Powyses) – and gives rise to strange apprehensions. Parent and child are subliminally conflated, so that (for example) the child's welcome in the world is quickly overstayed.

for fourteen volumes of non-fiction; I have taught at Swansea, Princeton, Cambridge, Vanderbilt, and Manchester. May I quote Anthony Burgess? 'Wedged as we are between two eternities of idleness, there is no excuse for being idle now.' I have been married four times (two of my wives are novelists), and I have eight children and seven grandchildren – so far. Oh, and I almost forgot to mention my *Collected Poems* (1979).

The writer described above is of course semi-imaginary. But such a phantasm, such a basilisk of longevity and industriousness, seems to exist in the minds, or in the anxiety dreams, of a tiny stratum: British – no, English – feature-writers who occasionally address themselves to literary affairs. Incidentally, this is what they're groping to express when they say I'm 'turning into Kingsley'. They should relax: I'm already Kingsley. In truth, it is easily the most unusual thing about me: I am the only hereditary novelist in the Anglophone literary corpus. Thus I am the workaholic and hypermanic – and by now very elderly – Prince Charles of English letters. And I have been about the place for much too long.

About 95 per cent of the coverage has passed me by, but some new tendencies are clear enough. What's different, this time round, is that the writer, or this writer, gets blamed for all the slanders he incites in the press. Some quite serious commentators (D.J. Taylor, for one) have said that I'm controversial-on-purpose whenever I have a book coming out. Haven't they noticed that the papers pick up on my remarks whether I have a book coming out or not? And how can you be controversial-on-purpose without ceasing to care what you say? The *Telegraph*, on its front page, offers the following: 'Martin Amis: "Women have too much power for their own good".' This would be the equivalent of 'Ian McEwan: "Climate change science is a vicious lie".' I suppose the *Telegraph* was trying to make me sound 'provocative'. Well, they messed that up too. I don't sound provocative. I sound like a much-feared pub bore in Southend.

And yet experienced journalists will look me in the eye and solemnly ask, 'Why do you do it?' They are not asking me why I say things in public (which is an increasingly pertinent question). They are asking me why I deliberately stir up the newspapers. How can they have such a slender understanding of their own trade? Getting taken up (and distorted) in the newspapers is not something I do. It's something the newspapers do. The only person in England who can 'manipulate' the fourth estate is, appropriately, Katie Price (a.k.a. Jordan). But there I go again – victimising Katie. No, the vow of silence looks more and more attractive. That would be a story too, but it would only be a story once. Wouldn't it?

To return briefly to the longevity theme – and all the stuff about streetcorner suicide parlours, and the 'silver tsunami' (demographer shorthand for what has been described as 'the most profound population shift in history'). The press reacted with righteous dismay; but I saw no recent headline saying 'Terry Pratchett is mad', by way of commentary on *his* remarks about euthanasia. In addition, it turns out that 75 per cent of Britons (but none of the political parties) agree with him and agree with me.

Thus the euthanasia question, eerily, is the reverse image of capital punishment at the time of its abolition. The people were still in favour of judicial killing, but the government insisted on reform. That was in 1968. Forty-odd years later, the people, while no longer keen on judicial killing, are strongly in favour of medical killing, or mercy killing, but this is a reform that no politician dares countenance.

Of course, Sir Terry's dignified statement was taken from a public lecture; mine was a mishmash of half-quotes from a sardonic novel. For the interested, the passage reads (I am referring to Europe's distorted age structures):

> Hoi polloi: the many. And, oh, we will be many (he meant the generation less and less affectionately known as the Baby Boomers). And we will be hated, too. Governance, for at least a generation, he read, will be a matter of transferring wealth from the young to the old. And they won't like that, the young. They won't like the silver tsunami, with the old hogging the social services and stinking up the clinics and the hospitals, like an inundation of monstrous immigrants. There will be age wars, and chronological cleansing …

Then, too, Sir Terry has Alzheimer's – a condition made yet more tragic by the liveliness of the mind it here afflicts (I am thinking also of Iris Murdoch and Saul Bellow). And Sir Terry is older than me. Or is he? Well, yes and no. I am eighty-eight – but I am also twenty-four (look at the photographs). A sixty-year-old grandfather, I am, in truth, still the 'bad boy' (not even the bad man) of English letters. Who could possibly 'manipulate' perceptions as chaotic as these?

Writers should come from nowhere. This sounds right as a slogan, and I like its spirit. Writers do almost always come from nowhere, the children of schoolteachers, entrepreneurs, accountants, traders, bankers, and (especially) miners. I didn't come from nowhere; an English novelist, I am the biological issue of an English novelist (and if you hold that these things can rub off by mere propinquity, then bear in mind that for a formative eighteen years I was the grateful stepson of yet another English novelist, Elizabeth Jane Howard). Anthony Trollope's mother Frances was in her day a well-known writer; we have the Alexander Dumas team, Sr. and Jr.; Auberon Waugh (son of Evelyn) looked the part for a while, but then gave up fiction; we also have Susan Cheever (and, briefly, David Updike). And that's about it, in any language. I accept that the two-generational thread is offensively unegalitarian, bearing the taint of inherited privilege. But perhaps its freakish quality is what some people find alien (and I too am sometimes disquieted by it). Writers *should* come from nowhere. But what at this stage am I meant to do about it?

Guardian 2010

On the Road: The Multicity Book Tour

A coinage has forged itself in the media community of the West Coast: 'O.J.', as a *verb*. Thus, 'to O.J'. Or, passively (and much, much more commonly), 'to be O.J.-ed' or 'to *get* O.J.-ed'. 'O.J.-ing', generally, has nothing to do with sports, with movies, or with sexual jealousy (let alone with orange juice). It has to do with media reschedulings caused by extra coverage of the O.J. Simpson trial.

'People are always getting O.J.-ed off of things,' explains Kathi Goldmark, my media escort in San Francisco.

'So for example you'd say …?'

'"Norman Mailer was going to do national TV, but he was O.J.-ed off of it."'

I glance at my schedule and say, 'Look! I'm meant to do a radio interview at eleven-thirty. Live. But it says here they'll tape it if I get O.J.-ed.'

Among other things, Kathi runs a band called the Rock Bottom Remainders, composed of writers – with, for instance, Stephen King on rhythm guitar and Amy Tan on backup vocals. Like Amy, Kathi is a Remainderette; she plays me a live tape of the band as we drive around town (Amy Tan's voice is hauntingly deep and steady). On her car phone Kathi calls Amy about something else (a favour: I want to pick Amy's brains). Kathi gets *Amy's* car phone, which is answered by Mrs Stephen King, who hands her over to Amy. And Kathi hands Amy over to me.

After my reading, at the bookstore in Berkeley, Kathi and I dine with Jessica Mitford. Kathi has recently started up a record company called Don't Quit Your Day Job. Jessica's nickname, Decca, happens to be the name of a record company, but it is on the Don't Quit Your Day Job label that Decca has just released her first CD: a stalwart rendering of 'Maxwell's Silver Hammer'. Decca is currently updating her classic study *The American Way of Death* (which reads like a nonfiction version of Evelyn Waugh's *The Loved One*). But there remains the question of the follow-up to 'Maxwell's Silver Hammer'. We tentatively decide on 'When I'm Sixty-Four', which should be appropriately retro, because Decca is seventy-seven.

I know all this will feel like a dream when I get back to England (to London and my study). For now, though, I think I like the hotels and the plane rides and the many fresh encounters; and I think I like the cultural unfastidiousness and the postmodern promiscuity. 'To O.J.', I think, is a *good* verb, and a welcome guest to my prose. But you do have to remind yourself, from time to time, that O.J. means someone accused of cutting his ex-wife's head off.

There he sits, magnificently, everywhere you happen to be – our contemporary Othello, our Moor of Venice.

*

UnO.J.-ed, in Los Angeles, I do Tom Snyder, but find that I have been fractionally Shirleyed – by Miss MacLaine. My spot dwindles as Shirley talks interestingly and at great length about *Terms of Endearment* and Jack Nicholson's various readings of the line 'To kill the bug that you have up your ass.' Remember? Come to Laugh, Come to Cry, Come to *Terms*. The movie wasn't any good and won about nineteen Oscars, and I particularly disliked the way Jack Nicholson read that (mediocre) line about the bug.

Our dedicated chauffeuring firm has nothing smaller, so the next morning I am stretched to the beautiful Art Deco toy town of Burbank Airport; all small airports are beautiful, and the smaller the better, but not many are pretty too, as Burbank is. Shortly after take-off, the person beside me swivels and says to the person behind me, 'Can I bug you for a couple of autographs?'

A moment later, I ask the person beside me about the person behind me.

'It's Jack Nicholson,' he whispers, and adds, not at all complainingly, 'He seems a little grouchy.'

I don't turn and stare at Jack. But I resolve to go amidships soon (for a ginger ale or the bathroom), so I can stare at him as I return to my seat. Then *Jack* goes amidships. He returns, and I stare at him: loose black suit, sunglasses, and the authentic movie-star aura − which comes from him seeming deeply familiar and deeply unfamiliar, simultaneously. He *does* seem grouchy − melodramatically so. For a while, he lingers in the aisle, flexing his face with great actorly glowers and frowns and sneers. He notices the book I am reading − *The Adventures of Augie March*, by Saul Bellow. As the proprietor of the movie rights to Bellow's *Henderson the Rain King*, Jack would notice this. The person beside me eventually gets his autographs, duly personalised.

We land and prepare to disembark. Nicholson turns up his grimace dial an additional notch. Uncharitably I assume that this is the look all movie stars wear when they find themselves on non-private aeroplanes. But later I learn that Nicholson has some heavy family trouble in this part of the world. He may be a movie star, but he, too, has his internal chores and labours.

As does O.J. − but he doesn't show it. O.J. is an actor, and he has been told to do Serenity. His profile is like something on an ancient coin. Innocent or guilty, he can't be *feeling* serene. Desdemona is gone, as is Cassio. But Iago is still around − inside his head.

On my way through the airport I see Jack backing into a toilet; his weary scowl has a cork-tipped cigarette in the middle of it and his lighter is cocked.

*

As a rule, writers scorn their youngers and revere their elders. This is a literary law; and I find myself propounding it almost nightly in the Q & A sessions that follow the readings − no doubt because its implications are still occurring to me.

'Does your father like your work?'

No, I explain. My father has read my first, third, and seventh novels, and none of the others. He can't get through them. He sends them windmilling through the air after twenty or thirty pages. But then my father, these days, mostly reads thrillers. Some time ago, he vowed to me that he would never read another novel unless it began with the sentence 'A shot rang out.'

More generally, I go on, older writers *should* find younger writers irritating, because younger writers are sending them an unwelcome message. They are saying, 'It's not like that any more. It's like this.'

In the present context, 'that' and 'this' can be loosely described as the thought-rhythms peculiar to the time. Implicit in these thought-rhythms are certain values, moral, social, and aesthetic.

Somerset Maugham had this to say about my father's first novel, *Lucky Jim*: 'Mr Kingsley Amis is so talented, his observations so keen, that you cannot fail to be convinced that the young men he so brilliantly describes truly represent the class with which his novel is concerned.' This (rather trundling) sentence has been widely quoted. But it is misleading. The next sentence runs as follows: 'They are scum.'

*

American cities are so much better, so much more *citified* than English cities. And, it has to be said, so much more glamorous.

London is the equivalent of New York. And that's fine. But then what do we have? Instead of Chicago we get Manchester. Instead of Washington we get York. Instead of Los Angeles we get Birmingham. Instead of Dallas we get Leeds. Instead of Boston we get Liverpool. Instead of Miami we get Bristol. Instead of New Orleans we get Portsmouth. Instead of Kansas City we get Stoke. Instead of San Francisco we get Grimsby.

*

In Boston I have breakfast with Saul Bellow, who turns eighty this year, and who, uncannily, continues to hear the thought-rhythms of the directly contemporary.

Along the way I also encounter two inadmissibly promising juniors, both of them English: Will Self, again in Boston, and Lawrence Norfolk, in Chicago. These younger writers cause me to defy my own literary law: I like them. They *aren't* scum; and they can write.

Examining the perverse affection I feel, I find that my protective instincts have been roused. Twenty-odd years ago, when I started out, you wrote a novel and handed it in and that was that. There was a coherent reading public, prompted by word of mouth. There was no fourteen-city tour. There was no collateral activity whatever. At thirty-something, Will Self and Lawrence Norfolk are already old hands on the circuit. For them, the current arrangement – whereby your personality (whatever that may be) undergoes public processing – is simply the air they breathe. I had ten years of quiet; but they were born into noise.

★

At the readings I continue to be surprised by the forceful laughter that greets the line 'Poets don't drive.' I am pleased to hear this laughter, but I don't understand it. Are they laughing because it's funny that poets don't drive? Or are they laughing because it sounds like a ridiculous generalisation?

Anyway, it's true. Poets don't drive. A vivid personification of this fact is my friend James Fenton, now Oxford Professor of Poetry, who has failed his test six times. But Fenton is hardly typical. Nearly all the poets I know have never even had a lesson. They just sense that they're not cut out for it.

Poets, of course, are in general great pashas (and great drinkers), who like being ferried about by their admirers. Novelists (those nerveless brutes, those veteran A-to-Z jockeys) bomb around the whole time in their Volvos and VWs. When you drive, the streets and their grids plug themselves into some low-rent section of the brain. Some dud bit of the brain. Novelists are pashas and drunks too; but they do have this dud bit of the brain. Poets don't have this dud bit – the bit marked AUTOMOBILE.

This picture may well be very different in the United States, where the cult of personal mobility – and the distances – are much more serious. Maybe, in America, poets drive, but drive badly. Did Lowell drive? Did *Berryman*? I want to see the math on this.

Poets shouldn't drive. And that's the truth. It took the twentieth century, with its cars, to tell us something about poets' brains.

My father is a poet as well as a novelist – a big difference between us. I know he is a real poet because he doesn't drive. He can drive (he veered around behind the wheel of a jeep once or twice in the war). He just doesn't.

★

Out in the Midwest, the word 'Johnson' is constantly in use. For a start, everyone is called Johnson. I am reminded of the old loggers' song lovingly quoted by Kurt Vonnegut:

107

My name is Yon Yonson
I come from Wisconsin
I work as a lumberjack there ...

Everyone is called Johnson. And everything is called Johnson. And everywhere is called Johnson: streets, forts, bridges, creeks.

Colloquially, 'Johnson' has two meanings. It signifies the male organ, as in this snippet of dialogue from Bellow's *The Dean's December*: 'I held the man's Johnson for him. You understand what I'm saying? I held his dick for him to pee in the flask.' A 'Johnson' is also a regular guy and a standup American. 'A Johnson honors his obligations,' writes William Burroughs in *The Place of Dead Roads*. 'A Johnson minds his own business, will give help when help is needed.' In Madison, I get a fax from Will Self, reminding me to look up his friend Paul Ingram at Prairie Lights bookstore in Iowa City. 'Paul Ingram,' writes Self, 'is a Johnson.' In Iowa City I have a lively dinner with Paul Ingram, in a joint called something like Johnson's. Paul is definitely a Johnson of the second kind.

By this stage of the tour, I am wondering what kind of Johnson *I* am: a robotically garrulous and insanely peripatetic hireling of my own novel. Later, on the West Coast, John Marshall of the Seattle *Post-Intelligencer* begins our interview by saying, 'The woman I share a desk with read that profile of you in *Vanity Fair* and said it made you seem like a real asshole.'

'That's true enough.'

Some interviewers have read your book twice and are bubbling with quotes. Others haven't even finished the dust jacket – or even started it. Mr Marshall is somewhere in the middle: robustly professional. I am a part of his weekly routine. Still, the hour and a half passes swiftly and pleasantly.

'Nice meeting you,' he says.

'Nice meeting you. Oh, and tell that bitch I'm not an asshole.'

Tell her I'm a Johnson.

*

People say that novelists, nowadays, are like rock stars.

On what planet are they living?

It's been that way for years.

This is my fourth or fifth World Tour, and there's *still* something I can never get right. Every evening, as I prepare to abandon the ruined hotel room and search for my signing pen among the crack pipes and the splayed and sated groupies (or 'inkies', as we novelists call them), I keep trying to throw the TV out of the window and into the swimming pool. And the TV always lands in the flower bed or on the patio. For some reason my aim is much truer with the fax machine and the minibar.

*

After reading at Book Soup, on Sunset Boulevard in Los Angeles, I eat there with an old school friend and his wife, the three of us roosting on stools at the bar in order to persist with our smoking. Seated in a line beside me are ten or eleven people, and everyone is displaying at least one copy of a book by me.

This sight gives me the purest rush of authorial megalomania. I think: That's what the world is *supposed* to be like. All the bars should be like this bar. And all the restaurants. Nobody should even think of going anywhere without a Martin Amis.

*

I enjoy getting out of the house and meeting people, partly because it is the opposite of what I do all day; and being sent on tour is a privilege. But I am trying to see the process from the outside. You are pinched and poked (as Updike put it), you are on exhibit, you are inspected, then politely lauded (or very occasionally traduced). All day you are talking into a mike: everything you say is amplified or recorded or transmitted. Everything you say is mediated.

This article insists that you are a Johnson of the second kind; that article insists that you are a Johnson of the first kind, and of the first order. You are quoted and misquoted, represented and misrepresented. You tell yourself to hold something back but you can't hold anything back – because your novel is out there too, on display, and your novel holds nothing back.

*

Earlier in the tour, the nightly reading felt like an ordeal, then a hurdle, then a testing routine. But by now it is almost as enjoyable as a bad habit; and I expect no grief at Denver's Tattered Cover. A writer is nothing without a reader. A reader is needed to close the circle. A story is nothing without a listener. And this is old knowledge. Yet in the age of publicity the bond seems to require public confirmation. 'Could you personalise that for me?' 'Sure. What's your name?' Meet the Author is becoming Meet the Reader. And I find it to be salutary.

I have long thought, in addition, that every instance of travel is a kind of short story. So a long book tour almost amounts to a collection. Pondering this, I assume that such a volume would be very repetitive. But it is all in the telling – as John Updike showed in *Bech: A Book*. Here is another elder I feel free to admire.

Earlier I said that the touring author is 'very occasionally traduced'. In the green room after a reading at the Miami Book Fair, I was confronted by a fellow author – she was about my age and robustly punklike in appearance – who said, 'In my opinion your stuff is shit.' I thanked her with a smile and a nod. 'Yeah!' she added as I made my way by. 'Not everyone thinks you're marvellous!' I turned and thanked her again.

Now she probably thought that my show of gratitude was politely insincere (just me being English). And so did I, at least to begin with. But her words, I soon decided, were just what I needed to hear. Because the idea was forming in me that everyone really did think I was marvellous. And how did that happen?

On any given day many thousands of writers are touring America; dozens or scores of them hurry past you in every major airport. The whole business is eased along by semi-professionalised rites of generosity and good will. And composers of literary fiction, perhaps, enjoy extra kudos, if only because they're not responsible for (I don't know) *Drapes and Upholstery* or *Getting the Most out of Your Rottweiler*.

Not everyone thinks you're marvellous. That's worth remembering. In a continent-wide country of 300 million people (which I keep flying over), a stretch of high modernity so multilayered and diverse, there are bound to be a few exceptions, scattered around here and there.

New Yorker 1995

The King's English

Kingsley Amis was a lenient father. His paternal style, in the early years, can best be described as amiably minimalist – in other words, my mother did it all. It should be noted, though, that if I did come across him (before he slipped back into his study), he always said something that made me laugh or smile. This went a long way. And the humour usually derived from the originality of his phrasing. When I was sixteen or seventeen, and started reading books for grownups, I became in his eyes worth talking to. And when, half a decade later, I started using the English language in the literary pages of the newspapers, I became worth correcting. I was in my early–middle twenties; my father was still amiable, but he was lenient no longer.

'Has your enormity in the *Observer* been pointed out to you?' he asked with enthusiasm over breakfast one Sunday morning (I had left home by then, but I still spent about every other weekend at his house). 'My enormity?' I knew he was applying the word in its proper sense – 'something very bad', and not 'something very big in size'. And my mistake was certainly humiliating: I had used *martial* as a verb. Later, while continuing to avoid *hopefully* (a favourite with politicians, as he insists), I pooh-poohed his reprimand about my harmless use of the dangling *thankfully*. I also took it in good part when, to dramatise my discipleship, as he saw it, of Clive James (a very striking new voice in the 1970s), Kingsley started reading out my reviews in an Australian accent.

But there was one conversation that I still recall with a sincere moan of shame: it concerned the word *infamous*. In a piece about the 'Two Cultures' debate, I referred to F.R. Leavis's 'infamous crucifixion of C.P. Snow'. 'You leave us in no doubt,' said Kingsley watchfully, 'that you disapproved of it.' I remained silent. I didn't say, 'Actually, Dad, I thought *infamous* was just a cool new way of saying *controversial*.' *Infamous* will in fact now serve as the reigning shibboleth (or 'test word', or giveaway). Anyone who uses it loosely, as I did, is making the following announcement: I write without much care and without much feeling. I just write like other people write. As Kingsley puts it in *The King's English* (and 'the King', by the way, was a nickname he tolerated):

> Both adjective and noun [*infamous* and *infamy*] used to be terms of extreme moral disapproval, equivalent in depth of feeling to 'abominable' and 'wickedness'. Then quite recently ... the adjective weakened in severity to something on the level of 'notorious' [or, he might have added, simply 'famous'] ... The noun *infamy*, although seemingly out of use, retains its former meaning, but *infamous* is now unusable through ambiguity.

Kingsley gives some good examples (so-and-so's undergraduate life in the 1920s 'is now infamous'). But I wish he were alive to savour what must surely be the final profanation of this blameless adjective. A distinguished *Guardian* sportswriter recently referred to Steve McLaren – the sacked manager of the national football team – and 'his infamous umbrella'. All McLaren had done with his umbrella was stand on the touchline under it, during a downpour (which was considered a little unmanly). With *infamous*, we see linguistic incuriosity in its most damaging form. A supposedly smart addition to the language becomes an inadvertent subtraction. 'Unusable through ambiguity': the same can be said of *brutalise*, *decimate*, *crescendo*, *dilemma*, *alibi*, *avid*, *oblivious*, *optimistic*, *eke out*, and *refute*, among many others.

Such a tendency is nowhere better caught in *The King's English* than in the entry under 'Déjà vu, an uncanny sense of':

> Its original application was to a transient psychological state, not uncommon among those under about forty, in which the subject feels that he has seen before some place where he has provably never been in this life (thus providing fanciful evidence for reincarnation). The journalistic contribution has been to apply this feeling to some event or situation a person *has* witnessed before ...

The journalistic contribution thus obscures the old meaning, while providing 'the needy with a useful and quite posh-looking alternative to "this is where I / we came in" and other tattered phrases'. Similarly with *jejune*. On its journey from meaning 'scanty, arid' to meaning 'immature, callow', *jejune* has acquired an extra vowel and an acute accent, plus italicisation as a Gallicism. Kingsley quotes the following beauty: 'Although the actual arguments are a little *jéjeune*, the staging of mass scenes are [*sic*] impressive.' We watch such developments (in this case the gradual 'deportation of an English word into French') as we would watch the progress of a virus; like babesiosis and fog fever, such viruses afflict cattle and buffalo and wildebeest; they are the maladies of the herd.

Kingsley's favourite dictionary was the *Concise Oxford*. 'It's all you really need,' he used to say, patting it or even stroking it. And the *Concise Oxford*, I see, has come to toe the line on *infamous, déjà vu,* and *jejune*, giving the new meanings pride of place. Kingsley would have offered no objection (though he did secretly pine for an extra dictionary 'label': namely, *illit.*, to go with *colloq.* and *derog.* and the rest). Usage is irreversible. Once the integrity of a word is lost, no amount of grumbling and harrumphing can possibly restore it. The battle against illiteracies and barbarisms, and pedantries and genteelisms, is not a public battle. It takes place within the soul of every individual who cares about words.

Rather bluffly, perhaps, Kingsley draws up the battle lines as a conflict between Berks and Wankers:

> *Berks* are careless, coarse, crass, gross and of what anybody would agree is a lower social class than one's own. They speak in a slipshod way with dropped Hs, intruded glottal stops, and many mistakes in grammar. Left to them the English language would die of impurity, like late Latin.
>
> *Wankers* are prissy, fussy, priggish, prim and of what they would probably misrepresent as a higher social class than one's own. They speak in an over-precise way with much pedantic insistence on letters not generally sounded, especially Hs. Left to them the language would die of purity, like medieval Latin.

These are richly symmetrical paragraphs. Still, they need a little renovation. The class system, nowadays, has been more or less replaced by the age system (with the young and youngish as the aristocrats); and I for one can't help seeing the slipshod / pedantic opposition in generational terms. So for berks and wankers I would substitute something like punks and fogeys. Amis was in his seventies when he completed *The King's English* (and it was published posthumously). But those who remember him as a reactionary – or, if you prefer, as an apoplectic diehard – will be astonished to discover how unfogeyish he is. With remarkably few exceptions, he takes the sensible and centrist course. He is also deeply but unobtrusively learned. As a result, this is not a confining book but a liberating one. All users of the language – no matter how green, no matter how grey – will be palpably strengthened by *The King's English*.

Let us get the fogey stuff out of the way, because there isn't much of it. For instance, Amis is surely taking on a lost cause with the five-syllable *homogeneous* (the population at large is quite happy with the 'incorrect' *homogenous*); no one rhymes the closing syllable, or syllables, of Perseus and Odysseus with Zeus; no one says *alas* with a long second *a*, and to pronounce medieval 'medd-eeval' (he prefers 'meddy-eeval') is hardly 'an infallible sign of fundamental illiteracy'; no one stresses *peremptory* on the first syllable, and few of us do the same for *controversy* ('only a berk stresses the second'); on the question of using nouns as verbs, *authored* and *critiqued* are regrettable, true, but only a wanker would now object, as Amis does, to *funded*.

Elsewhere, he is a pragmatist, and not infrequently an iconoclast. The split-infinitive taboo is ridiculed as a 'superstition', an 'imaginary rule'; similarly, you may end a sentence with a preposition (and you may start a sentence with Arabic numerals). Amis is being rather more radical when he bluntly states that 'the gerund' – a verbal noun with a possessive attached to it – 'is on the way out', so that *excuse my butting in* has been supplanted by *excuse me butting in*. This contravenes strict grammar, but a rule 'serves no purpose if nobody obeys it'. More broadly, 'the aim of language is to ensure that the speaker [or the writer] is understood, and all ideas of correctness or authenticity must be subordinate to it'.

The battle – the internal campaign – is in essence directed against the false quantity, in its non-technical sense. I mean those rhymes, chimes, repetitions, obscurities, dishonesties, vaguenesses, clichés, 'shreds of battered facetiousness' and 'shopworn novelties' (*past its sell-by date, Marxism lite, no-brainer*, and all other herd words and herd phrases): anything, in brief, that makes the careful reader 'pause without profit'. Naturally the other side of this circumspection is the acceptance, indeed the embrace, of positive linguistic change. Perhaps the most stirring passage in the book is the article on the word 'Gay':

> The use of this word as an adjective or noun applied to a homosexual has received unusually prolonged execration. The 'new' meaning has been generally current for years. *Gay lib* had made the revised Roget by 1987 and the word itself was listed in the 1988 *COD* under sense 5 as a homosexual ... And yet in this very spring of 1995 some old curmudgeon is still frothing on about it in the public print and demanding the word 'back' for proper heterosexual use ... [O]nce a word is not only current but accepted ... no power on earth can throw it out ... The word *gay* is cheerful and hopeful, half a world away from the dismal clinical and punitive associations of *homosexual*.

An 'old curmudgeon': towards the end of his life, Kingsley was monotonously so described. Brewer's *Dictionary of Phrase and Fable* defines curmudgeon as 'a grasping and miserly churl'. Whereas all careful readers of *The King's English* (and of his novels) will find themselves responding to a spirit of reckless generosity.

My 1998 paperback of this book is festooned with praise from various pens. These snippets have a warmed and excitable quality; they are also unusually perceptive. Candia McWilliam says that *The King's English* is a work of reference that 'may be read like a novel, from start to finish'. And David Sexton accurately recognises 'a late flowering of Amis's greatest gift as a novelist, his ability to draw out the implications of a whole life from a tiny detail of speech or behaviour'. Both these writers have identified the unique charm of this 'Guide to Modern Usage': its satirical expansiveness.

All my adult life I have been searching for the right adjective to describe my father's peculiarly aggressive comic style. I recently settled on 'defamatory'. And here is an example from 'Pidgin Latin':

> In origin ... the French language is a simplified and corrupt form of Latin once current between Roman troops or colonists or traders on the one hand and the local peasantry on the other ... One easily imagines dialogues between a scrounging legionary, perhaps a Vandal or a Parthian by origin, and a willing but benighted yokel.
>
> LEGIONARY (in vile Latin): I want water. Bring me water. *Aquam*.

YOKEL: Ugh?

L: *Aquam*! Say *aquam*, you bloody fool. Go on – *aquam*.

Y: O? (To be spelt *eau* when they get to the writing stage centuries later.)

L: Bring it to the high cliff. The high cliff. *Altum*.

Y: Ugh?

L: *Altum*! Say *altum*, you bumpkin. Go on – *altum*.

Y: O? (To be spelt *haut* when, etc.)

'A terrific book,' wrote another reviewer, Sebastian Faulks. The prose 'has that tense, sly quality of his very best fiction ... a marvellous and quite unexpected bonus from beyond the grave'. Mr Faulks couldn't be expected to know how true this was. Two months before he died, Kingsley had a heavy fall after a good lunch ('At my age,' as he used to say, 'lunch is dinner') and banged his head on a stone step. Thereafter, by degrees, he became a pitiable and painfully disconcerting madcap. He kept trying, he tried and he tried, but he couldn't write; he couldn't read, or be read to; and his speech was like a mixture of *The Cat in the Hat* and *Finnegans Wake*. Aged seventy-three, he had just finished a book on the King's English; and now English was a language the King no longer had. His fate was a brutal reminder. We are all of us held together by words; and when words go, nothing much remains.

Plans for Kingsley's memorial service were quite far advanced when the typescript of the present book (then hardly more than a family rumour) was delivered to my door. I picked it up with a trepidation that the first few pages briskly dispersed. Here it was again, my father's voice – funny, resilient, erudite, with touches of very delicate feeling (see the entries under 'Brave' and 'Gender'), and, throughout, sublimely articulate. In truth, *The King's English* contains more concentrated artistic thrust than any of the five novels that followed his masterpiece of 1986, *The Old Devils*. The reason for this is, I think, clear enough. Love of life, like all human talents, weakens with age. But love of language, in his case, never did begin to fade.

Guardian 2011[*]

*This piece was also the introduction to a paperback reissue of *The King's English* in the same year.

Postscript. I suppose it's just as well that Kingsley was never exposed to the idiolect of Donald Trump – an adventure playground for any pro-scriptive linguist. But he would have been ready for 'bigly'.* This is from the article headed 'Single-handedly': 'Some illiteracies are presented in the name of literacy, or at least of regularity and common sense ... Those who like to make words longer and more polysyllabic have not noticed or do not care that *single-handed* is already an adverb as well as an adjective ... There are plenty of other adverbs vulnerable to creative il-literacy through not ending in *–ly* ... When can we expect to see *quitely*? *Altogetherly*? What *nextly*?' I passed on to my father the fact that I heard the great Jessica Lange – who was thanking her team at an awards cere-mony – use the phrase *lastly but not leastly* (and I told him about the New York dentist who says, *Open widely*). What does Donald say when you ask him how he is? *Goodly*? Or perhaps (this is after all a man of some culture) *Finely*. Or perhaps the neologism *Wellly*.

---

*Trump's campaign spokeswoman, gruellingly, has put it about that the nominee is in fact saying 'big-league' (a useful variant on his tawdry 'big-time'), though 'big-league' in its adver-bial application is unknown to the lexicographers' database. And why in that case does he stress it as a trochee (tum-ti) and not as a spondee (tum-tum). Anyway, it *sounds* like 'bigly', even though the credulous may accept that *–gue* is silently 'understood'.

Twin Peaks – 2

Bellow's Lettres

Saul Bellow, *There Is Simply Too Much to Think About*

'The flies wait hungrily in the air,' writes Saul Bellow (in a description of Shawneetown in southern Illinois), 'sheets of flies that make a noise like the tearing of tissue paper.' Go and tear some tissue paper in two – slowly: it sounds just like the sullen purr of bristling vermin. But how, you wonder, did Bellow know what torn tissue paper sounded like in the first place? And then you wonder what this minutely vigilant detail is doing in *Holiday* magazine (in 1957), rather than in the work in progress, *Henderson the Rain King* (1959). It or something even better probably *is* in *Henderson*. For Bellow's fictional and nonfictional voices intertwine and cross-pollinate. This is from a film review of 1962: 'There she is, stout and old, a sinking, squarish frame of bones.' Two decades later the image would effloresce in the story/novella 'Cousins':

> I remembered Riva as a full-figured, dark-haired, plump, straight-legged woman. Now all the geometry of her figure had changed. She had come down in the knees like the jack of a car, to a diamond posture.

In 1958 a play by Gore Vidal was adapted into the famous western *The Left Handed Gun* (which starred his friend Paul Newman); and it has often been said that when writers of fiction turn to discursive prose 'they write left-handed'. In other words, think pieces, reportage, travelogues, lectures, and memoirs are in some sense strained, inauthentic, ventriloquial. In Vidal's case, literary opinion appears to be arranging a curious destiny. It is in the essays (or in those written before September 11, 2001) that he feels right-handed. His historical novels, firmly tethered to reality, have their place. But the products of Vidal's untrammelled fancy – for instance *Myra Breckinridge* and *Myron* – feel strictly southpaw. Bellow, by contrast, is congenitally ambidextrous.

He is also a rampant instinctivist. In this respect Bellow is quite un-like, say, Vladimir Nabokov and John Updike, to take two artist-critics of high distinction. In his voluminous *Lectures* Nabokov is idiosyncratic and often verbally festive, but he is always a sober and serious professional: a pedagogue. And Updike, in his equally voluminous collections of re-views, makes it clear that critics, unlike novelists, are somehow 'on duty': they have to wear their Sunday best, and can never come as they are. Bellow comes as he is. He is closer to D.H. Lawrence, and closer still to V.S. Pritchett. 'Let the academics weigh up, be exhaustive or build their superstructures,' Pritchett writes. 'The artist lives as much by his pride in his own emphases as by what he ignores; humility is a disgrace.' This is Bellow's way of going at everything. No tuxedo and cummerbund, no gowns and tasselled mortarboards. Whatever the genre, Bellow's sensor-ium, it turns out, is whole and indivisible.

Inherent in this approach is a candid opposition to the ivory tower. Although he taught literature throughout his adult life, Bellow was always and increasingly suspicious of the universities – long before ideological jumpiness had turned them into what he privately called 'anti-free-speech centers' (his short essay 'The University as Villain' is dated 1956). He is infuriated, maddened, by the sort of commentator who wants to tell you what Ahab's harpoon may or may not 'symbolise'. In 'Deep Readers of the World, Beware!' (1959) he imagines a classroom conversation:

> 'Why, sir,' the student wonders, 'does Achilles drag the body of Hector around the walls of Troy? . . . Well, you see, sir, the *Iliad* is full of circles – shields, chariot wheels and other round figures. And you know what Plato said about circles. The Greeks were all made for geometry.' 'Bless your crew-cut head', the professor replies, 'for such a beautiful thought . . . Your approach is both deep and serious. Still, I always believed that Achilles did it because he was so angry.'

Critics should cleave to the human element, and not just laminate the text with additional obscurities. The essential didactic task, Bellow im-plies, is to instil the readerly habits of enthusiasm, gratitude, and awe.

To accuse novelists of egotism is like deploring the tendency of cham-pion boxers to turn violent. And Bellow, naturally and enlighteningly, re-lies on his own evolution to establish core principles. 'Everything is to be viewed as though for the first time.' Assume 'a certain psychic unity' with your readers ('Others are in essence like me and I am basically like them'). Accept George Santayana's definition of that discredited word 'piety': 'reverence for the sources of one's being'. Cherish your personal history, therefore, but never seek out experience, or 'Experience', as grist. Some writers are proud of their 'special efforts in the fields of sex, drunkenness' and poverty ('I have even been envied my good luck in having grown up during the Depression'); but 'willed' worldliness is a false lead. Resist 'the heavy influences' – Flaubert, Marx, etc., and what Bellow, citing Thoreau, calls 'the savage strength of the many'. The imagination has its 'eternal naïveté' – and that is something the writer cannot afford to lose.

Bellow's nonfiction has the same strengths as his stories and novels: a dynamic responsiveness to character, place, and time (or era). All are on display in the marvellous vignette 'A Talk With the Yellow Kid' (1956). The Kid is an octogenarian Chicago swindler: all his life he has 'sold nonexistent property, concessions he did not own and air-spun schemes to greedy men'. Bellow is altogether at ease in this company, but he has the deeper confidence to acknowledge the Kid's elusive mystery: 'It is not always easy to know where he is coming from', because 'long practice in insincerity gives him an advantage.' And you wonder – what other highbrow writer, or indeed lowbrow writer, has such a reflexive grasp of the street, the machine, the law courts, the rackets? But then Bellow is abnormally alive to social gradations everywhere, in Spain (1948), in Israel (1967), in Paris (1983), in Tuscany (1992). This is from 'In the Days of Mr Roosevelt', the days being those between the crash and the war:

> The blight hadn't yet carried off the elms and under them drivers had pulled over, parking bumper to bumper, and turned on their radios ... They had rolled down the windows and opened the car doors. Everywhere the same voice, its odd Eastern accent, which in anyone else would have irritated Midwesterners. You could follow without missing a single word as you strolled by. You felt joined to these unknown drivers, men and women smoking their cigarettes in silence, not so much considering the president's words as affirming the rightness of his tone and taking assurance from it.

That relay, that gentle gantlet of car radios, perfectly encapsulates what F.D.R. had to give to America and Americans: continuity in troubled times.

There Is Simply Too Much to Think About is a slightly pruned, and then greatly expanded, version of *It All Adds Up*, Bellow's nonfiction compendium of 1994. 'Distraction', 'noise', 'crisis chatter': persistent enough in the earlier book, these themes have now become pervasive. 'The world is too much with us; late and soon,/ Getting and spending, we lay waste our powers'. This bothered Wordsworth around 1802, and it bothered Ruskin in 1865 ('No reading is possible for a people with its mind in this state'); meanwhile, unsurprisingly, things have not quieted down. 'The world is too much with us, and there has never been so much world,' Bellow writes in 1959. In 1975 he goes further: 'To say that the world is too much with us is meaningless for there is no longer any us. The world is everything.' And there is no escape, even in rural Vermont: 'What is happening everywhere is, one way or another, known to everyone. Shadowy world tides wash human nerve endings in the remotest corners of the earth.' Yes; but 'it is apparently in the nature of the creature to resist the world's triumph,' the triumph of 'turbulence and agitation' – and Bellow's corpus is graphic proof of that defiance.

One of the most audacious essays in the book is a seemingly modest little piece called 'Wit Irony Fun Games' (2003, and quite possibly the last thing he ever wrote). Elsewhere describing his own novels, or many of them, as 'comedies of wide reading', Bellow here insists that by a very considerable margin 'most novels have been written by ironists, satirists, and comedians'. I have been thinking that for years. Look at Russian fiction, reputedly so gaunt and grownup: Gogol is funny, Tolstoy in his merciless clarity is funny, and Dostoyevsky, funnily enough, is very funny indeed; moreover, the final generation of Russian literature, before it was destroyed by Lenin and Stalin, remained emphatically comic – Bunin, Bely, Bulgakov, Zamyatin. The novel is comic because life is comic (until the inevitable tragedy of the fifth act); and also because fiction, unlike poetry and unlike all the other arts, is a fundamentally rational form. This latter point is not the paradox it may appear to be. In the words of the artist-critic Clive James:

> Common sense and a sense of humour are the same thing, moving at different speeds. A sense of humour is just common sense, dancing. Those who lack humour are without judgment and should be trusted with nothing.

New York Times Book Review 2015

Nabokov's Natural Selection

Stalking Nabokov by Brian Boyd

> Jake Balokowsky, my biographer,
> Has this page microfilmed. Sitting inside
> His air-conditioned cell at Kennedy
> In jeans and sneakers, he's no call to hide
> Some slight impatience with his destiny ...

Philip Larkin intends that last line as an understatement. For Jake, the Larkin project is merely a path to tenure and a couple of semesters' leave, freeing him up to concentrate on something more interesting – i.e. 'Protest Theater' (the poem, 'Posterity', is dated 1968). So Professor Balokowsky's *Philip Larkin*, if he ever finishes it, will probably be nothing worse than an exercise in cynical toil, with the author's hostile condescension ('this old fart', 'this bastard') kept manfully in check. We may incidentally note, nevertheless, that in the course of eighteen lines the poet gives Jake considerable insight into his subject – far more than was shown by the critics who lined up to savage Larkin's reputation in the early 1990s, after the publication of the *Life* and the *Letters*. 'What's he like?' says Jake:

> [']Christ, I just told you. Oh, you know the thing,
> That crummy textbook stuff from Freshman Psych,
> Not out of kicks or something happening –
> One of those old-type *natural* fouled-up guys.'

Jake will be detained by Larkin for only a year, so the chances are that he won't be decisively embittered by the experience. Nowadays, in the real literary world, biographers typically immure themselves for a significant fraction of a lifetime, and the 'slight impatience' is given the leisure to metastasise (into 'pathography', as Joyce Carol Oates called it). Also, in a culturally egalitarian era, feelings of emulousness become harder to resist. Would-be Boswells start to wonder whether their particular Dr Johnson is really worthy of such protracted labour, and, being writers themselves, with a writer's ambitions and anxieties, they start to whimper with neglect. To this tendency we can offer a straightforward corrective: Dr Johnson did not write the monumental *Life of James Boswell*, and for obvious reasons. A similar thought experiment reveals the impossibility of *Andrew Motion: A Writer's Life* by Philip Larkin (or, say, *James Atlas: A Biography* by Saul Bellow). Jake Balokowsky merited a poem; he would not merit a monograph.

Vladimir Nabokov died on July 2, 1977. Before the month was out Andrew Field finally published *Nabokov: His Life in Part*. The book had been gestating since the mid-1960s; Nabokov first saw it in typescript in 1971, and responded with no fewer than 200 pages of corrections. Although Field is an interesting writer (why else would Nabokov have given him so much of his time?), we can safely say that he is not one of nature's bridesmaids. As it turned out, his biography became mildly famous for the tonnage of its inaccuracies (Field offers 1916 as the date of the Russian Revolution, and seems to think that Nabokov climbed trees when he hunted butterflies); but what concerns us here is its murky presumptuousness – and the depth of the affront it managed to cause. 'I cannot tell you how upset I am by the whole matter,' wrote Nabokov (to his lawyer); and a sense of waste and violation did much to becloud the last decade of his life.

Nabokov: His Life in Part opens with Field and Nabokov engaging in a stylised dialogue on the matter of methodology. Then, after nine pages of unfathomable tension, we come to what Field calls 'our little differ-ence' (a revealing phrase, though the contretemps remains obscure):

> Neither Nabokov nor I said a cross word to one another ... I was upset. There are, I must confess at the outset, ways (and I am not thinking now of his many virtues and attributes) in which I am too much like Vladimir Nabokov to judge him. I threw pieces of stale bread to the sea-gulls from the fourteenth-floor balcony ...

Etc., etc. (it takes him a further half a paragraph to calm down). How do we respond to this? With a compliant reverie about the foibles suppos-edly shared by a senior Russian-American novelist (pictured on the front cover) and an exceptionally shaggy Australian academic (pictured on the back flap)? No, of course not: we just rub our eyes at Field's attempt to claim a kind of parity of ego. The biographer is evidently unhappy with his station; and a part of his mind simply cannot understand why Nabokov will never write a book called *Andrew Field*. Actually, one can imagine such a text: it would take the form of a merciless novella. But why should the aged eagle spread its wings? Extreme and florid literary delusion was an area that Nabokov had already mapped and colonised – with Hermann Hermann in *Despair*, with the (real-life) Nikolai Chernyshevsky in *The Gift*, and most raucously with Charles Kinbote in *Pale Fire*.

*

The non-existence of Nabokov's *Stalking Boyd* has clearly never troubled the author of *Stalking Nabokov*. It was Brian Boyd who, in the late 1980s, put the Nabokov Life (and archive) in order, duly producing *Vladimir Nabokov: The Russian Years* (1990) and *Vladimir Nabokov: The American Years* (1991). These two volumes are thorough, vigorous, and of course pressingly readable: the flight of the nineteen-year-old poet and princeling from revolutionary Russia; the murder of his father, the liberal statesman V.D. Nabokov, in 1922; courtship, marriage, and parenthood in the flatlets and boarding houses of Berlin; the rise of another 'nauseous dictatorship'; the flight from France in 1940, with the Wehrmacht bearing down on Paris; heroic self-reinvention in America; world fame in the late 1950s, after forty years of uncomplaining penury; and then the hugely industrious twilight in the Montreux Palace Hotel, on Lake Geneva. It is a story that seems more and more fantastic as it recedes from us in time.

Boyd is impeccable on points of fact and tact. We can be quite certain of this, because his biography survived the scrutiny of Nabokov's widow. Although Véra Evseevna Nabokov was a beautiful, charming, and highly accomplished woman, her spousal protectiveness could justly (and admiringly) be described as barbaric. Even more to the point, Boyd's comportment is exemplary, and his prose is energised by an impassioned lectorial love. Here is a writer who has heeded Auden's requiem for Yeats, which ends: 'In the prison of his days / Teach the free man how to praise.'

In *Stalking Nabokov* Boyd attempts something fairly ambitious: he takes the titanic Nabokov and seeks to revise him upwards. As Boyd sees it, Nabokov is not only the greatest novelist of the twentieth century; he is also a considerable poet, an important scientist, a controversially original translator, a fearless and liberating critic, a learned psychologist (and not just a Freudophobe), a prolific playwright, an inimitable memoirist, and a humblingly tireless and eloquent literary correspondent. After this cannonade of accomplishments, it feels almost bathetic to be reminded that the chess problems Nabokov devised are widely considered to be 'world-class' (the chess problem, Nabokov writes in *Speak, Memory*, is 'a beautiful, complex, and sterile art' – but then so is chess, as he showed in his brilliant early novel *The Defence*). *Stalking Nabokov*, in the end, is a tribute not just to an extraordinary literary animal, but also to the size, force, and stamina of an extraordinary brain.

The Nabokovians among us now face a future more or less blotted out by the prospect of keeping pace with the master's scandalous fecundity – for Boyd gives us warning that there is much, much more to come. Future publications will include 800 pages of dramatic writings (including the two screenplays for Stanley Kubrick's *Lolita*); two thick volumes of notes to Pushkin's *Eugene Onegin*; three thick volumes of translations of Russian verse; an imminent *Collected Poems*; an expanded edition of the already sizeable *Short Stories*; the letters to Véra (and the letters to his mother, his father, his sister, his brother, and a wide circle of Russian friends), to go with the *Selected Letters* and *Dear Bunny, Dear Volodya: The Nabokov-Wilson Letters*; 'two or three volumes of new lectures', to go with *Lectures on Literature, Lectures on Russian Literature* and *Lectures on Don Quixote*; and *Think, Write, Speak*, a compendium of prose pieces and interviews to go with the glittering critical apologia, *Strong Opinions*.

This epic of hard graft should close with a whispered footnote. After the perfectly understandable nervous breakdown suffered by the French translator of *Ada or Ardor: A Family Chronicle* (the longest and most tortuous of the novels), Nabokov was getting up at five o'clock every morning in order to do the job himself. He had a year to live. He was seventy-six.

*

It must be admitted that *Stalking Nabokov* gets off to a decidedly shaky start. 'Since completing my biography,' Boyd writes, rather blithely, in his introduction, 'I have explored new fields, but Nabokov keeps pulling me back. By now I have published a pile of my own on him, some of it well known, some not. When recently I had reason to consult one of my less well-known efforts, I decided others might like to see this stuff.' And for some reason (it is not a chronological reason) he puts all the lightest and slightest stuff first – a toast he gave at a centennial dinner, a speech he gave at an award ceremony, and so on. Boyd's air of chummy informality leads to vulgarisms ('offers I cannot refuse', 'I kid you not'), ugly locutions like 'feedback' and 'inexhaustibleness', the odd unaccountable error (a Russian speaker ought to be doubly sure that there is no such thing as 'a gulag'), and a fair amount of shameless repetition. Some passages read as if they were knocked together in the conference minibus ('for the rights to Nabokov's butterfly papers for a volume for which'), others as if they were long pondered, under a hot lamp, back at the airport hotel:

> Does [Nabokov's] passion for papillons indicate that he is insufficiently interested in people? Or should we argue the opposite, that the way he used the butterfly net of his boyhood has no bearing on the way he flourished his pen? After all, Humbert pursued nymphets, not Nymphalids; Luzhin captured chessmen, not Checkerspots; Pnin accumulated sorrows, not Sulphurs.

And when, in one of his ill-advised asides, Boyd reveals that during 'the last eight of my nine years as a student, I had worn nothing but purple, tangerine, lime green, or scarlet overalls', we start wondering what we have let ourselves in for. At this point – page eighteen – Boyd is sprucing himself up for his first meeting with Mrs. Nabokov (you will be relieved to learn that he wore his only suit). As it happened, Véra Evseevna soon came to value him and to trust him; and we should follow her lead.

For much of the 1940s Nabokov worked at the Harvard Museum of Comparative Zoology, spending up to fourteen hours a day at the microscope, and writing several key papers (one of them a 'ninety-page monograph on the Nearctic members of the genus Lycaeides'). Professor Boyd, as the author of books on evolution and cognition, is well equipped to give us a real sense of Nabokov's scientific weight. Lepidopterists, he tells us,

> have recently reinstated Nabokov's Cyclargus after cladistic analysis of many anatomical features revealed that Cyclargus and Hemiargus are not even immediate sister genera … Johnson and Balint announce that they 'follow the methods of NABOKOV (1945) (the first reviser of the Neotropical polyommatines), who underlined the taxonomic importance of the genitalic armatures in lycaenid systematics …' Kurt Jonson commented that the results confirm 'that Nabokov's

contribution was significant, historic, and displayed remarkable, uncanny bioïlogical intuition'.

This is impressive, and not just incidentally impressive: it leads us to a Nabokovian difficulty that is (at least) two-ply, like a chess problem. Although he acknowledged the beauty and brilliance of Darwin's theory, Nabokov was incurably attached to a personal version of what we would now call Intelligent Design; and the basis of that attachment was the question of mimicry. In *The Gift* the young poet Fyodor Godunov-Cherdyntsev ponders

> the incredible artistic wit of mimetic design which was not explainable by the struggle for existence (the rough haste of evolution's unskilled forces), was too refined for the mere deceiving of accidental predators ... and seemed to have been invented by some waggish artist precisely for the intelligent eyes of man.

Boyd assures us that 'experimental work on the survival rates of camouflaged animals ... confirmed that even elaborate mimicry could be perfectly explained by natural selection', and goes on to wonder if Nabokov, or his ghost, would have capitulated to these findings. He thinks not – probably rightly. And Nabokov, after all, was a professional scientist. How do we account for the depth of his intransigence? Perhaps a naïvely 'biographical' explanation is for once in order. Nabokov lived in Berlin from 1923 to 1937. He witnessed 'social' Darwinism; the ideology of 'the struggle for existence' was what he heard from the rooftop loudspeakers.

The Third Reich would have been impossibly disgusting to him in any case; but we must bear in mind that he watched the passage of the Nuremberg Laws in the company of his *Jüdin* wife and their *Mischling* child (who was then aged one). Nabokov very seldom addresses the German question in his fictional prose – a single unforgettable paragraph in *Pnin*, an excoriating sentence in the five-page 'Signs and Symbols', and these lines from another story, 'That in Aleppo Once ...' (1943):

> Crushed and jolted amid the apocalyptic exodus [from Paris], waiting for unscheduled trains that were bound for unknown destinations, walking through the stale stage setting of abstract towns, living in a permanent twilight of physical exhaustion, we fled; and the farther we fled, the clearer it became that what was driving us on was

something more than a booted and buckled fool with his assortment of variously propelled junk – something of which he was a mere symbol, something monstrous and impalpable, a timeless and faceless mass of immemorial horror that still keeps coming at me from behind even here, in the green vacuum of Central Park.

And the narrator's gravamen is definingly Nabokovian: 'with all her many black sins, Germany was still bound to remain for ever and ever the laughingstock of the world.'

*

It is possible to be a pretty strenuous Nabokov enthusiast while remaining almost entirely ignorant of his verse. *Poems and Problems* (1970) comprised fifty-three poems and eighteen chess problems; and this playful-seeming configuration led many of us to assume that poetry, for Nabokov, was something of a sideline or even a hobby. But isn't that the assumption we made about his entomology? Boyd convinces us that Nabokov was incapable of the perfunctory: he went at everything he did with everything he had.

Still, there is one verse epic (it is a single pentameter short of a thousand lines) that all Nabokov's admirers will have read at least twice – namely 'Pale Fire'. The novel of that name requires us to leapfrog back and forth between John Shade's heroic couplets and Charles Kinbote's crazed 'Commentary' (which is a distraction in all three senses). The long and fervent essay in *Stalking Nabokov*, and Boyd's new edition of an unencumbered 'Pale Fire', compel us to reexamine the poem as something autonomous. And the exercise is epiphanic. 'Pale Fire' glows with fresh pathos and vibrancy – and so does *Pale Fire*. For the first time we see the poem in all its innocence, and register the vandalism of Kinbote's desperate travesty.

So at last the true dimensions of *Pale Fire* are more clearly revealed to us. And this feat of late-acting reinvigoration qualifies as one of Nabokov's most audacious gambles on greatness (see pages 7–8). In *Lolita* we are told of the heroine's fate in the 'editor's' Foreword:

'Louise' is by now a college sophomore. 'Mona Dahl' is a student in Paris. 'Rita' has recently married the proprietor of a hotel in Florida. Mrs. 'Richard F. Schiller' died in childbed, giving birth to a stillborn girl, on Christmas Day 1952, in Gray Star, a settlement in the remotest Northwest. 'Vivian Darkbloom' [anag.] has written a biography ...

Lolita does not appear under the guise of her married name until page 266. Any other writer would have hedged the bet with something like 'Mrs. "Richard F. 'Dolly' Schiller"'. But not Nabokov. Future readers, he intuited, would come to know that Lolita is dead before the story even begins. In 1958 he added an afterword, 'On a Book Entitled *Lolita*', in which he stressed that 'Gray Star' (mentioned only once) is 'the capital town of the book'. Dolores Haze, the obliterated heroine, only had to wait three years for her tragedy to be fully acknowledged. John Shade, the murdered hero, was obliged to wait half a century.

Books and reputations have afterlives. But do human beings have them too? John Shade strives to believe in some kind of resurrection, if only to assuage his grief for his lost daughter ('I'm reasonably sure that we survive / And that my darling somewhere is alive'). And Nabokov, from childhood on, was disposed to reject what Shade calls 'the inadmissible abyss' of oblivion. Formal religious faith, with its docile communalities, he of course dismissed as hopelessly undignified.

'The search for God: the longing of any hound for a master,' notes Fyodor in *The Gift*. 'I'm convinced that extraordinary surprises await us,' he says elsewhere: 'It's a pity one can't imagine what one can't compare to anything. Genius is an African who dreams up snow.' There is something inexorable about Nabokov's need to imagine African snow: it is an extension of his temperament, and of his supercharged sensorium. On the timbre of Nabokov's artistic spirit Boyd is fundamentally right-headed:

> He was a maximalist: someone who appreciated, as much as anyone has, the riches the world offers, in nature and art, in sensation, emotion, thought, and language, and the surprise of these riches, if we animate them with all our attention and imagination ... And his generosity to his readers matches and reenacts and pays tribute to what he senses is the generosity of our world.

This is a necessary iteration. It is time to deemphasise the allegedly cold, cruel, dark, daunting Nabokov, who is very largely a creature of myth (a myth rigged up as a kind of defence mechanism, perhaps, by readers who feel menaced by the strength of his penetration). Nabokov was a celebrator; and the secret of his prose is its divine levity.

Boyd tells us that *Mary* (1926), Nabokov's first novel, was provisionally entitled *Happiness* (similarly, the hero of *The Gift* wants to write 'a practical handbook: *How to Be Happy*'). Several of the early short stories – 'Gods', 'Beneficence', 'A Letter That Never Reached Russia' – are little more than dazed hymns to the bliss of existence. 'In life and in my whole mental makeup I am quite indecently optimistic and buoyant'; gloom and dejection (as Boyd puts it) are only for 'the ridiculously unobservant'. At the age of twenty-two Nabokov sent his mother a short poem – as proof 'that my mood is as radiant as ever. If I live to be a hundred, my spirit will still go around in short trousers'. 'This is ecstasy,' he writes in *Speak, Memory* (he is out hunting butterflies), 'and behind the ecstasy is something else, which is hard to explain. It is like a momentary vacuum into which rushes all that I love'. Towards the end of that book he discourses on 'the best things in life' (parenthood in a harmonious marriage, intelligent nature, and – surprisingly – inactivity), and concludes:

> 'Struggle for life' indeed! The curse of battle and toil leads man back to the boar, to the grunting beast's crazy obsession with the search for food … Workers of the world, disband! Old books are wrong. The world was made on a Sunday.

*

In case we forget: the lion's share of what we inherit from Nabokov comes in the form of fiction. Here, naturally, Boyd has his own predilections. He gravitates towards the teacherly or teachable Nabokov, the allusive, the punsome, the highly wrought – the silver-age or, in a word, the self-indulgent. Furthermore, he is committed to the interpretational approach, claiming, for instance, to have 'solved' the 'puzzle' of *Transparent Things*, and confessing (likably enough) that he still doesn't 'understand' *Lolita*. Among non-specialists, this kind of inductive reading has been dead for a generation; we no longer read novels to solve them or to understand them – if indeed we ever did.

Boyd is also something of an apologist for the only significant embarrassment in the Nabokov corpus. Of the nineteen fictions, no fewer than six wholly or partly concern themselves with the sexuality of prepubescent girls. In *Stalking Nabokov* the six are whittled down to three: Boyd ignores the paedophilia theme in *Transparent Things*, and accounts for its presence in *Look at the Harlequins!* and *The Original of Laura* by saying that Nabokov was merely trying 'to subvert our expectations'. The argument fails on two counts. Clearly, it doesn't make the two little girls go away (the paedophilia theme goes on being the theme). And it imputes a trivial and entirely implausible knowingness. Nabokov loved his readers; yet we may be sure that he never for a moment considered their 'expectations'.

To be as clear as one can be: the unignorable infestation of nymphets in Nabokov is not a matter of morality; it is a matter of aesthetics. There are just too many of them.

A confessedly 'artificial' but unusually helpful distinction is made in Boyd's pages between Nabokov the stylist and Nabokov the storyteller. One could go at it slightly differently, and divide Nabokov's endowment into a) what derives from genius, and b) what derives from talent – genius being the Godgiven altitude of perception and articulacy, talent being technique, and all the skills that come under the heading of Craft. Sometimes talent predominates, as in those two melodic but fiercely focused black farces, *The Enchanter* and *Laughter in the Dark*. Sometimes, as in those two would-be magna opera, *The Gift* and *Ada*, genius engorges itself and talent shrivels and dies (the same thing happens in *Finnegans Wake*). Much depends on how you feel about those two dystopian satires, *Bend Sinister* and *Invitation to a Beheading*, but it would seem that in about a dozen Nabokov novels (and we include *Transparent Things*) talent and genius are in near-perfect equipoise.

The delightfully painful short story 'Lips to Lips' (1932) opens with an aspirant novelist hunched over his desk:

> *The violins were still weeping, performing, it seemed, a hymn of passion and love, but already Irina and the deeply moved Dolinin were rapidly walking toward the exit ... Their two hearts were beating as one.*
>
> *'Give me your cloakroom ticket', uttered Dolinin* (crossed out).
>
> *'Please, let me get your hat and manteau'* (crossed out).
>
> *'Please', uttered Dolinin, 'let me get your things'* ('and my' inserted between 'your' and 'things').
>
> *Dolinin went up to the cloakroom, and after producing his little ticket* (corrected to 'both little tickets') –
>
> Here Ilya Borisovich Tal grew pensive.

While Nabokov – very wittily and tenderly – gives his ageing wordsmith an iota of genius ('descriptions of nature and emotions came to him with surprising facility'), he denies him even a lone neutrino of talent.

Poor Ilya Borisovich suffers hideously at the hands of his pronouns – 'she', for example, when there is another 'she' in the room, forcing him into gruelling variations like 'that lady' or 'her interlocutress'. He is all thumbs with the nuts and bolts of reality (doors, tickets, coats, 'things') – but 'luxury items', or so he fancies, appear 'to be much more compliant':

> and now, having ponderously finished with the cloakroom fuss and being about to present his hero with an elegant cane, Ilya Borisovich naively delighted in the gleam of its rich knob, and did not foresee, alas, what claims that valuable article would make, how painfully it would demand mention, when Dolinin, his hands feeling the curves of a supple young body, would be carrying Irina across a vernal rill.

It is a commonplace to say that Nabokov was blessed with a superabundance of genius. Yes; and he was also blessed with a superabundance of talent. His transitions from scene to scene and from one point of view to another, his pacing, his modulations, his stage management, his ever-alerting shifts of perspective, his freedom from inadvertency, his security of rhythm: all this feels quite frictionless.

At first 'Lips to Lips' strikes you as a scarcely credible feat of empathy: how did Nabokov, of all people, dream his way into the mind of a man who can't write? But there are days when every writer feels like Ilya Borisovich. As Boyd reminds us, a single sentence in *Lolita* (the important but hardly crucial evocation of the barber Kasbeam in Chapter 16) cost the author a month of work. 'My pencils outlast their erasers,' said Nabokov in *Strong Opinions*. 'I have rewritten – often several times – every word I have ever published.'

Panegyric is rightly regarded as the dullest and idlest of all literary forms. In our attempts to evaluate Nabokov's feverish shimmer, with its 'distant spasms of silent lightning', we have nothing to adduce but our own helpless subjectivism; that, and quotation.

So here is a personal or 'biographical' aside. The present writer (who as a young man worked for three years at the present periodical, and is archaically mindful of its conventions), the present writer, to resume, quite recently taught a course on First Novels (or Very Early Novels) – among them Waugh's *Decline and Fall*, Bellow's *Dangling Man*, Roth's *Goodbye, Columbus*, and Pynchon's *The Crying of Lot 49*. Although each of these maiden voyages contained rumbles and quickenings of things to come, only one novel, out of eight, and only one sentence, out of scores of thousands, gave the impression that something otherworldly was announcing its approach. That novel was *Mary* (1926), and that sentence (which, curiously, contains a technical error worthy of Ilya Borisovich – the repeated 'shaking') – comes on page 113: 'The black trains roared past, shaking the windows of the house; with a movement like ghostly shoulders shaking off a load, heaving mountains of smoke swept upward, blotting out the night sky.'

Vigilant Russian émigrés, in the shabby but dynamic literary circles of the German capital, would have been anxiously awaiting the second novel by the shadowy 'V. Sirin'. Upon opening it, they would have seen at once that the 'black train' had indeed arrived (and was again about to depart, exactly on time). *King, Queen, Knave* (1928), a tale of murder, madness, and dissolution, begins as follows:

> The huge black clock hand is still at rest but is on the point of making its once-a-minute gesture; that resilient jolt will set a world in motion. The clock face will slowly turn away, full of despair, contempt, and boredom, as one by one the iron pillars will start walking past, bearing away the vault of the station like blind atlantes; the platform will begin to move past, carrying off on an unknown journey cigarette butts, used tickets, flecks of sunlight and spittle; a luggage handcart will glide by, its wheels motionless; it will be followed by a news stall hung with seductive magazine covers – photographs of naked, pearl-gray beauties; and people, people, people on the moving platform, themselves moving their feet, yet standing still, striding forward, yet retreating as in an agonizing dream full of incredible effort, nausea, a cottony weakness in one's calves ... The entire old burg in its rosy autumn morning mist moved as well: the great stone [statue] in the square, the dark cathedral, the shop sign – top hat, a fish, the copper basin of a barber. There was no stopping the world now.

And it was a world that Nabokov was determined to see – in the words of *Mary*, a first novel mainly remarkable for its serenity – 'with a fresh, loving eye'.

Times Literary Supplement 2011

Americana (Stepping Westward)

Losing in Las Vegas

If for some reason you were confined to a single adjective to describe Las Vegas, then you would have to settle for the following: un-Islamic. And soon I'll return to that theme. But first I want to tell you what brought me to Sin City. I was here to compete in the annual World Series of Poker. All the intensive homework lay behind me, and I looked forward to the coming contest with unsmiling ambition.

Now I give you fair warning, I murmured as I deplaned into the walk-through casino that calls itself McCarran International Airport. *Don't figure me for dead money.* Purged of tells, tilts, overbets, limp-ins, cry-calls, gutshots, and long-odds suckouts, and purged, too, of all that defeatist and self-pitying 'bad beat' bunkum (when you whine about the cards), my poker had moved on to a new level. I had recently read dozens of anecdotal how-to books written or dictated by the stars and tsars of the green felt; and I had mastered, at least in theory, the technique of 'changing gears'. This was my strategy for the World Series: to kick off I'd go tight and leather-ass, and even on premium cards I'd sandbag and smoothcall; then I'd go loose and splash around and bump and bluff and bully; and then I'd go tight again – and so on. I hadn't journeyed to Vegas just to make it to the last table and then walk to the rail with a mere five hundred thousand. I was there for the $U.S. 10 million (which would then be doubled by a lavish and adoring sponsor). I was there for the bracelet. I was going to the Amazon Room (as they say) to take the whole enchilada.

Soon I'll be telling you about my bad beat with the three fives. But first, some observations on the Nevadan venue.

★

Las Vegas is really tremendously un-Islamic. When, on the airport fore-court, I climbed into one of the motorised fridges known hereabouts as taxis, I was asked if I wanted 'some music'. I said I didn't want some music, because I surmised that I was going to get some music everywhere I went, whether I wanted some music or not. This city is noisy. The whoops from the craps tables (all *yea* and *ooo* and *ow*), the continuous and cutely variegated birdsong of mobile phones ('What's good, buddy?'), and the madhouse nursery jingles of the slot machines, horribly prolonged and as pleasing to the ear as a defective car alarm, and then the cataract of coins into the acoustically enhanced money trays.

And some music. Osama Bin Laden advises us that music is 'the flute of the devil'. Islam also deplores any visual representation of the human form. Las Vegas would not be one of Bin Laden's favourite towns. Pneumatic décolletages and oiled derrières adorn the freeway billboards, to promote strip clubs, lap-dance parlours, topless cocktail bars, and all-nude harlequinades (this last, at least, being alcohol-free). At the Bellagio, where I put up, there are no half-nude girls dancing in the casinos – though every last waitress sports a gulch-like cleavage. At the Rio, home of the World Series of Poker (W.S.O.P), on the other hand, half-nude girls are part of the furniture; and, in addition, at regular intervals a kind of railway track is lowered from the ceiling for a re-enactment of the Rio carnival, with floats and steel bands and half-nude girls.

Prostitution is both illegal and ubiquitous in Clark County. The writer Marc Cooper called his book about Vegas *The Last Honest Place in America* because Sin City, by and large, is pretty light on hypocrisy. But anomalies remain, as the place evolves from Mob to nabob, from Little Italy to Wall Street, from Filthy Frank Giannatasio to Michael Milken. Vegas is supposedly down on sex, following its attempt to become a 'family' destination; this was aborted (a fun palace or two later) when it was realised that children don't gamble. Anyway, sex is all around you here, perhaps unavoidably, given its well-attested affinities with games of chance.

More than a hundred of the Las Vegas Yellow Pages are devoted to the exchange of sex for cash: Full Service Casino House Girls, Barely Legal College Cheerleaders, Full Service Barely Eighteen. The week I was there, all the waiters and fridgedrivers were talking about the guy who won big on the slots and then went upstairs with a swinger who doped his drink. She left him his passport, his car keys, and a single credit card. Las Vegans have a word for that kind of behaviour: *class*. More normally, you're lucky to be left with your underpants. As a fall-back, there is pornography in every hotel room. Much of it is billed as 'inter-active': viewers are granted something like editorial control over what they watch. This means that pointy-headed knowhow has given serious thought to the needs of the interacting vacationer.

The Taliban stamped out sports and used the stadiums for public floggings and executions. The Taliban would have warm work to do in Las Vegas. Everywhere there are multiple screens showing basketballers, golfers, baseballers in their sateen jumpsuits, and, of course, the encaged faces of the Darth Vaders of the grid. The extent of the addiction be-comes clear when you find yourself watching a televised tournament of Rock, Paper, Scissors; there is a bent and frowning referee, a clamorous crowd, and a barn-door-sized cheque for $50,000. In the post-playoff interview, the grinning winner doesn't find it at all easy to explain why he is so incredibly good at Rock, Paper, Scissors.

Then there is the gambling (or the 'gaming', in the term preferred by the industry), anathema to the Ayatollah Khomeini, for instance, who banned one of Islam's great inventions, chess, lest people put money on it. Gambling – and gambling spiced with profanity and free drinks. You have to queue for lots of things in Vegas, for restaurant tables, cups of coffee, Elton John, *Cats*, rhinestone-brassiere musicals, motorised fridges, stools at non-tournament poker meets; but you never have to queue for those games of chance in which the odds favour the house. What is most startling about the casinos of Las Vegas is their scale and how populous they are. The numbers are Third World. As you enter a hotel the size of the Pentagon and start looking for the right queue, you realise that you are in a queue already – that the entire multitude is queuing to queue.

*

To the poker wing of the Rio – for in-depth acclimatisation. This will be necessary if I am to do a Chris Moneymaker and take the bracelet at my first attempt. I quote from the PokerStars.com press release: 'When [in 2003] 27-year-old Tennessee accountant Chris Moneymaker turned a $39 online satellite tournament win on www.PokerStars.com into a $2.5 million windfall at the World Series of Poker, people around the world asked, "Why not me?"'

It seems a fair bet that the near-apocalyptic national upsurge in poker-mania is at least partly due to Chris Moneymaker's surname. What if he was called Chris Moneyloser or Chris Breadline or Chris Asshole? Pokerstars.com would have to rewrite some of its copy ('Pokerstars. com Launches Moneymaker Millionaire Tournament'), and Partygaming.com, when it went into flotation last year, might not have turned out to be bigger than Disney and British Airways.

The Rio's poker wing is a conference centre, and the theme, for now, is Texas Hold'Em. 'Your day job could be a distant memory,' say the posters. 'Chris Moneymaker – Accountant. Joe Hachem – Chiropractor. Greg Raymer – Patent Attorney'. And there is a billboard with the three champs glowering out at you, as in a boxing or wrestling head-to-head. But these men are just middle-class chubsters: accountant, chiropractor, patent attorney. And perhaps that's the point. There are opposed longings in the contemporary psyche: on the one hand, the need for enclosed anonymity within a clearly defined peer group; and on the other, a sweltering lust for celebrity. To be quite ordinary and yet wholly exceptional: nobody combines these conditions more seamlessly than the poker star – than Chris Moneymaker, the World Series accountant from Tennessee.

Like darts in the 1980s, poker is trying to clean up its image. Why, then, does it showcase itself in Las Vegas? And why does the trade-fair area have continuous bikini-babe footage on the plasma screens, and why are there dozens of chicks in general-issue satin hotpants, and why, at the Media Tournament later in the day, are the guest stars the softcore Shannon Elizabeth (*American Pie*) and the hard-core Ron Jeremy (by acclamation the grossest performer in the San Fernando Valley)? The master rule would seem to be that if you have a product to sell, then put some female flesh next to it. Besides, in glandular terms, poker is inseparable from the carnal energies: it is all heartbeat and hot palms. I am now old enough to inspect the attendant girls with an anthropologist's eye: astonishingly, the average set of vital statistics would go something like 38E-28-26. These top-heavy buttless wonders, incidentally, wouldn't turn any heads in the real Rio, where most of the surgical ballooning takes place below the waist.

It may seem perverse to take Las Vegas as the setting for a complaint about diminutive posteriors – Vegas, the holiday home of the truly astronomical rear end. Patent attorney Greg Raymer is no drink of water, but there is a woman in his autograph queue ('My husband's a great fan. You've inspired him, big-time') who has munched herself into a wheelchair: arms like legs, legs like torsos, and a torso like an exhausted orgy.

A male two-wheeler, in the forecourt beyond, succeeds in 'falling' from his vehicle even while it is stationary; passers-by shovel and bail him back into it, but his body is more liquid than solid, and it is simply seeking the lowest level, like a domestic flood coming down a staircase. Al-Qaeda remains silent on the question of obesity. But even the non-believer can contemplate such human forms with a sorrow that is almost religious. They are unbounded, infinity-tending, like a single-handed push for globalisation.

★

I faux-nonchalantly compete in the Media Poker Tournament, and am undiscouraged by my early exit. If money is 'the language of poker', and it is, then this session is dumbshow. The winnings are destined for charity. And what good is *that* to anyone?

On the eve of my first day at the W.S.O.P (winning it will take a whole week) I dine with Anthony Holden and James McManus – two of the top writer-players in pokerdom. Holden has of course picked up a title or two; and McManus, here in Vegas in 2000, made it all the way to the final table. My intention, as we know, is to do a little bit better than that.

'Be ultra-conservative while you get your bearings,' they tell me. 'It's ten players per table, so be prepared for more high stuff than you're used to. There are 169 possible opening hands. Only about a dozen are worth playing. Fold on everything except pocket jacks and up, A-K, or high-suited connectors. Later on, if you're behind the button [that is, to the right of the rotating dealer-position], don't always wait for premium cards. You can go with K-J or pocket eights. By then it's better to be too loose than too tight. Loose-strong. Avoid what Al did [Al Alvarez]. Avoid tight-weak.'

As the evening comes to an end, generous McManus clutches my arm. 'Don't be intimidated, man! Remember – you're Martin fucking Amis!'

★

Back in the Bellagio I continue with McManus's classic book about his classic run, *Positively Fifth Street*. And I am slightly concerned to discover how perpetually and implacably and worldbeatingly *brave* you have to be if you want to exist for ten minutes in No Limit, where every hand might be your last. Brave, and cool too: brave-cool. The other books haven't even mentioned this, because they take brave-cool for granted. Which is not to dismiss the more or less reliable intrepidity and calm that have served me pretty well, over the years, in various stressful kitchens in north London, where scores of pounds regularly change hands. Still, McManus's book also reminds me that after the first day I will be competing exclusively against passionate professionals in the poker equivalent of the Super Bowl.

It is perfectly true that I am Martin fucking Amis. But what about Chris fucking Moneymaker and Mike the fucking Mouth Matusow and Chris fucking 'Jesus' Ferguson – and, for that matter, what about Kathy fucking Liebert and Annie fucking Duke?

Vast serenity and a consciousness of simple heroism escort me into the Amazon Room just before noon the next day. My nostrils flare to the elegant scene: it is like the dining room of an ocean liner after an invasion by unusually pitiless pirates. About two thousand card sharps are jinking their chips (and there are another six thousand where they came from) – the sound of cicadas and rattlesnakes. This won't be a jokey works outing, like the media game. There'll be an edge; oh yes, there'll be some shit, what with the press tag and the English accent. I locate my seat and fine-tune my table presence.

We are nine, for now, and, disappointingly, all-male. I give my immediate neighbours a soldierly glance. The others, stretching away over the kidney-shaped baize, are an unsociable blur of speckle and bumfluff in mirror shades and sleeveless T-shirts, under baseball caps wedged into place by earphones the size of car clamps.

'Hi', says the sweet-faced, olive-skinned thirty-year-old to my right. 'I'm Josh. With a J.'

'Eccentric parents,' says the droll dealer, who is labelled Dan.

'They were hippies,' says Josh. 'What d'you expect?'

At this point, comforted by Josh, I relax enough to look around and beyond. Approximately one butter mountain per table, with his rump slobbering all over his stool; and the same proportion of snazzy-looking women – and twelve-year-old boys, who have apparently mistaken the Amazon Room for a family destination. I reflect that the kids must in fact be over twenty-one, or their presence in a casino would give rise to their arrest. Still, the age profile of poker is heading steadily down. These are the owls of the internet. Poker isn't about cards, says Doyle Brunson (the game's premier sage and gent): it's about people. But the web rats never meet any people. For them, poker isn't about people. It's about mathematics. They do the reverse implied pot odds on every pip.

Dan knocks on the table. 'Gentlemen? Cards in the air.'

*

I am now obliged to spend a long time describing the first deal – for mortifying reasons that will duly emerge. I peek: Ajax, A-J, unsuited. A trouble hand. My position is optimal, so when nobody raises I too call the big blind, or mandatory opener, of $50, along with four opponents. The flop comes up Q-10-K. And my epic calm and simple heroism flee with such a shriek that I immediately break the rules. I jerk back from the table with the cards held to my chest.

'Sir? Cards stay on the table!' says Dan. 'Really I should cancel your hand.'

Oh, don't do that, I almost yell – it's a high straight! I am all contrition and my cards are suffered to stand. Everyone checks to me. Then I find myself troubled by what in Las Vegas is a most unhelpful inhibition: puritan guilt (because my hand, strictly speaking, is null and void). So instead of transforming myself into a burp-gun of power raises, I check too – unforgivably. Fourth Street, the turn card, is a 3, and the board is a rainbow: no possible flush. Once again everyone checks and it is me to speak. I now see the true meaning of those four flat-calls and eight consecutive checks (a phenomenon that would not recur): there was practically nothing in the pot. We had two cards to come, and my best bet would have been a slow-play raise of a hundred, or maybe two or three to make it look like a positional steal. But it is my intention to scare off all the two-pairs and threes-of-a-kind I imagine are ranged all around me; so I bet a thousand, and everybody folds.

It seems to me that I now have a couple of alternatives. I can celebrate my win of $200 by standing on my chair and pumping my fist until the TV camera comes over and makes me famous. Or I can utter a four-letter word. In recent years, during the televised sequences, the players' transmitted conversations sounded like Morse code, so often was the bleeper needed ('Then the bleep makes his bleeping straight with a bleeping trey on the bleeping river'). So audible obscenities, now, earn you a ten-minute ban. A ten-minute ban is exactly what I want: time for a stabilising cigarette and some fresh air in the forecourt, where it is forty-four degrees centigrade.

Instead I go on tilt. For a whole round I am in the thick of it, eerily combining a trance of fear and a panic of greed with a boss pair (losing to trips), a boss double pair (losing to trips), and a post-flop ace-high four-flush, which, embitteringly, stayed that way on streets four and five. My game is all solecism: I bet out of sequence; I sit for a full minute, waiting, when it is my turn to say; and I fold when I could check. I am, in brief, a psychological ruin, and $3,500 down – just over a third of my complimentary stake.

'Have a white russian', Josh tenderly counsels. 'Have two – but not three. It'll smooth you out'.

But now I smooth out the hard and nauseous way, with successive hands (after a while I started writing them down) of 7-2, 8-3, J-4, 3-2, 5-4, 10-3, 7-3, 9-4, 8-2, Q-2, 9-3, 10-4, 3-2, J-5, 4-3, 10-2, 8-3, Q-2, 9-3, 10-2, and so on, for ten or eleven rounds. Then I cop 9-9, play it from a weak position, make a set, and tremulously prevail. This is to be my second and last win at the W.S.O.P.

Until now, the seat on my left has remained empty (its stack fractionally eroded by subtracted blinds). And the table, it seems, lacks a 'flair' personality. But here he comes, two hours late, gangly, punk-pretty, and fresh from Essex, England, with iPod, shades, and pink bandanna beanie, and calling himself Gar, with a G. And it seems that Gar's seat may remain unwarmed: still standing after his first flop, Gar is already going all-in.

'Here, Dave, I'm all-in!' hollers Gar to his friend four tables away. 'Dave! Dave! I'm all-in! That's the way I am,' he tells me. 'Tight-weak. Internet donkey!'

'Call,' says Josh, very still. And he pushes in his $9,500 to match Gar's.

The board reads A-4-J. There will be no more betting, so the players show their cards. Josh holds 4-4; Gar holds A-K. The turn is a 10. 'See you later, lads,' says Gar, backing away. But the river is a Q, and Gar shrugs, takes his seat, and starts stacking and riffling and pinging his chips. Josh staggers on, looking sick to his stomach, for two more hands. Then, after husky farewells, he is gone. Gar doesn't notice. He is going all-in again. He says: 'How much you got there? Ballpark.' Ballpark is Garspeak for 'approximately'. The table has found its flair.

After the lunch break, sucking his fingertips and shouting for a serviette, Gar comes back with a reeking paper plateful of medium-raw hamburger. And Josh's gentle gaze has been supplanted by the pocked scowl of Mike Woo. Wait. Isn't that Mike Woo as in Mike fucking Woo? Mike's a name, a face. And he is soon having a series of ferocious battles with Gar and with anyone else who dares come near him. By now I am dreading the sight of pocket aces – I'm that brave-cool. But it never happens. I play A-K, the Big Slick, twice, losing on both. And soon I am looking for something, anything, to go all-in on before my stack hits three figures.

J-2, 3-2, 8-3, 5-4, 9-3. Gar is gone, his pocket jacks hitting three overcards on the flop. Mike Woo is gone, his king flush succumbing to the case ace. 5-2, 8-6, 7-3, 5-4, 6-5. It is dawning on me that my best hand was my first: I didn't have the lock, the cinch, the stone-cold nuts – but I did have a straight. And since then? Three nines. Only once in my life have I had a session where God hated me as much as this, and I almost broke even; but today his wrath has No Limit. At last I get 5-5 and go all-in. My lone adversary, showing his A-6, is pairless after the flop. So I'm 11-10 favourite, I think. The flop is 5-J-6. I have 5-5-5. Fourth street is a Q. Fifth street is another 6. He has the mark of the beast (6-6-6). He has the boss set.

'It sucks so bad', said the man steering the fridge back to the Bellagio. 'Like a kick in the gut. I sympathise. Me, I went out yesterday on a mega-bad beat. I'm flying American Airlines [A.-A.] and I'm all-in. Guy calls with 5-5! Flop comes up A-4-2. The turn's another ass [A]! Four aces! But he's got four connected clubs! Then the prick makes the fucking steel wheel with the fucking blue trey on the fucking river. That was my bad beat. What was yours? ... I'm sorry. You don't want to talk, right? That's it, that's it. Let yourself go pale for a spell. Bleed it all out. Would you like some music?'

*

The nicest hotel in Las Vegas stands hard by the nastiest hotel in Las Vegas, on the northern extremity of the Strip. You can actually walk from one to the other without your destination eternally receding as you approach, and without finding, at the last moment, that you have to sprint across a twelve-lane highway. The nicest hotel is called the Wynn, after its owner, Steve (another matter-of-fact Vegas surname), and it is themeless: no Eiffel Tower or St Mark's Square, no medieval jousts or rubberised rainforests, no white tigers or shark tanks, no volcanoes or talking statues. At the Wynn, even the exterior is airconditioned: an alfresco fridge the size of two football fields. The swimming pools are lined with cabanas, like ritzy beach huts – masterful lairs of toupee and pedicure and minibar. All around there are tables for massage and baccarat. The Wynn is a monument to what physicists call negative entropy. Enormous outlays of power and expense create order and comfort, before dispersing themselves in chaos and waste.

In one area, 'European-style' sunbathing is permitted, but it is a freedom that goes unembraced. Locally, toplessness is considered menial: in Las Vegas, people get a wage for showing their breasts. I briefly regret this, because here we see the human form as nature might have conceivably intended: lean, toned, and bronzed, and expensively maintained. The humans are enjoying the neg-entropy – warmed pool water, cooled air, iced drinks; and they are blessed with wealth and youth. I am not at home, here at the Wynn.

The nastiest hotel in (uptown) Las Vegas isn't called The Looze. It is called The Frontier. And as I deflatedly approach it, Martin Moneymaker transmutes into Martin Moneyloser or Martin Asshole (and to hell with Martin fucking Amis). This is more like it: SHRIMP AND STEAK $8.95, says the neon sign. FAJITAS FEAST FOR TWO WITH 2 FREE RITAS $19.95. COLD BEER DIRTY GIRLS. LIVE MUD WRESTLING. BIKINI BUCKING BRONCO GIRLS. In the parking lot there is an aged white coupé suffering from spontaneous combustion: it has blown its hood. Under the withered hedge, two witch-like pigeons are pecking away at a handful of discarded Cheez-Its.

The Frontier once had a theme (the frontier), still detectable in the Tex-Mex snack bar and, I suppose, in the dusty plastic statuary of The Flintstones bingo nook. Now the theme is Travelodge or Indian-reservation HoJo. Dumpster-sized human shapes move around in the desperate murk of the cocktail lounge; there is a viscous gloom, moist and sooty to the senses. Its polities never had much luck with the notion, admittedly, but we all recall the primacy, in Islam, of the ideal of equality and justice. After The Wynn, The Frontier is a reminder that money and success, winning and losing, et cetera, are zero-sum. There is not enough to go around, and what is gained by one is lost by the other.

★

It is in the Frontier that I finally resolve to turn fulltime pro. I have the skills, clearly enough. All I need is the cards: American Airlines or suited Big Slick at least every other hand. My wife and daughters would be happy enough living with me here at The Frontier (and the Assholes, perhaps, would be given a preferential family rate).

I can see myself at the bar, enjoying a second skull-chilling margarita, plus a fajita and a mahaka and a gordita (but where is my enchilada?), before I head off to work. Some outfit called the D-Cup Divas would be warming up on the trampoline. And I'd tell anyone who'd listen about the time I sat down at a World Series that was mine for the taking, and caught that bad beat with the three fives.

Sunday Times 2006

Travolta's Second Act

He opened the door himself – so you walked straight into the icon. It was January 1995, and that morning he had begun work on *Get Shorty*, a major production (co-starring Gene Hackman, Rene Russo and Danny DeVito) based on Elmore Leonard's satirical thriller about Hollywood. A big book, a big film, and a big day. Thus I was naturally expecting a big wait – or a cancellation; or a bodyguard and a body search and, eventually (maybe), a big entrance in some Spanish-style den infested with the star's 'people' ...

But no. Here was John Travolta removing my coat from my shoulders and personally sliding it on to a hanger, and turning to me with the close-set deep-blue eyes that remind you of the phrase 'undivided attention'. Actors' eyes don't blink unless the actor tells them to; and Travolta's eyes don't blink. For me, it was like stepping into a Warhol poster – a Mao, an Elvis. It was like bumping into James Dean or Jimi Hendrix. You feel that John Travolta is so iconic that he ought to be dead. And he isn't: not any more.

In his early twenties Travolta was, by many magnitudes, the brightest star in the firmament: everyone wanted him in everything. 'It could be a role for an eighty-year-old woman,' his ex-girlfriend Marilu Henner has said, 'and John would be offered it.' By his mid-thirties, Travolta was simply a human vacuum, lost in Hollywood's interstellar void. (And *travolta*, we may be unsurprised to learn, means 'overturned', 'shook up', 'knocked down'.) Now he is forty, and his career has done something that the industry can barely find words for. 'Comeback' doesn't begin to cover it; nor does 'renaissance' or 'revival.' This product is flying direct from zero temperature to *dignity*.

What happened? The answer, of course, is *Pulp Fiction*. Another, more general answer is Quentin Tarantino. Smoothly Travolta guided me to a living room (this was a rented property in Beverly Hills, north of Sunset) and, his voice dropping to a whisper of gratitude, told me how it had gone – how 'it was *all* Quentin'. Or so it would now seem. Actually, even Quentin needed outside help. The latest phase in this inimitably American story also owes something to postmodernism – and to Scientology. How drunk was Scott Fitzgerald when he said that there were no second acts in American lives?

Two years ago almost to the day, John Travolta, apparently, had only one movie prospect. 'It was *Look Who's Talking 3*,' he said, with some resignation (but with insufficient embarrassment and scorn). That would be the one with the talking dogs. We can picture Travolta back then, in his twenty-room château in Penobscot Bay, Maine, or in his second home, in the Spruce Creek Fly-In development in Daytona Beach, Florida, or, indeed, en route between them, at the controls of one of his three aeroplanes, in actorly preparation for the dogs movie: thinking *dogs*.

As it happens, he was unprecedentedly rich and fat and happy in his private life, with his wife, the actress Kelly Preston, and his newborn son, little Jett. But he was about to make a film about talking dogs. 'I try to be realistic,' he said in his measured way. 'You know: you can't dance without legs. I would continue to work with the best that was offered. But I did think, Well, it's all over'. Then there came a succession of rumours that Quentin Tarantino, 'the hottest guy in town', wanted a meeting with John Travolta, the wintry relic with the vanished career. The meeting happened, and it lasted twelve hours.

'It didn't look as though he had a project in mind. He had started writing *Pulp Fiction*, but he kept talking about some horror movie. And I am not a horror kind of guy. His interest in me seemed to be ... generic.' The meeting began in Quentin's apartment – 'which turned out to be *my* apartment', he went on. 'The one I rented when I first came to LA, in 1974.' (Resolutely unflaky, Travolta didn't make much of the coincidence.) They talked, they had a glass of wine, they went out to dinner, they came back and played Tarantino's movie-buff board games, they went out to a coffee shop, they came back again. 'And then Quentin let me have it.

'He said, "What did you *do*? Don't you remember what Pauline Kael said about you? What Truffaut said about you? Don't you know what you *mean* to the American cinema? John, what did you *do*?" I was hurt – but moved. He was telling me I'd had a promise like no one else's. I went out of there with my tail between my legs. I was devastated. But I also thought, Jesus Christ, I must have been a fucking good actor.'

By now, we were seated at his circular dining table, drinking wine. The house was comfortable and anonymous, but there was still the sense of the movie star's in-depth backup: helpers, minders. It has been said that Travolta is a millionaire who lives like a billionaire. Still, here in LA everything is scaled down and streamlined for work – for *Get Shorty* – including the star himself. Although the energies of the house centre on Travolta, there is now another power source, who is fitfully sleeping. Kelly Preston – tousled, pretty, petite – appeared. Next came an earnest discussion about the imminence of Jett's return to full consciousness. Soon afterward, Jett duly presented himself, in his mother's arms, looking crumpled and slurpily applying himself to a bottle of juice. Many hugs and kisses and avowals. Jett's eyelashes are an inch long.

It occurred to me that Jett must be one of the most cosseted creatures on the entire planet. In Maine, evidently, he has his own Wonderland wing, where servants approach him bearing plates of tempura shrimp. Children, when they come, knock everybody sideways, but movie stars (with their expanded selves) have further to shift. So they tend to whale: movie stars' children *really* live like movie stars. Can you imagine how nice the *help* are to Jett Travolta? Wouldn't *you* be nice to someone called Jett Travolta?

We talked about parenthood. Travolta was eager to speak, eager to listen. The grotesque vicissitudes of his career must seem more distant now; but it's always possible that his objectivity is long established and secure. Something he once said struck me, and I quoted it to him over the cheesecake: "'You're assuming that a person is introverted and self-obsessed all the time ... He feels bad. He feels a loss. But give the guy the benefit of not being *insane*.'"

★

Tarantino's question remains, and remains unanswered. What *did* Travolta *do*? To curl up with a VCR and the Collected Movies, 1976–93, is to witness a trajectory of dizzy decline. In the firmament, as elsewhere, the brightest stars have the shortest lives: blue giant to black hole. But the universe isn't old enough to encompass the degeneration that Travolta managed. It will take ten billennia for our sun to reach its ultimate state, frozen in crystalline undetectability. He did it in ten years.

By 1980, John Travolta had made three movies that passed him straight into pop-culture immortality. You can summon them in stills.

First, in *Saturday Night Fever*, the polystyrene erection under the disco strobes, in the kind of shirt that reduces your nipples to blobs of plasma, on bricklike high heels, pointing skyward. Next, in *Grease*, the rocker with the cigarette in the corner of his knockout smile, the eyes mere slits of clichéd cool. And then, in *Urban Cowboy*, the proud, puzzled, romantically sculpted profile beneath the stiff rim of the cow-puncher hat. It is not just good looks and good lighting that give these images their durability. What we are seeing here is what the camera sees when it confronts a palpable charge of life. And in these films Travolta gives complete performances; they form a trilogy whose subject is masculine youth. In his thwarted frowns and glares, his tonguey cadences, his strut-ting uncertainty, in the italicisations of his forehead, Travolta contrives a mature commentary on what it is to be callow.

Now comes the transitional *Blow Out* (1981), overdirected and mis-erably underwritten by Brian de Palma, who launched Travolta in *Carrie* in 1976 (and whose career curve would take the same kind of turn). A scarecrow of ragged illogicalities, spruced up by Hitchcock via Antonioni, *Blow Out* was nonetheless a logical choice for Travolta, now twenty-seven and ready, it seemed, to receive his Italian-American inheritance. Pauline Kael, writing in these pages, compared him to Brando in *On the Waterfront* ('It's the willingness to go emotionally naked and the control to do it in character'); and there was a more general expectation that he would soon fall under the sway of directors such as Francis Coppola and Martin Scorsese. Instead, he fell under the sway of Sylvester Stallone. What this entrained, in any event, was catastrophic collapse.

Travolta, loyally, has never seen it this way. The way he sees it, he was more or less naturally displaced by a new generation of stars: Hanks, Cruise, Costner. One wonders about the nature of the initial attraction: Stallone is an icon, too, of course. Rambo, that lethal trapezium of organ meat; Rocky, out jogging with his dog. Maybe even the dog thing goes all the way back to Sly. Dogs, at any rate, were what Travolta started star-ring in, exclusively, after 1982.

In the space of one year, he made the Stallone-directed *Fever* follow-up, *Staying Alive* – a charmlessly muscular salaam to body-building and the Big Time – plus *Two of a Kind*, with Olivia Newton-John, a sort of wishful lube job on *Grease*. *Two*, one of the worst films ever made, opens in a celestial setting (clouds, white-smocked angels, a deep-voiced God off camera), and features Oliver Reed as the Devil. Can we fully imagine what kind of trouble a movie is in when it features Oliver Reed as the Devil? Oliver Reed in a ringmaster suit?

Next came the thoroughly average *Perfect*, which can be considered a local high point. Thereafter, Travolta was finding himself in the kind of films that get exclamation marks added to their titles when they expeditiously appear in the rental stores. I refer to what Columbia Tristar Home Video calls '*Look Who's Talking Now!* (A TOM ROPELEWSKI Film)'. *Look Who's Talking* (1989) showcased a garrulous baby; *Look Who's Talking Too* (1990) showcased a garrulous toddler plus a garrulous newborn. *Look Who's Talking Now* was the talkie with the dogs: simply an ad for the silent screen. And that was Travolta in 1993.

*

'The day Quentin finished writing *Pulp Fiction*, he sent it to me,' Travolta resumed. 'He said, "Look at *Vincent*."' Tarantino had adapted the part for Travolta; he believed in Travolta – 'but he was the only guy who was thinking that way. Which kind of shows you how my light had died. The studio wanted an actor with … a higher temperature. Quentin had much more to lose than I did. Finally, he told them, "You either do it with John Travolta or you don't do it."'

Simultaneously – and ridiculously, it might seem – Tarantino was having to win over *Travolta*. 'My doubts were not artistic doubts. They were moral doubts'. We live in an age of mass suggestibility, the argument went. And in his earlier days, in the days of Tony and Danny and Bud, Travolta's performances had an uncontrollable effect: they caused crazes. What kind of role model was Vincent, with his hypodermic and his handgun? The reservation seems responsible, but it hardly seems appropriate, given Vincent's fate (studded with bullets, on a toilet seat). Given, too, the quality of Tarantino's writing. As with David Mamet – as with Elmore Leonard – the burnished heartlessness of the dialogue is always pointing beyond itself, to the moral world it carefully excludes. In one scene, Vincent goes to score a few grams of 'madman' heroin from his dealer, Lance (the droll and Jesusy Eric Stoltz):

LANCE: Still got your Malibu?
VINCENT: Oh man. You know what some fucker did the other day?

LANCE: What?

VINCENT: Fuckin keyed it?

LANCE: Oh man. That's fucked up.

VINCENT: Tell me about it. I had it in storage for three years. It was out five days and some dickless piece of shit fucked with it.

LANCE (*weighing out the powder*): They should be fuckin killed, man. No trial, no jury. Straight to execution ... What a fucker.

VINCENT: What's more chickenshit than fucking with a man's automobile? I mean, *don't* fuck with another man's *ve*hicle.

LANCE: You don't do it.

VINCENT: It's against the rules.

(*Drugs and cash exchange hands.*)

LANCE: Thank you.

VINCENT: Thank *you*. Mind if I shoot up here?

It seems that by this stage in his career Travolta was almost incapable of accepting a good script – or of rejecting a bad one. He saw the irony of it even then. 'I was saying to Quentin, "No. I'll do *Look Who's Talking 4* instead. In which the *chairs* talk."' But when I asked him, the next day, about the long list of parts he had mistakenly turned down, Travolta mentioned *Arthur* and *Splash* before throwing in *Prince of the City* and *Midnight Express* – and he blandly dismissed *An Officer and a Gentleman* and *American Gigolo*. Travolta is thoughtful and articulate, but he is also obtuse and something of a point-misser.

The talk turned to *Get Shorty*. (Travolta had just finished an interim project, *White Man's Burden*, a drama about the racial divide, produced by Tarantino's stablemate Lawrence Bender.) I said what I believed to be true: that Elmore Leonard was one of the greatest popular writers of all time; that *Get Shorty* was a masterpiece; and that Travolta's mother (working closely with Travolta's agent) couldn't have come up with a better Travolta role than the one he was playing – that of Chili Palmer, the Miami loan shark with big ideas about making movies.

'I turned it down at first.'

'You what?'

'I turned it down. Then Quentin called and said' – Travolta's voice became a wheedling whisper – '"This is not the one you say no to. This is the one you say yes to. I'm not going to *let* you make this mistake."'

'You've lost weight for Chili, I see.'

'That was Quentin, too. He said lose about fifteen pounds. I lost *exactly* fifteen pounds.'

★

While writing *Pulp Fiction*, Tarantino must have instinctively grasped that Travolta could never 'come back' in any conventional sense. The rebirth had to be a revamp, and a kind of travesty. Accordingly, the physically graceful but emotionally gawky American calf – Tony / Danny / Bud – was obliged to reappear as a corrupt and jowly journeyman. This is why the dance scene with Uma Thurman is central: it is a post-modern coup de théâtre, in which the audience archly colludes. Every moviegoer knows what Travolta can do on a dance floor. Watching his drugged gyrations is like watching the aged Picasso drawing a stick man. 'Stephanie, I want to ask you something, all right?' pleads Tony Manero in *Saturday Night Fever*. 'Do you think that I am either interesting or intelligent?' Tarantino provides the heartless – and contemporary – destination for that old American quest. All that Vincent knows, after three years in Europe, is how to order a big Mac in French.

Yet Tarantino's simpler aim was just to get Travolta in front of the camera with some lines worth saying. And we find that the talent was always there, unimpaired and entire: concentration, timing, fluidity and wit. In his preparations for the part, Travolta mingled not with Mob executioners but with heroin addicts. There he found a fear of full consciousness – a fear of the intelligence that Tony / Danny / Bud liked to hope would be waiting for them. From then on, with Vincent, it is all in a twitch, a roll of the dead eyes.

'Pauline Kael said you had the "gift of transparency". What do you think she meant by that?'

'It doesn't take much for a thought to be seen. I keep having to talk directors out of talking me into overacting. I say, "You won't see it on the set. You'll see it in the editing room."' And he adds, with an emphasis quieter than the italics I give it, 'I have an ability to be it, and *it will read*.'

★

Get Shorty has a beautiful premise. If Hollywood is full of cheats, liars, hustlers, and double-crossers – if movies are made by crooks – then why can't a crook make a movie? Chili Palmer, ex-wise guy and general Mob hard-on, a shylock who gives loans at 150 per cent, chases a debt to Hollywood, and sticks around. The business practices look pretty familiar, though even Chili can sense subtleties he has yet to master:

> Other things to remember: you don't 'take a meeting' any more, you say you have 'a two-thirty at Tower'. If a studio passes on a script, you don't say 'they took a Pasadena'. That was out before it was in. Like 'so-and-so gives good phone' ... There were a lot of terms you had to learn, as opposed to the shylock business where all you had to know how to say was 'Give me the fuckin money'.

Usually, on movie sets, the visiting journalist hangs around for thirteen hours and then, when the cameras are finally rolling, watches an extra tying up his shoelace. But Travolta was as obliging as ever. I arrived at the multi-storey parking lot at LAX in time to watch several takes of a funny, dramatic and salient action sequence during which Chili Palmer taunts, works over, and finally befriends a menacing lunk (an ex-stuntman) called the Bear. Travolta was wearing silks and loafers (what he calls 'a street guy's idea of *GQ*') and a pitying sneer, recalling Jack Nicholson in *Chinatown*—the sneer that says 'You're even dumber than you think I think you are.' The two actors rehearse. A kick, a punch, a knee in the face, and the Bear goes down. Chili crouches over him and says,

> 'How many movies have you been in?'
> 'About sixty'.
> 'No shit. What're some of them?'
> '*Saturday Night Fever*,' ad-libs the Bear.

On the set Travolta is candidly regal. He is a prince mingling with his subjects. Wearing the high finish (and light makeup) of intransigent stardom, he triggers hysteria wherever he goes. ('I've walked down the street with some big stars, O.K.?' Tarantino has said. 'I cannot walk *two feet* down the street with John Travolta. People stop their cars. People are clawing all over him.') The day before, a production assistant warned the extras that they would be fired if they asked for more autographs. 'No, no. You will *not* be fired,' Travolta said, and continued signing. Today, on my arrival, Travolta veers off to secure me a cappuccino, confronting a flock of paparazzi; and then I sit beside him (while the makeup woman copes with some subatomic blemish) on a director's chair. Wait: not a director's chair. *The* director's chair – Barry Sonnenfeld's chair.

'Why is it that you seem to be the *people's* star?' I asked. 'It certainly isn't your lifestyle. They love you as if you still lived with your brothers and sisters in Englewood, New Jersey.'

'It works the other way. You know: quintessentially American, living out your dreams. They don't *want* you to be humble.'

Twenty minutes later, I learn something – something entirely ludicrous – about not being humble. In his public dealings, Travolta is polite, considerate, even courtly. But he doesn't make the mistake of the movie star in *Get Shorty*, who, in Chili's view, 'wanted people to think he was a regular guy, but was too used to being who he was to pull it off'. You cannot combine being a movie star with being a regular guy. You cannot combine being a movie star with not being a movie star.

A chauffeur-driven car appears. I assume that we are going to be chauffeured to the Travolta trailer (saving ourselves a three-minute stroll). It turns out that we are going to be chauffeured to the *elevator*, which is a hundred and fifty yards away. En route, we pass the Bear. Travolta asks the driver to stop and lowers his electric window. Gently and, I think, unironically, he asks this powerhouse if he 'wants a ride'. The Bear says it's OK: he's good. We reach the end of the journey and climb out. As the elevator doors open, we are joined by a couple of members of the crew. And by the Bear.

*

'John,' I tell him, 'I find I'm in a terrible position.' By making things easy for me, Travolta has made things hard for me. For two decades, on and off, I have been interviewing famous people. And I have to confess that I have never interviewed anyone as generous as Travolta: generous with his time, his trouble, his attentiveness. When I came to Los Angeles to interview Brian de Palma, years ago, things went rather differently. I arrived on the set, as arranged – and he cancelled. This was what Hollywood was *supposed* to be like. (I was delighted. The piece wrote itself.) 'A journalist,' I explained, 'doesn't want to discover that John Travolta is a nice guy. That's not a story.'

'What gets written about me is one of the things I can't control. So I thought I'd just put a lot into it from my end and see what happened.'

Was this postmodernism? 'Control': was this Scientology? We had tackled Scientology the night before, during our second dinner. As interpreted by John Travolta, at least, Scientology came across as stolidly, even boringly, uncreepy: self-management on a buddy network, with an emphasis on communal therapy (but with full reliance on modern medicine). Some people are drawn to religion – and a religion is what Scientology now is, officially, tax-deductibly – not in a search for God but because they like group systems. If we read Nirad Chaudhuri we find that Hinduism, for instance, is worldly: Do right by that cow, and you will get one over on your neighbour. But Scientology in its doctrines is basic survivalism. It teaches you how to pay the rent and not go crazy. 'Without it,' Travolta said, 'I wouldn't have lived any longer than John Belushi.' Well, as they say – whatever works.

The star's trailer is a luxurious version of Buddy's mobile home in *Urban Cowboy*: plush carpet, microwave, VCR. There is pizza, there is iced tea. Duly prompted, Travolta tells the story about making an emergency landing in his Gulfstream at Washington's National Airport with his wife and child on board.

'I had the equivalent of seven failures – contagious failures.' The talk turns technical: his 'transducer rectifier' wasn't functioning. 'I claimed an Emergency over the radio. And then *everything* went. I had one gyro. No flaps. No reverse thrust. When I fly, I find great objectivity up there. And I found I was calm. In flying school, they give you what they call a black cockpit. So I felt I'd been there before.'

This story sounds to me like a pretty good figure for Travolta's career. The steep takeoff, the high altitude, the contagious failures, the black cockpit, the half-blind but eventually triumphant landing. Nonchalantly, Travolta now reveals that he has just been offered eight million dollars (twice his current rate) to star in a movie with Sharon Stone – 'That was an hour ago'. Sharon Stone? Here in Hollywood, there are two directions you can disappear in. My protective instincts are stirred. Tony and Danny and Bud all longed for guidance. The baffled sweetness of the young Travolta's smile I take to be real, and durable. He is also a terrifying achiever who has learned to be calm. But he does need guidance; he does need his transducer rectified. By now, of course, I am ready to offer my mentorship to John – my words of advice. Instead, I will offer them to Quentin Tarantino. All will be well. Just don't let Travolta out of your sight.

New Yorker 1995

Postscript. As it turned out, Travolta's resurgence lacked staying power. His last really good thing was *Primary Colors* (1998), where he gave us a rendering of Bill Clinton (with plenty of Bubba mixed in with the charismatic Big Dog). Since then, the only strong glimmer came with a return to Elmore Leonard and Chili Palmer in *Be Cool* (2005). This is a pity. But it is not to be compared with the death of Jett Travolta, in 2009 (a seizure, related to his autism). Jett was sixteen.

In Pornoland: Pussies are Bullshit

1. PUSSIES ARE BULLSHIT

Pussies are bullshit. Don't let them tell you any different.

'Answer me something,' I said to John Stagliano, the creator of *Butt-man*. We were stepping out of the porno home – onto the porno patio with its porno pool. This was Malibu, California. Down the slope and beyond the road lay the Pacific Ocean; but the Staglianos have no access to its porno shore. In the evening they can watch the porno sunset with its porno pink and mauve and blood-orange, and then linger awhile, per-haps, under a porno moon. 'Answer me something. How do you account for the emphasis, not just in your ... work but in the industry in general, how do you account for the truly incredible emphasis on anal sex?'

After a minimal pause and a minimal shrug Stagliano said, 'Pussies are bullshit.'

Now John was being obedient to the dictionary definition of 'bullshit': nonsense intended to deceive. With 'vaginal', Stagliano elab-orated – well, here you have some chick chirruping away. And the genu-inely discerning viewer (jack-knifed forward in his seat) has got to be thinking: Is this for real? Or is it just bullshit?

With 'anal', on the other hand, the actress is obliged to produce a dif-ferent order of response: more guttural, more animal. As Stagliano quaint-ly but brightly puts it, 'Her personality comes out!' (And her personality, after all, is what the viewer of porno is so anxious to see.) He goes on: 'You want guys who can fuck really good and make the girls look more ... virile.' Virile, of course, means manly; but once again Stagliano is using the King's English. You want the girls to show you 'their testosterone'.

The name of Rocco Siffredi, again and again, was wistfully and rev-erently conjured. Siffredi, the grotesquely endowed Italian, is porno's premier 'buttbanger' or 'assbuster'.

'Rocco has far more power in this industry than any actress,' said Stagliano, pleased to be pulling one back for the boys (generally speaking, male performers are the also-rans of porno). 'I was the first to shoot Rocco. Together we evolved toward rougher stuff. He started to spit on girls. A strong male-dominant thing, with women being pushed to their limit. It looks like violence but it's not. I mean, pleasure and pain are the same thing, right? Rocco is driven by the market. What makes it in today's market place is *reality*.'

And assholes are reality. And pussies are bullshit.

2. BUSH AND GORE

There are, at present, two types of mainstream American pornography: Features and Gonzo.

Features are sex films with some sort of resemblance to 'narrative': settings, storyline, characterisation. 'We don't just show you people fucking,' said a Features executive. 'We show you *why* they're fucking.' These movies are allegedly aimed at the 'couples market.' Couples, it is asserted, want to know *why* people are fucking. I can give these couples a three-word answer that will hold true in every case: for the money.

In *Flashpoint* (Wicked Pictures), for instance, a bunch of porno stars are dressed up as firefighters. As the film opens, we see the porno stars sliding down the pole and boarding the crimson firetruck. An exploding car, a colleague (not a porno star but an ageing extra) falling in the line of duty. There follows an insanely boring funeral, which includes the whole of the Lord's Prayer and the slow and solemn furling, by a porno star, of the American flag. Porno star Jenna grieves for the fallen extra. After returning from the funeral she finds herself alone with another porno star dressed up as a firefighter. He seeks to assuage her grief, and in return she grants him fellatio plus full intercourse. The next sex scene, which occurs about a millennium later, is also triggered by grief counselling. Here a male porno star comforts two female porno stars, one of them anally ...

After a while you begin to think that porno stars, despite being very bad at acting, are very good at acting in one particular: they can keep a straight face. But then humourlessness, universal and institutionalised humourlessness, is the lifeblood of porno.

Films like *Flashpoint* go out to the video stores and, in the soft version (where the hard action is tastefully obscured by some stray object – a fireman's hat, say, or a fireman's boot), are sold to cable and to hotel-chain franchises, and so on. Features owes the humiliating fatuity of its conventions to an old legal precedent called the 'Miller Test'. Miller v California (1973) established that a dirty movie was obscene if it was 'utterly' without social, literary, artistic, political, or scientific 'value'. In juridical terms, the key word here, of course, is 'utterly', and millions of dollars have been spent on its definition.

With a wife as earnest and active as Hillary, Bill Clinton could never be a true pal of porno, but he largely left it alone on First Amendment grounds. Unlike his two predecessors, who systematically harassed the industry with confiscations, multiple prosecutions, fines, jail terms. It's a fair guess that porno never felt more gorgeously secure than when Clinton, in his second term, became in effect the porno president.

Now porno is tensed and braced for changes. It feared Gore. It dreaded Bush. Gonzo porno is also known as 'wall-to-wall'. It shows you people fucking without a care for the reason why. There are no Lord's Prayers, no furled American flags in Gonzo. Features porno is much, much dirtier than it used to be, but Gonzo porno is gonzo, or remorselessly transgressive; and the new element is *violence*.

3. TEMPTRESS AND JONATHAN MORGAN

I had lunch with Temptress (Features). I had lunch with Chloe (Gonzo). And the next day I joined Chloe on the set of *Welcum To Chloeville*.

My lunch with Temptress was a relatively sedate affair. At first I was reminded of the time I interviewed Penny Baker, a Playboy Playmate of the Year: within a minute I had run out of questions. Temptress, like Penny, seemed to be inhibited by the presence of a company executive – in this case Steve Orenstein of Wicked Pictures, for which she is a contract player. But Temptress loosened up.

'Tell me, Temptress,' I said (having apologised for the corniness and awkwardness of my enquiry), 'what *won't* you do?'

'I won't do anal,' said Temptress. 'They keep trying to coax me into it. You know: "Just a finger or a tongue. Or just a little bit: just the tip." But I won't, I used not to do facials. But I do them now.'

Temptress is not talking about beauty treatments. She is talking about the destination of what is variously referred to as the 'pop shot' or the 'money shot': the ejaculation of the male.

'What happens,' I asked, 'when a co-star can't get hard?'

The fiasco used to be the nemesis of porno. A penile no-show could make the difference between profit and loss. But the situation has changed, I was told, thanks to Viagra. On Viagra, the actor performs forty-five minutes behind schedule, with a flushed face and a headache. 'You also lose a dimension,' John Stagliano would explain. 'The guy's fucking without being aroused!' He's just 'showing off' – and pretty soon you're back to bullshit.

Another thing with Viagra is that the guy can have a problem with the pop shot, thus endangering the facial.

'What do you do then, Temptress?'

'They give you a gulp of pina colada mix. The cock's in your mouth and you let it like *ooze* out around it.'

Physically Temptress made you think of a sophomore gussied up for a ball. She didn't sound shy, but she looked it. With her long straight hair frequently steered over her shoulders by her slow-moving hands, with her face unglazed by cosmetics, with her gently narrowed eyes, she exuded what Philip Larkin called the 'strength and pain / Of being young'. I asked about her history and she told me something of it. And there was strength and there was pain (and there was certainly youth: Temptress is twenty-one).

'But I don't want you to write about that. And could you not mention my real name? ... I don't have relationships any more. They make life unstable. The only sex I have is the sex on screen.'

Temptress is one of the lucky ones. She's a star. After lunch I went to Wicked Pictures and had a talk with Jonathan Morgan (performer turned director) in a computerised cutting-room while he edited his latest Feature, a fantastically unfunny comedy called *Inside Porn*.

'Ah,' said Jonathan. 'Now here we have a double anal.'

A double anal is not to be confused with a DP (double penetration: anal and vaginal delivered simultaneously by a two-man team). A double anal is a double anal. And there have been triple anals, too.

'The girls could be graded like A, B and C,' said Jonathan. 'The A is the chick on the boxcover. She has the power. So she'll show up late or not at all. Ninety-nine point nine per cent of them do that.'

He gestured at the screen and said, 'Here you have a borderline A/B doing a double anal. Directors will remember that. She'll get phone calls. For a double anal you'd usually expect a B or a C. They have to do the dirty stuff or they won't get a phone call. You've had a kid, you've got some stretchmarks – so you're out there doing double anal.

'Some girls are used up in nine months or a year. An eighteen year old, sweet young thing, signs with an agency, makes five films in her first week. Five directors, five actors, five times five: she gets phone calls. A hundred movies in four months. She's not a fresh face any more. Her price slips and she stops getting phone calls. Then it's, "Okay, will you do anal? Will you do gangbangs?" Then they're used up. They can't even get a phone call. The market forces of this industry use them up. It just uses them up.'

I thanked Jonathan for his candour. But he wasn't as candid as Chloe. We met in the lobby of my hotel and we strolled out to her Mustang.

'See that?'

The number plate said: STR82NL.

'Straight to anal,' said Chloe.

And she hadn't even got started.

Chloe was Gonzo. She gave me the truth.

4. EXTREME PRODUCTIONS: MAX HARDORE AND KHAN TUSION

A single issue of *Adult Video News* (April 2000) yields the following.

Last October porno star Vivian Valentine attended the XXX-Treme Adults Only vacation in Mexico sporting the black eye she copped from Jon Dough in *Rough Sex* (Anabolic Video). 'I have no regrets or bad feelings about it,' said Vivian.

Regan Starr who worked on the second film in this 'line', *Rough Sex 2*, had a different take. 'I got the shit kicked out of me,' she said. 'I was told before the video – and they said this very proudly, mind you – that in this line most of the girls start crying because they're hurting so bad … I couldn't breathe. I was being hit and choked. I was really upset, and they didn't stop. They kept filming. You can hear me say, "Turn the fucking camera off," and they kept going.' The director of the Rough Sex series (now discontinued), who goes by the name of Khan Tusion, protests his innocence. 'Regan Starr,' Tusion claims, 'categorically misstates what occurred.'

If you don't like Khan Tusion, you won't like Max Hardcore. *AVN*'s regular 'On the Set' column carries a cheerfully scandalised account of the making of *Hollywood Hardcore 13*. In this scene, actor-director Hardcore is having rough sex with Cloey Adams, who is pretending to be under age. 'If you're a good girl, I'll take you to McDonald's later and get you a Happy Meal.' Hardcore then 'proceeds to piss in her mouth'. Addressing the camera, Cloey Adams says, 'What do you think of your little princess now, Daddy?' Nor is Hardcore done with her. 'Turning to the crew, he calmly says, "I'll need a speculum and a hose" ... One of Max's favourite tricks is to stretch a girl's asshole with a speculum, then piss into her open gape and make her suck out his own piss with a hose. Ain't that romantic?'

Now. American porno (and how could it be otherwise?) is *market-driven*. We can see what the above tells us about porno. But what does it tell us about America? And if America is more like a world than a country, what does it tell us about the world?

- The average American spends four hours and fifty-one minutes of every day watching porno (video and internet).
- The average non-homeowning American male spends more on porno than he spends on his rent.
- Porno accounts for 43.5 per cent of the US Gross Domestic Product.

Like pussies, the above statistics are bullshit. I made them up. But the true figures are similarly wild, similarly dizzying, similarly through-the-roof. This *isn't* bullshit:

- Porno is far bigger than rock music and far bigger than Hollywood.
- Americans spend more on strip clubs than they spend on theatre, opera, ballet, jazz and classical concerts combined.
- In 1975 the total retail value of all the hardcore porno in America was estimated at $5–10 million. Last year Americans spent $8 billion on mediated sex.

Whatever porno is, whatever porno does, you may regret it, but you cannot reject it. To paraphrase Falstaff: Banish porno, and you banish all the world.

5. CHLOE

'I have herpes,' said Chloe as she drove me to a smoker-friendly bar. 'After you've been in this business for a while, you have herpes. Everyone has herpes. On the set sometimes you'll say to a guy, "What's this?" And he'll say, "What's what? That? It's a fuck spot." And it may well be a fuck spot, you know, a fuck sore, what with all the traffic. But it's more likely to be a herpes sore, and that guy shouldn't be working. My movies are all-condom, but condoms won't protect you from herpes. They don't cover the base. Sometimes when you're doing girl-girl you'll say, "Honey, I think you should go and see someone." It can be a very stinky scene down there. I'll send her to a porno-friendly doctor (the others treat you like shit) and she'll come out holding her Flagyll prescription with multiple refills.'

Chloe is twenty-six. For ten years she trained as a ballerina; then, at seventeen, she got into drugs, mostly speed ('I'd fuck for like *seventy-two hours*'); at twenty she started shooting up heroin and was already in the industry by the time she quit, over two years ago. Chloe has fair, fine red hair and a warm and clever face. She has a ballerina's body: strong legs, a full muscular backside, and –

'– and no tits. It's true that some Features companies urge the girls to have implants and offer to pay for it. On the road [i.e., stripping] girls used to boast about the cubic capacity of their titjobs. "I've got 840s." "I've got 1220s." One of them turned to me and said, "Get tits or just suck cock." I'd rather just suck cock. I really would.'

If you're going to be a porno star, what do you need? It's pretty clear by now. You need to be an exhibitionist. You need to have a ferocious sex drive. You need to suffer from *nostalgie de la boue* (literally 'mud nostalgia': a childish, even babyish delight in bodily functions and wastes). And – probably – you need damage in your past. You also need to be humourless. Chloe is not humourless. When she talked to me she was like someone peeping over the wall that demarcates two different worlds, and telling me stories about the other side.

'I *like* to be peed on. I like being spat on: it feels like come on your chest. I like to be choked. I like to be fisted. Here we have the "no-thumbs" rule? A girl can have sixteen fingers up her. But no thumbs.' She laughs, and continues: 'For vaginal I prefer a girthy kind of dick. And some of these guys' – Chloe seizes the broad base of a water glass on the table before us – 'are like *this*. For anal I prefer a longer, thinner kind of dick.'

'So when you do DP you get one thick one and one thin one?'

'Right ... No. Come to think of it,' she said happily, 'I get two thick ones. I like to feel *crammed*. You know, I did my first anal for $200? I still can't believe that.'

'And what are your rates now, Chloe?'

'In Gonzo, you're paid, not by the picture, but by the scene. So it's girl-girl: 700, plus 100 for an anal toy. Boy-girl: 900. Anal: 1,100. Solo [a rarity]: 500. DP: 1,500. I won't do anal fisting or double anal. People ask me how I can hang on to my title as Anal Queen of LA when I won't do double anal. But I have hung on to it.'

In common with about 10 per cent of the porno girls (her estimate), Chloe retains the approval of her parents (and so does Temptress). In fact, Chloe's guardians are Gonzo. She recently shot a film out near their place, and her stepfather (while absenting himself from his stepdaughter's scenes) 'was like a towel-boy'. And Chloe's mother, for two years running now, has marched out of the *AVN* Awards, brandishing her daughter's Best Anal trophies above the heads of the crowd.

*

After lunch we drove to Chloe's residence: barred gates, the feel of a two-floor motel, a modest, comfortable, orderly apartment, featuring a cute black cat with a porno name: Siren. Chloe thinks that some porno girls get their names by looking out of the window at the road signs: Laurel Canyon, Chandler, Cherry Mirage.

For a while Chloe talked about her love life. She is torn, at present, between the neglectful Chris, a rock musician (bass), and the attentive Artie, a fellow performer. She suspects that Chris just strings her along because it's a status symbol for a rock star to have a porno-star girlfriend. Chris, I think, knows about Artie. But Artie doesn't know about Chris.

'And with Artie, he comes over and I'm horny as hell and he says, "I can't. I have to do two scenes tomorrow."'

'With private sex, is there a crossover in your head?'

'Oh yeah. I find myself thinking, "*Fuck*. I should be being paid for this." Or "*Fuck*. I wish I had a camera."'

'I'd better not write about Chris and Artie.'

'Go ahead. They'll both soon be over. Here, it doesn't last.'

Chloe was unforgettable. I won't forget the way she said this (she said it with sorrowful resolve): 'We're prostitutes ... There are differences. You can choose your partners, and they're tested for Aids – you won't get your john to do that. But we're prostitutes: we exchange sex for money.'

'You've thought this through.'

'I looked it up in the dictionary and that's what it says.'

In etymological terms *pornography* is what *I'm* doing: I'm writing about whores.

I will see Chloe on set tomorrow morning. The scene they'll be shooting? Gonzo girl-boy-girl anal.

6. MISTER MONSTER

Towards the end of *Rabbit at Rest*, John Updike writes:

> Rabbit thinks of adding $5.50 to his bill to watch something called *Horny Housewives* ... The trouble with these softcore porn movies on hotel circuits, in case some four-year-old with lawyers for parents happens to hit the right buttons they show tits and ass and even some pubic hair but no real cunt and no pricks, no pricks hard or soft at all. It's very frustrating. It turns out pricks are what we care about, you have to see them. Maybe we're all queer, and all his life he's been in love with Ronnie Harrison.

Or, as a friend would put it to me later that week: 'It's no good without Mister Monster. You *must have* Mister Monster.'

Must you? Gore Vidal once said that the only danger in watching pornography is that it might make you want to watch more pornography; it might make you want to do nothing else but watch pornography. There is, I contend, another danger. As I sampled some extreme productions on the VCR in my hotel room, I kept worrying about something. I kept worrying that I'd *like* it. Porno services the 'polymorphous perverse': the near-infinite chaos of human desire. If you harbour a perversity, then sooner or later porno will find it out. You'd better hope that this doesn't happen while you're watching a film about a coprophagic pig farmer – or about an undertaker. That week in Los Angeles I found out what I don't like. I don't like Mister Monster.

High up in higgledy-piggledy Hollywood Hills, I hobnobbed with Andrew Blake, the Truffaut of porno, and two incredibly beautiful girls in incredibly expensive underwear (and six-inch heels). Strictly speaking, Blake's work is Gonzo: scriptless, storyless, with the performers interacting with the camera. But Blake is pre-eminently 'high-end'. His actresses look like voluptuous fashion models, and he flatters and glorifies them on the screen, with oils, unguents, silks, cords, ribbons, textures.

'I hired Monica because she has these beautiful breasts,' he told me, 'and that's what we're going to be concentrating on. I've never worked with Adriana before but she seems to be ... really something.'

Laconic, gruff, direct, and, of course, humourless, Blake goes about his business.

'Now put your hand into her panties ... And maybe a nipple comes out, a nipple is revealed? ... Squeeze them, caress them, do the whole nine yards with them ... Try opening your legs. Kind of tease the panties ... Don't smile so much. Just kind of be into yourself ... So is the bra ready to ride? Kiss the nip ... Arch up your butt a little more ... Cross and uncross your legs. Show a little pussy ... Now this is the panties coming off ...'

Behold. A platonically perfect pubis, wearing nothing but the latest hairstyle, a minimal mohawk.

'This must be a tough day's work for you,' said the makeup girl amiably. 'Someone's got to do it. Right?'

Her remark obliged me to examine my 'affect', or feeling-tone. I admit to a strong sense of furtive beauty-assimilation. But the instinct being aroused in me was not sexual so much as protective. Naked Adriana was twenty years old. And the very last thing I wanted to see, just then, was Mister Monster.

Outside, during an intermission, Blake said in his flat, declarative style, 'I'm into looking at woman. Not all this "pissing and fisting". I've never had any legal problems. We await the election. The SM bubble will burst.'

7. WORK PERMIT

A 'tough' day's work for me, then, and the same could be said for Adriana and Monica. They weren't being slapped around by Khan Tusion or peed on by Max Hardcore. But were they being 'used up'?

If you're a porno performer, your latest HIV test is your work permit. Two years ago the actor Marc Wallice started to become evasive about his documentation. He was using an out-of-town health centre and seemed to be fudging his results. By the time he was found out, Wallice's condition was fulminant. He infected six actresses.

'The tests we take only test for Aids,' says Chloe. 'We've contained Aids in the industry but what about all the others? You know we're now up to Hepatitis G.?

'You should be at least twenty-one before you work in this industry. You should know your body, understand your body. But that would wipe out half of San Fernando Valley. There are whole *lines* on the eighteen-pluses.'

And there are: *Dirty Debutantes, Nasty Newcomers, Filthy First Timers.* Actresses described as 'barely legal' are barely eighteen.

One of the actresses infected by Marc Wallice (his condition now is so pitiful that no one thinks him worth persecuting) is Mrs John Stagliano. Stagliano himself, the pioneer of Gonzo, is HIV-positive (he contracted the virus recreationally, in a Rio bordello). A medium-sized fortune has been made by Stagliano, in a business where, contrary to popular belief, very few fortunes are made. But I often think of the Staglianos, out by the pool, gazing at an ocean to which they have no access.

8. GONZO GIRL–BOY–GIRL

Chloe's shoot is in a rented property on Dolorosa Drive: Pain Street.

The porno house, the porno fish in the porno tank (the fish are porno-coloured: yellow, mauve, blood-orange), the porno TV set (as big as a double refrigerator), the porno deck, the porno pool, with a plastic duck floating around in it. Beyond the fence stands the house of the much-hated neighbour who keeps climbing on to the roof, with a mouthful of nails, to get himself shocked enough to call the police.

Girl-boy-girl: the girls are Chloe and Lola (a friendly Amerindian-style beauty); the boy is Artie (Chloe's offscreen lover: tattooed, muscular, balding). Artie seems to be a nice guy, but he keeps talking with a jokey French accent. Porno performers are great ones for funny voices, funny faces. German scientists, Russian spies, French connoisseurs; in Features they can keep it up all movie long.

There is a crew: the DP (for the time being this means Director of Photography) and his sound-recordist, who go about their business like middle-aged handymen; a plump youth who seems to be there for general work experience; and Chloe's sister, Shannon, caterer and towel-girl. Chloe will soon be calling out to Shannon, 'Stop that phone!' Shannon: 'It's the home phone! There's like *nine* of them!'

Artie is giving us more French accent, then more French accent, while Chloe and Lola strip for the 'pretty girl' shots that will go on the box-cover. Chloe, with whom I spent five hours the previous day, walks past me, naked. It doesn't bother her that she's naked. She *doesn't know* she's naked.

The porno stills by the porno pool. 'See pink? Want lots of pink?' 'Let's have some booty.' 'Open it? You want it *all*?'

It is barely ten o'clock in the morning, and I am, I realise, experiencing the kind of anxiety that usually precedes a mild ordeal. A line is about to be crossed. I shouldn't be here. None of us should be here. But we all have work to do.

*

Fifteen minutes later, referring to the recent achievement of Lola, Chloe stabbed a hand through the air at me, and shouted with joy and triumph (Chloe is the director, remember, and she was thrilled to have secured such footage): '*That's* the kind of blowjob I was telling you about *yesterday*!'

I reeled out into the yard with my notebook, laughing and shaking my head. There are plenty of jests and japes on a porno set, and there is much raucous mirth. But only a Chloe, only an exception, could inject real humour. She sounded like Mel Brooks in *The Producers* saying, '*That's* our Hitler!'

The kind of blowjob Chloe was telling me about yesterday was this kind of blowjob. It is as if the girl's passionate – indeed desperate – intention is to reach and then actually consume the boy's lower viscera. But she faces an obstacle. She can't go around it. She has to go through it. 'I mean,' Chloe had said admiringly, 'some of these girls *go down*. Drooling and slobbering, saliva everywhere, choking, dry-heaving. I've tried my hardest but I just *can't* do it.'

A pause, a rest, and now the troilism scene is about to begin. Understandably anxious, Artie asks Lola if she wouldn't mind topping up his erection (by applying 'some head'), and Lola, with a soft grunt of colle-

172

gial amenability, briskly obliges. The three of them get under way – and with every appearance of feral and escalating passion.

'Choke her!' 'Spit inside me!' 'Break me! You can't break me! Try!'

'... *COMING!!!*'

Chloe screamed this last word like a mother answering a child's despairing cry from the other end of the house. Then, to Lola, 'Choke me!' And then Chloe's entire upper body flushed with pink, and she seemed to swoon ...

Another turn around the yard, another cigarette. 'I mean, pleasure and pain', propounded John Staglione at the outset, 'are the same thing, right?' And I thought: *No they're not.* The distinction between them has always been perfectly clear, whatever 'the market' might choose to claim. I satisfied myself that porno, naturally male-chauvinist in origin and essence, is now so baldly misogynistic that the only desire it arouses is a desire to be elsewhere. I would indeed soon be elsewhere; but not quite yet.

*

Back in the bedroom the post-coital breather is winding up. 'I want to piss,' said Artie.

For a moment the DP's eyes widened in alarm. He thought, wrongly, that Artie wanted to piss mid-scene – on Lola, on Chloe. Artie disappeared. 'Pissing is as bad as coming,' the DP wearily confided. 'They're supposed to piss and they can't. They go off to the shower, then they say they can. And they still can't. It's as bad as coming.'

Artie trudged back from the toilet. 'God I'm old', he muttered as he returned to the workspace.

Well I'm old too, and so I blew a kiss at Chloe and took my leave – before the anal and the money shot. Shannon kindly drove me to the hotel. Poor Shannon: she was having one of those days. First, shopping in a health-food store, she dropped an enormous jar of wheatgerm on her foot (she limped all day and now in the car had difficulties with the pedals). Next she discovered that her boyfriend was cheating on her – and she finished it. Contemplating the suspension of her love life, Shannon said sadly, 'And when you compare it to *that*' – meaning Chloe's threesome – 'the sex doesn't seem much anyway.'

I knew what she meant, in a sense. Chloe-Artie-Lola made me feel like a shrinking violet, like a virgin who had never been kissed.

9. PUSSIES ARE BULLSHIT

Later that afternoon I journeyed from San Fernando to Pasadena. I was expected at a five-day symposium on 'The Novel in Britain, 1950–2000' at the Huntington Library. After some prompting, I told a gathering of delegates about my recent experiences. And 'Pussies are Bullshit' duly became the running joke of the conference.

To exchange one philosopher for another, to exchange Buttman for Friedrich Nietzsche, a joke is 'an epitaph on the death of a feeling'. In other words, the best jokes are always new lows. It is utterly characteristic that the coiner of 'pussies are bullshit' had no idea he was being funny. In any case, porno is littered – porno is heaped – with the deaths of feelings.

Every time a porno megastar opens a megastore – or advertises a line of perfume, or does a walk-on in a TV show – porno people start saying that porno is 'mainstream', that porno is hip, that porno is cool. Is masturbation hip? It doesn't *feel* hip. And it doesn't look hip either, which is why you never see anyone doing it. Porno cannot possibly be mainstream, partly because of the contrarian nature of the form. For porno to become mainstream, humankind would have to change, abjuring for ever their grasp of the ridiculous.

Porno people: *they've* changed. In the yard of the house on Dolorosa Drive, during one of the many breaks in filming (typically the shooting of a single scene expends at least three hours), Chloe, Artie, and Lola stood there naked by the pool, discussing a new rollercoaster ride called Desperado. They were all smoking. I came across many a good little smoker in pornoland. What with the risks they run already, who cares that much about smoking? Then it was cigarettes out and back to work. And I do mean work. Porno is also a *proletarian* form. And porno people are a hard-grafting, ill-paid, gradually unionising contingent who, by and large, look out for each other and help each other through. They pay their rent with the deaths of feelings.

No, Chloe, you are not a prostitute, not quite. Prostitution is the oldest profession; and market-driven porno is, perhaps, the newest profession. You are more like a gladiator: a contemporary gladiator. Of course, the gladiators were slaves – but some of them won their freedom. And you, I think, will win yours.

Talk 2000

Literature – 2

Literature 2

Don DeLillo: Laureate of Terror

The Angel Esmeralda: Nine Stories by Don DeLillo

When we say that we love a writer's work – yes, even when we say it hand on heart – we are always stretching the truth. What we really mean is that we love about half of it. Sometimes rather more than half, sometimes rather less: but about half. The gigantic presence of Joyce relies pretty well entirely on *Ulysses*, with a little help from *Dubliners*. You could jettison Kafka's three attempts at full-length fiction (unfinished by him, and unfinished by us) without muffling the impact of his seismic originality. George Eliot gave us one readable book, which turned out to be the central Anglophone novel. Every page of Dickens contains a paragraph to warm to and a paragraph to veer back from. Coleridge wrote a total of two major poems (and collaborated on a third). Milton consists of *Paradise Lost*. Even my favourite writer, William Shakespeare, who usually eludes all generalisations, succumbs to this law. Run your eye down the contents page and feel the slackness of your urge to reread the comedies (*As You Like It* is not as we like it); and who would voluntarily curl up with *King John* or *Henry VI, Part III*?

Proustians will claim that *In Search of Lost Time* is unimprovable throughout, despite all the agonising longueurs. And Janeites will never admit that three of the six novels are comparative weaklings (I mean *Sense and Sensibility, Mansfield Park*, and *Persuasion*). Perhaps the only true exceptions to the fifty-fifty model are Homer and Harper Lee. Our subject, here, is literary evaluation, so of course everything I say is mere opinion, unverifiable and also unfalsifiable, which makes the ground shakier still. But I stubbornly suspect that only the cultist, or the academic, is capable of swallowing an author whole. Writers are peculiar, readers are particular: it is just the way we are. One helplessly reaches for Kant's dictum about the crooked timber of humanity, or for John Updike's suggestion to the effect that we are all of us 'mixed blessings'. Unlike the heroes and heroines of *Northanger Abbey, Pride and*

Prejudice, and *Emma*, readers and writers are not expressly designed to be perfect for each other.

I love the work of Don DeLillo. That is to say, I love *End Zone* (1972), *Running Dog* (1978), *White Noise* (1985), *Libra* (1988), *Mao II* (1991), and the first and last sections of *Underworld* (1997). The arc of this luminous talent, as I see it, reached its apogee toward the close of the millennium, and then partly withdrew into enigma and opacity. What happens, then, when I read *Ratner's Star* (1976) or *The Names* (1982) or *Cosmopolis* (2003)? Novelists can be likened to omnicompetent tour guides – as they gloss and vivify the wonders of unfamiliar terrains, the marketplaces, the museums, the tearooms and wine cellars, the gardens, the houses of worship. Then, without warning, the suave cicerone becomes a garrulous rogue cabdriver, bearing you off on a series of sinister detours (out by the airport, and in the dead of night). The great writers can take us anywhere; but half the time they're taking us where we don't want to go.

*

The Angel Esmeralda: Nine Stories, surprisingly, is DeLillo's first collection. In the course of his career he has published twenty shorter fictions, so there has already been a paring down. A halving, in fact, though the book, to my eye and ear, is a faithful alternation between first- and second-echelon work – between easy-chair DeLillo and hard-chair DeLillo. The stories come in order of composition, with dates, and in three sections, each of them flagged by a quietly resonant illustration (a view of the planet from outer space, a heavily restored classical fresco, a painting of a spectral cadaver). As a package, the book feels both pointed and secretive, both airy and airtight. The arrangement holds the promise of a kind of unity, or a kind of cumulative artistic force; and the promise is honoured. These nine pieces add up to something considerable, and form a vital addition to the corpus.

Three stories focus on, or at any rate include, erotic encounters, and two of them run into the additional hazards that beset this sphere. Unless sexuality is the master theme of a narrative (as in *Lolita*, say, or *Portnoy's Complaint*), it will always feel like a departure or a parenthesis. In 'Creation', the earliest story (1979), the protagonist uses the chaos of inter-island Caribbean travel to engineer an adulterous fling with another stranded passenger. The frustration, the suspension in place and time ('We'll get the two o'clock flight, or the five, depending on our status. The important thing right now is to clarify our status'), and the sensuality of the landscape supposedly conspire to make the episode seem inevitable; but the reader's naïve and no doubt vulgar curiosity (what for? and then what?) goes ungratified. The story feels bleached of past and future, of context and consequence.

I long ago assented to DeLillo's unspoken premise – that fiction exaggerates the ever-weakening power of motive in human dealings. Yes, it does; but there's a reason for that. Motive tends to provide coherence, and fiction needs things that cohere. 'The Starveling' (2011, and the most recent story) gives us a middle-aged retiree named Leo Zhelezniak. Beginning at around nine in the morning, Leo spends all day, every day, in the cinemas of New York. Why? His ex-wife, Flory, with whom he cohabits, likes to speculate:

> He was an ascetic, she said. This was one theory. She found something saintly and crazed in his undertaking, an element of self-denial, an element of penance ...
>
> Or he was a man escaping his past ... Was he at the movies to see a movie, she said, or maybe more narrowly, more essentially, simply to be at the movies?
>
> He thought about this.

Readers may like to ponder that question in tandem with another (while bearing in mind that Leo once took a course in philosophy): 'If we're not here to know what a thing is, then what is it?'

Next, and again for no clear reason, Leo starts taking an obsessive interest in another obsessive *cinéaste*, another haunter of Quads and Empires (she is pale, gaunt, faceless, and young). He follows her from theatre to theatre, follows her home, follows her, finally, into a multiplex toilet (the Ladies'), where he unburdens himself of an erratic, free-floating five-hundred-word monologue – and then she flees. Now DeLillo, in 'The Starveling' (this is Leo's name for his quarry), avowedly abjures all cause and effect ('There was nothing to know'; 'There was nothing to trust but the blank mind'), and enters the void of the motiveless. Most readers, I think, will find this region arid, and inherently inartistic. All it can give us is a rendering of the functionally insane – insanity being the sworn foe of the coherent.

'Baader-Meinhof' (2002), the third negotiation of the sexual theme, is, by contrast, an alarming success. 'She knew there was someone else in the room,' it begins. The young woman is in a Manhattan gallery, transfixed by 'a cycle of fifteen canvases' – paintings of the dead Andreas, the dead Ulrike. The 'someone else' is an unnamed young man. They start to talk. They go to a snack bar:

> She drank her apple juice and looked at the crowds moving past, at faces that seemed completely knowable for half a second or so, then were forgotten forever in far less time than that.

Suddenly, they are in her apartment, and the veneer of normality is soon losing its glow. 'I sense you're not ready,' he says, 'and I don't want to do something too soon. But, you know, we're here.' A page later, he is 'all around her'. '[He] looked at her so levelly, with such measuring effect, that she barely recognized him' – and we are back on Seventh Avenue with the illusorily 'knowable' faces of the passers-by, back in the gallery with those murderous free spirits Baader and Meinhof, and we remember the girl saying that the paintings made her feel 'how helpless a person can be'.

*

DeLillo is the laureate of terror, of modern or postmodern terror, and the way it hovers and shimmers in our subliminal minds. As Eric Hobsbawm has said, terrorism is a new kind of urban pollution, and the pollutant is an insidious and chronic disquiet. Such is the air DeLillo breathes. And so strong is this identification that we feel slightly dislocated when, in 'The Ivory Acrobat' (1988), he confronts a form of terror that is 'natural' and therefore ancient and innocent: the earthquake. Set in Athens during a time of tremors, and told, with great inwardness, from a woman's point of view ('Something had basically changed. The world was narrowed down to inside and outside'), the story is expertly realised; but it is not pressingly DeLilloan. 'Now that Terror has become local, how do we live?' the old nun, Sister Edgar, asks in 'The Angel Esmeralda' (first published in 1994 and later incorporated into *Underworld*) – and we feel we are back in the right barrio. 'What is Terror now? Some noise on the pavement very near, a thief with a paring knife or the stammer of casual rounds from a passing car.'

The barrio is the South Bronx, where Sister Edgar and her young colleague, Sister Gracie, are going about their good works. They visit the diabetic amputee, the epileptic, the 'woman in a wheelchair who wore a FUCK NEW YORK T-shirt'; they move among congenitally addicted babies, among 'junkies who roamed at night in dead men's Reeboks', among 'foragers and gatherers, can-redeemers, the people who yawed through subway cars with paper cups'. Every time a child dies in the projects (a frequent occurrence), 'graffiti writers spray-painted a memorial angel' on a dedicated tenement wall, pink for girls, blue for boys, giving age, name, and cause of death: 'TB, Aids, beatings ... left in dumpster, forgot in car, left in Glad bag Xmas Eve.'

'I wish they'd stop already with the angels,' says Sister Gracie, who is something like the voice of reason. ('It's not surreal,' she shouts at the tour bus with a sign above the windshield that reads 'SOUTH BRONX SURREAL'. 'It's real, it's real. You're making it surreal by coming here. Your bus is surreal. You're surreal.') But Sister Edgar is more susceptible. Later, when a twelve year old, Esmeralda, is raped and thrown off a roof, her image 'miraculously' appears on a nearby 'billboard floating in the gloom', and Edgar goes to join the crowds that gather and stare at what is actually nothing more than an ad for Minute Maid orange juice. DeLillo fractionally overloads his title story with some high-style editorialising ('And what do you remember, finally, when everyone has gone home and the streets are empty of devotion and hope, swept by river wind?'). We don't need the big voice. All we need is Gracie's 'The poor need visions, okay?' and Edgar's rejoinder, 'You say the poor. But who else would saints appear to? Do saints and angels appear to bank presidents? Eat your carrots.'

'The Runner' (1988) gives us a seven-page snapshot of another act of local terror: a little boy is snatched from a city park, in daylight, while his frozen mother looks on. Our witness to the abduction, a young man out on his evening jog, is approached by a middle-aged woman, her head tilted 'in the hopeful way of a tourist who wishes to ask directions':

> She said pleasantly, 'Did you see what happened? ... The father gets out and takes the little boy ... Don't we see it all the time? He's unemployed, he uses drugs ... The mother gets a court order. He has to stay away from the child ... There are cases they walk in and start shooting. Common-law husbands.'

Still jogging on the spot, the young man demurs:

'You can't be sure, can you? ... All right, we're looking at a woman in a terrible stricken state,' he said. 'But I don't see a common-law husband, I don't see a separation, and I don't see a court order.'

As it happens, the runner is right ('It was a stranger,' a policeman later confirms). But he doesn't disabuse the spooked woman, allowing her to cleave to her consoling fiction. 'It was definitely the father,' he tells her as he finishes his run. 'You had it just about totally right.'

This is a recurrent itch in DeLillo – the need to flesh out and piece together the half-glimpsed lives of others. In 'Midnight in Dostoevsky' (2009), two solemn young pedants, Todd and Robby, slouch around a wintry upstate campus. On one of their ponderous rambles, they see a middle-aged woman unloading grocery bags onto a baby stroller:

> 'What's her name?'
>
> 'Isabel', I said.
>
> 'Be serious. We're serious people. What's her name?'
>
> 'Okay, what's her name?'
>
> 'Her name is Mary Frances. Listen to me,' he whispered. '*Mar-y Fran-ces*. Never just Mary.'
>
> 'Okay, maybe.'
>
> 'Where the hell do you get Isabel?'
>
> He showed mock concern, placing a hand on my shoulder.
>
> 'I don't know. Isabel's her sister. They're identical twins. Isabel's the alcoholic twin. But you're missing the central questions.'
>
> 'No, I'm not. Where's the baby that goes with the stroller? Whose baby is it?' he said. 'What's the baby's name?'

Their restless fantasies come to centre on 'the hooded man', an elderly gentleman in an anorak ('He doesn't have the bearing of a Russian ... Think about Romania, Bulgaria. Better yet, Albania'), and his supposed connection to their logic professor, Ilgauskas (a virile mystagogue given to whole-sentence pronouncements like 'The causal nexus' and 'The atomic fact'). The phrase 'midnight in Dostoevsky', we're told, comes from a poem, and is probably intended to conjure some epiphany of willed despair. Yet DeLillo's story ends in one of his more sumptuous registers, sad, warm, and buoyant.

Such a register sustains the even more enchanting 'Human Moments in World War III' (1983). A 'mission specialist' and his young sidekick, Vollmer (one of DeLillo's comically intimidating nerds, like Heinrich in *White Noise*), are up in Tomahawk II, orbiting the earth and gathering intelligence, tricked out with their suction clogs, modal keys, sense frequencers, and quantum burns. The specialist is monitoring data on his mission console when a voice breaks in, 'a voice that carried with it a strange and unspecifiable poignancy'. He checks in with his flight-dynamics and conceptual-paradigm officers at Colorado Command (and we ask ourselves – has there ever been a more distinctive exponent of dialogue than Don DeLillo?):

> 'We have a deviate, Tomahawk.'
> 'We copy. There's a voice.'
> 'We have gross oscillation here.'
> 'There's some interference. I have gone redundant but I'm not sure it's helping.'
> 'We are clearing an outframe to locate source.'
> 'Thank you, Colorado.'
> 'It is probably just selective noise. You are negative red on the step-function quad.'
> 'It was a voice,' I told them.
> 'We have just received an affirm on selective noise ... We will correct, Tomahawk. In the meantime, advise you to stay redundant.'

The voice, in contrast to Colorado's metallic pidgin, is a melange of repartee, laughter, and song, with a 'quality of purest, sweetest sadness': 'Somehow we are picking up signals from radio programs of forty, fifty, sixty years ago.' Meanwhile, there is the blue planet, tenderly rendered, with its 'sediment plumes and kelp beds', 'lava flows and cold-core eddies', 'storm-spiraled, sea-bright, breathing heat and haze and color'. And meanwhile, 'Vollmer drifts across the wardroom upside down, eating an almond crunch.' Occasionally, the two astronauts put aside their pulse markers and systems checklists, and reach for something more intimate:

> [Vollmer] talks about northern Minnesota as he removes the objects in his personal-preference kit, placing them on an adjacent Velcro surface ... I have a 1901 silver dollar in my personal-preference kit

... Vollmer has graduation pictures, bottle caps, small stones from his back yard. I don't know whether he chose these items himself or whether they were pressed on him by parents who feared that his life in space would be lacking in human moments.

In common with his extraordinary ear for jargon (not least the jargon of everyday life), DeLillo's predictive powers have been much remarked. To take one graphic instance, it is clear that he never regarded the World Trade Center as a pair of buildings: to him they were always a pair of bull's-eyes. In the novel *Players* (1977), Pammy Wynant works in the W.T.C. for a grief-management firm: 'The towers didn't seem permanent. They remained concepts, no less transient for all their bulk than some routine distortion of light.' This is certainly very striking – though we may wonder if the quoted lines shine the brighter *as prose* because they happened to come true. DeLillo said long ago that the mood of the future would be determined not by writers but by terrorists; and those who mocked him for this forecast must have felt even worse than the rest of us did on September 12, 2001.

*

Although the story 'Hammer and Sickle' was published in 2010, by which time the fraying of Western economies was far advanced, DeLillo is already sensing the vague insurrectionary stirrings that are a more recent phenomenon. I would nevertheless submit that it is his general receptivity to the rhythms and atmospheres of the future that we should value, rather than the slightly carny business of confirmable outcomes. And here DeLillo's angle of indirection is inimitably acute. Jerold Bradway is in a correctional facility for financial felons – in other words, part of a whole prisonful of Bernie Madoffs. Each weekday, the flabby culprits gather in the common rooms to watch a market report on a cable channel. The presenters are two little girls. 'Did it seem crazy, a market report for kids?' Indeed – and the more so when we learn that the girls are Jerold's daughters, Kate, twelve, and Laurie, ten:

'The word is Dubai ... Dubai,' Laurie said.
'The cost of insuring Dubai's debt against default has increased one, two, three, four times.'

'Do we know what that means?'

'It means the Dow Jones Industrial Average is down, down, down.'

'Deutsche Bank.'

'Down.'

'London—the FTSE One Hundred Index.'

'Down.'

'Amsterdam – the ING Group.'

'Down.'

'The Hang Seng in Hong Kong.'

'Crude oil. Islamic bonds.'

'Down, down, down.'

'The word is Dubai.'

'Say it.'

'Dubai', Kate said.

And we are invited to look even further ahead: these, after all, are the reproving voices of our swindled children.

In the end, 'Hammer and Sickle' errs on the side of overexcitement (at about the point where the girls' duologues start to rhyme); but overexcitement is something that the DeLillo faithful will be exhilarated to see. Creative gaiety, a sense of fun and play, has been too firmly suppressed by the almost morbid tentativeness of his latest novels and novellas. Literature seeks to give 'instruction and delight': Dryden's tag, formulated three and a half centuries ago, has worn pretty well. We reflect, all the same, that whereas instruction doesn't always delight, delight always instructs. Very broadly, we read fiction to have a good time – though this is not to deny that the gods have equipped DeLillo with the antennae of a visionary. There is right field, and there is left field. He comes from third field – aslant, athwart. And I love *The Angel Esmeralda: Nine Stories*.

New Yorker 2011

J.G. Ballard: From Outer Space to Inner Space

I first came across Jim Ballard when I was a teenager. He was a friend of my father's, and Kingsley championed his early work, hailing him as 'the brightest star in postwar SF' (all purists call science fiction SF, and have nothing but contempt for 'sci fi'). Physically Ballard was a rare case, a man peculiarly beautified by his own temperament; he had a marvellously full, resonant face, with high colour and hot eyes. He talked in the cadences of extreme sarcasm, with very heavy stresses – but he wasn't being sarcastic; he was just gorging himself on ironic possibilities. The Jim–Kingsley relationship did not survive Ballard's increasing interest in experimentalism (which my father always characterised as 'buggering about with the reader'). But I was always delighted to see Jim later on. He was, equally, vigorous and invigorating. Funnily enough, he was an unusually lovable man with an instinctive common touch, despite the extreme unsociability of his imagination.

His imagination was formed by his wartime experience in Shanghai, where he was interned by the Japanese. He was thirteen at the time and took to the life in the camp as he would 'to a huge slum family.' But it wasn't just the camp that formed him – it was the very low value attached to human life, something he saw throughout his childhood. He told me that he'd seen coolies beaten to death at a distance of five yards from where he was standing, and every morning as he was driven to school in an American limousine there were always fresh bodies lying in the street. Then came the Japanese. He said 'people in the social democracies have no idea of the daily brutality of parts of the east. No they don't, actually. And it's as well that they don't.'

It is interesting that his two most famous novels were filmed by famous (and interesting) directors: *Empire of the Sun* by Steven Spielberg (an essentially optimistic artist who regularly steels himself for stringent historical themes), and *Crash* by David Cronenberg (a much darker artist, and one who specialises in filming unfilmable novels). *Crash* is the more typical Ballard piece. It is animated by an obsession with the sexuality of the road accident, reminding you that the word *obsession* derives from the Latin *obsidere*, which means 'to lay siege to'. Ballard is beleaguered by his obsessions. Mood and setting, in him, are identical. He has very little feel for human beings in any conventional sense (and no ear for dialogue); he is remorselessly visual.

Empire of the Sun – his greatest success – came as a strange kind of backhander to his more cultish admirers. This novel, which is utterly realistic for all its wild exoticism, seemed a betrayal of the Ballardian faith. The cultists felt that *Empire* (as he used to call it) showed – all too intelligibly – how Ballard's imagination had been warped into such a curious shape. The novel was a naturalistic explanation of how his imagination got that way. For the cultists (not very logically), again, it was like the witch doctor revealing how he faked his cures.

Ballard began as an exponent of hardcore SF. His very early short stories, on familiar themes such as overpopulation, societal decay, and so on, are as good as anything in the genre. But the genre couldn't hold him. There followed four novels of glazed apocalypse – *The Wind from Nowhere* (1961), *The Drowned World* (1962), *The Drought* (1964), *The Crystal World* (1966) – where the mother planet is destroyed by wind, by water, by heat, and by mineralisation. Then came his brutalist period, beginning in 1970 with *The Atrocity Exhibition*. The titles of two stories from that book give the tone of the collection: 'The Facelift of Princess Margaret' and 'Why I Want to Fuck Ronald Reagan.' Then the mortar-and-steel period extends itself with *Crash* (1973), *Concrete Island* (1974), and *High-Rise* (1975). The next period can again be evoked by another title: *Myths of the Near Future* (1982). He was still in this period when he died (despite the moving and beautiful memoir *Miracles of Life*, published in 2008). The last novels – including *Cocaine Nights* and *Super Cannes* – were about the violent atavism of corporate and ultra-privileged enclaves in a different kind of near future.

On my desk I have a printed postcard from Ballard which represents 'the future' in mathematical terms: *the future equals sex times technology squared*. In his work he kept asking: what effect does the modern setting have on our psyches – the motion sculpture of the highways, the airport architecture, the culture of the shopping mall, pornography, and cyber-space? The answer to that question is a perversity that takes various mental forms, all of them extreme. When he broke away from rigid SF, Ballard said that he was rejecting outer space for 'inner space'. This has always been his fief. Ballard will be remembered as the most original English writer of the last century. He used to like saying that writers were 'one-man teams' and needed the noisy encouragement of the crowd (i.e., their readers). But he will also be remembered as a one-man genre; no one else is remotely like him. Very few Ballardians (who are almost all male) have been foolish enough to emulate him. What was influential, though, was his prose (characterised by Peter Straub as both 'creamy and precise'), and the weird and sudden expansions of his imagery.

Ballard was a great exponent of the Flaubertian line – that writers should be staid and predictable in their lives, so that they can be savage and original in their work. He lived in a semi-detached in Shepperton, which might as well have been called 'Dunroamin', and there was the tomato-red Ford Escort parked in its slot in the front garden. When I wrote a long profile of him in 1984, I arrived at eleven in the morning and his first words were 'Whisky! Gin! Vodka!' He told me that '*Crash* freaks' from, say, the Sorbonne would visit him expecting to find a miasma of lysergic-acid and child abuse. But, in fact, what they found was a robustly rounded and amazingly cheerful – positively sunny – suburbanite. In 1964 his wife Mary died very abruptly, on a family holiday, so Ballard raised their three children himself. To begin with he could only manage to do this by drinking a Scotch every hour, starting at nine in the morning. It took him quite a while to push this back to six o'clock in the evening. I asked him if that was difficult, and he said: 'Difficult? It was like the Battle of Stalingrad.' Becoming a full-time parent and house-mensch was, he said, 'the best decision of my life'; and I think his three children would agree.

The last time I saw Ballard, three or four years ago, was when my wife Isabel Fonseca and I, together with Will Self and Deborah Orr, had dinner with him and his partner of forty years, Claire Walsh. He revealed in the Shepherd's Bush restaurant that he probably had 'about two years to live'. This was said with innate courage, but with all the melancholy to be expected of a man who loved life with such force.

Guardian 2009

Early Ballard: *The Drowned World*

Is prescience a literary virtue? And should the work of J.G. Ballard be particularly prized (as some critics maintain) for the 'uncanny' accuracy of its forecasts? The answer to both these questions, I suggest, is a cheerful no.

In *The Atrocity Exhibition* (1970) Ballard famously tapped Ronald Reagan for president. His *Hello America* (1981), on the other hand, surmised that the United States in its entirety would be evacuated by 1990. The meteorological cataclysms envisaged by his first four novels still look plausible. But the social crisis envisaged by his last four novels – violent and widespread anomie brought about by a glut of leisure and wealth – now looks vanishingly remote.

So here's a prophecy: fictional divination will always be hopelessly haphazard. The unfolding of world-historical events is itself haphazard (and therefore unaesthetic), and 'the future' is in a sense defined by its messy inscrutability. Besides, the art of fiction owes allegiance to a muse, a goddess as pure as her nine sisters, and not to some bustling Madame Sosostris (Eliot's 'famous clairvoyant', with her 'wicked pack of cards'). Nevertheless there are certain writers whose visionary power is indifferent to the corroboration of mere upshots – writers who seem to be able to feel, and use, the 'world hum' of the 'near-after'. That first quote is from Don DeLillo, who is one such; the second quote is from James Graham Ballard (1930–2009), who is another.

Ballard foresaw manmade climate change, not in *The Drowned World* (1962), but in *The Drought* (1964). In *The Drought* (originally entitled *The Burning World*), industrial waste has thickened the mantle of the oceans and destroyed the precipitation cycle, transforming the planet into a wilderness of dust and fire. In *The Drowned World*, ecological catastrophe has a quite different set of causes. The median temperature at the Equator is 180 degrees and rising, the polar ice caps and the permafrost have melted, Europe is 'a system of giant lagoons', the American Midwest is 'an enormous gulf opening into the Hudson Bay', and the global population (down to five million) huddles within the Arctic and Antarctic Circles (where the thermometers, for now, record a 'pleasant' eighty-five). And how did all this come about? Solar instability, pure and simple, with no help whatever from *Homo sapiens*. So, on the basis of this one novel, Ballard could unobtrusively add his voice to the current Republican debate on global warming – slightly to the left of Rick Perry and Michele Bachmann, true, but slightly to the right of Mitt Romney.

This is an irony we need not fear: indeed, it speeds us on our way to more central questions. As a man (and as a good Green), Ballard was naturally on the side of the angels; but as an artist he is unconditionally of the Devil's party. He loves the glutinous jungles of *The Drowned World* and the tindery deserts of *The Drought* – just as he loves the superhurricane, or express avalanche, of *The Wind from Nowhere* (1961) and the mineralised multiplicities of *The Crystal World* (1966). It is the measure of his creative radicalism that he welcomes these desperate dystopias with every atom of his being. He merges with his conjured futures, internalising them in a kind of imaginative martyrdom. The fusion of mood and setting, the mapping of a landscape of the troubled mind – this is what really matters in Ballard. It gives the novels their tight clench of waywardness and fixity.

'Soon it would be too hot' is the laconic first sentence of *The Drowned World*. Its hero, the marine biologist Robert Kerans, is staring out from the balcony of his suite at the Ritz; he is the only (mammalian) occupant of the hotel; the rising water is ten storeys from his feet.

> Even through the massive olive-green fronds the relentless power of the sun was plainly tangible. The blunt refracted rays drummed against his bare chest and shoulders ... The solar disc was no longer a well-defined sphere, but a wide expanding ellipse that fanned out across the eastern horizon like a colossal fire-ball, its reflection turning the dead leaden surface of the lagoon into a brilliant copper shield.

The sun is alarmingly distended. It is also alarmingly *noisy*; it 'thuds' and 'booms'; we hear 'the volcanic pounding' of its flares.

There are mosquitos the size of dragonflies, hammer-nosed bats, wolf spiders. There are iguanas and basilisks – at one point a large caiman sees Kerans 'waist-deep among the horse-tails' and veers towards him, 'its eyes steadying' (that 'steadying' is awfully good). The water gives off an unendurable reek, 'the sweet compacted smells of dead vegetation and rotting animal carcases'. Kerans watches the 'countless reflections of the sun move across the surface in huge sheets of fire, like the blazing faceted eyes of gigantic insects'. Beneath the lagoon is a city: 'Free of vegetation, apart from a few drifting clumps of Sargasso weed, the streets and shops had been preserved almost intact, like a reflection in a lake that has somehow lost its original'. The city is London.

Kerans is nominally engaged with a team of scientists on a waterborne testing station, but the work has become pointlessly routine. Fauna and flora are faithfully following 'the emergent lines anticipated twenty years earlier', namely an accelerated counter-evolution, a retrogression into a world of lizards and rainforests under a Triassic sun. The human actors have embarked on a parallel process – within the diameter of their own skulls. Early on we learn that something has gone wrong with *sleep*: at night, the protagonists enter the 'time jungles' of uterine dreams, descending into their amniotic past and also into the past of the species, experiencing the 'archaic memories' (the 'organic memories' of danger and terror) encrypted in their spinal cords. Some fear these dreams. Kerans, of course, embraces them, and yearningly submits to their domination of his waking mind:

> Guided by his dreams, he was moving backwards through the emergent past, through a succession of ever stranger landscapes, centred upon the lagoon ... At times the circle of water was spectral and vibrant, at others slack and murky, the shore apparently formed of shale, like the dull metallic skin of a reptile. Yet again the soft beaches would glow invitingly with a glossy carmine sheen, the sky warm and limpid, the emptiness of the long stretches of sand total and absolute, filling him with an exquisite and tender anguish.

Ballard gives *The Drowned World* the trappings of a conventional novel (hero, heroine, authority figure, villain), and equips it with a plot (jeopardy, climax, resolution, coda); but all this feels dutiful and perfunctory, as if conventionality simply bores him. Thus the novel's backdrop is boldly futuristic while its mechanics seem antique (with something of the boys'-own innocence we find in John Buchan and C.S. Forester). In addition, Ballard's strikingly 'square' dialogue remains a serious lacuna. Here as elsewhere, his dramatis personae – supposedly so gaunt and ghostly – talk like a troupe of British schoolteachers hoisted out of the 1930s: 'Damn' shame about old Bodkin', 'Capital!', 'Touché, Alan'. (Cf. DeLillo, whose dialogue is always fluidly otherworldly.) We conclude that Ballard is quite unstimulated by human interaction – unless it takes the form of something inherently weird, like mob atavism or mass hysteria. What excites him is human isolation.

The 'otherness' of Ballard, his mesmeric glazedness, is always attributed to the two years he spent in a Japanese internment camp in Shanghai (1943–45). That experience, I think, should be seen in combination, or in synergy, with the two years he spent dissecting cadavers as a medical student in Cambridge (1949–51). Again the dichotomy: as a man he was ebulliently social (and humorous), but as an artist he is fiercely solitary (and humourless). The outcome, in any event, is a genius for the perverse and the obsessional, realised in a prose style of hypnotically varied vowel sounds (its diction enriched by a wide range of technical vocabularies). In the end, the tensile strength of *The Drowned World* derives not from its action but from its poetry.

'Soon it would be too hot.' Yes, and soon it will be time to abandon the lagoon and the drowned city; they will evacuate north, to one of the last human redoubts, Camp Byrd, in Arctic Greenland. There are, after all, pressing reasons to go: the mutating mosquitos and mutating malarias, the new skin cancers caused by the evaporating cloud cover, the increasingly brazen encroachments of the reptiles, the coming of the Equatorial rain belts and the Equatorial heat. Kerans is, inevitably, the last to leave. He does so on foot (on foot singular, with an infected leg wound and a crutch). And which way is he heading, as the novel closes? Even a reader quite new to Ballard will by this stage consent to the logic of it. 'There isn't any other direction.' He is heading south.

Guardian 2011

The Shock of the New:
A *Clockwork Orange* Turns Fifty[*]

The day-to-day business of compiling a novel often seems to consist of nothing but decisions – decisions, decisions, decisions. Should this paragraph go here? Or should it go there? Can that chunk of exposition be diversified by dialogue? At what point does this information need to be revealed? Ought I to use a different adjective and a different adverb in that sentence? Or no adverb and no adjective? Comma or semicolon? Colon or dash? And so on.

These decisions are minor, clearly enough, and they are processed more or less rationally by the conscious mind. All the major decisions, by contrast, have been reached before you sit down at your desk; and they involve not a moment's thought. The major decisions are inherent in the original frisson – in the enabling throb or whisper (a whisper that says, *Here is a novel you may be able to write*). Very mysteriously, it is the unconscious mind that lays down all the foundations. No one knows how it happens. This is why Norman Mailer called his (excellent) book on fiction *The Spooky Art*.

When, in 1960, Anthony Burgess sat down to write *A Clockwork Orange*, we may be pretty sure that he had a handful of certainties about what lay ahead of him. He knew that the novel would be set in the near future (and that it would take the standard science-fictional route, developing, and fiercely exaggerating, current tendencies). He knew that his vicious anti-hero, Alex, would narrate, and that he would do so in an argot or idiolect that the world had never heard before (he eventually settled on a blend of Russian, Romany, and rhyming slang). He knew that it would have something to do with Good and Bad, and Free Will.

[*]This is my introduction to the 'restored' Anniversary Edition (Heinemann 2012).

And he knew, crucially, that Alex would harbour a highly implausible passion: an ecstatic love of classical music.

We see the wayward brilliance of that last decision when we re-acquaint ourselves, after half a century, with Burgess's leering, sneering, sniggering, snivelling young sociopath (a type unimprovably caught by Malcolm McDowell in Stanley Kubrick's uneven but justly celebrated film). 'It wasn't me, brother,' Alex whines at his social worker (who has hurried to the local jailhouse): 'Speak up for me, sir, for I'm not so bad,' But Alex *is* so bad; and he knows it. The opening chapters of *A Clockwork Orange* still deliver the shock of the new: they form a red streak of gleeful evil.

On their first night on the town Alex and his *droogs* (or partners in crime) waylay a schoolmaster, rip up the books he is carrying, strip off his clothes, and stomp on his dentures; they rob and belabour a shop-keeper and his wife ('a fair tap with a crowbar'); they give a drunken bum a kicking ('we cracked into him lovely'); and they have a ruck with a rival gang, using the knife, the chain, the straight razor: this 'would be real, this would be proper, this would be the nozh, the oozy, the britva, not just fisties and boots ... and there I was dancing about with my britva like I might be a barber on board a ship on a very rough sea.'

Next, they steal a car ('zigzagging after cats and that'), cursorily savage a courting couple, break into a cottage owned by 'another intelligent type bookman type like that we'd fillied [messed] with some hours back', destroy the typescript of his work in progress, and gang-rape his wife:

> Then there was like quiet and we were full of like hate, so [we] smashed what was left to be smashed – typewriter, lamp, chairs – and Dim, it was typical old Dim, watered the fire out and was going to dung on the carpet, there being plenty of paper, but I said no. 'Out out out out,' I howled. The writer veck and his zheena were not really there, bloody and torn and making noises. But they'd live.

And all this has been accomplished by the time we reach page twenty.

Before Part One ends, thirty-five pages later, with Alex in a *rozz-shop* smelling 'of like sick and lavatories and beery rots [mouths] and disinfectant', our 'Humble Narrator' drugs and ravishes two ten year olds, slices up Dim with his britva, and robs and murders an elderly spinster:

… but this baboochka … like scratched my litso [face]. So then I screeched: 'You filthy old soomka [woman]', and upped with the little malenky [little] like silver statue and cracked her a fine fair tolchock [blow] on the gulliver [head] and that shut her up real horrorshow [good] and lovely.

In the brief hiatus between these two storms of 'ultra-violence' (the novel's day one and day two), Alex goes home – to Municipal Flatblock 18A. And here, for a change, he does nothing worse than keep his parents awake by playing the multi-speaker stereo in his room. First he listens to a new violin concerto, before moving on to Mozart and Bach. Burgess evokes Alex's sensations in a bravura passage which owes less to *nadsat*, or teenage pidgin, and more to the modulations of *Ulysses*:

The trombones crunched redgold under my bed, and behind my gulliver the trumpets three-wise silverflamed, and there by the door the timps rolling through my guts and out again crunched like candy thunder. Oh, it was wonder of wonders. And then, a bird of like rarest spun heavenmetal, or like silvery wine flowing in a spaceship, gravity all nonsense now, came the violin solo above all the other strings, and those strings were like a cage of silk round my bed.

Here we feel the power of that enabling throb or whisper – the authorial insistence that the Beast would be susceptible to Beauty. At a stroke, and without sentimentality, Alex is decisively realigned. He has now been equipped with a soul, and even a suspicion of innocence – a suspicion confirmed by the deft disclosure in the final sentences of Part One: 'That was everything. I'd done the lot, now. And me still only fifteen.'

In the late 1950s, when *A Clockwork Orange* was just a twinkle in the author's eye, the daily newspapers were monotonously bewailing the rise of mass delinquency, as the post-war Teddy Boys diverged and multiplied into the Mods and the Rockers (who would later devolve into the Skinheads). Meanwhile, the literary weeklies were much concerned with the various aftershocks of World War II – in particular, the supposedly startling coexistence, in the Third Reich, of industrialised barbarism and High Culture. This is a debate that the novel boldly joins.

Lying naked on his bed, and thrilling to Mozart and Bach, Alex fondly recalls his achievements, earlier that night, with the maimed writer and his ravaged wife:

> ... and I thought, slooshying [listening] away to the brown gorgeousness of the starry [old] German master, that I would like to have tolchocked them both harder and ripped them to ribbons on their own floor.

Thus Burgess is airing the sinister but not implausible suggestion that Beethoven and Birkenau didn't merely coexist. They combined and colluded, inspiring mad dreams of supremacism and omnipotence.

In Part Two, violence comes, not from below, but from above: it is the 'clean' and focused violence of the state. Having served two years of his sentence, the entirely incorrigible Alex is selected for Reclamation Treatment (using 'Ludovico's Technique'). This turns out to be a crash course of aversion therapy. Each morning he is injected with a strong emetic and wheeled into a screening room, where his head is clamped in a brace and his eyes pinned wide open; and then the lights go down.

At first Alex is obliged to watch familiar scenes of recreational mayhem (tolchocking malchicks, creeching devotchkas, and the like). We then move on to lingering mutilations, Japanese tortures ('you even viddied a gulliver being sliced off a soldier'), and finally a newsreel, with eagles and swastikas, firing squads, naked corpses. The soundtrack of the last clip is Beethoven's Fifth. 'Grahzny bratchnies [filthy bastards],' whimpers Alex when it's over:

> 'Using Ludwig van like that. He did no harm to anyone. He just wrote music'. And then I was really sick and they had to bring a bowl that was in the shape of like a kidney ...
>
> 'It can't be helped', said Dr Branom. 'Each man kills the thing he loves, as the poet-prisoner said. Here's the punishment element, perhaps. The Governor ought to be pleased.'

From now on Alex will feel intense nausea, not only when he contemplates violence, but also when he hears Ludwig van and the other starry masters. His soul, such as it was, has been excised.

We now embark on the curious apologetics of Part Three. 'Nothing odd will do long', said Dr Johnson – meaning that the reader's appetite for weirdness is very quickly surfeited. Burgess (unlike, say, Franz Kafka) is sensitive to this near-infallible law; but there's a case for saying that *A Clockwork Orange* ought to be even shorter than its 141 pages. It was in fact published with two different endings. The American edition omits the final chapter (this is the version used by Kubrick), and closes with Alex recovering from what proves to be a cathartic suicide attempt. He is listening to Beethoven's Ninth:

> When it came to the Scherzo I could viddy myself very clear running and running on very light and mysterious nogas [feet], carving the whole litso of the creeching world with my cut-throat britva. And there was the slow movement and the lovely last singing movement still to come. I was cured all right.

This is the 'dark' ending. In the official version, though, Alex is afforded full redemption. He simply – and bathetically – 'outgrows' the atavisms of youth, and starts itching to get married and settle down; his musical tastes turn to 'what they call *Lieder*, just a goloss [voice] and a piano, very quiet and like yearny'; and he carries around with him a photo, scissored out of the newspaper, of a plump baby – 'a baby gurgling goo goo goo'. So we are asked to accept that Alex has turned all soft and broody – at the age of eighteen.

It feels like a startling loss of nerve on Burgess's part, or a recrudescence (we recall that he was an Augustinian Catholic) of self-punitive religious guilt. Horrified by its own transgressive energy, the novel submits to a Reclamation Treatment sternly supplied by its author. Burgess knew that something was wrong: 'a work too didactic to be artistic', he half-conceded, 'pure art dragged into the arena of morality'. And he shouldn't have worried: Alex may be a teenager, but readers are grownups, and are perfectly at peace with the unregenerate. Besides, *A Clockwork Orange* is in essence a black comedy. Confronted by evil, comedy feels no need to punish or convert. It answers with corrosive laughter.

In his book on Joyce, *Joysprick* (1973), Burgess made a provocative distinction between what he calls the 'A' novelist and the 'B' novelist: the A novelist is interested in plot, character, and psychological insight, whereas the B novelist is interested, above all, in the play of words. The most famous B novel is *Finnegans Wake*, which Nabokov aptly described as 'a cold pudding of a book, a snore in the next room'; and the same might be said of *Ada: A Family Chronicle*, by far the most B-inclined of Nabokov's nineteen fictions. Anyway, the B novel, as a genre, is now utterly defunct; and *A Clockwork Orange* may be its only long-term survivor. It is a book that can still be read with steady pleasure, continuous amusement, and – at times – incredulous admiration. Anthony Burgess, then, is not 'a minor B novelist', as he described himself; he is the *only* B novelist. I think he would have settled for that.

New York Times Book Review, 2012

Sport

Three Stabs at Tennis

I. THE PERSONALITIES OF THE COURT

I have a problem with – I am uncomfortable with – the word *personality* and its plural, as in 'Modern tennis lacks personalities' and 'Tennis needs a new star who is a genuine personality.' But if, from now on, I can put 'personality' between quotation marks, and use it as an exact synonym of a seven-letter duosyllable starting with 'a' and ending with 'e' (and also featuring, in order of appearance, an 'ss,' an 'h,' an 'o,' and an 'l'), why, then 'personality' and I are going to get along just fine.

How come it is always the old 'personalities' who lead complaints about the supposed scarcity of young 'personalities'? Because it takes a 'personality' to know a 'personality'? No. Because it takes a 'personality' to *like* a 'personality'.

Ilie Nastase was a serious 'personality' – probably the most complete 'personality' the game has ever seen. In his memoir, *Days of Grace*, Arthur Ashe, while acknowledging that Nastase was an 'unforgettable personality', also recalls that Ilie called him 'Negroni' to his face and, once, 'nigger' behind his back. Ilie, of course, was known as a 'clown' and a 'showman'; i.e., as an embarrassing narcissist. Earlier this year, his untiring 'antics' earned him a dismissal and a suspension as Romania's Davis Cup captain ('audible obscenities and constant abuse and intimidation'). Ilie is forty-seven. But true 'personalities' merely scoff at the passage of time. They just become even bigger 'personalities'.

Jimmy Connors: another total 'personality'. Imagine the sepsis of helpless loathing he must have inspired in his opponents during his 'great runs' at the US Open. There's Jimmy (what a 'personality'), orchestrating mass sex with the Grandstand Court. It's great for the mild-mannered Swede or Swiss up at the other end: he double-faults, and New York goes *wild*. Jimmy was such an out-and-out 'personality' that he managed to get into a legal dispute with the president of his own fan club. Remember how he used to wedge his racket between his legs with the handle protuding and mime the act of masturbation when a call went against him? *That's* a 'personality'.

Twenty-odd years ago, I encountered Connors and Nastase at some PR nightmare in a Park Lane hotel. Someone asked these two bronzed and seersuckered 'personalities' what they had been doing with themselves in London. 'Screwing each other,' Nastase said, and collapsed in Connors' arms. I was reminded of this incident when, last fall, I saw an account of a whistle-stop tour undertaken by John McEnroe and Andre Agassi. Questioned about their relationship, Agassi described it as 'completely sexual'. Does such raillery inevitably come about when self-love encounters mutual admiration? Or is it part of a bonding ritual between 'personalities' of the same peer group?

By turning my TV up dangerously loud, I once heard McEnroe mutter to a linesman (and this wasn't a Grand Slam event but one of those German greed fests where the first prize is something like a gold helicopter), 'Get your fucking head out of your fucking ['personality'].' Arthur Ashe also reveals that McEnroe once called a middle-aged black linesman 'boy'. With McEnroe gone, it falls to Agassi to shoulder the flagstaff of the 'personalities' – Agassi, the Vegas traffic light, the 'Zen master' (B. Streisand) who used to smash forty rackets a year. And I don't think he has the stomach for it, funnily enough. Nastase, Connors, McEnroe, and Agassi are 'personalities' of descending magnitude and stamina. McEnroe, at heart, was more tremulous than vicious; and Agassi shows telltale signs of generosity – even of sportsmanship.

There is a 'demand' for 'personalities', because that's the kind of age we're living in. Laver, Rosewall, Ashe: these were dynamic and exemplary figures; they didn't need 'personality' because they had character. Interestingly, too, there have never been any 'personalities' in the women's game. What does this tell us? That being a 'personality' is men's work? Or that it's boys' work?

We do want our champions to be vivid. How about Pete Sampras, then – so often found wanting in the 'personality' department? According to the computer, Sampras is almost twice as good as anyone else in the sport. What form would his 'personality' take? Strutting, fist-clenching, loin-thrashing? All great tennis players are vivid, if great tennis is what you're interested in (rather than something more tawdrily generalised). The hare-eyed Medvedev, the snake-eyed Courier, the droll and fiery Ivanišević, the innocent Bruguera, the Wagnerian (and Machiavellian)

Becker, the fanatical Michael Chang. These players demonstrate that it is perfectly possible to have, or to contain, a personality – *without* being an asshole.

New Yorker 1994

2. MY AD

Every couple of years, I improve and update the Tennis Monster. The Tennis Monster is the kind of ultimate player that Baron Frankenstein might assemble, working in close conjunction with some Floridian guru like Nick Bollettieri. Here's how he's looking.

Head: Muster. Legs: Chang. (This is already a fine start.) Hands: Stich. Armpits: Courier (still the number-one sweater boy). Torso: Becker. To wire the actual shots, one would simply cannibalise the top two Americans. First serve, second serve, overhead: Sampras. Forehead, backhand, return of serve: Agassi. And then you'd loot Edberg for the volleys.

This year, at Wimbledon, I suspected that Baron Bollettieri had gone into the lab and come up with the hulking violence of Mark Philippoussis. You could practically see the bolts sticking out of his neck. But then the Baron calmed down, and produced Richard Krajicek. *That* explained the mysterious absence, in the later stages, of all the major stars: they were lying in bits on the Baron's slabs.

Krajicek, however, is not the Tennis Monster. No, Richard Krajicek is not that player. I think you'll find that I, the undersigned, am that player. Krajicek may be strong, but I am stronger – in at least two departments. First, my confidence (*so* crucial in sports) belongs to a different league. Krajicek was surprised to win Wimbledon! Yet when my turn comes, I will take my triumph humourlessly in stride. Second, Krajicek keeps getting injured. And I don't.

True, the near-immobilising back pain I suffer from is probably the result of playing too much tennis. Or any tennis whatever. And both my knees hurt a lot all the time. But I never get *injured*. Of course, I can already hear the doubting Thomases who will soon be telling me that I have left it too late to make a serious bid for world dominance. It's perfectly possible, they claim, that I might not make the top three, or even the top ten. I have nothing to say to this. Because I prefer to do my talking on the tennis court.

In preparation, I am taking the trouble to compile my entry for the ATP Tour *Player Guide*. Here's how it's looking:

Birth date: 25/8/49. Height: 5' 6¼". Weight: 150. Plays: Right-handed. Career winnings: A cruise around the British Isles. Career losings: About £200 (gambling on Martin Amis).

Career highlights: 1989 – Playing in Morocco, took a game off the hotel pro, Kabir, who once warmed up with Yanick Noah. 1991 – Beat a sixty year old to reach career-best second round of Paddington Sports Club Over 35s. 1993 – Beat Zach, David and Andy on consecutive Sundays at PSC. 1995 – Partnered by Peter Fleming, caused a venerable publisher to cramp on match point, winning first ProAm event (and the waived cruise around the British Isles). 1996 – Took a set off Chris at PSC, causing him to break two new racquets. Beat Ray at PSC.

GRAND SLAM HISTORY

	'94	'95	'96
AUS. OPEN	–	–	–
FRENCH OPEN	–	–	–
WIMBLEDON	–	–	–
US OPEN	–	–	?

Readers will notice that intriguing question mark, which whispers, 'Amis for the US Open – in '96?' But I skipped the Olympics, and I have now pulled out of the Open. My plan is to conserve myself for Wimbledon '97. There is still a weakness in my game – one I am resolved to eliminate.

Frankly, it's my return of serve, which is not as good as Andre Agassi's. I sometimes think that in this department I'm not much better than Jimmy Connors. A serve is by definition a short ball, but my reply still tends to be hurried. I particularly notice this when I face players who are taller than me (or insufficiently shrunken by age). So I usually settle for a kind of chip.

But there's only one server who really worries me. Not Sampras. Because Sampras is only six feet one. I know he can jump higher than Air Jordan and hasn't missed an overhead in ten years. But I'd precision-lob him, or else dink my returns to his feet, making Pete crazy. Courier can expect the same treatment.

At Wimbledon, I will probably be unseeded, and may face quite reasonable players in the early rounds. I can see it now: towards dusk on the opening day, on court thirteen, in poor light. We have reached the inevitable first-set tiebreak. I peer over the net, and focus. Grass is my opponent's best surface, and he's playing out of his skin. Goran Ivanišević is preparing to serve *with new balls* ...

Yet Goran's nerve will fail him, as it always does. And my confidence will start to soar. I don't foresee a problem until the round of sixteen, at which stage I may get taken to four sets by someone like Stich or Kafelnikov. Then Edberg in the quarters; then Pete or Andre – whichever – in the semis. By now Baron Bollettieri will be sniffing around my locker room. He'll be after my big shots: that lob, and the little pat I give the spare ball at the end of a service game. He'll be hoping to reënmonster Krajicek for the final. Well, let them patch him up all they like. I don't want a neo-Boris Becker out there, for that rendezvous on centre court. I want Boris Karloff. I wouldn't have it any other way.

New Yorker 1996

3. THE TIMS

Over the past twelve months Tim Henman has accumulated much praise: praise for his bowshot serve and his matador backhand; praise for his 'boyish' good looks and his sound choice of girlfriend; and praise for the way he 'handles' the heavy burden of a nation's hopes. But these are mere details. In my view, Tim's real distinction has never been properly assessed – or even mentioned. It is an achievement that transcends the realm of sport and aspires to something world-historical. And it has to do with his *name*.

I don't mean the 'Henman' bit, which presumably denotes an interest in poultry among his earliest forebears. Although 'Henman' isn't particularly appealing or mellifluous, it doesn't amount to a congenital handicap. But 'Tim' does. And this is what gives Henman his true paramountcy. He is the first human being called Tim to achieve anything at all.

Already, as I type, I can hear people clucking away at this slur. Special outrage is to be expected from the Tims themselves – to whose troubles I am seeming to add. The Tims don't need the extra aggravation; and I understand. But look at it the other way: with Henman at the helm, this is a time of *hope* for the Tims. Maybe the Tims are starting to turn it around. There's one thing I'm already prepared for: the somewhat boorish suggestion that the Martins aren't that great either. Not so. A minute's thought gives me Luther, Heidegger, Ryle, Scorsese, and Martin Luther King. Who can the Tims bounce back with? Tim Calvin? Tim Schopenhauer? Tim Hubble? Tim Ford Coppola? Tim X?

'Tim', I fear, just doesn't have that ring to it. The name lacks all gravity. It's easy enough to see how it happened: the Tims of this world had all their ambitions crushed, all their aspirations dashed, by being called 'Timmy' during childhood. The association with 'timid' and 'timorous' (from the Latin *timere:* 'to fear') was obviously much too strong. 'Hello, Timmy!' – imagine what that does to you, after the first few thousand times. The real puzzle is that the Tims do as well as they do, many of them leading reasonably active lives, holding down jobs, getting to meet girls, and going on to have children of their own.

Do I expect them to be taking this lying down, over at Tim HQ? I do not. In the 1970s, in London, there was a brief craze for Rock Concerts Against Ginger-Haired People. The occasional carload of ginger-haired people used to patrol these events, taking vengeance when and where they could ('I'd just left the hall and these four ginger-haired geezers were all over me'). Still, going proactive, with vigilante gangs of Tims on the prowl, doesn't sound like the Tims' style. As I browsed through the dictionary, looking for more dirt on Tims, I came across the word *timocracy*. It doesn't mean 'rule by Tims' or 'rule by Tim'. It means rule by people 'motivated by love of honour'. This is surely the gentler, more Tim-like course, and the clear way forward for the Tims.

In my own sphere, that of writing, I have already noticed a solidification of Tim talent. There are four British Tims who make a living from their pens: Messrs. Binding, Jeal, Garton Ash, and Mo. This is a start. The next step would be to internationalise the upswing and extend it to the United States, where Tim O'Brien is rather desperately holding the fort. One difficulty here is that American writers tend to have formidably bold and percussive surnames; the Tims would certainly wilt in such an unequal clinch. Tim Mailer? Tim Updike? Tim Heller? Tim Bellow?

There *is* a Tim Roth, but he's an actor (and unusually diminutive even for a movie star). I think I can see a way out of this. It's a solution suggested to me by the example of Thomas Pynchon.

For the time being, at any rate, the Tims should all change their first names to Tom. Are you listening, Mr Henman? And while we're at it let's change the name of 'tennis', too. 'Tennis' ('appar. from OFr. *tenez*, "take, receive" (called by server to his opponent), imper. of *tenir*, "take"') sounds hopelessly fey and effete. I no longer want to play or watch a game called 'tennis'. I demand a name that sounds more macho and up-to-date. Volleyball has preëmpted 'volleyball'; 'powerball' is promising; and what about 'crackball', which, moreover to recommend it, sounds like a drug likely to enhance performance? I'd ask the Tims to send in some suggestions, but I don't think this is the sort of thing they'd be any good at.

Henman must act fast, because Wimbledon is almost upon us. He needs to jump in a cab and get down to Somerset House and start filling in all those forms.

And after that I'll say, 'So how about it, Tom? Anyone for smackball?'

New Yorker and *Evening Standard* 1997

Postscript. I have gone on idly brooding about the place of the Tims in literature – the Tims as opposed to the Toms. Who would have suspected that a lone vowel could make so much difference? Consider the essential unlikelihood of *Tim Sawyer, Uncle Tim's Cabin, Tim Brown's Schooldays*, and that seminal prose epic of 1749, Henry Fielding's *Tim Jones*. Tim Paine, Tim Wolfe, Tim McGuane, Tim Clancy, Sir Tim Stoppard? And it would be tasteless, quite frankly, to go on at any length about all the Thomases – Moore, Wyatt, Gray, Hobbes, Hardy, Mann, Thomas Stearns Eliot ... No, in this sphere the Tims have a lot of ground to make up. But elsewhere they're suddenly rampant. In show business Tim Roth can now grandly mingle with the likes of Tim Burton, Tim Spall, and Tim Robbins; the Tims have a boxer (Witherspoon), a historian (Snyder), and even a vice-presidential pick, if you please, in Tim Kaine ... But doubts remain. I sometimes think (perhaps I'm very old-fashioned) that everyone was more relaxed – more content, more reconciled – in the old days, when the Tims knew their proper place.

The Champions League
Final, 1999

Bayern Munich	1–2	**Manchester United**
Basler (6)		Sheringham (90+1)
		Solskjaer (90+3)
Nou Camp, Barcelona		Att: 92,000

We are all aware of the massed ferocity of the football crowd, and much has been written about its causes. What is it that makes the bescarved, bobble-hatted multitudes steam on by, trampling all in their wake – alienation, tribalism, lost empire? I have a simpler explanation. The roots of football hooliganism lie in football matches, and in what it's like to attend them.

Yes, I Was There – for the fairytale, for glory night on the magic field of impossible dreams. And apart from a few half-hearted punch-ups over the forged tickets, it was a volatile but unviolent occasion (because we won), and the tabloids got their shots of sombreroed lads cavorting on Las Ramblas. For me, though, the evening amounted to ninety seconds of in-credulous euphoria sandwiched by thirty hours of torment. A few more experiences of that order and I too would be down on the high street stoving in the shopfronts, throwing bricks at enemy supporters, attacking my darker-skinned compatriots, and sieving the internet (the horde's new rumpus room) for lots more about the National Front and Combat 18.

To feint sideways for a moment: the reason people who hate Man U. hate Man U. is that Man U. are the footballing future, and they have been the future for quite a while. It used to be said that their players were just a troupe of itinerant mercenaries, with little grasp of the local identity and the local traditions (slow to develop the right kind of contempt for Manchester City and the right kind of loathing for Liverpool). But that general description now holds for all the other clubs in the top half of the Premiership – while Man U. have moved on.

The Reds keep finding new ways of being ahead of their time. They are a *brand* – computerised, digitalised, corporatised. They can afford to buy the big stars (Cantona, Ince, Mark Hughes), but their wealth has allowed them to circle back in the other direction: they grow their own, with that naggingly productive youth-development machine (Ryan Giggs, Gary Neville, Paul Scholes, David Beckham). On the one hand, the car park at the training ground is infested with Ferraris; on the other, the twelve-year-old bootboys will soon have their own penthouses, racehorses, and supermodels.

That's the team. What about the fans? Themselves widely travelled and cosmopolitan (hailing from South Africa, from Japan, from Equador), are they similarly evolved? As I made my way to the airport last Wednesday morning, I expected, or half-expected, to hobnob with a new elite, a strolling fraternity of football connoisseurs who had long transcended the lumpen peer-pressures of the herd.

Manchester United vs. Bayern Munich was, in addition, England vs. Germany. There were wounds to heal and scores to settle (Euro 96, Italia 90, World Wars II and I). But here also, surely, was a chance for burnished technique and the sober delectation of the beautiful game.

*

Whereas the snow leopards and mountain lions of the United team had processed south from Heathrow by Concorde, a dawn start saw me in the departure lounge at Stansted with the other clients of Sports Mondial's 'private charter' to Spain. I did notice the odd fan who might have looked at home in the twenty-first century: gym-fit, spruced, tanned, thirtyish, with cupped mobile, gleaming shell-suit, twinkly white trainers, and one of those wallet-belts round the waist like a detachable beergut. But that was it. Everyone else seemed either a) dowdily and comfortably middle-aged or b) anonymously liveried from head to foot in club merchandise. Many a red jersey featured, across the shoulderblades, the name of a famous favourite: in the bar (at ten in the morning) a SHERINGHAM sat slumped over a pensive pint of lager; in the McDonald's a KEANE enjoyed successive Big Macs.

To begin with the pre-boarding atmosphere was reminiscent of any jaunt to the Costa Brava: mildly raucous with excited anticipation. Then came the series of 'delays' – owned up to by a Sports Mondial representative – which mysteriously blossomed into a six-hour wait. The brochure had said (untruthfully) that the flight would be teetotal, but now there was plenty of time to down the 'few' with which the Britisher typically girds himself for foreign travel. Some of the more impatient travellers found it a bit much when the Caribbean steel band (what was *that* doing there?) started playing 'Viva España'. 'Are they taking the fucking piss or fucking what?' enquired the worst man in our party of his bro or cuzz, who was the next-worst man in our party. 'They lucky there's not a fucking winduh unbroken in this fucking place."Viva España".What the fuck?' The worst man and the second-worst man repaid close study: gracelessly ageing skinheads, tubby but muscular, and taut with uncontainable energy.

By 2.30 we were on the buses to the plane. Dispersed in the lounge, the fans were now coalescing into a pack. 'Ryan Giggs, Ryan Giggs, coming down the wing' (to the tune of 'Robin Hood'). 'We shall not, we shall not be moved … We are going to win the fucking Cup'. Or, alternatively, 'the fucking lot' – for United were on the brink of a unique treble (having already won the FA Cup and the league title). 'We shall *not be moved*! Re-Darmy, Re-Darmy, Re-Darmy …' Singing, or chanting, or bawling, is supposed to be one of the folklorish charms of the game; but an immoderate hatred of musicality, of tone and rhythm, seems to part of the fibre of the terraces. While we were stalled on the runway there was a ragged attempt at a slow handclap; it sounded like scattered applause.

Once we were airborne, of course, herd spirit was doubled, or squared. There was much hollered one-lining (typically a TV-tie-in soundbite with a 'fucking' added to guarantee a laugh). And now the buoyant clamour intensified when it was announced that we would land, not in Gerona, as advertised, but in Barcelona itself, to make up time; why, the coaches that were meant to meet us were even now speeding to the airport, with our tickets safely on board. But then negative rumours started reeling drunkenly through the plane. The lowpoint was a chorus of 'Tickets at Stansted' sung to the tune of 'There's only one Keane-oh' (or, more remotely, of 'Guantanamera'). On disembarkation we were told that our coaches were late, or lost, so we journeyed to the rendez-vous near the town centre in approximately thirty taxi cabs.

Outside the Hotel Juan Carlos there was an altercation between an embattled rep and the next-worst man. The next-worst man, who had always looked as though he would soon have his shirt off, had his shirt off. (What is it about bare-chestedness at football matches? More me? More

this?) 'I know', began the representative, 'that you're all fucked off but ...'
'Fucking right we're fucked off! Where's the fucking tickets?' 'Things are
fucked up because ...' 'The fucking tickets. Get the fuckers down line.
The fucking *tickets*, for fuck's sake'.

It was now an hour before kick-off. The forecourt jostling had quickly
produced a police presence, and the police did some jostling of their own. I
went and sat on the grass; then the police told me to get off the grass; then
the police told everyone to get on the grass; then the police told everyone to get off the grass ... At last the tickets arrived, and it was proposed
that they be dispensed in alphabetical order. 'Amis!' Feeling sorry for the
fans, if any, called Zygmunt, I hurried off, arriving sweat-soaked at the
stadium in time for ten minutes of the duster-twirling cheerleaders, a diva
in a golfcart, and Freddie Mercury on the twin screens like a phantom of
the opera, his voice a distant croon among the raw throats of 92,000 souls.

★

Every time it strikes me, with all the freshness of revelation: going to watch
a football match is the worst possible way to watch a football match. Never
mind the business of getting to the ground (and getting back again), never
mind the lost two days and the vast expense, never mind being crushed and
cordoned with all the civility generally accorded to a riot-prone rabble of
thugs and sociopaths. When you find your seat, up on the cliff of the bleach-
ers, you attend to your nosebleed and your hypothermia, and you peer down
on a flea circus in a misty abyss; and whenever anything happens, everyone
jumps to their feet, so you're obliged to rubberneck through a shifting collage of hair frizz and earring. Yes, TV, as well as being close by and free of
charge, is hugely superior – in every respect but one. You don't get the crowd.

And the crowd is the engine of this experience. It is asking something of you: namely the surrender of your identity. And it will not be
opposed – it cannot be opposed. The crowd is a wraparound millipede,
and it is thrillingly combustible. With relief, with humiliation, with terror, you lose yourself in the body heat of innumerable torched armpits,
in the ear-hurting roars and that incensed whistling like a billion babies
joined in one desperate scream. All we lacked was the prospect of victory.
And now the sands of time were running out.

In the eighty-fifth minute a fat red shirt waddled past making the
'tosser' gesture and, for clarification, yelling: 'Fucking *wankers*!' No one

followed him. And how unforgettable it was, in those last moments, to be caught up in the fabulous lurch of emotion, when hatred and despair became their opposites. Stranger turned to stranger with love and triumph. All were subsumed in the great red sea.

*

On my way into the Nou Camp I asked a Sports Mondial rep where I would find the coach when the game was over. I was assured that it would be 'waiting outside' the stadium. (Imagine: after the Carnival the coach will be 'waiting outside' Notting Hill.) After a long and fruitless trek I recognised two fellow passengers, a red-shirted father and his red-shirted son. 'Let's have a wander down here,' said the dad chirpily, as we began an eighty-minute trudge through a fuming bus park. Three hours later, we spotted the frazzled rep, and numbly climbed aboard.

Sports Mondial then subjected us to two relatively trivial vagaries: a leisurely tour of Barcelona before we chanced upon the Gerona road, and a controversial M-way rest-stop to ease the boiling bladders of a YORKE and a STAM. Then they delivered us to the general disaster of cynicism and scorn (and Spanish paranoia) of the airport. Here, perhaps two thousand fans were being forced to spend the rest of the night in the parking lot, sleeping in heaps. One old man, contemplating a shivering child, repeatedly intoned, with deliberation and justice, 'They're treating ooz ... like foogging shite.' And they were, too. Flightload by flightload we crossed the police line – and slept in heaps in the departure lounge (one man slept downward-slanted on the little slide in the kiddie playroom). At last the call came: 'RN240. Destinationuh Esstansteduh.' The plane landed six hours late.

When you talk to a member of the crowd he immediately becomes an individual. This didn't work with the worst man and the next-worst man, who would not disclose themselves and remained thin-lipped and hard-eyed; they were fizzers, part of that 'tiny minority' you keep hearing about; and they would have had warm work to do if United hadn't won. Everybody else in my party submitted to the herding with resignation and dour humour. 'What if we'd lost?' I asked a fan, as we surveyed the human desolation of the car park. 'Well it doesn't bear thinking about,' he said. 'Does it?'

All cheerfully agreed that it had been 'a crap match', apart from injury time and its immortal drama. 'Crap match. Great result.' As expected, United missed their chain of steel in midfield, Keane and Scholes; possession was fitful, and the passing game never flowed. But this team really believes that it can do it on will. The crowd believed it; and Bayern (after the substitution of Matthaus) felt that concentrated unanimity still coming at them, and were unhinged by it.

The supporters cannot join with the team in dexterity or athleticism, but they can be part of its will. I have felt the atavistic lusts of the football fan, the turgid passions of religion and war. Nationalism by itself doesn't quite explain it, though I derived harsh pleasure from seeing those Germans with their faces in the mud (after the second goal the ref had to help some of them to their feet; they were gone, dead). And the powerless man, by giving his identity to the Saturn of the crowd, has helped administer this slaughter. Soon he must return to the confines of his mere individuality. But for ninety minutes – ninety seconds – he has known prepotence.

Observer 1999

Postscript. The 'I' of this piece should really be a 'we': I went to Barcelona with my two sons, aged fourteen and twelve (and kept quiet about it because they both bunked off school). Their tribal loyalties and mine lay elsewhere – with Newcastle, with Liverpool, with Tottenham Hotspur – but I admired Man U.'s style and personnel (Yorke, Sheringham, Scholes, Schmeichel), and I wanted them to win. That rather abstract preference became a matter of dire urgency as the game progressed. Indeed, by the end of normal time I was feeling a hormonal preparedness for violence, for a great sprawling, swearing ugliness with my boys in the middle of it. As we now know, the night passed without that core component of mayhem, which is defeat ... Our plane, which had taken off six hours late, returned six hours late, maintaining symmetry, and leaving me less than a day to write 2,000 words. My sons catalogued the Barcelona experience as a fitfully intriguing ordeal. I have to admit, though, that I felt a strangely durable exaltation. George Best, a Man U. hall-of-famer so totemic that he has a major airport named after him (in Belfast), left the ground five minutes early and, to his lasting grief, missed that utterly implausible comeback. In essence, the hardened traveller-fan is engaging in an act of self-sacrifice; those who stayed till the end earned the pride of the martyr (which means 'witness') and the enduring honour of grim perseverance – of Being There, all the way, with the madding crowd.

In search of Dieguito Maradona

There is a truly terrifying photograph of Diego Armando Maradona, dating from 2000, the year of his first heart attack. He is wearing: a reversed baseball cap which reveals a squirt of hair, dyed the punk colour of baby shit; dark glasses; a drummer's sleeveless T-shirt, giving full play to the tattoo of Che Guevara on his right shoulder; and a defiant, slack-mouthed sneer. Then you come to the massive emplacement of the gut.

It would be hard to exaggerate the ubiquity of the diminutive (-ito, -ita) in Latin-American Spanish, which originates from the extreme reverence and indulgence accorded to the young. You are always coming across grown men with nursery names – strapping Sergitos, hefty Hugitos (and I'm friends with a sixty-year-old called, simply, Ito). But it would choke you, these days, to call Maradona 'Dieguito'. The figure still frequently seen, on television, wobbling through airports or wedged into golfcarts, has his old hair-colour back, and is more soberly dressed; yet his bulk remains prodigious and unignorable. It visibly tortures him. And you can still glimpse Dieguito, walled up in his new carapace, pining, suffering – but unresisting. Inside every fat man, they say, there is a thin man trying to get out. In the case of Maradona, it seems, there is an even fatter man trying to get in.

Maradona's autobiography, *El Diego*, was about to be published, and there was talk, down here, of his giving an interview in Buenos Aires (I happened to be living in the neighbourhood: Uruguay). When he suddenly decamped to Cuba, his second home (or sanatorium) since 2002, I blithely followed. Maradona had already had a drug-induced heart attack in April, true; but it was put out that this particular trip was routine – a dryout, or a decoking. A man describing himself as his agent, a Dieguito-shaped youngster called Gonzalo, received me at his hotel, and we seemed to be moving cautiously forward. I got my answer the next day, on the evening news. The doctors – Fidel's doctors – at the Centro de Salud Mental were emphatic. The patient was wired up like an astronaut, and would be seeing no one. Maradona retired in 1997. In 2001, he played (rather tubbily, I admit) in a televised football match. Now, in 2004, he needs medical permission to *watch* a televised football match. He is forty-three. Oh, Dieguito – where did he go?

*

In South America it is sometimes said, or alleged, that the key to the character of the Argentinians can be found in their assessment of Maradona's two goals in the 1986 World Cup. For the first goal, christened 'the Hand of God' by its scorer, Maradona dramatically levitated for a ballooned cross and punched the ball home with a cleverly concealed left fist. But the second goal, which came minutes later, was the one that [England manager] Bobby Robson called the 'bloody miracle': collecting a pass from his own penalty area, Maradona, as if in expiation, put his head down and seemed to burrow his way through the entire England team before flooring Shilton with a dummy and stroking the ball into the net. Well, in Argentina, the first goal, and not the second, is the one they really like.

For the Argie macho (or so this slanderous generalisation runs) foul means are incomparably more satisfying than fair. 'It's the same in government and business,' you're told. 'They don't just tolerate corruption. They worship corruption.' It is a proclivity that extends into the sexual arena, with the high value assigned, in macho circles, to heterosexual sodomy – something noticed in his travels by V.S. Naipaul and, more surprisingly (this was in the 1920s), by Jorge Luis Borges, who thought it the essence of the cult of 'taking advantage'. In Maradona's personal lexicon, the same word does duty for both goalscoring and fornication. (The word is 'vaccinate': an odd choice, given that Diego was so often the pre-match recipient of the six-inch painkilling needle, driven into the inflamed kneecap, the suppurating big toe.) By this logic, the second goal against England was a languid, erotic epiphany; the first was a knee-trembler in a back alley; and each has its points. More broadly, there is in this culture a humiliation, an abjectness, in always playing by the rules.

By the time we reach the England game in *El Diego*, the reader is in any case wholly seduced by the story and by the turbulent naïvety with which Maradona tells it. To begin with, the passions involved in Argentina v. England were not merely ludic: 'In the pre-match interview we had all said that football and politics shouldn't be confused, but that was a lie. We did nothing but think about that. Bollocks was it just another match!' And it wasn't only the Malvinas (the Falkland Islands), either: it was to be the historic *revancha* of a subjugated and immiserated population. So, having exulted at length in the second goal ('I wanted to put the whole sequence in stills, blown up really big, above the headboard of my bed'), Maradona turns his attention to the first: 'I got a lot of pleasure from the other goal as well. Sometimes I think I almost enjoyed that one more.' And the reader can only assent, by now, to the contented urbanity of his conclusion: 'They [the two goals] both had their own charm.'

In other words, all's fair – all's sweet – in love and war. And, for some reason, that's what football is, and those are the energies it calls upon: the energies of love and war.

*

It was a childhood without insulation, in all senses. If the society had its sicknesses, then nothing stood between them and Dieguito. 'Everyone goes on about role models. Role models my arse! In Argentina we don't have a single living role model so stop breaking my balls about it.' The beautiful game was a way out of the slums, but it was hardly a beacon of probity for the growing boy. Football was as corrupt and rapacious as everything else. Here (it was well known) was a league where players had to bribe the manager to get on the team sheet – where Patrick Vieira, say, has to slip a bung to Arsène Wenger or else languish in the reserves.

Maradona's Buenos Aires barrio was Villa Fiorita ('little bloom'), a festering wilderness in the 1960s (and, these days, a Saddam City of weaponised crime). 'My parents were humble working folk,' he writes, but the stock phrase is barely adequate. All ten Maradonas occupied a three-room lean-to where the only running water was the torrent that came through the roof ('you got wetter inside than out'). The obsession with football seems utterly inborn; no memories precede it, and no other interests compete with it. Whenever the infant Diego ran errands, he did so playing keepie-uppie with an orange. On his third birthday a cousin gave him his first leather ball ('I slept with it hugged to my chest'). And when he went for his first trial, aged nine, he was so advanced that the coach seriously suspected that he was a dwarf. He made the senior side at fifteen, and with his first wages he bought a second pair of trousers, to supplement the turquoise cords with the big turn-ups.

His ascendancy, thereafter, was perfectly designed to detach him from reality – and reality, then, included the Dirty War and the terror and the 30,000 *desaparecidos* [disappeared]. At the age most kids hear stories (read one headline), he hears ovations. Three months after his debut he was training with the national team, up against Daniel Passarella and Mario Kempes. At eighteen, after a win over US Cosmos, he swapped shirts with Franz Beckenbauer; at nineteen, he scored his hundredth goal. He was already the face of Coca-Cola, Puma, Agfa …

Marginal and relatively impoverished, South American leagues act as a training and recruitment ground for the clubs of Europe, and in 1982 Maradona duly moved to Barcelona for $8m (£4.4m). When he went to Napoli two years later he was on $7m a year, plus $3m from Italian television (there was also $5m from Hitachi). An International Management Group poll named him 'the best known person in the world', and he was offered $100m for his 'image rights'; he turned it down, for patriotic reasons (IMG wanted him to take out dual nationality). 1986 brought him his nationalist apotheosis: he captained Argentina in the World Cup, and they won it. He was twenty-five.

El Diego is a transparent narrative, and you keep seeing in its interstices a startling inner chaos – acute and chronic flaws of character and judgment, and above all a self-knowledge that remains perennially absentee. When Maradona was fourteen he fell under the sway of his first manager, an old mentor with the unencouraging name of Jorge Cyterszpiler. You can see it coming when, early on, Maradona boasts that they 'handled everything on the basis of friendship, not a single piece of paper was signed'. Sure enough, when he arrives in Naples ten years later he bewilderingly reveals that, 'Cyterszpiler had had such bad luck with figures that I was down to zero'. Or less than zero. Cyterszpiler's bad luck with figures, his investments in Paraguayan bingo halls and the like, additionally devoured Maradona's slice of his transfer fee together with his ten-bedroom house in Barcelona. 'What's done is done,' shrugs Diego, insisting that every investment (every bingo hall) was the result of his own decision. Much later on, when Maradona undertakes a fitness drive, he hires a trainer: Ben Johnson. 'Yes, Ben Johnson! The fastest man on earth, whatever anyone says.'

It is the same with the Camorra – the Mob – in Naples. 'They offered me things but I never wanted to accept them: because of the old dictum that first they give and then they ask … whenever I went to one of those clubs they gave me gold Rolexes, cars'. He didn't 'want' to accept them;

but he accepted them. It is the same with fouls, and referees. When Maradona forms a judgment, you feel you are watching one of his 'mazy runs':

> That bastard Luigi Agnolin, the Italian ref, wrongly overruled one of my goals. I never stamped on Bossio, no way. I beat him because I jumped over him. It was never an intentional stamp ... that Agnolin, he was a fucker. We tried to pressurise him from the start but the Italian wasn't a man to be intimidated ... He pushed Francescoli, he pushed him! He even elbowed Giusti. I liked Agnolin ...

Maradona's anarchistic streak also reveals itself in the contempt – no, the disgust – with which he regards the law. On the occasions when he attracts the attention of the police he can barely bring himself to say why. 'I was arrested, arrested!' he says, and briefly describes the ensuing 'farce'; meanwhile, with a polite cough, a footnote steps in to divulge the charge (possession of cocaine). Later, back in Argentina, after being incessantly doorstepped, 'I reacted ... I reacted in the way anyone might. It was the episode with the air rifle, yeah, that's right.' And again the footnote, itself evasive, adds that this was the 'affair' when Maradona fired an air rifle at congregated journalists, without adding that he hit four of them and received a suspended three-year sentence.

Then, too, there are frequent glints of what one might call exceptionalism – or low-level megalomania. Maradona routinely refers to himself in the third person, not just as Maradona ('We made him bigger than Maradona', 'That's the most important thing Maradona can have', and, amusingly, 'The drug trade is far too big for Maradona to stop it'), but also as El Diego: 'Because I am El Diego. I too call myself that: El Diego'; 'Let's see if we can get this point across once and for all: I am El Diego'; 'I am the same as always. I'm me, Maradona. I am El Diego.' After a while it stops sounding like self-aggrandisement, and starts sounding like self-hypnosis.

Passarella was 'a good captain, yes', El Diego allows, but 'the great captain, the true great captain, was, is and always will be me'. This form of words finds an echo, later on, in 1996, when Maradona launched a national anti-drugs campaign by saying, 'I have been, am and always will be a drug addict.' The twelve-stepper's mantra, usually a mock-humble boast of hard-won continence, feels in this case more like a statement of irreducible truth. Maradona has been using drugs for twenty years: it resulted in a fifteen-month ban (in Italy), ejection from the 1994 World Cup ('I was given [sic] ephedrine, and ephedrine is legal, or ought to be'), and a career-ending scandal on his swansong return to Boca Juniors in 1997. The habit, after all, can no longer be described as recreational. This is a man who regularly snorts himself into a cardiac arrest. It seems that only a life-threatening debauch can recreate the intensities – the heart-bursting highs, the abysmal lows – of his vanished pomp.

This is an operatically emotional book, and also an exceptionally vivid one. The exoticisms of the Maradona idiolect are balanced by the oath-crammed clichés of football, which would appear to be universal ('the crowd went mental'; 'that wanker'; 'sorted'; and manager Carlos Bilardo's nicely implausible 'Leave it out, Diego'). But there are intimations, too, of a stronger level of perception. Pre-match funk in the changing-room: 'I felt a silence, too deep, too cold. I looked out at some faces and saw them pale, as if they were tired already.' A bad injury: 'I sprinted after a lost ball and I heard the unmistakable sound of a muscle tearing, like a zip opening inside my leg.' As for the emotion, Maradona cries himself a river on every other page. And the prose poems to his wife and to his family are all the more affecting because you know that he is now divorced, and estranged from both his brothers; and because you know that all the ties of love have failed to hold him in his orbit.

Many sportsmen claim to be champions of the people, but Maradona's populism is underwritten by his itinerary – the proletarian strongholds of Buenos Aires, Naples, and now Havana (and the only French club he flirted with, indicatively, was Marseille). In B.A., if you ask around, the response to Diego is always thoughtful, always sympathetic; and the Havanans, who have never known a non-decadent Maradona, seem to be unreserved worshippers ('I am Maradona fanatic'). Cuba is perfect for him; he can be a man of the people and a man of the president, hobnobbing with that other world-class scapegrace, Fidel Castro.

The great player Jorge Valdano said a good thing about Maradona, and in the Latin high-style: 'Poor old Diego. For so many years we have told him repeatedly, "You're a god", "You're a star" ... that we forgot to tell him the most important thing: "You're a man".' But we're not quite there yet. In Italy they used to tell him, 'Ti amo piu che i miei figli' – I love you more than my own children. It's not as blasphemous as it sounds. With his tantrums, his self-injuries, and his unassuageable sweet tooth, Maradona has remained 'El Pibe d'Oro', the child of Gold. He is still Dieguito.

Guardian 2004

On the Court: My Beautiful Game

I took up tennis, from scratch, quite late in my teens, and began with a series of lessons. First, at an indoor club, with Harry, the kind of middle-aged ruin who drank a bottle of port with his breakfast; and then with elderly Syd, a public-park freelance whose startlingly bandy legs were, moreover, incapable of bending at the knee. Harry and Syd were, by then, deplorable physical specimens, but they shared the characteristic that marks the talented player: they knew exactly where your reply was going to go, and flowed towards it with leisurely economy. And at the net they both had 'soft hands' – blotched and dappled in the case of Harry, gnarled and claw-like in the case of Syd, but undeniably soft, and supply responsive to the feel and pace of the ball. Your hardest forehand would be met by their racket heads quite soundlessly, and the ball would drop, die, and slowly roll halfway to the service line.

Harry, at least, gave me some reasonably sound advice. When serving, he said, imagine you are throwing your whole racket across the net at its target; on groundstrokes, make a full circular swing as the ball starts its journey towards you. Syd's teachings, I now know, were hopelessly antique. 'Stand tall at the net. However low the ball is, just look down your nose at it.' (In fact your head should be level with the point of impact.) He was traditionalist in other ways. 'Come *on*,' Syd once softly snarled, as he watched me struggling against Linda, a well-schooled ex-girlfriend. 'They don't *want* to win. And you shouldn't *let* 'em.' Later, I used to bear Syd's words in mind while being regularly and eagerly slaughtered by my pal Kate.

When I turned thirty I stopped hiring teachers and started hiring 'hitters' (who are much cheaper and barely say a word). So in an hour you make about 600 strokes. But hitting, I slowly realised, has a fundamental flaw. Stored in a kind of spindly trolley, the tennis balls fired at you vary in quality, some as good as new, some bald, some limp and soggy (as if prised out of a dog's mouth six months ago). They all bounce at different heights; thus the supposed goal of getting 'grooved', of acquiring 'muscle memory', is entirely delusive. I stopped learning, and stopped hitting, and just went on playing, sometimes as often as six times a week.

My first serve was necessarily flat (I am five foot six), my second a weak but reliable kicker. My volleys were always jittery, though my smash usually worked. My looping forehand had 'quite a lot on it', as they say; my backhand was an accurate slice, and I later developed the topspin variant (deployed only against midcourt longhops). My defensive lob, far and away my most effective weapon, developed likewise. One time I topspin-lobbed a very good, very fit, and very tall opponent when he was standing on the service line. He didn't jump, he didn't even turn; he just clapped his hand against his racket. That's what an average player's career finally amounts to: the cherishing, in the memory, of perhaps a dozen shots. That angled drop half-volley, that topspin backhand down the line, that wrongfooting drive that put the other guy flat on his arse ...

I peaked at the age of forty. One legendary summer I performed on the court like a warrior poet, with ichor streaming through my veins, and a visionary gleam in my concentrated eyes – and carried my Wilson for five months without losing a set. At the end of that year I recorded what was perhaps my greatest victory, against Chris, one of the burlier and wittier first-teamers at Paddington Sports Club. It was just the one set, that day, and I had a plan: I moonballed him into a frenzy (while his piss-taking peers looked on). Chris stood there with his hands on his hips and his head down, waiting (and swearing), while the ball descended from the troposphere. When we shook hands at the net (7–5), Chris said: 'Well played, Mart. You're fucking useless, and if I don't beat you six–love, six–love next time I'm giving up the game.' Next time he won 6–0, 6–1. Chris did not give up the game.

But I did – by degrees. In my mid-forties I noticed that I was losing to my erstwhile equals; then I started losing to people I had never lost to; then I started losing to absolutely everyone. And each match, for me, became an increasingly effortful passion play about the ageing process. You become slower, of course, and clumsier, and your pelvic saddle hurts a lot all the time, and you simply don't want a second set, let alone a third. But the most terrible symptom of all is the retardation of your reflexes.

The ball comes over the net like a strange surprise: you just stand there and watch until, with a senescent spasm, you bustle off to meet it. This tendency manifested itself elsewhere. One afternoon I was watching a tense football international with my sons, and halfway through the second half the elder said: 'In the sixty-third minute, Paul Scholes scored for England. And in the sixty-fifth minute, Dad leapt to his feet.'

About a year ago I came to the convenient conclusion that the day wasn't long enough (and life wasn't long enough) for tennis: changing, driving, parking, stretching, playing, losing, stretching, driving, showering, and changing – not to mention the hours spent at the hands of sadistic physiotherapists. Maybe, one day, I'll start limping back on to the lined court. But for now I just miss it. Tennis: the most perfect combination of athleticism, artistry, power, style, and wit. A beautiful game, but one so remorselessly travestied by the passage of time.

Guardian 2009

More Personal – 2

Writing *Time's Arrow*

'Why did you decide to write a novel about the Holocaust?' This challenge, which I still sometimes hear, can only be answered as follows: 'But I never did.' Similarly, I never decided to write a novel about teenage sexuality, or Thatcher's England, or millennial London, or, indeed, about the Gulag (which I nonetheless completed in 2006). With its hopelessly inapposite verb, and presumptuous preposition, the question reveals an understandable naïvety about the way that fictions are made. For the novel, as Norman Mailer put it, is 'the spooky art'.

Deciding to write a novel about something – as opposed to finding you are writing a novel around something – sounds to me like a good evocation of writer's block. No matter what its length (vignette, novella, epic), a work of fiction begins with an inkling: a notion that is also a physical sensation. It is hard to improve on Nabokov, who variously described it as a 'shiver' and a 'throb'. The throb can come from anywhere, a newspaper report (very common), the remnants of a dream, a half-remembered quote. The crucial, the enabling fermentation lies in this: the shiver must connect to something already present in the subconscious.

Time's Arrow depended on a coincidence, or a confluence. In the mid-1980s I started spending the summers in Cape Cod, Massachusetts, where I made friends with the distinguished 'psychohistorian' Robert Jay Lifton. Bob was and is the author of a succession of books on the political horrors of the twentieth century: books on thought reform in China, on Hiroshima, on Vietnam. And in 1987 he gave me a copy of his latest (and perhaps most celebrated) work, *The Nazi Doctors: Medical Killing and the Psychology of Genocide*.

Here, Lifton's historiographical mission is to establish Nazism as an essentially *biomedical* ideology. It is there in *Mein Kampf*: '*anyone who wants to cure this era, which is inwardly sick and rotten, must first of all summon up the courage to make clear the causes of this disease.*' The Jew was the agent of 'racial pollution' and 'racial tuberculosis': the 'eternal bloodsucker', 'germ-carrier', the 'maggot in a rotting corpse'. Accordingly, the doctor must become a 'biological soldier'; the healer must become a killer. In the camps, all the non-random murders were supervised by doctors (and so were the crematoria). As one of their number put it, 'Out of respect for human life, I would remove a gangrenous appendix from a diseased body. The Jew is the gangrenous appendix in the body of mankind.'

That year, too, I already had it in my head that I might attempt a short story about a life lived backwards in time. This tenuous proposition appealed to me as a poetic possibility – but it seemed fatally frictionless. I could find no application for a life so lived. Which life? As I began *The Nazi Doctors*, I found myself thinking, most disconcertingly, *This* life. The life of a Nazi doctor. 'Born' in New England, as an old man; 'dying' in Austria, in the 1920s, as a baby boy ...

After more than a year of further reading, and of daily struggles with a sense of profanity and panic (by what entitlement could I address this sepulchral subject, and from such an apparently 'playful' vantage?), I began to write. And at once I made an emboldening discovery: the arrow of time turns out to be the arrow of reason or logic, expectably enough; but it is also the arrow of morality. Set the cinema of life in reverse motion, and (for example) the city of Hiroshima is created in a single moment; violence is benign; killing becomes healing, healing killing; the hospital is a torture chamber, the death camp a fount of life. Reverse the arrow of time, and the Nazi project becomes what Hitler said it was: the means to make Germany whole. Which still strikes me as some kind of measure of this terminal and diametrical atrocity: it asked for the arrow of time to point the other way.

We often ask ourselves, Who was worse, the little moustache or the big moustache, Hitler or Stalin? Well, fifteen years later I wrote a novel about the Russian Holocaust, too (*House of Meetings*); and the latter, incidentally, was the more difficult to write, because it focused on the victims and not the perpetrators. But that is by the way. In our hierarchy of evil, we instinctively promote Hitler. And we are right.

The Gulag – and this is not widely grasped – was first and foremost a system of state slavery. The goal, never achieved, was to make money. Still, this is a motive we can recognise. The German idea, with its 'dreams of omnipotence and sadism' (Lifton), was utterly inhuman, or 'counter-human', in Primo Levi's judgment, like a counter-clock world.

The Nazis were on the intellectual level of the supermarket tabloid. It shouldn't surprise us to learn that there was a government department, in Berlin, set up to prove that the Aryans were not descended from the apes; no, they came from the lost continent of Atlantis, in the heavens, where they were preserved in ice from the beginning of time.

Guardian 2010

Marty and Nick Jr. Sail
to America

I paid my first visit to America in 1958, at the age of nine; and I liked it so much that I stayed for almost a year. Before we embarked on the *Queen Elizabeth*, I and my brother Philip (aged ten) took the wise precaution of changing our names. For me it was quite straightforward: I would be known, stateside, as Marty. Philip was more imaginative, adapting one of his middle names and coming up with Nick Jr. – while boldly ignoring the fact that there was no Nick Sr. *My* middle name, I later realised, would have been perfect just as it was: Louis (my parents were admirers of Louis Armstrong). Anyway, when the great liner approached the glittering immensity of New York, Nick Jr. and Marty were fully prepared.

We came from Swansea in South Wales. This was a city of such ethnic homogeneity that I was already stealing cash and smoking the odd cigarette before I met – or even saw – a person with black skin. My baptism of fire came in 1956, when my father took me along to visit an academic from what was then Rhodesia (now Zimbabwe). On the way, as we rode the scarlet double-decker, he delivered a patient and, I thought, rather repetitive tutorial on what lay ahead of me. 'He's got a black face,' he said. 'He's black.' And so on. I entered the little apartment – and immediately burst into tears. Nor did I mince my words: 'You've got a black face!' 'Of course I have,' said the visiting professor, when he had finished laughing. 'I'm black!'

My father, in 1958, was also a visiting professor – he had come to teach creative writing at Princeton, NJ. By the time we started school at Valley Road, Nick Jr. had made my mother buy him his first pair of long trousers; Marty turned out to be the only human being in the entire establishment who was wearing shorts (plus Clarks sandals and floppy

228

grey socks). At Valley Road there were plenty of black pupils – though, as I recall, no black teachers; and at home I was soon on excellent terms with our cleaning lady, May, who drove over from Trenton two or three times a week in her sensational pink Cadillac.

In fourth grade I made friends first with Connie, then Marshal, then Dickie. After a while I became enamoured of a black boy – called Marty. Marty wore his name with some panache (whereas, in my case, Marty had reverted to Mart, just as Nick Jr. had reverted to Phil). One day, using the come-on line favoured by British children, I said to Marty,

'Would you like to come to my house for tea?'

'Mm. I prefer coffee.'

'I meant high tea. With cakes and buns. You can have coffee.'

'Nah. Your mother wouldn't like me.'

'Why not?'

'Because I'm black.'

'... My mother won't even *notice* you're black.'

So Marty came to tea, and it was, I thought, a complete success. Then I went to Marty's. He lived in Princeton's black neighbourhood (which, I gather, is now mainly Hispanic). And as I ate the evening meal with Marty's large family, and played basketball in the back alley with his brothers and his friends, I most certainly noticed I was white, and with a physical intensity that I will never forget. *The only boy in the school wearing shorts*: take that blushful isolation and multiply it by a thousand. This was my *skin*. And what I endured was a three-hour attack of self-consciousness so crushing that I feared I might faint dead away. And I later wondered: was this how Marty felt at my house? Was this how Marty felt on Main Street?

In 1967 my father took another teaching job in America – 'at Vanderbilt University at Nashville, Tennessee', according to his *Memoirs*, 'an institution known, unironically I suppose to some, as the Athens of the South.' Princeton started admitting black students in the mid-1940s. Two decades later my father asked if there were any 'coloured' students at Vanderbilt. 'Certainly,' came the unsmiling reply. 'He's called Mr Moore.' Nor did the SCR, in the department of the humanities, provide any kind of counterweight to the 'values' of the surrounding society – i.e., the raw prejudices of the hogwallow and the gutter. The culprit in the following anecdote was a novelist and a teacher of literature called Professor Walter Sullivan:

Whenever I tell this story, as I frequently do, I give him a Dixie chaw-bacon accent to make him sound even more horrible, but in fact he talked ordinary American-English with a rather attractive Southern lilt. Anyway, his words were (verbatim),

'I can't find it in my heart to give a negro [pron. nigra] or a Jew an A.'

The strong likelihood of hearing such unopposed – indeed, widely applauded – sentiments, at each and every social gathering moved my father to write that he considered his period in Nashville to be 'second only to my army service as the one in my life I would least soon relive'.

All this happened a long time ago, and I can prove it. During that year in Princeton the Amis family – all six of us – went on a day trip to New York City. It was an episode of joy and wonder, and of such startling expense that we talked about it, incredulously, for weeks, for months, for years. What with the train tickets, the taxi fares and ferry rides, the lavish lunch, the lavish dinner, and the innumerable snacks and treats, the Amises succeeded in spending no less than *one hundred dollars*.

When he got back to the UK in 1967 my father wrote a longish poem about Nashville, which ends: 'But in the South, nothing now or ever. / For black and white, no future. / None. Not here.' His despair, it transpired, was premature. One of the most marked demographic trends in contemporary America is the exodus of black families from the northern states to the southern. Nevertheless, those of us who believe in civil equality are suddenly in need of reassurance. I refer of course to the case of Trayvon Martin. Leave aside, for now, that masterpiece of jurisprudence, Stand Your Ground (which pits the word of a killer against that of his eternally wordless victim), and answer this question. Is it possible, in 2012, to confess to the pursuit and murder of an unarmed white seventeen year old, and then be released without charge? Ease my troubled mind, and tell me yes.

New York Times 2012

You Ask the Questions (2)

Are you an Islamophobe?
Alisdair Gray, Edinburgh

No, of course not. What I am is an Islamismophobe. Or better say an anti-Islamist, because a 'phobia' is an irrational fear, and there is nothing irrational about fearing people who say they want to kill you. The form that vigilante xenophobia is now taking – the harassment and worse of Muslim women in the street – disgusts me. It is mortifying to be part of a society in which any stratum feels under threat. On the other hand, no society on earth, no society imaginable, could frictionlessly absorb a day like July 7, 2005. Anti-Islamism is not like anti-Semitism. There is an empirical reason for it.

More generally, the difficulty has to do with versions of national identity; and the American model is the one that we (and everyone else) should attempt to plagiarise. A Pakistani immigrant, in Boston, can say 'I am an American', and all he is doing is stating the obvious. Can his equivalent, in Bradford, say the equivalent thing in the equivalent way? Britain needs to become what America has always been – an immigrant society. That, in any case, is our future.

The phrase 'horrorism', which you invented to describe 9/11, is unintentionally hilarious. Have you got any more?
Jonathan Brooks, by email

Yes, Jonathan, I've got another one for you (though I can hardly claim it as my own): fuck off. And incidentally 'horrorism' is a word, not a phrase.

I wasn't describing '9/11'. I was describing suicide bombing, or suicide-mass murder. And the distinction between terrorism and horrorism is real enough.

If for some reason you were about to cross Siberia by sleigh, you would be feeling 'concern' or even 'anxiety'; when you started out, and you heard the first howl of the wolves, your anxiety would be promoted to 'fear'; as the pack drew closer and gave chase, your fear would become 'terror'. 'Horror' is reserved for when the wolves are actually there. Some acts of terrorism are merely terrible. Suicide-mass murder, the act of self-splattering in which the assailant's blood and bones and organs become part of the political argument, is always horrific.

Something like four fifths of all suicide bombings in history have occurred post-September 11. Suicide bombing is new; and I have to say that I can't think of any greater defilement of the human image.

What do you think should be done about Israel and Iran's looming nuclear stand-off? Would you support an Israeli preemptive nuclear strike?
Clive Marr, Cambridge

Mahmoud Ahmadinejad, after that goons' rodeo in Tehran (where Islamist scholars gathered to question the historicity of the Holocaust) and his recent electoral reverses, is probably on the wane; but even Rafsanjani, Iran's most prominent (and corrupt) 'pragmatist', has said that a nuclear attack on Israel would obliterate the Jewish entity, whereas any retaliatory strike, however devastating, would be 'absorbed' by Greater Islam.

It is understandable that Israel should be far from enthusiastic about the emergence of a suicide bomb that can be measured in megatons. The only way forward, I think, is diplomacy, and it has to be led by America, which, in turn, must recognise that the West's two-tier nuclear position is a moral and philosophical non-starter. The West must give some *face* (do they realise how crucial this is?), and start cutting arsenals with a view to the utopian goal: the zero option, worldwide.

Can the war on terror be won?
Amber Alwan, by email

When historians come to write about this era (I persistently imagine), they will begin by saying that, in the early stages, the West panicked and wildly overreacted; and they will go on by saying that the strategy for defeating or containing terrorism was slow to crystallise. That strategy hasn't yet emerged, but we are slowly narrowing in on it. Remember the axiom: the deeper danger of terrorism lies not in what it inflicts but in what it provokes. September 11 could be sustained and survived; the ramifications of the Iraq War are still unknowable, and are already vast and multiform. Islamism has received a great boost from its rejection of reason and its embrace of death, both of which are hugely energising, as Lenin and Hitler well understood.

Islamism, jahadi-ism, now, its warriors obedient to a famous manual called *The Management of Savagery*, is simply too poisonous to survive for very long. What happened within Islam was not a civil war (between the moderates and the radicals); it was more like an October revolution (a revolution which is already starting to devour its children). We'll never 'win', exactly. But the Age of Vanished Normalcy will gradually become a thing of the past.

Have you made up with your old friend Christopher Hitchens after your spat over Stalin?
Marlijn Evans, London

We never needed to make up. We had an adult exchange of views, mostly in print, and that was that (or, more exactly, that goes on being that). My friendship with the Hitch has always been perfectly cloudless. It is a love whose month is ever May.

Which is your favourite of your own novels and why?
Richard Long, by email

Your novels are like your children, so you don't have a favourite. But you will certainly nurse a soft spot for the one that had the hardest time of it. So I will go for *Yellow Dog*. My fellow novelist Tibor Fischer contributed a gun-jumping hatchet job; and, after that, everyone who could hold a pen was suddenly feeling brave. For writers, a grudge is a terrible drag (though I hereby embrace the opportunity to repeat that Fischer is a creep and a wretch – and, oh yeah, a fatarse). Didn't he say somewhere that he wrote the review just to stir things up and make a name for himself? Well, there's some transient reassurance to be gained from the likelihood that he will be remembered for nothing else. But grudges should be quickly evacuated, as if they were poisons. These acrimony pageants bother you to no purpose: as Robert de Niro says in *Goodfellas*,

'Don't give them the *satisfaction*.' I doubt that there is any satisfaction in it for anyone.

Although I was fond of *Yellow Dog* and still am, it wasn't my favourite – not until I had to watch it being taunted and scragged in the schoolyard.

How do you think you might have ended up spending your working life if your father hadn't been a famous writer?
John Gordon, Eastleigh

Well, John, that would wholly depend, as must be obvious, on what Kingsley had chosen to do instead. If he had been a newsagent, then he would have fixed me up with a delivery round. If he had been an estate agent, then I would have walked into a job at, say, Stickley & Kent. If he had been a philosopher of sub-atomic thermodynamics, then I would have ...Are you beginning to get the idea?

No. It is in ourselves that we are thus and thus.

Now that Saul Bellow has passed away, who do you regard as the greatest living American novelist(s)?
Philip East, by email

John Updike, and then your namesake, Mr Roth. With Don De Lillo coming up on the flank. That's just my opinion. Time will sort it out. Bellow's pre-eminence, while he was here, seemed to me conclusive; it stared me in the face. As Matthew Arnold said of Shakespeare, 'Others abide our question. Thou art free.'

Why are you such a snob?
Beatrice Franks, by email

In the USSR a very high status was accorded to 'hereditary proletarians.' I can't aspire to that, but I have certain credentials. My father was a lower-middle-class scholarship boy from South London (Norbury). So it would hardly be my place, would it, to go and give myself airs?

A snob is 'a person who has an exaggerated respect for high social position or wealth and who looks down on those regarded as socially inferior'. In *Yellow Dog* I described the institution of the monarchy as 'a wank' – a designation free, I think, of exaggerated respect. As for the so-called 'socially inferior', I have devoted many hundreds of pages of fiction to them, and only a novelist *manqué* can write with a sneer on his face. If you want to learn about the human disaster of snobbery, read Trollope. Apart from anything else, snobbery is a full-time job: you're never off-duty. You never have a moment's peace.

On the other hand, I think snobbery is due for a bit of a comeback. But not the old shite to do with 'class'. 'There is a universal eligibility to be noble,' said Bellow rousingly. There is clearly a universal eligibility to be rational and literate. Sometimes snobbery is forced upon you. So let's have a period of exaggerated respect for reason; and let's look down on people who use language without respecting it. Liars and hypocrites and demagogues, of course, but also their fellow travellers in verbal cynicism, inertia, and sloth. 'High social position' brings no immunity. Princess Diana was also the princess – no, the empress – of secondhand speech, of mouldering novelties, of gullible vulgarisms, of what might be called herdwords and herd-phrases. Seen it, done it, been there, got the T-shirt, had a banana. No-brainer. I don't think so.

What's the worst thing that's ever happened to you?
Nesa Gardezi, by email

One day I returned home from a book tour in the US, and I suddenly noticed that the leading edge of the toilet roll in the bathroom wasn't folded into an inviting V – as it was in all those American hotels.

Not only that. I then had a tedious five minutes issuing instructions about the new arrangement to my wife and all the servants.

Is it true that the Lorne Guyland character in Money *was based on Kirk Doug-las and, if so, did old Kirk really stand naked in front of you and ask, 'Is this the body of a sixty-five-year-old-man?'*
John Niven, by email

Lorne Guyland, let us say, was made possible by Kirk Douglas. Kirk didn't disrobe for me personally, but, on the set, he was always ripping his clothes off. Movie stars are funny that way (or they used to be). During the same shoot I had dinner with Harvey Keitel in his room at Clar-idge's, and he was stripped to the waist throughout. It was a hot night, I allow. Kirk was very bright and very sweet in his way. As he said to the director (who was soon to be fired), 'The thing is, John, I'm unbelievably insecure.' He was, again, naked at the time.

Do you ever worry you have inherited some of your father's misogyny? Wasn't Julie Burchill right that Nicola Six, in London Fields, *is a murderer's dream-girl?*
Jenny Donovan, Cardiff

Try telling my fully politicised wife that I'm a misogynist – and see what you get.

To spell this out: I am not only a feminist – I am a gynocrat. That is to say, I believe in rule by women. Feminism is in fact the subject of my next novel, which is called *The Pregnant Widow*. Why the title? The Russian thinker Alexander Herzen said that after a revolution we should, on the whole, be braced by the fact that one order has given way to another; but what we are left with, he added, is not a birth, not a newborn child, but a pregnant widow – and there will be much grief and tribulation before we hear the baby's cries. In other words, consciousness is not revolutionised by the snap of a finger. And feminism, I reckon, is about halfway through its second trimester.

If you think that Nicola Six is a misogynistic creation, try reading *The Driver's Seat* by Muriel Spark. And I love this stuff about 'dream-girls'. The heroine of *House of Meetings*, too, has been described, here and there, as a 'male fantasy figure'. All they're saying is that she's pretty. I think that certain reviewers have subconsciously persuaded themselves that male novelists are by definition physically unattractive, and so consort, willy-nilly, with the physically unattractive, and when alone are reduced to having male fantasies about male fantasies.

How has your motivation for writing changed throughout your career?
Bob Swankie, Dundee

I don't think 'motivation' is quite the right word. Writing fiction is less mental and more physiological than is generally understood – once you're started, decisions and calculations, matters of reason, hardly ever come into it. It took me years to find out how true this is. When I was younger, I would come up against a difficulty in the narrative and I would beat my head against it for hours and days at a time. Now I feel prompted to leave my desk and pick up a book; and I don't return to my desk until my legs take me there. When they do, I find that the difficulty has been resolved. Your unconscious does it. Your unconscious does it all.

How did you research your new novel, House of Meetings. *You have not, I believe, ever been to Russia?*
Oksana Everts, London

No. I did it by reading (and imagining). The *Daily Mail* school of criticism would have it that all writers are sneak thieves and bagsnatchers – that they simply ponce off non-fiction. But reading is the other half of writing, or the other third: you write, you read, and you live. Also, Oksana, it got to the point where I thought a visit to Russia (very desirable in itself) would only confuse and impede me.

What is the most depressing thing about Britain you have observed since your return? And the best?
Grant Mullin, Surrey

I lived in Uruguay for nearly three years. Since my return, the most depressing thing was the sight of white middle-class demonstrators, last August, waddling around under placards saying, We Are All Hizbollah Now. Well, make the most of being Hizbollah while you can. As its leader, Hasan Nasrallah, famously advised the West: 'We don't want anything from you. We just want to eliminate you.' Similarly, when I went on *Question Time* the other week, a woman in the audience, her young voice quavering with indignation, presented the following argument: since it was America that supported Osama bin Laden when he was fighting, or rather peppering, the Russians, the US armed forces, in response to September 11, 'should be dropping bombs on themselves!' And the audience applauded. It is quite an achievement. People of liberal sympathies, stupefied by relativism and white guilt, have become the apologists for a creedal-political wave that is racist, misogynist, homophobic, totalitarian, imperialist, inquisitorial, and genocidal. To put it another way, they are up the arse of those who want them dead.

That was the most depressing thing. The best thing has been to find myself living in what, despite its faults (despite a million ills), is an extraordinarily successful multiracial society. This is a beautiful idea, with a good chance of becoming a beautiful reality, too.

Independent 2007

Politics – 2

Ivan Is Introduced to the USSR: All Together Now

Voices of Revolution, 1917, edited and introduced by Mark D. Steinberg

This is a formidably boring book – which is itself of some interest, given the desperate fascination of the historical moment. The documents collected here allegedly vivify 'the experiences, thoughts, and feelings of the Russian people – workers, peasants, soldiers' during that 'landmark' year in a 'rich and complex language'. And even as one toils, tills, and battles one's way through Mark D. Steinberg's introduction and the first of his three scene-setting historical essays, one still imagines that a great feast lies in store.

The sense of anticipation, as is meet, seems strongly progressive and egalitarian in tendency. You think: down with the pontifications of arid academics; let us hear from the salt of the earth ... What we get, of course, is another revolution that failed. With a handful of exceptions, the words of the people are even more boring than Professor Steinberg's. This has very little to do with the fact that the contributors are 'lower-class' (a shocking designation in the context of the author's sanitised editorials. How about 'unempowered'?). It is more fundamental than that; and more integral, too.

If we exclude the poems (which there are good reasons for doing anyway), then the great majority of the documents are not 'voices'; they are choruses. They are resolutions, appeals, protocols, petitions, and 'instructions' from various councils, initiative groups, general meetings, commissions, regimental associations, and village assemblies. 'A joint resolution', then, 'of the Executive Committee of the Soviet of Workers' and Soldiers' Deputies and of the Executive Committee of the Soviet of Peasants' Deputies'; or prepare yourself for the stifling intimacy of a 'Resolution Passed at the General Meetings of 3 and (illegible) August 1917 by the Cultural-Educational Commission Under the Executive

Committee of the Soviet of Workers' Deputies of the Factory of the Rozhdestvensky Manufacturing Company of P.V. Berg in Tver'. 'In the name of ...' 'We, the undersigned ...' Elias Canetti told us something about crowds and power. Professor Steinberg tells us something, with mad iteration, about crowds and prose: they can't do it. This book demonstrates that writing is somehow synonymous with the isolated self. And one wonders afresh whether collaboration, in literature, has ever produced anything better than the workaday.

Most readerly responses can be dramatised by quotation – but not boredom. Of the three categories, the workers are the most committed to collective utterance, and their texts are therefore more boring than those of the soldiers and the peasants. So here (by reverse psychology) is the most interesting paragraph from the shop floor:

> Citizens! Like a venerable oak standing in the middle of the forest, the giant Putilov factory stands in the middle of state industry, making the earth quake with the heavy blows of its hammers. From all ends of Russia, workers have come to work in it, and while they are working they think thoughts: to the whistle of the saw, the screech of the drive belts, the dispiriting sight of the gun carriages and cannons, gloomy thoughts creep into your mind. In work as hard as prison labor, the mothers and fathers who gave us birth die, and we too are dying right here: in despairing alienation from the joys we envy, from the wealth and culture that is enjoyed not far from us – separated only by a fat monument, the old Narva Gates – by the rich, 'educated' minority.

Despite the swift breakdown of the opening simile, there is much to admire here (or there is if you are on page 187 of *Voices of Revolution, 1917*): the pride, the anger, and the sacrificial heroism which the Bolsheviks would go on to demand and enforce; it also reads like the work of an individual. Elsewhere, minor anomalies ('Approved unanimously; opposed 1') and stray vehemencies ('The Duma must die!!!') get you through another couple of inches of text. Usually, and essentially, though, the workers are simply listing their demands: food, higher wages, peace (ritually 'without annexations or indemnities'), plus all power to the Soviets, and long live the Constituent Assembly (promised for November). From the outset – March 1917 – the proletarian rhetoric feels third-hand. We know that factory, and what it makes is boilerplate.

As already noted, the soldiers and peasants are more inclined to wander off on their own, and very occasionally they give us what we realise we are missing: details, anecdotes – non-abstractions. There is a stunned, numbed letter from a soldier who has just witnessed the murder of three officers suspected of treachery in the Kornilov affair: 'Vasiliev the general was dragged over the pavement: he was covered with blood and asked for nothing, just kept crossing himself.' This is a lonely example of unselfconscious observation, from a lonely pen. In the main, one relies on mere accumulation of instances for one's sense of the terrifying squalor of the front. The army was of course almost entirely made up of peasants. Those that remained in the countryside were the elderly, and those that returned to it were the wounded (together with growing stream of deserters). The communications from the 'esteemed reapers' (in Stalin's facetious phrase) are written by the literate minority, who for obvious reasons sought a left-leaning cohesiveness. This voice or chorus is revealing only when it shows exasperation and then alarm at the extent of rural unpreparedness for the great experiment:

> I categorically declare that in our the village (*sic*) of Belogorenka ...
> we do not have any provocateurs ... Comrade soldiers, I beg you to
> send provocateurs here because I can't deal with this alone and I
> don't know what's going on there in Petrograd ....

He means 'propagandists': educators, indoctrinators, radicalisers. There were plenty of propagandists in the cities and (more spottily, true) at the front.

Steinberg's book gets livelier in the final section, oddly called 'Soviets in Power: From the October Revolution to the closing of the Constituent Assembly' (oddly, because the Soviets, in this period, were joining the long queue to the ash-heap of history), and livelier still after the Bolsheviks began to show their hand. A letter to Trotsky: 'I am sending you a New Year's greeting from the whole Russian people. God damn you to hell!' A letter to Lenin (the pre-obscenity endearment is superb):

> It's been four whole days since we've had a glimpse of bread, we are
> walking around naked and barefoot ... If you've picked up the reins

then go ahead and drive, and if you can't, then, honey, you can take a flying fuck to hell, or as we say in Siberia, you're a goddamned motherfucker, son of an Irkutsk cunt, who'd like to sell us out to the Germans.

It is clear, incidentally, from another volume in the Annals of Communism series, *The Unknown Lenin: From the secret archive* (edited by Richard Pipes), that the Bolsheviks took money from the German 'scum' before and after October. This was opportunism on Lenin's part, not the high treason of which he was widely accused. If the socialist experiment had gone to schedule, then Germany would have staged a cooperative revolution in 1918, and the clandestine payments would have been just another brilliancy in what Lenin, referring to another deception, called 'a beautiful plan'.

Communism was a beautiful plan. And for once a beautiful intention, in its way (if you happen to be attracted to a creepy utopia where, according to Trotsky, your neighbours will all be Shakespeares and Beethovens). Similarly, a book representing the soliloquys of the common dramatis personae of 1917: *that* would have been nice, too. But in revolutionary times, it seems, the inner voice has to sleep in the dark, and the self is inevitably folded outwards to the world, and expresses itself collectively. Steinberg's contributors are under the impression (and it is not quite an illusion) that their two bits might shape the destiny of a great nation. This whiff of power, in any case, is enough to overload the individual. The poems included here are similarly distorted; they are marching-songs, or factory hooters, or unearned excursions into the high style, in which the authors speak not for themselves but for Russia – or for all humanity.

So-and-so's 'language is marked by the richness of visual imagery that typifies folk language', writes Ekaterina Betekhtina in a supplementary essay called 'Style in Lower-Class Writing in 1917'. Having chainsmoked his way through that, the present reviewer was moved to recall how little he had relished the essays by Professor Steinberg (which amount to some 130 pages). Steinberg is also a politicised being. To the grim piety long associated with history 'from below' he adds his peculiar moral bloodlessness. And if he has simply succumbed to the advice of the editorial board, then we are left staring at another example of the literary anti-talent of committees.

The Bolsheviks were, as Lenin said, 'a party of a new type'. Steinberg writes as if he honestly didn't know anything about the great census-slashing deformity that was about to enfold. His tone, indeed, would be appropriate to an account of a complicated reshuffle in a provincial guildhall. In this historiographical world, with its apparent dread of controversy, nobody is to blame for anything. Nor does Mark Steinberg seem aware that his 'voices' have one overriding poignancy, in that they were all of them destined for silence.

Times Literary Supplement 2002

Is Terrorism 'About Religion'?

History is accelerating; and so with every passing day the future becomes more and more unknowable. Among our foremost thinkers, we find only one presentiment that is universally shared. This turns out to be a sinister variation on the idea of 'convergence'. Not the convergence of nations and polities, whereby the world's autocratic regimes would gradually align themselves with the democratic and contentedly globalised mainstream. This particular expectation, even neoconservatives now concede, was a triumphalist fantasy of the 1990s – that curious holiday from what Philip Roth has called 'the remorseless unforeseen'.

The convergence we have now come to anticipate is the convergence of international terrorism and weapons of mass destruction – of IT and WMD. Even strictly parallel lines, I was taught, meet and cross in infinity. And the paths of IT and WMD are visibly inclined, like the sides of a tapering spire. Their eventual convergence is guaranteed by the simplest of market forces. Marginal costs will fall; and demand will climb.

It has not been widely realised, even now, that America has already suffered a terrorist deployment of WMD – as we have just been reminded by the one-man suicide mission of the troubled germ-scientist, Bruce E. Ivins, in Frederick, Md. (July 29, 2008). The WMD attack began on September 18, 2001. The cost in blood was five dead and seventeen seriously infected. The cost in treasure was over a billion dollars (the cost to the perpetrator, in a vibrant asymmetry, was estimated at the time to be about $2,500). And there was a third impact: the cost in fear. Anthrax is not contagious; but fear is. The scale of the attack was minuscule, yet for a while the terror filled the sky.

Unlike the poet, the novelist (see Auden's lustrous sonnet of that name) assumes that his or her reactions to the main events (in life, in history) are utterly median, average – predictably and dependably human. I am confident that my reaction to September 11 was quite normative:

a leaden and sourly mineral incredulity. It is with rather more diffidence that I divulge my reaction to September 18: I followed the example of that large and flightless African bird which, when sighting a threat to its existence, chooses to bury its head in the sand. Rather than keep my eyes open, I accepted a mouthful of grit.

This was the kind of datum I was unable to contemplate (from an official 'projection'):

> *Using one aircraft dispensing 1,000 kg of anthrax spores.* Clear calm night. *Area covered (sq. km)*: 300. *Deaths assuming 3,000 – 10,000 people per sq. km*: one million to three million.

The affective content of September 18 ran as follows: you must abandon for ever the notion that you can protect your loved ones. Staggering, too, was the perceived magnification of the enemy's power. Al Qaeda swelled like a Saturn; and for a while they seemed to be everywhere on earth – the whisperers, the nightrunners of Osama. September 18 was very cheap, very terrifying, and durably elusive. It entrained over 9,000 interrogations and 6,000 grand-jury subpoenas; and the case is not yet closed.

The anthrax letters contained two near-identical cover notes. The first said:

09-11-01
THIS IS NEXT
TAKE PENACILIN NOW
DEATH TO AMERICA
DEATH TO ISRAEL
ALLAH IS GREAT

After the ebbing of panic (the widely reported 'sub-clinical hysteria'), no one took the cover note seriously, let alone literally. 'Take penacilin now': this was sound medical advice (anthrax is a bacterium, not a virus), but the misspelling was obviously tactical – a false lead, a false flag. The perpetrator was not a zealot; he was a scowl in a lab coat, a Unabomber, a Timothy McVeigh with a Ph.D. And so it proved – or so it seems.

September 18, we concluded, was 'not about religion' ('Allah Is Great' was a blind). Was September 11 about religion? This is still controversial. Both President Bush and former British PM Tony Blair, who are religious, were very quick to say that September 11 was 'not about religion' ('religion', hereabouts, being a euphemism for Islam). A gathering concensus then emerged that September 11 *was* about religion – or, at least, was not *not* about religion. But in the last year or two, evidently, we have gone back to saying that September 11, and March 11 (Madrid, 2004), and July 7 (London, 2005), and all the rest, were 'not about religion'.

The two most stimulating IT-watchers known to me are John Gray and Philip Bobbitt. Professor Gray (*Straw Dogs, Al Qaeda and What It Means to Be Modern*, and *Black Mass*) and Professor Bobbitt (*The Shield of Achilles* and the masterly *Terror and Consent*) are utterly unalike, except in brainpower and literary panache. Bobbitt is a proactive and muscular Atlanticist, whereas Gray is almost Taoist in his scepticism and his luminous passivity. Bobbitt is religious, and Gray is at least philo-religious (secular, but wholly reconciled to the inexorability of 'faith'); but neither man is an exponent of relativist politesse. And they assert, respectively, that international terrorism is 'not about Islam' and that IT has 'no close connection to religion'.

Al Qaedaism, for them, is an epiphenomenon – a secondary effect. It is the dark child of globalisation, and, equally, the mimic of modernity: devolved, decentralised, privatised, outsourced, and networked. According to Bobbitt (rather more dubiously), Al Qaeda not only reflects the market state: it *is* a market state ('a virtual market state'). Globalisation created great wealth and also great defencelessness; it created a new space, or a new dimension. Thus the epiphenomenon is not about religion, they argue; it is about human opportunism and the will to power.

Then what, you may well be wondering, was all that about jihad and infidels and Allahu Akbar and crusaders and madrasas and sharia and *fiqh* and *takfir* and the scriptural prophecies and the cleansed caliphate and the martyrs' paradise? Why did people write whole books with titles like *A Fury for God* and *The Age of Sacred Terror*? There are several reasons for *hoping* that international terrorism is not about religion – chief among them the immense onerousness, the near-impossibility, now, of maintaining any kind of discourse that involves creedal 'convictions' and (I'll put this simply) *less than reverent generalisations about non-white foreigners*. Al Qaedaism may evolve into not being about religion, about Islam. But one's faculties insist that at the very least it is not not about religion *yet*.

Let me devote a paragraph to the British perspective. In the UK, in 2007, there were 203 arrests on terrorism charges, nearly all of them connected to radical Islam. It is possible to open your newspaper (the *Independent*) and read about three thwarted or bungled cases of jihadism on a single day (May 24, 2008). The main purpose of the Quilliam Foundation, recently established, is to deradicalise young British Muslims. And consider the otherwise extraordinarily weak motivation of the four men responsible for July 7. Experience of conflict or of foreign occupation? No. A set of demands or the prospect of benefits? No. Community support? No. Familial heroisation *post mortem*? On the contrary.

Then, too, the rise of suicide attacks *directly targeting civilians* is astonishing – and it is also astonishing how unastonished we claim to be in the face of it. Many commentators like to remind us that this tactic is a) nothing new, and b) non-theological, and then follow that up with a perfunctory reference to the Tamil Tigers, the godless Sri Lankan separatists who have been blowing themselves to pieces since 1987. The relevant essay in *Making Sense of Suicide Missions* (edited by Diego Gambetta and updated in 2006) states, of the Tigers: 'There are no clear examples of civilians being directly targeted.' Moreover, one database (quoted in the *Times Literary Supplement*) concludes that 'over 80 per cent of all suicide attacks in history have taken place since 2001'. Suicide bombing is a cult. And Gambetta makes the haunting point that this weapon, unlike any other, is self-replenishing. The bomber uses up one martyr, but he creates many others; and 'we know that the number of volunteers soars immediately after Ramadan ...'

It may also emerge that the use of religion is, or is becoming, merely a means of mobilisation. Religion is for the footsoldiers, supposedly, and not the masterminds. At some later date we may see that religion provided the dialectical staircase to indiscriminate death and destruction. The idea, for instance, that democracy (fundamentally unclean) inculpates every citizen in its nation's policies; the idea (or ancient heresy) of *takfir*, whereby the jihadi pre-absolves himself of killing fellow Muslims. Interestingly, though, Ayman al-Zawahiri is currently squirming about in a theological debate with the venerable cleric, Sayyid Imam al-Sharif, as Al Qaeda itself is having to defend its religious legitimacy. Osama bin Laden is often similarly embroiled. Even Abu Musab al-Zarqawi, the Jordanian jailbird proudly known as 'the sheikh of the slaughterers', constantly sought doctrinal ballast. Are these masterminds persuaded that terror is not 'about religion'?

We can further expect IT to become much more diffuse in its motivations, reflecting changes in the contemporary personality. John Gray has identified a vein of what he expressively calls 'anomic terrorism'. This would be the carnage inspired by alienation, the self-extending despair evident in the random serial stabbings in the cities of Japan, or in the campus massacres in the US – or indeed in the threats voiced by Dr Ivins during the weeks before his death. The historian Eric Hobsbawm believes that the pandemic collapse of moral inhibition has to do with a general coarsening, the desensitisation of violence brought about by the mass media (and of course the internet). This prompts some further points.

It is Bobbitt's thesis (which Gray, incidentally, tends to pooh-pooh) that the current conflicts are epochal, having to do with a shift in the constitutions of the polities of the West. As the welfare state evolves into the market state, it abandons many of its responsibilities to its citizenry, and concentrates above all on the provision of opportunities to the individual. This, I think, has clear consequences for the self: there is simply more pressure on it. In *Mr Sammler's Planet*, which appeared at the end of that great spurt of narcissistic eccentricity known as the 1960s, Saul Bellow has his elderly hero reflect (with delightful restraint) that mass individualism is relatively new and, perhaps, 'has not been a great success'.

Joseph Conrad's *The Secret Agent* (1907), with its dank crew of self-righteous anarchists, is horribly prescient. Here we find (for example) the observation that merely to erect a building is to create a new vulnerability; here we find a revolutionist observing that the power of life is far, far weaker than the power of death. In his reading of the terrorist psyche, Conrad persistently stresses the qualities of vanity and sloth – i.e., the desire for maximum distinction with minimum endeavour. In other words, the need to make an impression is overwhelming, and a negative impression is much more easily achieved than a positive. In our era, this translates into an ungovernable thirst for fame. Probably no one under thirty can fully grasp it, but fame has become a kind of 'religion' – the opium, and now the angel dust, of the mass individual.

By some accounts it took the Ayatollah Khomeini several nauseous years of war with Iraq before he came to see the theological viability of nuclear fission (and the groundwork was then begun). Osama bin Laden has never made any secret of his admiration for WMDs: 'It is the duty of Muslims to prepare as much force as possible to terrorise the enemies of God' (statement entitled 'The Nuclear Bomb of Islam', 1998). All these tools are now for sale; and how very remarkable it is, in the larger scheme, that the world's first megadeath madam, the metallurgist A.Q. Khan, is 'a national hero' in Pakistan.

There is another good reason for wanting international terrorism to stop being 'about religion'. One can think of scenarios of extortion, compellance, and ransom, but only an eschatological dream could justify the clear calm night and the three million dead. On the other hand, the actors would unquestionably make an impression; and it would be super-geohistorical in size.

International terrorism, for now, represents a puny apocalypse. Philip Bobbitt is as droll about this as anybody: since September 11, 'the total number of persons worldwide who have been killed by terrorists is about the same number as those who drowned in bathtubs in the US'. But at any moment it – IT – could go from nothing to everything. After an untraceable mass-destructive strike on one of its cities, what political system would ever know itself again? And all other nation states would be unrecognisable too, as would relations between them.

Wall Street Journal 2008

In Memory of Neda Soltan
(1983–2009): Iran

The writer Jason Elliot called his recent and resonant Iranian travelogue *Mirrors of the Unseen*; and I should say that I'm aware of the dangers generally associated with writing about the future. But what we seem to be witnessing in Iran is the first spasm of the death agony of the Islamic Republic. In this process, which will be very long and very ugly, Mir Hossein Mousavi (the recently defeated moderate) is likely to play a lesser role than Neda Agha Soltan.

According to *Time* magazine, it was 'probably the most widely witnessed death in human history'. There she is, in the amateur video, spiritedly present on the periphery of a demonstration (which was being broken up); then comes the jolt of the gunshot wound to the chest. '*NeDA!*' cries her avuncular companion (in fact her music teacher). The bullet was fired by a paramilitary policeman. She died in two minutes. 'I'm burning, I'm burning,' she said.

Her metamorphosis (from youth, hope, and beauty to an agonised end) unforgettably crystallised the core Iranian idea – the Shia tragedy and passion – of martyrdom in the face of barbaric injustice. A traveller, a linguist, a performing musician, and a divorcee, apolitical but civic-minded, a defiant individualist (in dress and mores), a questioner, Neda Soltan embodied something else, too: she was the gentle face of the modern. Jason Elliot's title should again be borne in mind as we consider the June Events of 2009, which are open to two interpretations.

Quite possibly, things are more or less as they look: the results of a fraudulent election were presented to the people with indecent haste and indecent flippancy (with, in other words, contempt for the democratic participants); civil unrest was then followed by the application of state violence. Now consider. If, after the usual interval, Supreme Leader

Ali Khamenei had soberly announced a 51 per cent win for President Ahmadinejad, then Iran, and the world, might well have bowed its head and moved on. Just as possibly (the Islamic Republic being what it is), the landslide was ostentatiously rigged and vaunted, to bring on the unrest, the terror, and the crackdown, which continues.

Back in 1997, the regime felt confident enough to sanction the surprise victory of Muhammad Khatami, who won by the same landslide margin of 69 per cent in a joyous election that no one disputed. Khatami, a cleric, had nonetheless far stronger liberal credentials than the technocrat Mousavi (who, during the Iran–Iraq war, was well to the right of Khamenei). Lovingly hailed as 'Ayatollah Gorbachev', Khatami was soon talking about the 'thoughtful dialogue' he hoped to open with America. It seemed possible that international isolation, which so parches and de-oxygenates the Iranian air, was about to be eased.

Everyone understood that this process would take time. In June 2001, Khatami was re-elected with a majority of 78 per cent. Seven months later came George W. Bush's 'axis of evil' speech (one of the most destructive in American history), and the Tehran Spring was at an end. In truth, Bush was heaven-sent for the Iranian right; without meaning to, he greatly enhanced Iran's regional power (with the adventurist, indeed experimentalist war against Iraq), and at the same time remained sufficiently 'arrogant' (the most detested of all attributes in the Shia-Iranian sensorium) to maintain and service popular hatred.

Today, the mullahs are aware that the new president is for several reasons much more formidable. Had Mousavi won, Obama would have rewarded Iran, and in a way palpable to every Iranian. Such a 'linkage' – liberalisation equals benefits – would have fatal consequences for the regime. The earth is already stirring beneath their feet, with the pro-Western, anti-Syrian, anti-Iranian election in Lebanon. And other historical forces are conspiring to rattle the armed clerisy of Iran.

For the mullahs now know that they are afloat on an ocean of illegitimacy. The great hawsers of the revolution of 1978–79 are all either snapped or silently rotting. Of the four foundational narratives, three are myths: the 'Islamic Revolution' was not an Islamic revolution; the Iran–Iraq war (1980–88), which destroyed a generation, was not the 'Imposed War', as it is still called; and Ayatollah Ruhollah Khomeini was not the infallible, the inerrant 'Divine Authority' (Khomeini, as every inquisitive Iranian has long understood, was a world-historical monster).

Perhaps most importantly of all, for now, the fourth narrative, or thread (anti-Americanism – anti-'Westoxication', and 'Death to America!', an old battle-cry still chanted by schoolchildren), has been severed by the person of Barack Obama.

Over the course of the summer and autumn leading up to November 8, 2008, opinion polls in the Middle East showed a near-unanimous certainty that in America 'they' would never let a black man take possession of the White House. But there he was, with his democratic super-legitimacy glittering all about him, and he spoke to Islam in a new voice, a voice of historical awareness and respect. When, in July of 2008, President Sarkozy received Obama in Paris, he said in greeting, 'This is the America we love.' It was a sentiment very likely to find an echo from the youth in the cities of the Middle East.

Which brings us to two other hasteners of theocratic doom: globalised modernity (instant communications) and the future imposed by demography. For Iran, one of the oldest nations on earth, is getting younger and younger.

*

'In the history of the Iranian plateau,' writes Sandra Mackey in her stylish and magisterial classic, *The Iranians: Persia, Islam, and the Soul of a Nation*, 'the sun has risen and set on nearly a million days'. And a million days is longer than we think – 2,739 years. If we date the birth of the country from its unification in 625 BCE, then the millionth dawn will come in 2114. What will the sun see as it patrols that Iranian plateau?

Let us examine the three main lies that undergird the Islamic Republic.

The 1979 revolution wasn't an Islamic revolution until it was over. In its origins, it was a full-spectrum mass movement, an avalanche of demonstrations and riots, and strikes so relentless that they blacked out the Peacock's palace; the military, moreover, was sustaining a thousand defections per day. The June Events of 2009 constitute a mere whisper of demurral when set against the unyielding crescendo of 1978. The noise was not made for clerical rule; the noise was made because a decadent monarchy had lost the *farr* – the inherent aura of kingship.

It is instructive to compare the Iranian revolution with the two Russian revolutions of 1917: the February revolution, a popular revolt, and

the October revolution, a Leninist coup (with an impotent Provisional Government in the interim). Trotsky said that the Bolsheviks found
power lying in the street and 'picked it up like a feather'. And then, of
course, the really warm work began – against the Whites, against the
Greens (the peasantry), against the trade unions, against the church, and
so on, until every alternative centre of power (and opinion) was eradi-
cated, down to and including any gathering of three. The popular revolution gave way to a clique; in Iran it gave way to an echelon, an echelon
led by one of the great charismatics of the twentieth century.

On January 16, 1979, Muhammad Reza Shah flew out of Tehran – to
exile in Cairo. On February 1, Ayatollah Khomeini flew into Tehran –
from long exile in Paris (where one of his more regrettable neighbours,
I feel obliged to mention, was Brigitte Bardot). Thus the political revolution was over; now the cultural revolution began. The Provisional Government was successively eroded by the *komitehs* (mosque-based militias,
later the Basij), by the Revolutionary Guards (later the Pasdaran, or the
Iranian army), and by the revolutionary tribunals (which dealt out rough
justice to survivors of the old regime and to various other undesirables).
On November 4, a group of pious students spontaneously infiltrated the
US embassy and seized the fifty-three hostages. Khomeini manipulated
this V-sign directed at the Great Satan to such effect that in the imminent
referendum on the new constitution '99.5 per cent' of a turnout of 17
million gave their blessing to Islamic autocracy.

But there was still that '0.5' to deal with. And Khomeini faced vigorous opposition from almost every quarter – most formidably from the
Mujahedin-e Khalq. Established a decade and a half earlier, in opposition
to the Shah, the Mujahedin (Marxist, left-Islamic, and committed to
women's rights) had half a million adherents and could field a guerrilla
army of 100,000 experienced fighters. When Khomeini excluded them
from the new political order as 'un-Islamic', they rose up.

In 1981, if you recall, the Mujahedin were blowing mullahs to bits
by the dozen (seventy-four in a single strike in Tehran); and they went
on to assassinate more than a thousand government officials in the latter
months of that year. What followed was terroristic civil strife. By September, Khomeini's Revolutionary Guards were executing fifty people a
day for 'waging war against God' (the same crime, and the same punishment, now being invoked by the clerics of 2009). Fired by a zeal both
revolutionary and religious, the mullahs bloodily prevailed.

Revolutions, almost by definition, are fiercely anti-clerical. As late as 1922 (to take the fiercest possible example), Lenin executed 4,500 priests and monks, plus 3,500 nuns in that year alone. Contrarian Iran, on the other hand, swam upstream. By December 1982, Khomeini had more or less secured the monopoly of violence, and the Iranian people found themselves living under the world's only revolutionary theocracy. The Islamic Republic was Islamic, now, but it was no longer a republic. And by 1982, besides, they had something newly pressing to think about. When the eight-year war began, the Iranians were the defenders of their homeland; now they were the invaders of Iraq.

The Iran–Iraq war can rightly be thought of as the Imposed War, but only if we understand that the war was imposed by Khomeini. It tests the historical imagination to get a sense of the horrified dismay engendered, throughout the region, by the advent of the meshuga ayatollah. Stalin, after a while, was content with 'socialism in one country'. Khomeini, proclaimedly, wanted Shia theocracy in every country on earth. Throughout the course of the Iran–Iraq war, Khomeini put himself about elsewhere, with bombings, assassination attempts, and armed subversion, in Bahrain, Kuwait, Lebanon, and Saudi Arabia. In Mecca, the *hajj* became the scene of annual agitation; in 1987, a clash between Iranian militiamen and Saudi riot police left more than 400 dead.

And Iraq? In 1979 Saddam Hussein reached out a trembling hand of friendship to the new Iran, and was clearly hoping for the continuation of the détente he had established with the Shah. Iran responded by resuming support for the separatist Kurds (suspended since 1975) and for the Shia underground; there were assassination attempts on the Iraqi deputy premier and the minister of information, and the successful murder of at least twenty prominent officials in the single month of April 1980. Khomeini, meanwhile, withdrew his ambassador from Baghdad; in September, Iran shelled the border cities of Khanaqin and Mandali.

In *The Iran–Iraq War, 1980–1988*, Efraim Karsh lists in his chronology eight Iraqi offers of ceasefires, the first on October 5, 1980, twelve days after the war began, the last on July 13, 1988, five weeks before it ended. Khomeini's war aim was the theocratisation, or de-Satanisation, of Iraq; thus the war became a (failed) test of Islam, and devolved, in Sandra Mackey's words, into 'a daily enactment of Shia themes of sacrifice, dispossession, and mourning'. So: twelve-year-olds were attacking Iraqi machine gun emplacements on bicycles, and 750,000 Iranians filled the multi-acre cemeteries, and perhaps twice that number were left crippled in body or mind. Eleven months later, Khomeini himself joined the fallen in the land of the dead.

*

What remains, then, visitors might wonder, as they deplane at Tehran's Imam Khomeini International Airport and enter a city where no cab-driver will stop for a cleric – what remains of the legacy bequeathed by the Father of the Revolution, or (alternatively) by 'that fucking asshole', as he is reflexively called, in loud English, by the youth of the cities of Iran? Khomeini's notion of the Velayat-e Faqih, or rule by the vice-regent of God (i.e., the top mullah, i.e., Khomeini), was so unhistorical that many of its angriest opponents came from the clergy. Political participation, in Shia theology, is seen as a contaminant. And with good reason: power corrupts, and absolute power (absolute corruption) combined with absolute self-righteousness, defined the insane nightmare of Khomeini's rule.

His moral imbecilities provide a rich field. I will confine myself to two examples. After President Carter's 'fiasco in the desert', the failed 'Entebbe' raid of April 1980, Khomeini announced that God had personally thrown sand into the helicopters' engines to protect the nation of Islam. To hear this kind of talk from an eight-year-old is one thing; to hear it from a bellicose head of state, on public radio, is another. The second example comes from Mackey (the time is 1981):

> A film run on government-controlled television showed a mother denouncing her son as a Marxist. The son, sobbing and grabbing for his mother's hand, desperately tries to convince her that he has given up Marxist politics. The mother rejects his pleas saying, 'You must repent in front of God and you will be executed.' The picture fades to Ayatollah Khomeini telling the people of Iran, 'I want to see more mothers turning in their children with such courage without shedding a tear. This is what Islam is.'

Well, it may or may not be what Islam is. But it is not what Iranians are.

*

Iran is one of the most venerable civilisations on earth: it makes China look like an adolescent, and America look like a toddler. And its 2,600-year history is sliced almost exactly in two by the rise of Islam. Accordingly, the Iranian heart is bipolar, divided between Xerxes and Muhammad, between Persepolis and Qom, between the imperially sensuous (with its luxury and poetry) and the unsmilingly pious. You will, I think, acknowledge that dividedness when I tell you that the author of this quietly beautiful quatrain –

> I am a supplicant for a goblet of wine
> From the hand of a sweetheart.
> In whom can I confide this secret of mine,
> Where can I take this sorrow?

– is the Ayatollah Khomeini.

Not Ferdowsi, not Rumi, not Hafez, not Omar Khayyám: Khomeini. It is perhaps the most beguiling single feature of Iranian life that its people go on pilgrimages, not only to the shrines of their martyrs and imams, but also to the shrines of their poets. The Iranian-Persian soul resembles the goddess Proserpina in Ted Hughes's masterly *Tales from Ovid*:

> Proserpina, who divides her year
> Between her husband in hell, among spectres,
> And her mother on earth, among flowers.
> Her nature, too, is divided. One moment
> Gloomy as hell's king, but the next
> Bright as the sun's mass, bursting from clouds.

In 1935, Iranians found themselves living in a different country – not Persia but Iran, the specifically pre-Islamic 'land of the Arians'. This was the work of Reza Shah (the army strongman who seized the throne in 1925). Reza Shah was a modernist and seculariser – Iran's Atatürk or Nasser. He was also a friend of Nazi Germany (and was deposed by the Allies in 1941). In 1976, Iranians found themselves living in a different millennium, not 1355 (dated from the time of the Prophet) but 2535 (dated from the time of Cyrus the Great). This was the work of Reza Shah's son. Installed by the coup of 1953 (the West's very grave historical crime, whose sequelae are still with us), Muhammad Reza Shah was a 'miserable wretch', as Khomeini rightly called him; but he was quite closely attuned to Iran's divided self. Reza Shah beat women who wore the veil; Khomeini beat women who didn't; Muhammad Reza Shah beat neither.

After 1979, Iran was subjected to militant and breakneck re-Islamisation. The Zoroastrian era was declared to be *jahiliyyah*, a benighted slum of ignorance and idolatry, and a dire embarrassment to all good Muslims. In the mid-1990s, for example, the historian Jahangir Tafazoli was put to death simply because he was the best-known specialist on ancient Iran. We would call this 'killing the messenger', and we would call the entire tendency 'delusional denial'. The thirty-year suppression of the mixed Iranian soul – which says yes to freedom and tolerance, yes to love and life and art, yes to Islam, and yes to modernity – provided the energy and courage of the June Events, and entrained the hideous murder of Neda Soltan.

∗

So now we have another four years of Mahmoud Ahmadinejad, who will be more purple-gummed with insecurity than ever, and another four years of troubled dreams about the Iranian bomb. I find that the one thing Ahmadinejad mandates, with full legitimacy, is a tone of ridicule – because it is impossible to write solemnly about the man who, among other absurdities, clinched the 2005 election by the simple feat of not having a Jacuzzi. And you needn't reread that sentence: the 'Jacuzzi moment', or the no-Jacuzzi moment, when the candidate revealed that yes, he had no Jacuzzi, was broadly credited with securing his majority. This was enough, apparently, to make him shine out in the smog of pelf and hypocrisy that passes for the Islamic Republic.

The American politician whom Ahmadinejad most closely resembles – in one vital respect – is Ronald Reagan. General similarities, I agree, are hard to spot. Ahmadinejad doesn't live on a ranch with a former starlet. Reagan didn't have a degree in traffic control. Ahmadinejad doesn't use Grecian 2000 (as his rapidly greying hair triumphantly attests). Reagan, as a young man, wasn't involved in the murder of political adversaries. And so on. But what they have in common is this: both figures are denizens of that stormlit plain where end-time theology meets nuclear weapons.

Now we can return, for a while, to dissimilarities. Ahmadinejad is not checked and balanced by democratic institutions. Reagan did not actually spend public money on civic preparations for the Second Coming, and was not the product of a culture saturated in ecstatic fantasies of morbid torment. Ahmadinejad does not have a temperament in which 'simple-minded idealism' (in Eric Hobsbawm's formulation) might lead him to recognise 'the sinister absurdity' of the arms race. And Reagan was not answerable to some millenarian vicar in the holy city of, say, Lynchburg. Finally, whereas Reagan wielded enough firepower to kill everyone on earth several times over, Ahmadinejad does not yet have his Button.

Jesus Christ, according to both presidents, is due very shortly, but in Ahmadinejad's vision the Nazarene will merely form a part of the entourage of a much grander personage – the Hidden Imam. Who is the Hidden Imam? In the year 873, the bloodline of the Prophet came to an end when Hasan al-Askari (in Shiism, the eleventh legitimate imam) died without an heir. At this point, among the believers, a classic circularity took hold. It was assumed that there must *be* an heir; there was no record of his existence, they reasoned, because extraordinary efforts had been made to conceal it; and extraordinary efforts had been made because this little boy would be an extraordinary imam – the Mahdi, in fact, or the Lord of Time.

In Shia eschatology the Mahdi will return during a period of great tribulation (during, say, a nuclear war), will deliver the faithful from injustice and oppression, and will then supervise the Day of Judgment. Not only Ahmadinejad but members of his cabinet have been giving the Hidden Imam 'about four years' – well within the president's second term. And where has the Hidden Imam dwelt since the ninth century? In 'occultation', wherever that may be. The Hidden Imam is at least intelligibly called the Lord of Time: he is 1,136 years old.

Rule number one: no theocracy can ever be permitted to get its hands on nuclear weapons. And Iran, we respectfully suggest, is not yet ready for the force that drives the sun. We all know what Ahmadinejad thinks of Israel (and we remember his Islamists' conference, in Tehran, on the historicity of the Holocaust). Yet this is what Ali Rafsanjani thinks of Israel – Rafsanjani, the old, much-jailed revolutionary chancer, a pragmatist and reformer, hugely worldly, hugely venal: 'The use of even one nuclear bomb inside Israel will destroy everything', whereas a counterstrike on Iran will merely 'harm' the Islamic world; 'it is not irrational to contemplate such an eventuality.' Indeed, given the Shia commitment to martyrdom, mutual assured destruction, as one Israeli official put it, 'is not a deterrent. It's an incentive.'

Nuclear weapons, it seems, were sent down here to furnish mankind with a succession of excruciating dilemmas. Until recently the mullahs' quest for the H-bomb seemed partly containable: the nuclear states could give face to Tehran, and begin to scale back their arsenals towards the zero option. But now those states include North Korea (already the land of the living dead); and the Islamic Republic, in any case, no longer seems appeasable. Equipped with weapons of fission or fusion, the supreme leader may delegate first use to Hizbollah, or to the Call of Islam, or to the Legion of the Pure. Or he may himself become the first suicide bomber to be gauged in megatons.

*

Meanwhile, the memory of the June Events, and of Neda Soltan, will do its work, and add weight to the mass of unendurable humiliations meted out to the Iranian people. Meanwhile, too, the senescent regime (I again warily predict) will reach beyond crackdownism for the supposedly unifying effects of war. Not a war against someone its own size, or someone bigger. Tiny Bahrain, which is 60 per cent Shia, looks about right.

As for apocalyptic Islamism, in all its forms, I cannot improve on the great Norman Cohn. This is from the 1995 foreword to *Warrant for Genocide* (1967), where the subject is the Tsarist fabrication *The Protocols of the Elders of Zion* and what Jewry calls the Shoa, or the Wind of Death:

> There exists a subterranean world where pathological fantasies disguised as ideas are churned out by crooks and half-educated fanatics [notably the lower clergy] for the benefit of the ignorant and superstitious. There are times when this underworld emerges from the depths and suddenly fascinates, captures and dominates multitudes of usually sane and responsible people, who thereupon take leave of sanity and responsibility. And it occasionally happens that this underworld becomes a political power and changes the course of history.

Guardian 2009

On Jeremy Corbyn, Leader of Her Majesty's Opposition

When I was a ten-year-old resident of Princeton, NJ, I used to crouch by the radio on Saturday mornings to hear the children's songs, and I was always anxiously hoping for 'Carbon the Copy Cat'. You can find an intriguing rendition of 'Carbon' on YouTube by Tex Ritter, a vocalist who could impart a touch of gravitas and woe to the simplest chant or lullaby. The version I thrilled to, in 1959, was much smoother and jollier; whereas Tex was a Texan, the 'cover' was the work of an unnamed Midwesterner, who pronounced Carbon 'Carbin' (cf. 'Wimbledin', 'commitmint', 'pregnint'). Is it any wonder, then, that I have been going around the place this summer singing Corbyn the Copy Cat?

The comparison is far from airtight, I admit, but the example of the Copy Cat still has much to teach us. In the song, Carbon is a bloody fool of a feline who wants to join, or at least to imitate, animals from other species.

> Like a sheep he tried to baa (baa, baa)
> Like a bird he tried to chirp (chirp, chirp)
> Like a dog he tried to bark (bark, bark).
> He tried and tried the best he knew how.
> It always came out meow, meow, meow.

Jeremy Corbyn learned to say meow early on in life (coached, at several removes, by a certain German economist); and it has never even occurred to him to try saying anything else.

We are exact contemporaries (born 1949, along with NATO); and for the lion's share of my twenties I found myself close to the epicentre of the Corbyn milieu. For I was on the staff of the *New Statesman* – attending party conferences, drinking with parliamentary correspondents, and playing regular games of cricket and football against *Tribune* and other loose confederations of the left. There were identikit Corbyns everywhere – right down to the ginger beard, the plump fountain pen in the top pocket, and the visible undervest, slightly discoloured in the family wash.

Weedy, nervy, and thrifty (you often saw a little folded purse full of humid small change), with an awkward-squad look about them (as if nursing a well-informed grievance), the Corbyns were in fact honest and good-hearted. Politically, they were the salt of the earth – 'those to whom', at some stage and on some level, 'the miseries of the world / Are misery, and will not let them rest' (John Keats). What the exponents of the old left were like humanly depended – with mathematical precision – on how doctrinaire they were. You sought the company of Alan Watkins and Mary Holland, among many others; you avoided the company of Corin Redgrave and Kika Markham (as well as the more driven Corbyns).

All this was during the later 1970s – the apogee and swansong of the old left. Harold Wilson's short third term after the interregnum of Ted Heath; James Callaghan (1976–79), and work-to-rule, the miners' strike (Arthur Scargill), the three-day week, plus a class war whose tremors you felt a dozen times a day; then came Margaret Thatcher (1979–90). Everyone was old left. It was generally felt at the *Statesman* that the proletariat deserved to win, this time: now there would at last be moral redress.

My closest office colleagues were old left too, with variations. I agreed with James Fenton, pretty much, when he calmly stated: 'I want a government that is weak against the trade unions.' Julian Barnes clashed with a certain *Staggers* hardliner when he revealed that he had once voted Liberal. That hardliner was Christopher Hitchens. Throughout his polemical career Christopher maintained his peculiar blend of irony and granite. When he came up to the books and arts department, there would always be an exchange of taunts and teases. 'You want rule by yobs,' I used to tell him: 'Not just rule in their interests and in their name – but rule *by* yobs.' 'That's it,' he'd answer, with his equivocating smile: 'I live for the day when the berks are finally in the saddle.'

It is one of the most saliently endearing facts about Christopher – that he never, ever, stopped loving Trotsky. Everyone else was old left too, though by then largely shorn of utopian romance. And everyone who looked in on the weekly editorial meetings, who dropped by with pieces entitled 'An End to Growth' and 'Whither the Closed Shop?', was Jeremy Corbyn. Or were they? Corbyn himself wouldn't have joined us, as all the others did, in the pub or in the Bung Hole wine bar (he's TT), nor in the Italian café where we all lunched on the full English breakfast (he's vegetarian). Then, too, the bods who came to Great Turnstile were, once you got to know them, congenial types who, in addition, could put an argument together on paper, often with some panache. And Jeremy? After thirty-odd years as a safe-seat backbencher (Islington North), Corbyn is the fluky beneficiary of a drastic elevation. So it is time to take a serious look at his flaws.

*

First, he is undereducated. Which is one way of putting it. His schooling dried up when he was eighteen, at which point he had two E-grade A-levels to his name; he started a course at North London Polytechnic, true, where he immersed himself in trade union studies, but dropped out after a year. And that was that. Corbyn says he enjoys 'reading and writing' (listing them, I thought, as if they were hobbies, like potholing and trainspotting); to my eyes, he doesn't have the eager aura of an autodidact. It is a fair guess that his briefcase, or his satchel, contains nothing but manifestos and position papers. In general, his intellectual CV gives an impression of slow-minded rigidity; and he seems essentially incurious about anything beyond his immediate sphere.

Second, he is humourless. Many journalists have remarked on this, usually in a tone of wry indulgence. In fact it is an extremely grave accusation, imputing as it does a want of elementary nous. To put it crassly, the humourless man is a joke – and a joke he will never get. When he was collared by a TV team and asked to say something about Tony Blair's wearily witty attacks on him, Corbyn straightened up and said he would respond only to 'substantive' questions. In his face there was not the slightest glint of amusement or defiance or spirit. And Blair's criticisms contained plenty that was 'substantive', including the charge that everything Corbyn says, without exception, is pallidly third-hand – his championship, for instance, of Clause 4 (on public ownership), which was first formulated in 1918. 'I don't do personal,' Corbyn has explained, shoring up one's surmise that he is 'modern' only in the up-to-date vulgarity of his syntax. When he found himself arguing for a UK where every house has a garden, Corbyn elaborated as follows: 'Anyone who wants to be a beekeeper should be a beekeeper.' Nobody with a sense of humour could possibly have said that.

Third, he has no grasp of the national character – an abysmal deficit for any politician, let alone a torchbearer. The idea of dismantling Trident looks set to gain a clear plurality on practical grounds; but his proposal to leave NATO ('a Cold War organisation'), and so paralyse the special relationship, causes only exasperated tedium in London and suspicious dismay in Washington. As for his proposal to scrap the army (last articulated in 2012): this would be a veritable spear through the British soul. It shows an indifference to both the past and the future. Philip Larkin spoke for the country, as he often did (it is both a strength and a weakness), in 'Homage to a Government' (1969):

> Next year we shall be living in a country
> That brought its soldiers home for lack of money.
> The statues will be standing in the same
> Tree-muffled squares, and look nearly the same.
> Our children will not know it's a different country.

The national character contains nationalism, naturally; and the British temper is above all gradualist. Enormous powers of suasion are needed to induce an electorate to waive what it values most, which is continuity.

Turning to Corbyn's foreign policies – well, here I'll deal only with the thing they call IT (international terrorism). When at last he managed to make himself clear about what he hoped would happen in the Middle East, Corbyn's vaunted 'friendship' with Hamas and Hizbollah became roughly intelligible. Far more damningly and tellingly, he often implied that July 7, 2005, was an act of revenge, a calibrated tit-for-tat, for the invasion of Iraq. We see here the dismally reflexive mental habit of seeking moral 'equivalence' at every opportunity; thus the glitteringly murderous theists of Isis are indistinguishable from the coalition troops in Falluja. And heed his Churchillian call for 'political compromise' with Abu Bakr al-Baghdadi and his genocidaires in Raqqa and Mosul.

*

Generously equipped with the demerits – the encysted dogmas – of the old left, Corbyn nonetheless gawkily embodies one of its noblest themes: the search for something a little bit better than what exists today: more equal, more gentle, more just.

If, as every commentator seems to agree, the current Corbyn is obviously unelectable, then in what direction will he be obliged to move? The recruitment of Seumas Milne (a far-left intellectual) as media manager changes nothing, though it does defer the prospect of a slicked-up, business-friendly Corbyn with a new suit and a new smile. That was always close to inconceivable. It is far easier to imagine a Labour party that devolves for now into a leftist equivalent of the American GOP: hopelessly retrograde, self-absorbed, self-pitying, and self-righteous, quite unembarrassed by its (years-long) tantrum, necessarily and increasingly hostile to democracy, and in any sane view undeserving of a single vote. Under him, the Labour Party is no longer Her Majesty's Opposition. There is no opposition; Labour is out of the game.

For all his charming insecurities, Carbon the Copy Cat boldly roamed the rural farmsteads, and showed an ardent interest in the exotic, the other – the mooing cows, the clucking hens, the quacking ducks. In contrast to the coal-black Carbon, Corbyn is a marmalade cat, homebound, perched like a tea cosy on the kitchen radiator, and contentedly wedded to the things he already knows.

Sunday Times 2015

The Crippled Murderers of Cali, Colombia

1. EXIT WOUND

It was a *bala perdida* that almost did for little Kevin: the stray bullet went in through his nape and came out through his brow. That was a year ago, when he was four. The incident took place a few yards from where we now sat: in a front room that felt like a car-less garage, with its damp cement floor, and a series – almost a pattern – of scorched light fixtures along its walls and ceiling. Kevin's grandmother runs a modest line in second-hand clothes; there was a stretched wire with some coat hangers on it, and a plastic bag stuffed with espadrilles and flip-flops. The family dog, small, frazzled, and elderly, was still growling at us after half an hour, even while scratching its ear with a raised hind paw.

Kevin was playing in the street when the car sped by (it never became clear to me what, if anything, the *muchachos* were trying to hit). At the hospital, his twenty-year-old mother was told that Kevin had five minutes to live. They operated; and, after a five-day coma, a silent and unsmiling spell in a wheelchair, and a course of rehabilitation, Kevin seems to have re-emerged as a confident, even a stylish little boy.

For months Kevin was deeply withdrawn; he responded only listlessly to other children, and was indifferent to adults. When he divided his toy soldiers into goodies and baddies, the baddies always won.

*

What happened to Kevin was an accident: an accident in a very accident-prone city, but an accident. Another child, ten-year-old Bryan, will find it harder to gain the (in fact nonexistent) consolation of 'closure'. He was shot in the back by his best friend. Bryan's offence? It wasn't as if he threatened to take his football home – all he did was say he didn't want to play any more. Bryan now has a palsied gait (a slow, bobbing hop) and a face deprived of symmetry; and he looks blind, too (though he isn't), because his gaze seeks nothing. Kevin, on the other hand, amiably complied when his grandmother, parting his hair and lifting his fringe, showed me the entry wound, the exit wound; they looked like vaccination scars. As we took our leave, the dog gave us an eloquent snarl: good riddance to bad rubbish. The dog, it seemed, had taken on the fear and distrust that ought to belong to Kevin.

In the forecourt of the house opposite, a fully adult male (statistically quite a rarity in this neighbourhood) was closing up his house for the night; he stared at us with frank but nonspecific hostility, all the while rearranging the contents of his crimson running shorts.

Some residents try to disguise it with fancy grilles and lattices, but most of the houses in non-downtown Cali are wholly and candidly encaged. The male adult across the street now proceeded to wall himself up in his personal penitentiary. In El Distrito, the boys rage all night and sleep all day (in their coffins and crypts); and at dusk they all turn into vampires.

We always had to be out by five – but wait. There was still time to visit Ana Milena. Some years ago her sister had been paralysed after being shot in the throat by a neighbour; she died of depression and self-starvation in 1997. Seven years later, Ana broke up with her boyfriend. So he attacked her in broad daylight at a bus stop, stabbing her in the navel, the neck, and twice in the head. Their daughter (then nearly three) stood and watched, and hid her face. She still insists that her mother was hit by a car.

Gang slang for a home-made gun is *una pacha*: a baby bottle. The violence starts at once and doesn't go away. Kevin's scars are not at all disfiguring. He has an entry wound and an exit wound. His was easily the most hopeful story I heard in Cali. In general, you assent to the existence of entry wounds; but when you consider the effects – emotional, psychological, and (almost always) physical – you doubt the existence of exit wounds. The thing is never over.

2. LA ESPERANZA

Occupying about a quarter of Colombia's third city, Aguablanca (Whitewater) consists of about 130 barrios; each barrio has two or three gangs, and all the gangs are theoretically at war with all the others. What do they fight about? They don't fight about drugs (ecstasy and dope are universally popular, but the cocaine trade is reserved for the criminally mature). They fight about turf (a corner, a side street); they fight about anything at all to do with disrespect (what might be called 'eyebrow' clashes); and they fight about the fight that went before (*venganza* operates like a series of chain letters).

Yet the main fuel of the murder figures, here as elsewhere, is the fantastic plenitude of weaponry. A home-made gun costs just over £20, a hand grenade just over £12 (a hand grenade is what you'll be needing if, for instance, you gatecrash a party and get turned away). 'Guns don't kill people. People kill people,' argued Ronald Reagan. You could take this line further, and say that people don't kill people either. Bullets kill people. In Cali they cost fifty cents each, and can be sold to minors individually, like cigarettes.

Three teenage girls, acting as the representatives of a barrio called El Barandal (The Rail), advised us not to enter; but a couple of hundred yards further down the road, at La Esperanza (Hope), we were casually welcomed. I asked what had made the difference, and our driver said that El Barandal was even poorer and dirtier and, crucially, fuller; there was more humiliation, more wrath, and more guns. Sara, the friendliest of the Esperanzans, had a different emphasis: '*Somos todos negros, y somos buena gente.*' We're all black, and we're good people. And good people they would need to be.

Every South American country has its own name for places like this. In Bogotá the word is *tugurio* (hovel), but the Chilean version best evokes La Esperanza: *callampa* (mushroom). 'Whitewater' suggests a fast-flowing river, or even foaming rapids. The marshlands where the barrios sprouted up, in the 1980s, are now whitened by their own putrefaction. The endless ditch isn't deep enough to submerge the tubs and tyres that disturb its caustic mantle. Yet the egrets still consider it worth their while to paddle in it and peck in it; when they flap their wings you expect them to fly off on half-corroded stilts.

The people here are *desplazados*, displaced peasants, mainly from the country's Pacific coast. Cali contains about 70,000 of the displaced. Some are pushed from the land by that irresistible modern force, urbanisation; others are fleeing what may be the final convulsions of a civil war that began in 1948. But here they are, with no money and no jobs. Colombia does not provide free health care or free education for its citizens; and the first explanation you reach for is the enormous South American lacuna – taxation. Taxation, necessarily of the rich, is not enforced. To paraphrase the former president Lleras Camargo, Latin Americans have gone to jail for many strange reasons, but not one, in the whole continent, has ever gone to jail for tax fraud.

Of the four houses I ducked into at La Esperanza, Sara's, counter-intuitively, was easily the worst. Your first step took you on to a nail bed of chipped, upward-pointing tiles on bare soil: this was clearly a work in progress, but for a moment it felt like a booby trap. Then a communal area, and a dorm of crushed cots. Then, finally, out towards the water, a kitchen-bathroom, with lots of exposed (and ingenious) plumbing, a hotplate, a heap of compost in the corner and a largely ornamental fridge with four eggs in its ever-open door. A huge negress, already stripped to the waist, pushed past us and disappeared into a wooden wigwam. There came a gush of water and a burst of song.

Outside, the ladies laugh, and playfully squabble about whose house is the prettiest. La Esperanza's lone shop has only a handwritten sign on its door, saying *no fio* (no credit), and sells only tobacco and starch, but the residents call it their *supermercado*. As for the rancid water, into which the barrio seems about to collapse – you just tell yourself, said Sara, that it's a nice sea view.

Colombia has the Atlantic on its right shoulder and the Pacific on its left (and its neck goes straight to Panama). It also straddles the equator. At noon, on a clear day, your shadow writhes around your shoes like a cat. We paid our visit on one of the cooler mornings (the clouds were the same colour as the water); and it was onerous to imagine the barrio under a sky-filling sun. Just back down the road, at the entry point to Aguablanca, the smell of the blighted canal, with its banks of solid rubbish, grips you by the tonsils. This smell is La Esperanza's future.

3. STAG NIGHT

The classic *venganza*, in Cali gangland, is not a bullet through the head but a bullet through the base of the spine. Some thought has gone into this. 'One month after the attack,' says Roger Micolta, the young therapist from Médecins Sans Frontières (MSF), 'the victims ask me, "Will

I ever walk?" Two months after, they ask me, "Will I ever fuck?"' The answer to both questions is invariably no. Thus the victims not only have to live with their wound – they have to wear it, they have to wheel it; and everybody knows that they have lost what made them men.

At the municipal hospital in Aguablanca, at therapy time in the mid-afternoons, crippled innocents, like limping Bryan, are outnumbered by crippled murderers – by cripples who have done much crippling of their own. They go through interminable sets of exercises: pull-ups, sideways rolls. Girlfriends and sisters take hairbrushes to their legs, to encourage sensation. One young man, inching along the parallel bars, keeps freezing and closing his eyes in helpless despair. Another has a weight strapped to his ankle; he is watched by his mother, who reflexively swings her own leg in time with his.

In the back room there is a storyboard used for psychosexual counselling. '*Lo mas frustrante: estar impotente. No poder sentir, no comprension, no tener ganas.*' (to be unable to feel, to understand, to have no desire.) The MSF educational posters, too, rightly and aggressively zero in on the question of testosterone. A typical specimen shows a pistol with its shaft curling into a droop: 'To carry a gun doesn't make you a man.' Another shows a series of waistbands with the gun positioned behind the belt buckle and pointing straight downwards. In Cali, all the stuff you have ever read or heard about male insecurity, phallic symbols, and so on, is almost tediously verified, everywhere you look.

*

Nearby, in the market streets, the shops are disconcertingly full of goods, essentials and nonessentials – cheap cameras, exercise gear, shower organisers (an item badly needed in La Esperanza). The armless, headless mannequins are faithful to the indigenous female type: high and prominent backsides, hefty breasts with nipples the size of drawer pulls. At the patisserie there is an elaborate cake representing a thonged *muchacha*. Another represents a penis. The testicles are hirsute with squiggles of chocolate; the blancmange-hued helmet bears a thin swipe of cream, appreciatively indicating the slit. A hen-night item, you might suppose. The inscription says '*Chupame, cario,*' in a toilingly decorative hand (suck me, honey). There is no female form for it in Spanish – no *caria*. But you wonder. In Cali, maybe the tackle cake is meant for the stags.

That night there was a cookout on a downtown rooftop. Our fellow guests were professionals, academics; there was music and some dancing – very chaste and technical. Yet even here a sexual trap door can open up beneath you. At one point a young woman began an innocent conversation with a handsome young guest, and after some joking in male undertones she was grinningly handed a paper napkin. The suggestion was that she would now be able to wipe away her drool.

All the outer walls around us were topped by spikes of glass, varying dramatically in size, shape, and thickness. If glass-topped walls constitute a kind of architecture, then here we had it in its gothic phase. In Britain this form of crime prevention was a very frequent (and very stimulating) sight in my childhood – but not in my youth. Again and again you kept vaguely thinking: two or three generations, forty or fifty years – that's how far back they are. Just now, Colombia seems to be poised to turn from oligarchy to something more progressive. If there is a current theme in the evolution of South America, it appears to be this: the vested interests (very much including the United States) are tolerating an improvement in the calibre of the political leaders, with Kirchner in Argentina, Lula in Brazil, and now, perhaps, Uribe in Colombia.

Beyond the shard-studded walls you could see an entire mountainside of lights. This was the *callampa* of Siloe, which, I am told, is roughly twice as violent as Aguablanca.

4. THE CENTRAL DIVIDE

We were on the central divide of the dual carriageway, about 300 yards from one of the most decidedly non-enterable barrios. Three *muchachos* approached. When I offered Marlboros, I got two takers; they lowered their heads as they smoked, embarrassed by the fact that they didn't inhale. The third boy declined. He didn't say '*No fumo*', he said '*No puedo fumar*'. It wasn't that he didn't smoke. He couldn't smoke – much as he'd like to.

Then he lifted his T-shirt and showed us why. His right shoulder, his right breast and his right armpit, where he had recently been shot, formed an unmade bed of bandages and brown sticky tape. He had recently been stabbed too, and with a vengeance. From his sternum to his navel ran the wound, not yet a scar, pink and plump, like a garden worm.

He turned out to be a patient of Roger Micolta's (one of the less tractable). His name was John Anderson. This was by no means the first time he had been shot, nor the first time he had been stabbed. He was sixteen.

Like everyone else, they were keen to be photographed, but first they had to go and get their weapon. After rooting around in a rubbish dump across the road, they returned with a sawn-off shotgun. John posed, with his flintlock, his knife wound (like an attempt at vertical seppuku), his stupidly wonky hairstyle, his trigger-happy stare. Abruptly you were struck by the thinness and inanity of it: an existence so close to nonexistence.

It couldn't have been clearer that John Anderson had only weeks to live. To say this of human beings is to say both the best and the worst. They can get used to anything.

5. THE LESS-INTERESTING CRIPPLED MURDERER

And I got used to it too. You find yourself thinking: if I had to live in El Distrito, I wouldn't stay at Kevin's but at Ana Milena's, where they have cable TV and that nice serving hatch from the kitchen to the living room. And if I had to live in La Esperanza, I would gently but firmly refuse Sara's offer and try to bribe myself into the place four houses along, where the man has a working fridge and a working fan (and ten dependents). Similarly, I now found myself thinking: you know, *this* crippled murderer isn't nearly as interesting as the crippled murderer I interviewed the day before yesterday. And so it seemed. Raul Alexander was nothing much, compared to Mario.

When we called, Raul was lying on his bed watching *The Simpsons*. In Kevin's house, in Ana's house, in Sara's house, there were never any young men. When there is a young man in the house, it's because he can't walk away from it. He will certainly be a cripple, and very probably a crippled murderer.

With his buzz-cut hair and ingenuous little face, Raul looked like the kind of waiter you might grow fond of at a resort hotel. It sounds tactless, but the truth was that we were settling for Raul. We had hoped for Alejandro. Alejandro was the crippled murderer who, in his prime, couldn't get to sleep at night if he hadn't killed someone earlier that day.

But we'd already skipped an appointment with Alejandro, more than once, and when we did appear his mother told us he had taken the dog to the vet. Was this a particularly savage Latino anathema, or just a weak excuse? I thought of the gang verb *groseriar* (*no respetar*). And it was a relief, in the end, to make do with Raul.

Asked about his childhood, he described it as *normal*, which it seemed to be, except for a father who remained in situ well into Raul's teens. He started stealing car parts, then cars, then cars with people inside them. 'One on Monday, one on Thursday.' Then he got competitive with a friend: there would now be six armed carjackings a day. He started stealing money that was on its way to or from shops, factories, banks. He did nine months in prison and emerged, predictably fortified. By now the bank deliveries were oversubscribed, with queues of blaggers in the street; so Raul started venturing within. These weekly capers were not to last. He did thirty months, came out for three days, and went back in for three years. During his last stretch, Raul killed a man, for the first time, he claimed: payback for a stabbing.

Blooded, his bones made, Raul took a job in an office. That last sentence may look slightly odd to a non-Caleo, but when someone around here says that they worked in an office or did 'office work', you know exactly what they did: they sat by a phone, on a retainer (£250 a month), and did targeted assassinations through an agent for a further £100 a time. Boys who work in offices, incidentally, are not called 'office boys', so far as I know, but boys, very young boys, are valued in office work, because they are cheap, fearless, and unimprisonable till the age of eighteen. Raul would at this stage have been in his twenties. The most popular day for office murders, incidentally, is Sunday: that's when people are most likely to be found at home.

Raul's downfall? By this point my faith in his veracity, or in his self-awareness, never high, began to dwindle. How did he tell it? He had some trouble with a guy who shot his cousin, a murder that a friend of his (Raul's) impulsively avenged. There was this consignment of marijuana. Raul circled and meandered, and it all seemed to come down to *una problema*, a poker game, a spilt drink – an 'eyebrow' *venganza*.

We took our leave of Raul Alexander heartlessly early (one of us had to get to the airport), and filed through a sunny nook containing his wheelchair and his walking frame. When, minutes earlier, I asked him how many people he had killed, he pouted and shrugged and said:

'Ocho?' You thought: oh, sure. But even if Raul was dividing his score by two, or by ten, he was nothing much, compared to Mario.

6. MARIO

He, too, is lying on his bed – apparently naked but for a pale-blue towel draped over his waist. The reproductions on the wall of the adjacent sitting room – a wide-eyed young princess, a wooden cottage near a water-fall, a forest with a white horse picked out by opalescent sunbeams – prompt you, in describing Mario, to seek the heroic frame. You think of the fallen Satan, hurled over the crystal battlements. Mario was once very radiant and dynamic; but he has made the journey from power to no-power, and now he lies on his bed all day with his clicker and his Cartoon Network.

Although the long legs are tapering and atrophying, Mario's upper body still ripples. The armpits, in particular, are unusually pleasing; they look shaved or bikini-waxed, but a glance at the half-naked relative in the kitchen, who has his hands clasped behind his head, confirms that the abbreviation is natural. Mario's trouble, his difficulty, begins with his face. With its close-set eyes divided by a shallow bridge, its very strong jaw (full of avidity and appetite), Mario's is the face of a mandrill. If you'd seen Raul Alexander coming for you, on the street, in a bar, or standing in your doorway, you would have tried to resist him, or reason with him, or buy him off. If you'd seen Mario coming for you, in his pomp, you wouldn't have done anything at all.

As a seven-year-old, he hid under a cloth-covered table and listened while nine peasants, two of them women, killed his father. Mario is now about thirty years old: this would have happened during the period known as *La Violencia* (though there is barely a period of Colombian history that could not be so called). When he was twelve he made a start on his *venganzas*, killing the first of the nine peasants with a knife. He then went on to kill the other eight. Then he gravitated to Cali. That's who they are in Aguablanca, in Siloe: peasants, and now the children of peasants, drastically citified.

After a spell in carjacking, then in kidnapping (a vast field), Mario was called up for military service. On his discharge he took his improved organisational skills and 'went to the woods', supervising the production and transfer of *talco* (cocaine) in rural Colombia and in Ecuador. This was itself a kind of military tour; your adversary was not the police but the army.

Mario speaks of his time in the woods with fondness and awe. 'The cocaine came in blocks, all stamped – very pretty [*muy bonita*], how it shines [*como brilla*],' he says. 'Once I saw a whole *room* full of money.'

He came back to Cali, equipped with discipline, esprit and (one imagines) a ton of pesos, and started 'enjoying life'. It is not hard to imagine Mario enjoying life: in a city full of terrifying men, he would have been universally feared. He took a job in an office, and in this capacity he killed about 150 people in six years. But that's a lot of *venganza* to be storing up, and in December 2003 they came for him in force. He was at a stoplight when four men on two motorbikes pulled up on either side of the car.

★

Now Mario's sister served coffee – a profound improvement on the Tizer and Dandelion & Burdock you are usually offered in Colombia. It seems deeply typical of Aguablanca that there is never any coffee; you trudge from place to place whining for a cup.

Time to go. I asked Mario to describe the difference between his first murder and his last, and he said: 'The first, with the knife? It was awful. I had bad dreams. I cried all day. I had paranoia. But the last time? *Nada*. You do it and you just think, "Now I get paid."'

Mario called for his cloudy trophies, and lay half-immersed in them: his handgun (very heavy – to its wielder it must have had the divine heaviness of gold), his X-rays (the lucent second bullet in the arched thorax), and his stainless police record (which cost him £750). He also had his clicker, his clock, and, of course, his transparent wallet of urine, taped to the side of the bed.

They are still after Mario, so it was a double deliverance to get out of his house. When I thought about it later, though, it seemed to me that Mario, with his provenance, was entitled to his hate; and that the non-monstrous Raul, with his slight frame and his bellhop's smile, was the more representative figure – a leaf in the wind of the peer group.

Machismo, in its Latin American mutation, has one additional emphasis, that of indifference – unreachable indifference. You felt that indifference very strongly with John Anderson, the sixteen-year-old on the central divide. Any kind of empathy is not just enfeebling – it is effeminate. You have no empathy even for yourself.

So it appears that the Aguablancans are playing a children's game – kids' stuff – of dare and taunt and posture, in which they all feel immortal. Except that the sticks and stones are now knives and guns and hand grenades.

As you drive back into the heart of the city, you see boys – jugglers – performing for the spectators who sit wedged in their cars. They are not juggling with clubs or oranges, but with machetes and brands of fire.

7. THE RETURN OF DEATH

On my last day I went to the MSF exhibition of photographs and case histories. There were familiar names and faces: Ana Milena, little Kevin. On the night the exhibition opened, all the featured victims attended, except Edward Ignacio. Still recovering from his multiple panga wounds, Edward was shot dead earlier that day.

From there to the cemetery in the middle of town, a small, crowded plot of land between the football ground and the busy Texaco. Its entrance was almost submerged by roadworks: a steamroller, a cement mixer, hillocks of hot tar. Tradesmen had gathered with soft drinks and ice cream. A storm was coming, and you could smell the moisture in the dust.

The cemetery was more like a morgue than a graveyard, with the dead stacked into a series of thick blocks, each berth not much bigger than a paving stone. Every panel had something written on it (at the minimum just the name and the year of interment) in Magic Marker; others were more elaborate, with framed photographs, poems, avowals ('*yo te quiero*'), figurines, crosses, hearts, angels. We had come with a woman called Marleny Lopez. Her husband was one of the few who had been buried in the earth. The tombstone gave his name and dates, Edilson Mora, 1965–1992. This was an engraver's mistake. Edilson was in fact thirty-seven when he died, two years ago. He was playing dominoes with a policeman, and he won. This was perhaps survivable; but then the loser had to pay for the beers.

Most of the other dates showed a shorter span than Edilson's: 1983–2001, 1991–2003. On the whole they got longer as you moved deeper in and further back in time. Further back in time, too, the names ceased to be Anglophone. And so went Diesolina, Arcelio, Hortencia, Bartolomé, Nieves, Santiago, Yolima, Abelardo, Luz, Paz ...

*

I returned from one of the back alleys and found myself in the middle of a burial service. There was a coffin, with four bearers, and scores of people had come to mourn. This wasn't a gang slaying, a drive-by, a *bala perdida*. A woman had died of a heart attack at the age of twenty-eight: 1976–2004.

What happened next happened suddenly. I had spent the recent days making believe that death didn't matter. Now a bill was presented to me. I felt – suddenly inconsolable. It was a great chastisement to see the bitter weeping of the husband, the bitter weeping of the mother. It was a great chastisement, long overdue, to see death reassuming its proper weight.

Sunday Times 2005

Literature – 3

Philip Roth Finds Himself

Roth Unbound by Claudia Roth Pierpont

American anti-Semitism, which was running a high fever throughout the 1930s, steadily heated up after the onset of war. During the entire period, polls showed, well over a third of the populace stood ready to back discriminatory laws. Nor was this a mere offshoot of the general xenophobia spawned by isolationism. Every synagogue in Washington Heights was desecrated (and some were smeared with swastikas); in Boston, beatings, wreckings, and defilements had become near-daily occurrences by 1942. This woeful delirium, which ruled out all but a trickle of immigration and so cost countless lives, reached its historic apogee in 1944. The Holocaust proper began in the summer of 1941, and was fitfully winding itself down by the beginning of 1945 – thus the temperature surge in the American temper exactly coincided with it.

And what of the media? News of the mass killings of Jews emerged in May/June 1942: a verified report with a figure of 700,000 already dead. The *Boston Globe* gave the story the three-column headline 'Mass Murders of Jews in Poland Pass 700,000 Mark', and tucked it away at the foot of page 12. The *New York Times* quoted the report's verdict – 'probably the greatest mass slaughter in history' – but gave it only two inches. We may venture to say that such reticence is slightly surprising, given that the historiography of the events outlined above now runs to many tens of thousands of volumes.

Philip Roth would use this soiled and callous backdrop in *The Plot Against America* (2004), his twenty-sixth book; but anti-Semitism and its corollary, anti-anti-Semitism, wholly dominated the publication of his first, *Goodbye, Columbus and Five Short Stories* (1959). 'What is being done to silence this man?' asked a rabbi. 'Medieval Jews would have known what to do with him.' Roth's cheerful debut, some thought, shored up the same 'conceptions ... as ultimately led to the murder of six million in our time'. So he wasn't only contending with a 'rational' paranoia; he was also ensnared in the ongoing anguish of comprehension and absorption, as the sheer size of the trauma inched into consciousness. After a hate-filled public meeting at Yeshiva University in New York in 1962, Roth solemnly swore (over a pastrami sandwich) that he would 'never write about Jews again'.

It was a hollow vow. But Roth, remember, was still in his twenties; and one of the snags of starting young is that you're obliged to do your growing up in public. He was a proud American, as well as a Jew; a robustly bloody-minded talent, such as his, would have known at once that fiction insists on freedom: that, indeed, fiction *is* freedom, and freedom is indivisible (hence, later on, his passionate support for the writers of Czechoslovakia). Still, it could be argued that with one thing and another Roth took about fifteen years to settle into his voice. The later career was conventional; the early career was wildly eccentric – a mysterious and fascinating flail.

Claudia Roth Pierpont (no relation), in her lively and clever monograph, says that Roth's first full-length novel, *Letting Go* (1962), is 'about *not* letting go': not letting go of responsibility, obligation, a general frowning, crew-necked earnestness – and, importantly, not letting go of Henry James. Here, the large cast is pluralist; but ethnic anxieties seemed to linger. So what next? Well, at this point Roth put aside a book called 'Jewboy', and after 'years of misery' (five of them) produced *When She Was Good*, a straight-faced, all-goy saga set in a prim and mannerly Midwestern town. And here we were given our first real glimpse of the succubus that was eating his soul.

I remember thinking at the time that there was something extreme and frighteningly inordinate about the heroine, Lucy Nelson (she is adhesive, devouring, remorseless); I remember thinking, too, that she was only a part of an untold story. It is a profound portrait – flaringly alive in a book that often struggles for breath. Critics said that *When She Was Good* could have been written by a woman, others that it could have been written by a WASP (Sherwood Anderson, perhaps). Still, what the reader was looking for, around then, was a novel that could only have been written by Philip Roth.

That novel was *Portnoy's Complaint* (1969) – a time bomb of cawing, stinging comedy (it is even typographically explosive, setting the aggregate record, in mainstream fiction, for exclamation marks, block caps, and italics). Here the tensions and conflicts of the Jewish-American experience are reduced to their core: shiksas. The word's Yiddish root means 'detested thing'; by matrilineal logic, male gentiles are tolerable suitors for Jewish girls, but for Jewish boys shiksas spell a) apostate off-spring and b) assimilation, and shiksas are therefore taboo. Forbidden, detested – and all the more hotly desired. Roth attacked this crux with incomparable energy; and it seemed that a turbulent and directionless talent had finally found perfect pitch.

Now the story becomes strange, becomes passing strange. *Portnoy*, readers assumed, was Roth's real letting-go. But it turned out there was something else, and something quite intrinsic, to be let go of. Having ceased to care about that chimera called 'good taste' (a shallow con-sensus of the *bien pensant*), Roth ceased to care about literary value. He ceased to care about Henry James. *Our Gang*, written in 'a mere three months', is a grimly unfunny satire of the Nixon administration ('Trick E. Dixon'?); *The Breast*, written in 'a few weeks', transforms its hero into a giant mammary gland (an abnormally unpromising donnée); and *The Great American Novel*, 382 pages about baseball, is a hobbyist's exercise in virtuoso facetiousness. It was, you might say, remarkably bold: in tight succession, 1971, 1972, 1973, Roth – clearly something of a genius – pulled off three unqualified duds.

★

The lurid light surrounding Lucy Nelson, the five-year hiatus, the sense of an unaired wound, the mad cackle of *Portnoy*, the revolt against high seriousness and the embrace of frivolity: now the answers started com-ing in with *My Life as a Man* (1974). This tells the tale of Roth's 'horrific' first marriage and its aftermath, a relationship that began in 1956 and ended only with an accidental death in 1968. It is a novel you read between the fingers of the hand you keep raising to your face. The cen-tral puzzle is that Roth evidently colluded in his own entrapment; and the explanation, as his proxy in *My Life*, Peter Tarnopol, puts it, is that 'literature got me into this'. The attraction to difficulty, to complexity, even to agony is real enough in an intensely bookish young man; there are numerous instances of writers who hunt down the most fantastic entanglements; they make misery their muse, or they try. So the dud triptych – *Our Gang*, *The Breast*, *The Great American Novel* – can be re-garded as Roth's vandalous revenge on the literary.

He had found his subject, which is to say he had found himself. And the self, seen through an intricate mesh of personae, doppelgängers and noms de guerre, would provide the framework (with a couple of exceptions) for his remaining nineteen novels. John Updike once argued that although fiction can withstand any amount of egocentricity, it is wholly allergic to narcissism. There is no narcissism in Roth; the creature in the mirror is given merciless and unblinking scrutiny. Updike again: 'Who *cares* what it's like to be a writer?' The short answer is, We care, for all sorts of reasons, when that writer is Jewish. (Jewish-American literature is above all *new*: it began with Saul Bellow, circa 1950.) And Updike appeared to concede the point when he created Henry Bech, giving his Jewish writer three full-length excursions (and wistfully awarding him the Nobel Prize).

Portnoy was described in *Haaretz* as 'the book for which all anti-Semites have been praying', more toxic even than that (ridiculous) fabrication *The Protocols of the Elders of Zion*. But over the years the job of chorically attacking Philip Roth, increasingly skimped by Jewry, has been taken up by Feminism. Pierpont conscientiously deals with these objections as and when they arise, rightly pointing out that Roth's women cover a very broad range. But I think the charge of misogyny, etc., is just a straightforward category error. As with the rabbinical critique, there is some historical justification, but both are sociopolitical, not literary; they are in fact anti-literary. Besides, isn't women's fiction crammed with male louts and rats? Isn't men's? The right-on heroine (a harp-playing, corporation-running mother of five, say, with an enlightened husband and a virile young lover called Raoul) is of no conceivable interest to any genuine writer; besides, she is well-represented in any number of admiring narratives – and you can get all you want of them at the airport.

★

Roth Unbound is a critical biography of the old school, though one invaluably topped up with reported comments and judgments from the Philip Roth of today. Eighty years old, and 'done' with writing (or so he says), he comes across as droll, sagacious, securely self-deprecating (of the early books and the early marriage), relaxed, high-spirited, and warm. By the end one consents to the verdict of the Roth impersonator in *Operation Shylock* (1993), who says to the 'real' Roth:

But your eyes melt a little too, you know. I know the things you've done for people. You hide your sweet side from the public – all the glowering photographs and I'm-nobody's-sucker interviews. But behind the scenes, as I happen to know, you're one very soft touch, Mr Roth.

The corpus, it seems, is now complete. Roth tends to divide opinion – because high originality is, and should be, fairly tough to digest. Apart from *Portnoy* and the balefully powerful *My Life as a Man*, there are, by my count, three further magna opera. I am thinking of the lapidary burnish of *The Ghost Writer* (1979), the daunting intellectual rigour of *The Counterlife* (1986), and the lush Victorian amplitude of *American Pastoral* (1997). And, throughout, there are certain motifs that unfailingly ignite Roth's eloquence: Israel; ageing and mortality; sickness and suffering; this whole business with parents; and, most surprisingly, this whole business with children.

In *Sabbath's Theater* (1995), the rebarbative hero is shamefaced about having once had a wife, and consoles himself with the thought that at least he never had a child – he's not *that* stupid. Novelists don't always need to try things out for themselves (and believing otherwise brought him his 'Lucy Nelson' and twelve blighted years). Here we see the routine and elementary miracle of fiction. Look at Swede Levov and Merry in *American Pastoral*. You can write beautifully about children without having had any; you simply apply to the surrogate mother of the imagination.

New York Times Book Review 2013

Roth the Elder: A Moralistic Investigation

The Dying Animal by Philip Roth

The most significant page in any novel precedes the text and is tradition-
ally headed 'By the same author.' *Goodbye Columbus* (1959), of course,
lacked such a page, but the absence was still eloquent: it told us that an
original and menacing intelligence now roamed the land. Philip Roth
has recently been tampering with his introductory CV. Instead of simply listing his publications in sequence, he has corralled them into four
different sections: Zuckerman Books, Roth Books, Kepesh Books, and
Other Books. Well, you think, the author is approaching his seventieth
year; perhaps there is an urge to codify the corpus and to prompt the
pens of the dissertators. Later it strikes you that Roth has done away
with chronological order. His fiction, and his talent, are defying time.

It is in the Kepesh Books section that *The Dying Animal* belongs,
together with *The Professor of Desire* and (fittingly) *The Breast*. Actually
The Breasts, plural, would have served perfectly well for the new novella.
In the earlier book David Kepesh, then a young academic, is metamor-
phosed not into a beetle (or, in one Kafka translation, 'into a monstrous
vermin') but into a giant mammary gland. In *The Dying Animal*, which
is social-realist in genre, Kepesh merely becomes obsessed with the contents of a particular brassiere. And toward the end, horribly and harrow-
ingly, those breasts are fated to be reduced to the singular.

Unlike Roth, Kepesh is seventy already. As the book opens he is
looking back on an affair that began nearly a decade earlier. It lasted a
year and a half and took twice that long to recover from. The owner of
the brassiere, which is exhaustively established as 'a D cup' – 'powerful,
beautiful breasts', 'gorgeous breasts', 'really big, beautiful breasts', 'the
most gorgeous breasts I have ever seen', 'they're so beautiful, her breasts.
I cannot say it often enough' – is a bourgeois Cuban-American called

Consuela, and she is, or was, twenty-four. This is not a book (and this is not a book review) for leg men, or for butt men, or for prudes.

Kepesh is mainly a radio and TV pundit nowadays, but he still does a senior seminar called Practical Criticism. 'I attract a lot of female students,' he notes on page one. 'They are helplessly drawn to celebrity, however inconsiderable mine may be.' These young women are gallantly described as 'meat'. For some years now, what with all that harassment-hotline claptrap, Kepesh has been postponing his approaches until he is 'no longer officially in loco parentis' – 'so as not to run afoul of those in the university who, if they could, would seriously impede my enjoyment of life'. When Consuela comes to his office he keeps the door open, making sure that 'all eight of our limbs … [are] visible to every Big Brother of a passerby'. After the grades are in he always throws a party at his duplex for the purposes of decompression and weeding-out. Consuela seems game. And during their first date she sits on his sofa 'with her buttocks sort of half turned to me':

> All that we'd talked about, all that I'd had to listen to about her family, none of it has interfered. She knows how to turn her ass despite all that.
>> Turns in the primordial way. In display. And the display is perfect.
>> It tells me that I need no longer suppress the wish to touch.

Consuela is still a student. And although Kepesh is no longer her teacher, she's still in need of tuition. Generally speaking, hers is 'a generation of astonishing fellators', yet Consuela, at first, 'would move her head with a relentless rat-a-tat-tat rapidity' and then go passive at the key moment. 'I could have been coming into a wastepaper basket.' And we can't have that. 'No one had ever told her not to stop working then' – until her professor enlightens her. It still isn't that great (too efficient and narcissistic), but then 'something happened. The bite. The bite back. The biting back of life.'

I propose to quote from this episode at length (and bear in mind that Roth has always been a *transgressive* writer):

> [I] shoved a couple of pillows back of her head, propped up her head like that, angled it like that up against the headboard, and with my knees planted to either side of her and my ass centered over her, I

leaned into her face and rhythmically, without letup, I fucked her mouth. I was so bored, you see, by the mechanical blow jobs that, to shock her, I kept her fixed there, kept her steady by holding her hair, by turning a twist of hair in one hand ... like the reins that fasten to the bit of a bridle.

A sixty two year old 'so bored' by blow jobs? A sixty two year old not only still screwing his students but still headboarding them? To adopt a Portnoyan formulation, Kepesh puts the sex back into sexagenarian. He records Consuela's response:

After I came, when I drew away, Consuela looked not just horrified but ferocious. Yes, something is finally happening to her ... I was still above her – kneeling over her and dripping on her – we were looking each other cold in the eye, when, after swallowing hard, she snapped her teeth. It was as though she was saying, That's what I could have done, that's what I wanted to do, and that's what I didn't do.

And this changes everything for the sexually adversarial hero. Her 'elemental response' (and she will get even more 'primordial') awakens an elemental response in him: love.

Many readers, perhaps, will be feeling that some moral accountancy is long overdue. Now, it would be priggish, and philistine, to cluck at this if Kepesh were a major and powerfully functioning artist (like Philip Roth, for instance). But Kepesh is not an artist; with his Porsche, his piano, and his punditry, he is just another cultural middleman. He has a friend who is a poet as well as a fellow satyromaniac, and that's his only claim to the licence of bohemianism. Once the girls get their grades, remember, Kepesh considers that he is 'no longer officially in loco parentis'. All that means is that he is now unofficially in loco parentis: thus he acts in clear and serial violation of authority and trust.

There is no indication in the text that Kepesh has ever troubled his head with this question. He imagines that he is rendering Consuela a great service; he it was who 'fired up her senses, who gave her her stature, who was the catalyst to her emancipation'. Similarly, when wondering why a young woman would want to go to bed with an old man, he neglects the obvious idea that it has to do with filial confusion. Consuela's parents – rich, churchgoing, and Hispanic – seem to have been designed for maximal, indeed sanguinary outrage if they learned of their daughter's affair, but Kepesh admits to no unease. Towards the end he has a crisis encounter with Consuela, now thirty-two, who reveals that her subsequent affairs were all 'no good'. Kepesh doesn't feel guilty; he just feels jealous. Rounding out the long list of things that never occur to him is a political objection: gender asymmetry. Show me the lady prof of sixty (or seventy: read on) who still splashes her way through her male students.

Curiously, and however slantedly, Kepesh sees the whole deal as political – as revolutionary, in fact. When the 1960s happened, the professor of desire made a pig of himself, like everyone else, but did so with a steely eye. Here was an opportunity 'to live out my own revolution': 'How does one turn freedom into a system?' He left home ('I have a son of forty-two who hates me') and went on systematising freedom into his 'unmonastic' old age. He realises that his behaviour is repellent to the conventional world, but the feeling is mutual. The wife-child stuff is itself 'childish', an 'archaic addiction' to 'the pathos of feminine need'. His mission is 'to live intelligently beyond the blackmail of the slogans and unexamined rules' – particularly the one about May and December.

Roth, then, does not equip Kepesh with moral clarity. He goes at it the other way. He equips him with rationalisations – and with suffering. When love enters the Dec–May picture, the only possible outcome is continuous pain. An adored twenty-four year old, it turns out, does not make an old man very happy. She makes a happy man very old, saturating him with an awful dreamlike weakness and a sense of desperate fragility. The refinements of this pain, its pathos and bathos, are presented with decisive force. So much so that the book tops up one's view that marriage (to adapt Churchill on democracy) is the worst imaginable kind of human arrangement, except for all the other kinds. But Kepesh wouldn't be a Roth hero if he weren't absolutely incorrigible. This is a 'spoken' novel, addressed to an unidentified listener. We learn that the listener is young, and we know that the listener is unlikely to be male. Then we click: she's the next one.

A spoken novel needn't be underwritten. *Portnoy's Complaint* was spoken (to Dr Spielvogel), but Roth stylised the confession and was able to write flat-out. *The Dying Animal* is candidly conversational, and such stylisation as it deploys tends to take it even nearer to the top of the head, with outbreaks of mere telegramese. This isn't surprising, perhaps, after the high style, the big prose game, of what I will venture to call Roth's American Century trilogy, namely (in reverse order) *The Human Stain*, *I Married a Communist*, and *American Pastoral*. And it may be that the nature of Kepesh's tale precluded the need for a dignified verbal surface. Of course, I am perfectly aware that Roth might well be more 'with' Kepesh than I think he is – that ageing and death are such hopeless propositions that they justify any gratification along the road. Anyway, the moralist reading is there, and the existence of the above-named trilogy remains my best reason for thinking it is the right one. A further hunch: if Roth were genuinely 'with' David Kepesh he would have called him Nathan Zuckerman.

'Can you imagine old age? Of course you can't.' Actually I can, now. One of the eternal limitations of literature is its failure to prepare you for what you haven't experienced. The best pages of *The Dying Animal* prepare you, and I will continue to depend on Roth's miraculous energy. Such intimidating illumination can only be greeted equivocally, with something like – No thanks, but thanks.

Talk 2001

Updike's Farewell Notes

My Father's Tears and Other Stories by John Updike

The following wedge of prose has two things wrong with it: one big thing and one little thing – one infelicity and one howler. Read it with attention. If you can spot both, then you have what is called a literary ear.

> ... Craig Martin took an interest in the traces left by prior owners
> of his land. In the prime of his life, when he worked every weekday
> and socialised all weekend, he had pretty much ignored his land.

The minor flaw is the proximity of 'prior' and 'prime'. This gives us a dissonant *rime riche* on the first syllable; and the two words, besides, are etymological half-siblings, and should never be left alone together without many intercessionary chaperones. And the major flaw? The first sentence ends with the words 'his land'; and so, with a resonant clunk, does the second. Mere quibbles, some may say. But we are addressing ourselves to John Updike, who was perhaps the greatest virtuoso stylist since Nabokov – who, in his turn, was perhaps the greatest virtuoso stylist since Joyce.

So, the portrait of the artist as an old man: this is a murky and glutinous vista (and one of increasingly urgent interest to the present reviewer, who is closing in on sixty). My broad impression is that writers, as they age, lose energy (inspiration, musicality, imagistic serendipity) but gain in craft (the knack of knowing what goes where). Medical science has granted us a new phenomenon: the octogenarian novel. And one thinks, with respect, of Saul Bellow's *Ravelstein* and Norman Mailer's *The Castle in the Forest*; yet no one would seriously compare these books to *Humboldt's Gift* and *Harlot's Ghost*. Updike was seventy-six when he died. And for many years he suffered from partial deafness. I don't know (perhaps nobody knows) whether the two afflictions are connected, but the fact is that Updike, in *My Father's Tears and Other Stories*, is in the process of losing his ear.

This piece would have gone unwritten if its subject were still alive. In the last three decades I have published about 15,000 words of more or less unqualified praise of John Updike, and his achievement remains immortal. The most astonishing page in the new collection is the one headed 'Books by John Updike': sixty-two volumes, many of them enormously long. His productivity was preternatural: it made you think of a berserk IVF pregnancy, or a physiological condition (pressure on the cortex?), or – more realistically, given his Depression-shadowed childhood – a Protestant work ethic taken to the point of outright fanaticism. *My Father's Tears* is Updike's last book, and perhaps his least distinguished. But it ends, all the same, with the glimmer, the thwarted promise, of a happier ending.

Readers must now prepare themselves for quotation, and a blizzard of false quantities – by which I mean those rhymes and chimes and inadvertent repetitions, those toe-stubs, those excrescences and asperities that most writers hope to expunge from their work (or at least radically minimise: you never get them all). Updike's prose, that fantastic engine of euphony, of first-echelon perception, and of a wit both vicious and all-forgiving, has in this book lost its compass. Formerly, you used to reread Updike's sentences in a spirit of incredulous admiration. Here, too often, you reread them wondering a) what they mean, or b) why they're there, or c) how they survived composition, routine reappraisal, and proof-checking without causing a spasm of horrified self-correction.

Consider:

> ants make mounds like coffee grounds ...
> polished bright by sliding anthracite ...
> my bride became allied in my mind ...
> except for her bust, abruptly outthrust ...

This quatrain is not an example of Updike's light verse; the lines consist of four separate examples of wantonly careless prose. Similarly: 'alone on a lonely afternoon', 'Lee's way of getting away from her', 'his rough-and-tumble, roughly equal matches with women', and 'a soft round arm wrapped around her face'. One sentence contains 'walking' and 'sidewalk'; another contains 'knowing' and 'knew'; another contains 'year', 'yearbook', and 'year'.

'For what is more intimate even than sex but death?' Well, you know what he means (after a moment or two), but shouldn't that 'but' be another 'than' (which, I agree, wouldn't be any good either). 'Fleischer had attained, in private, to licking her feet.' Attained? And we surely don't need to be told that Fleischer isn't licking her feet in public. Or take this (from the title story) as an example of a sentence that audibly whimpers for a return to the drawing board:

> He was taller than I, though I was not short, and I realised, his hand warm in mine while he tried to smile, that he had a different perspective than I.

This isn't much of a realisation; and by the time you get to the repeated 'than I', the one-letter first-person pronoun (which chimes with 'realised' and 'mine' and 'tried' and 'smile') is as hypnotically conspicuous as, say, 'antidisestablishmentarianism'. Let us end these painful quotes with what may be the most indolent period ever committed to paper by a major pen (and one so easy to fix: change the first 'fall' to the Englishism 'autumn', or, if that's too onerous, change the second 'fall' to 'drop'): 'The grapes make a mess on the bricks in the fall; nobody ever thinks to pick them up when they fall'. The most ridiculous thing about this sentence, somehow, is its stately semi-colon.

★

Considered as mere narratives, the stories are as quietly inconclusive as Updike's stories usually are; but now, denuded of a vibrant verbal surface, they sometimes seem to be neither here nor there – products of nothing more than professional habit. Then, too, you notice a loss of organisational control and, in one case, a loss of any sense of propriety. This is 'Varieties of Religious Experience', which concerns itself with September 11. First we get a strongish eyewitness account of the falling towers; then Mohammed Atta ordering his fourth Scotch in a Floridan gogo bar; then an executive in the North Tower minutes after impact; then United 93 and the passengers' (weirdly telescoped) revolt. This story appeared in November 2002: fatally premature, and fatally unearned. Death, elsewhere appropriately seen as infinitely mysterious, august, and royal – as 'the distinguished thing', in Henry James's last words – is treated here without decorum and without taste.

I said earlier that *My Father's Tears* contains the rumour of a happier ending. These stories are presented in chronological order, and after a while the reader feels a disquieting suspense. How far will the degeneration advance? Will the last few pages be unadorned gibberish? This doesn't happen; and the lost trust in the author begins to be partly restored. The prose takes on solidity and balance; Updike, here, is attempting less, and successfully evokes the 'inner dwindling', the ever-narrower horizon imposed by time. This perhaps would have been Updike's very last phase. And the reader closes the book with a restive sadness that death has deprived us of it.

'The Full Glass', the final story, seems to me to be quietly innovative, like the ending of 'The Walk with Elizanne' (where the literary imagination boldly rescues a failing memory). V.S. Pritchett, on his ninetieth birthday, said to me in an interview:

> As one gets older one becomes very boring and long-winded to oneself. One's thoughts are long-winded, whereas before they were really rather nice and agitated. The story is a form of travel ... Travelling through minds and situations which reveal their strangeness to you. Old age kills travel.

I suggest without irony that Updike's last challenge might have been to turn long-windedness into art – and to make boredom interesting.

Age waters the writer down. The most terrible fate of all is to lose the ability to impart life to your creations (your creations, in other words, are dead on arrival). Other novelists simply fall out of love with the reader; this was true of James, and also of Joyce (who never much cared for the reader in the first place: what he cared for was words). Not so with Updike, even in these loose and straitened pages. As you might see on a signpost in his beloved American countryside (while approaching some stoical little township), the stories here are 'Thickly Settled'. Updike's creations live, and authorial love is what sustains them. He put it very plainly in his memoir, *Self-Consciousness*: 'Imitation is praise. Description expresses love.' That love, at least, never began to weaken.

Guardian 2009

Rabbit Angstrom Confronts Obamacare

America is sick about health: America, where strokes and heart attacks come with a price tag, and where the doctors carry on like slum landlords or war profiteers. And Americans *admire* it – this triage of the wallet.

John Updike, or John Updike's ghost, would be interested (but not surprised) to learn that the year of his death saw a kind of grass-roots rebellion *against* the health-care system favoured by the current administration: Obamacare – the first step towards a system long-established in every other country in the First World. Americans believe in decentralised authority, individual choice, and what they call 'fiscal responsibility' (or very low taxes); they dislike the 'nanny state', which, scandalously, coddles the apathetic citizen 'from cradle to grave'. Americans pay for their coming hither and for their going hence – costly entrances, truly exorbitant exits. It is the American way, and they're wedded to it.

My only extended meeting with John Updike – a two-hour interview – took place in a Massachusetts hospital (where, for the record, he was scheduled to have a pre-cancerous wart excised from his right hand). That was in 1987; I was thirty-eight, and he was fifty-five. And twenty-two years later, on January 27, 2009, Updike succumbed to lung cancer and breathed his last – in a Massachusetts hospital.

I do see that the coincidence is hardly staggering. It's not as if I once went bungee jumping with John Berryman, or tasted the twin barrels of a shotgun while playing Russian Roulette with Ernest Hemingway. Nevertheless, in the year of his passing, I have of course been thinking about my interlude with this great American presence – a presence which is now an absence of the same dimensions. And I have been thinking about Updike, and Updike's art, in the hospitalic setting. Furthermore, our long encounter, at the Wang Ambulatory Care Center in

Mass. General, Boston, contained its modest portent, its token omen, of a death foretold.

*

On that summer day the hospital cafeteria, shockingly vast, was the scene of every variety of enfeeblement. I delegate the task of describing it, not to Updike, for now, but to his one living superior (at the time), Saul Bellow. This is from *Augie March*:

> Shruggers, hobblers, truss and harness wearers, crutch dancers, wall inspectors, wheelchair people in bandage helmets, wound smells and drug flowers blossoming from gauze, from colorful horrors and out of the deep sinks.

And in this galère of morbidity Updike was intensely *alive*. The hyperactivity of his sense-impressions was palpable – almost audible. I felt I was in the presence of a great array, a NORAD of data-gathering and micro-inspection.

'My God,' he said joyously, 'we're surrounded by all kinds of sick Americans! Look at that woman's *glasses*.' A lady groped by in what could have been a pair of welder's goggles. 'I guess she really doesn't want any light in her eyes ... My God, look at *him*. Look at his shoulders! Look at that girl's *legs*.'

On the question of why we like certain literary characters (the vibrantly corrupt Becky Sharp, for instance) and dislike others (for instance, the deadeningly pious Little Nell), Updike, *qua* critic, is definitive: 'what we like is life'. What we like is life; and life is still life, especially so, perhaps, when it is menaced not only by infirmity but also by the sharpest financial strain. Yes, this is America, where illness is a dual disaster (and where medical costs contribute to 62 per cent of all bankruptcies). The endless edifice of Mass. General, like a vast and prosperous concentration camp, with its innumerable subsections for hearts, lungs, kidneys, bladders, brains, additionally resembled an emporium or even a mall, where sick Americans, free-enterprising individualists to the last, shopped for longevity.

I said, 'I read "The City" yesterday. A work of Joycean perfection'.

'Thank you. We'll come back to Joyce. Look at that lady who's just come out of the elevator. The one with the ...'

Updike was elated, fascinated, riveted; Updike was among the living.

*

We remember the somatic mutinies, the horrible turns, and the epic hospitalisations endured by Rabbit Angstrom – Rabbit, as buoyant and dynamic (and as lax and sclerotic) as the America he personifies. And medical dramas and anxieties increasingly intrude on Updike's later fiction, in the same way that they retard and burden the conversations of everybody over fifty-five. But perhaps 'The City', the 1981 short story from the collection *Trust Me* (1987), stands out as Updike's most sharply crystallised visit to the land of the sick.

'A work of Joycean perfection,' I said. Actually it is not quite perfect, and it is not at all Joycean, to its credit; in my view Updike frittered away several years of his prime in a fruitless attempt to transfer the thought-rhythms of Leopold Bloom to the stolid adulterers of suburban America (*Couples, Rabbit Redux,* and more spottily *The Maples Stories*). 'The City' is pure Updike: it is both embarrassingly intimate and grandly universal.

The first sentence gives us *onset* ('His stomach began to hurt on the airplane, as the engines changed pitch to descend' – to descend into the city we will never see), and the second sentence gives us the first twitch of *denial*, or the quest for proximate cause: 'Carson [Bob Carson, a mid-echelon computer salesman] at first blamed his pain upon the freeze-dried salted peanuts', of which, on the plane, he has consumed two whole packets, along with a mid-morning whisky sour.

As he disembarks, Carson vindictively continues to hold the peanuts responsible – the peanuts, the drink, the drone of the aircraft, the corpulent elbows on both his armrests, and then, a little later, and more self-pityingly, the tedium of the middle life: 'showering and shaving in the morning and putting himself into clothes and then, sixteen hours later, taking himself out of them'. In the taxi queue, the first decisive epi-symptom persuades him to skip his appointments and go straight to the hotel: 'A sudden transparent wave of nausea, like a dip in the flight of the 747 ...'

The stricken creature wants to seek its bedding; first, though, we have the phantasmagoric biliousness of the hotel, where, as Carson follows the 'maroon-clad bellhop down the orange-carpeted corridor, not only were the colours nauseating but the planes of wall and floor looked warped, as if the pain that would not break up were transposing him to a set of new coordinates ...' New coordinates, queer perspectives:

> For variation, Carson stretched himself out upon the cool bathroom floor, marvelling at the complex, thick-lipped undersides of the porcelain fixtures, and at the distant bright lozenge of the foreshortened mirror.

Denial is now diversified by *blind faith in resurgence,* just as Carson's identity, too, diversifies and bifurcates: the hastily rescheduled appointments bother him only 'remotely, for it would all be taken care of by quite another person – his recovered, risen self'. He visits the hotel pharmacy (shocked by a lobby mirror and the image of 'a thin-limbed man in shirt sleeves, with a pot belly and a colourless mouth tugged down on one side like a dead man's'), and buys the *familiar patented remedy*: a bottle of Maalox. 'The medicine tasted chalky and gritty and gave the pain, after a moment's hesitation, an extra edge, as of tiny sandy teeth.' By now *habituation* is doing what little it can. 'In the room's shadowy spaces his pain had become a companion'; 'he let the afternoon burn down into evening and thought how misery itself becomes a kind of home'.

★

Gathering the last shreds of his willpower (and wanting to hear a human voice), Carson calls the front desk. A young clerk breezily recommends the emergency clinic at the city hospital. It is the spur meek Carson has been waiting for, because habituation is ready to glissade into *capitulation.* After a cab ride of 'surprising' duration, he reaches the 'vast and glowing pile'; he expects – he hopes – 'to surrender the burden of his body utterly, but instead found himself obliged to carry it through a series of fresh efforts – forms to be filled out, proofs to be supplied of his financial fitness to be ill ...'

This last phrase, with its sheepish little irony, is the story's first acknowledgment of the peculiar American barbarism: that is to say, the fatal synergy of public health and private gain. Still, the peculiarity, mentioned again only once, is from here on quietly dramatised. Updike, as a man, accepts the American way; but as an artist he is alive to its deformations. His subliminal mind knows that being ill in America is not like being ill anywhere else. And it can't be right, can it – that inequality should dog you to your deathbed?

The medical operatives who go on to process Carson show no trace of vocational sympathy; they are 'elusive' apparitions who give the impression that they have far better things to do and should really be somewhere else entirely – at a dinner party, say, or otherwise immersed in 'a festive domestic world' from which Carson has 'long fallen'. Getting sick invariably involves a demotion of the self; if you're an American, the demotion is also socio-economic. Carson, after all, is petit-bourgeois (not high-bohemian, like his creator). 'Slowly Carson dressed again, though the clothes looked, item by item, so shabby as to be hardly his.' It's straightforward enough: if you feel poorly in America, then you're going to feel poor, too.

After a battery of tests, Carson is given a bed in a holding area, with other patients who moan, plead, and retch. 'Carson was comforted by these evidences that at least he had penetrated into a circle of acknowledged ruin.' At some point in the night he opens his eyes and a new and grander doctor (another refugee from the beau monde) is gazing down at him:

> Carson wished to make social amends but was in a poor position to, flat on his back and nearly naked ... He was very aware that, though the debauched hour and disreputable surroundings had become his own proper habitat, the doctor was healthy and must have a decent home, a family, a routine to return to.

Appendicitis (with one well-understood complication) is triumphantly diagnosed; the godlike sawbones will operate at once; Carson's 'promotion in status' infuses the medical team with a new esprit de corps; 'on soft swift wheels' he floats 'feet first' into the theatre:

> A masked and youthful population was already there, making chatter, having a party. 'There are so many of you!' Carson exclaimed; he was immensely happy. His pain had already ceased.

The happiness persists and ramifies, and the second half of 'The City' is one of Updike's odes to communitarian rebirth – rebirth, in the harmonial American setting. Carson's internal vandal, 'the burning, undiscourageable demon he had carried', is tamed by medical science, reduced to 'cool facts', and this 'vindicated Carson. For the sick feel as shamed as the sinful, the fallen.' Further vindication is delivered during a late-night visit from a beautiful nurse, whose 'queenly smooth black face' smiles wordlessly down at him; '*I forgive you*, her presence said.'

Rebirth involves regression. The suave surgeon gives him brief tutorials 'about eating and walking and going to the bathroom – all things that needed to be learned again'. Carson, touchingly, becomes absorbed in a jigsaw he finds in the recreation room. At night he is comforted by unseen presences. 'Lights always burned; voices always murmured in the hall; this world no more rested than the parental world beyond the sides of a crib.'

Now reality conspires to delight him; and his gratitude is circumambient. 'A television had been mounted on the wall opposite him and was obedient to a panel of buttons that nestled in his palm'; at night the 'set became an even warmer and more ingratiating companion, with its dancing colors and fluctuant radiance'. Carson exercises, as he must, hampered at first by the 'spindly, rattling IV pole', but he finds that there's 'a certain jaunty knack to it', and his handling of the 'faithful' apparatus comes to seem positively 'debonair'.

By this stage, Carson is haemorrhaging nothing more dangerous than dollars and cents. His nonchalant doctors, always about to 'take off' and go somewhere nicer, look in on him – for a price. But Carson is an American, and doesn't notice. Watch the way his mind wanders even as he draws attention to the twinkly avarice of his carers:

> ... there materialised a host of specialists in one department of Carson's anatomy or another, so that he felt huge, like Gulliver pegged down in Lilliput for inspection. All of them payed their calls so casually and pleasantly – just dropping by, as it were – that Carson was amazed, months later, to find each visit listed by date and hour on the sheets of hospital services billed to him in extensive dot-matrix printout – an old Centronics 739 printer, from the look of it.

I am suddenly reminded of a sentence I wrote about *Lolita*, and the meticulous moral reckoning to which Nabokov subjects Humbert

Humbert: 'As in an American hospital, every tear-stained pillowslip, every scrap of soiled paper tissue, has eventually to be answered for.'

Carson is being rebaptised – purification, regeneration, readmission. His favourite perch is the external staircase:

> The raw outdoor air had raked through his still-drugged system like a sweeping rough kiss, early-fall air mixing summer and winter, football and baseball, stiff with chill yet damp and not quite purged of growth.

From the staircase he can glimpse the city that he never knew and will never know again:

> The drab housing and assembled rubble that he saw through the grid of the cement barrier, which permitted no broader view, nevertheless seemed to Carson brilliantly real, moist and deep-toned and full. Life, this was life. This was the world.

*

'Joycean, you think?' said Updike, as our meeting drew to an end.

'In its perfection. Or near-perfection.'

'Well, nothing's perfect. A short poem can be perfect, but a short story of any length is soon open to "the natural sin of language". In Eliot's phrase.'

I said, 'You know Nabokov, when he taught, he used to grade the stories they studied. The worst mark he gave was a Z-minus, but Joyce got an A-triple-plus for "The Dead". He might've given you the same for "The City". He said he loved your prose, isn't that right?'

'He did. He signed off his little letter "cordially". It was pretty minimalist, that note. Making me suspect that Nabokov only loved my prose when it was lauding the prose of Nabokov. I've been meaning to ask. Have you read *Finnegans Wake*?'

'All of it? No. Just the beginning and the end and some bits in between'.

'Me too. Mm. Surprising. I thought you had about you the air of a man who had read *Finnegans Wake*.'

I felt flattered – probably mistakenly. What sort of air would that be, after all? Obsessive, thick-spectacled, onanistic. 'Nabokov called *Ulysses* "a noble book",' I said. 'But he called *Finnegans Wake* "a snore in the other room" ... I can't get over how cheerful everyone looks. They're in hospital. And it's costing them an arm and a leg.'

'When the bill comes – that's the really painful part. But Americans are all insured. Except of course for the millions who aren't.'

'It seems grotesque to me. Paying to be ill.'

He said, 'Socialised medicine would seem grotesque to *us*. Not to pay, not to be able to pick and choose, not to have your panoply of discretionary powers – when it's something as important as life and death. That'd be un-American.'

Present-day readers of 'The City' will be surprised to see how much *smoking* gets done in Updike's hospital. But there was a smoking section in the cafeteria at Mass. General, too, and after some hesitation I asked if we could move into it for ten minutes.

'While I have a cigarette.'

'Yes of course,' he said. Updike welcomed the move to another table: it gave him more sick Americans to look at.

'This is grotesque too,' I said. 'Smoking in hospital. Well, I suppose it's good for business.'

'I envy you. I quit.'

Updike quit; but lung cancer is the marathon runner of fatal diseases. It took human beings quite a while to discover that smoking – the metronomic ingestion of mouthfuls of formaldehyde and benzene – was bad for their health. The official declaration came in 1964, when Updike was thirty-one, and already the veteran of many cigarettes (and then many cigars).

'That woman – see the size of the brace she has to wear? That man in the hat. He's got a loudspeaker screwed into his throat. The old guy with the ...'

Looking, now, at the yardage of Updike's books on my shelves, I find it hard to believe that he was ever addicted to anything except the work ethic. Oh, and to life, of course. Those busy eyes of his, the set of the mouth (as if containing, with difficulty, a vast and mysterious euphoria), his turban-shaped hair still forcefully thriving, his hands on the tea tray so much firmer than my own ('Why don't *I* carry that') – my own, which trembled at the size and vigour of his presence and his talent. That day at Mass. General, John Updike was alive.

Areté 2009

Postscript. Nikolai Gogol (1809–52) was a passionate Slavophile, a devout Orthodox Christian, and a convinced Tsarist. He was a defender of serfdom, allowing only that its practices might be made more profitable. And yet his *Dead Souls* (1842) was the bible of the Abolitionists (serfdom, after seven centuries, was abolished in 1861), and reads today like a ruthless satire on that peculiar institution. As a citizen, Gogol accepted state slavery; as an artist, he rejected it. The man said yes, but the talent said no. The same duality applies to Updike and the American system of health care.

Jane Austen and the
Dream Factory

Jane Austen, as they might say in Los Angeles, is suddenly hotter than Quentin Tarantino. But before we try to establish what the Austen phenomenon is, let us first establish what it is not.

About eighteen months ago (in the summer of 1996) I went to see *Four Weddings and a Funeral* at a North London cineplex. Very soon I was filled with a yearning to be doing something else (for example, standing at a bus stop in the rain); and under normal circumstances I would have walked out after ten or fifteen minutes. But these weren't normal circumstances. Beside me sat Salman Rushdie. For various reasons – various security reasons – we had to stay. Thus the Ayatollah Khomeini had condemned me to sit through *Four Weddings and a Funeral*; and no Iranian torturer could have elicited a greater variety of winces and flinches, of pleadings and whimperings. So one was obliged to submit, and absorb a few social lessons.

It felt like a reversal of the Charles Addams cartoon: I sat there, thoroughly aghast, while everyone about me (save the author of *The Satanic Verses*) giggled and gurgled, positively hugging themselves with the deliciousness of it all. The only good bit came when you realised that the titular funeral would be dedicated to Simon Callow. I clenched my fist and said *yes*. No particular disrespect to Simon Callow – but at least *one* of them was going to die.

'Well,' I said, when it was over, 'that was bottomlessly horrible. Why is it so popular?'

'Because', said Salman, 'the world has bad taste. Didn't you know that?'

Still, 'bad taste', all by itself, won't quite answer. I can see that the upper classes might enjoy watching the upper classes portrayed with such whimsical fondness. But why should it appeal to four hundred berks from Hendon? In any postwar decade other than the present one, *Four*

Weddings would have provoked nothing but incredulous disgust. A Sixties audience would have wrecked the cinema. Yet now it seems that the old grievances have evaporated, and 'the million', as Hamlet called them, feel free to root for the (congenital) millionaires. They can lapse into a forgetful toadyism, and abase themselves before their historical oppressors.

Class is harmless, class is mildly cool; class is even felt to be ... *classy*. *Four Weddings* is of course deeply 'sentimental' in the colloquial sense: it displays a false and unworthy tenderness. But it is sentimental in the literary sense, too: an old form has been speciously revived. Houses, parties, house parties, amorous vicissitudes in opulent drawing rooms and landscaped gardens, do's and don'ts, 'p's and 'q's, old money, and unlimited leisure. It is Jane Austen's world, in a sense; but the invigorating intelligence is gone, to be supplanted by a simper of ingratiation. Here, the upper crust is playing cute. Dilemmas and entanglements are not admitted to *Four Weddings*. Nothing weighs anything at all.

*

Persuasion has recently been filmed, and so has *Sense and Sensibility*, and there are three versions of *Emma* in the works (not to mention *Clueless*), and no doubt someone will soon knock off the tartly mock-Gothic *Northanger Abbey*, and someone else will find the nerve to tackle the problematic austerities of *Mansfield Park* – and that will be that (except for the little-known fragment *Lady Susan*). *Pride and Prejudice* has been comprehensively taken care of in the BBC's six-part, nine-and-a-half-million-dollar serial, which has been emptying the streets of England every Sunday night (and which will arrive on American screens in January 1998).

Austen fever, or more particularly Darcymania, is upon us. Features editors have been reduced to commissioning interviews with lorry drivers and insulation engineers who happen to be *called* Darcy. Tourist pilgrimages to Jane Austen's house (in Chawton, Hants) were up about two hundred and fifty per cent in October, and sales of Austen tote bags, Austen crockery, Austen sweatshirts, Austen tea towels, and Austen aprons and pinafores were comparably brisk; while you're listening to *The Jane Austen Music Compact Disc* (stuff she might have heard or played), you can rustle something up from *The Jane Austen Cookbook* (all ingredients have been modernised); and so on.

Much of this enthusiasm is, of course, collateral enthusiasm, or Heritage enthusiasm: a blend of disembodied snobbery and vague post-imperial tristesse. No doubt, too, many of the serial's ten million viewers watched it in the same spirit as they watched *Four Weddings* – contentedly stupefied by all the eccentricity and luxe. But such wastage is inevitable, and even appropriate. *Sense and Sensibility* and *Persuasion* play at the art houses. *Pride and Prejudice* plays in your living room; and – true to the book – it comes at you with a broad embrace.

*

Some may be funnier than others, but all Jane Austen's novels are classical comedies: they are about young couples finding their way to the festive conclusion, namely marriage. Furthermore, all Jane Austen's comedies are structurally the *same* comedy. There is a Heroine, there is a Hero, and there is an Obstacle. The Obstacle is always money (not so much class – Mrs Bennet's origins are in 'trade', but so are Mr Bingley's). With the exception of Emma Woodhouse, all the Heroines are penniless and have no dependable prospect other than frugal spinsterhood.

As the Hero heaves into view, he will appear to be shadowed by a female Rival – schemer, heiress, or vamp. The Heroine, for her part, will be distracted, tempted, or merely pestered by a counterfeit hero, a Foil – seducer, opportunist or fop. The Foil can be richer than the Hero (*Persuasion, Mansfield Park*) and, on the face of it, much better fun (*Mansfield Park*). The Hero can also be uglier than the Foil. In her adaptation of *Sense and Sensibility* (which has a double Heroine), Emma Thompson does what she can to spruce up Colonel Brandon – the part is given to Alan Rickman – but the novel makes it plain that he is an old wreck at thirty-five. Brandon represents authorial punishment for Marianne's unrestrained infatuation with her Foil, John Willoughby (played in the film by the charmlessly handsome Greg Wise). The flaws of the Foil will highlight the Hero's much solider merits. While the Heroines have their foibles, the Heroes are all near-paragons. Two of them – Henry Tilney and Edmund Bertram, both well-born younger sons – are vicars of the Church of England.

In *Pride and Prejudice*, Austen turned up the dial that controls the temperature of comedy, giving it some of the fever of what we would now call romance. Both Rival and Foil are almost melodramatically garish figures: the self-woundingly feline Caroline Bingley, the debauched and self-pitying

George Wickham. They create logistical difficulties, but neither is capable of mounting a serious threat to the central attraction. For Elizabeth Bennet is the most frictionlessly adorable Heroine in the corpus – by some distance. And, as for the Hero, well, Miss Austen, for once in her short life, held nothing back: tall, dark, handsome, brooding, clever, noble, and profoundly rich. He has a vast estate, a house in town, a 'clear' ten thousand per annum. His sister Georgiana has thirty thousand pounds (the same as *Emma*) – whereas Elizabeth's dowry amounts to about a quid a week. No reader can resist the brazen wishfulness of *Pride and Prejudice*, but it is clear from internal evidence alone that Austen never fully forgave herself for it. *Mansfield Park* was her – and our – penance. As her own prospects weakened, dreams of romance paled into a modest hope for respectability (or a financial 'competence'). *Persuasion* was her poem to the second chance. And then came death.

★

This autumn, as the new serial got into its stride, distressed viewers rang up the BBC in tears, pleading for the assurance that fate would smile on the star-crossed pair and that all would yet be well. I was not among these callers, but I sympathised. And I quite understood why the *Pride and Prejudice* video, released midway through the run, sold out in two hours. When I was introduced to the novel, at the age of fifteen, I read twenty pages and then besieged my stepmother's study until she told me what I needed to know. I needed to know that Darcy married Elizabeth. (I needed to know that Bingley married Jane.) I needed this information as badly as I had ever needed anything.

Pride and Prejudice suckers you. Amazingly – and, I believe, uniquely – it *goes on* suckering you. Even now, as I open the book, I feel the same tizzy of unsatisfied expectation, despite five or six rereadings. How can this be, when the genre itself guarantees consummation? The simple answer is that these lovers really are 'made for each other' – by their creator. They are *constructed* for each other: interlocked for wedlock. Their marriage has to be.

Andrew Davies, who adapted the novel for television, was shrewd enough to regard his function as largely obstetrical – to get the thing out of the page and onto the screen in as undamaged a state as possible. After all, he had before him the example of the Olivier-Garson version of 1940 (based on a script by Aldous Huxley, among others): cold proof that any tampering will reduce the original to the emollient and the inconsequential. Huxley's reading is fatally winsome; even Lady Catherine de Bourgh is a good egg. Still, the adapter has to do what the adapter has to do. The pious and vigilant Janeite looks on, ever ready to be scandalised by the tiniest breach of decorum.

Very early on, we see Elizabeth in the bedroom she shares with Jane, saying, 'If I could love a man who would love me enough to take me for a mere fifty pounds a year, I should be very well pleased.' This puts us in the financial picture (and we will soon be seeing Mr Bennet sighing over his account book); but it commits Elizabeth to a predisposed mooniness quite at odds with her defiant self-sufficiency. Later, when the scandal of Lydia's elopement breaks, and Darcy gauntly takes his leave of Elizabeth in the inn near Pemberley, Austen writes, 'Elizabeth felt how improbable it was that they should ever see each other again on such terms of cordiality as had marked their several meetings in Derbyshire.' This translates as a one-line soliloquy: 'I shall never see him again!' Austen's lines show a brave face in social adversity, Davies's an admission of a love Elizabeth does not yet feel. Each shifted brick threatens the whole building.

TV is TV, and TV demands visual equivalents for every 'it', for every 'that'. And the visual is always literal, funnily enough. Any protracted passage of background explication is accorded a lavish collage. Darcy's letter to Elizabeth, with its revelations about Wickham's character, inspires a scene set in Cambridge: Darcy in his gown and mortarboard, striding through a colonnade, mounting the stairs – and surprising Wickham, who has a half-clad scullery maid on his lap. We see Lydia and Wickham's midnight flit (la, how they cuddle in the carriage!), we see Darcy pacing the festering streets of London in search of them, and we see the runaways in their bedroom at the rude tavern. From the start, Elizabeth and Darcy don't just think about each other, they have hallucinations about each other, thus unavoidably indicating romantic obssession. But he isn't in love for quite a while, and she isn't in love till much later on. These two slow-built awakenings are the heart of the book.

Davies's more minor interpolations are usually pretty deft and sometimes downright felicitous; he is an expert who has midwifed much of the British canon on to the screen. But every Janeite is like the Princess tormented by the Pea – we are so tender, so delicate ... Elizabeth would never say (sceptically), 'Astonish me!' Even the lascivious Lydia would not yearningly repeat the (invented) line, 'A whole campful of soldiers ...' Nor did she or would she say, 'We shall have some laughs!' When

Elizabeth refuses Darcy's first offer of marriage, he notes that she spurns him 'with so little *effort* at civility', whereas the book has the clearly superior 'so little *endeavour* at civility'. A few pages earlier, a beguiling subjunctive is lost when 'I expected at least that the pigs were got into the garden' becomes 'the pigs had got into the garden'. I could go on.

And I would go on, indefinitely – but I'm loath to abuse the reader's patience. A deep immersion in Jane Austen tends to transform me into something of a Regency purist. Indeed, I start to find that her rhythms are entirely displacing my own; normal social intercourse becomes increasingly strained and long-winded. If, for example, the editress had called, hoping for news of the near-completion of this piece, I would have been like to reply, 'Nay, Madam, I find I get on exceedingly ill. I need more sequestration with Miss Jane. May I extort, therefore, the indulgence of a further se'nnight?' This is of course anachronistic of me. And Jane Austen is not – and will never be – an anachronism.

*

In David Lodge's novel *Changing Places* (1975), a tweedy little British academic goes to teach at Euphoric State University in California, while a big brash American academic goes to teach at a rain-sodden redbrick called Rummidge. The American, Morris Zapp, wearily begins his seminar:

> 'What are you bursting to discuss this morning?'
> 'Jane Austen,' mumbled the boy with the beard ...
> 'Oh yeah. What was the topic?'
> 'I've done it on Jane Austen's moral awareness.'
> 'That doesn't sound like my style.'
> 'I couldn't understand the title you gave me, Professor Zapp.'
> 'Eros and Agapé in the later novels, wasn't it? What was the problem?' The student hung his head.

The immediate joke here is the contrast in literary-critical situations, the British still struggling in the ethical battlefields patrolled by F.R. Leavis, the Americans vaulting off into the architectonics of myth and structure. But Lodge's deeper point is that Jane Austen is weirdly capable of keeping everybody busy. The moralists, the Eros-and-Agape contingent, the Marxists, the Freudians, the Jungians, the semioticians, the deconstructors – all find a happy home in six samey novels about middle-class provincials in early nineteenth-century England. The critics are kept at it because the readers are kept at it; with every generation Austen's fiction effortlessly renews itself.

Each age will bring its peculiar emphasis, and in the current Austen festival our own anxieties stand fully revealed. Collectively, we love to wallow in the accents and accoutrements of Jane's world; but for the closeted reader the response is predominantly sombre. We notice, above all, the constriction of female opportunity: how brief was their nubility, and yet how slowly and deadeningly time passed within it. We notice how plentiful were the occasions for inflicting social pain, and how interested the powerful were in this infliction. We see how little the powerless had to use against those who might hate them. And we wonder: who on earth will marry the poor girls – the *poor* girls? Poor men can't, and rich men can't (except in novels), so who can? We fret and writhe at the physical confinement (how understandably desperate these filmmakers are to get their cast out of doors). Of all virtues Jane Austen valued 'candour'; but candour, as we understand it, has no social space in which to exercise itself. One honest exchange between Anne Elliot and Frederick Wentworth and *Persuasion* disappears. We long to give them our liberties. We wonder at their self-repression. And we are chilled by their circumambient boredom.

The BBC's new serial has been touted in the press as revealing the latent 'sensuality' of Jane Austen's world; naturally it reveals much more about the blatant sensuality of our own. Austen, after all, is notoriously cerebral – a resolute niggard in her descriptive dealings with food, clothes, animals, children, weather, and landscape. But we in the 1990s will not have it so.

Thus at the outset, on our television screens, Darcy and Bingley thunder towards Netherfield Park on their snorting steeds, while Elizabeth enjoys a hearty tramp on a nearby hillside. Later, climbing from the bath, Darcy looks out of the window and sees Elizabeth romping with a dog. Lydia is surprised half-clad by Mr Collins – and gigglingly confronts him with her cleavage. In the throes of his imprudent passion for Elizabeth, Darcy takes up fencing. 'I shall conquer this,' he mutters. 'I shall.' Returning to Pemberley, unshaven, with the hot horse between his thighs, he dismounts and impetuously plunges into a pond. Here, clearly, we are moving away from Jane Austen, towards D.H. Lawrence – and Ken Russell. 'There is a lot of pent-up sexuality in Austen's work,' Davies has said, 'and I have let it out.' But why stop there? Why not give her a course of Vitamin C and a backrub? Austen's characters resist the ministrations of the therapy age, the 'venting' age. As literary creations, they *thrive* on their inhibition. It is the source of all their thwarted energy.

Now for the performances, which are a testimony to great strength in depth and to the accuracy and inconspicuousness of Simon Langton's direction. Jennifer Ehle (pronounced 'Ely') is not quite the perfect Elizabeth, for such a creature could not exist; Elizabeth, simply, is Jane Austen with looks, and such a creature could never have created Elizabeth. Ehle, like Debra Winger, is one of those actresses whose presence floods the screen. She has the spirit and the warmth; she has a smile of almost orgasmic sweetness; she contrives to look voluptuous *and* vulnerable in the egg-cosy maternity outfits that 'authenticity' has reduced her to; and she has the eyes; but she cannot quite inhabit the surrogate wit. Colin Firth is an insidiously persuasive Darcy, as he makes his journey from probity to democratic right feeling. To know her heart, all Elizabeth needs is the facts before her. Darcy has to complete two centuries of internal evolution.

The ensemble players are led by Alison Steadman. Some dull dogs have found her Mrs Bennet too broad, too Dickensian, but in fact she establishes a miraculous equipoise between bitterness and boiling vulgarity (and this balance is stabilised by clear traces of her past allure). Susannah Harker makes a languid, comfortably ponderous Jane; Julia Sawalha gives us Lydia's 'high animal spirits'; David Bamber is a marvellously contorted and masochistic Mr Collins; and Anna Chancellor locates an unexpected pathos behind Caroline Bingley's expert taunts. The one important failure is Mr Bennet. Benjamin Whitrow's line readings are thoughtful and confident, but he is too quick to take refuge in wryness and twinkle. The most disillusioned character in all Jane Austen, Mr Bennet is the dark backing behind the bright mirror. He, too, is very close to his creator, and Jane Austen feared his weakness in herself. Mr Bennet sees the world as it is, and then makes sport of his own despair.

*

The sensualism imported by Davies and Langton brings one unarguable gain: all those creamy, dreamy scenes in the bedroom shared by Elizabeth and Jane, with the candles lit and the hair down, make us feel the crucial heaviness of their sisterly love. We are reminded that the emotional argument of the book is intimately bound up with this relationship; and we feel its weight without realising why it weighs so much. Watching Marianne's near-death scene (lovesickness, fever) in *Sense and Sensibility*, I wondered why I was so pierced, and so desolated, when Elinor addresses her sister as, simply, 'My dearest.' We are moved because the soft words are literally true – and may well remain true, for life.*

With the unmarried, no reconfiguration awaits the pattern of their love; their nearest are their dearest, and that is the end of it. In *Persuasion* we sense Anne Elliot's further privation as she probes for warmth in the humourless solipsism of her sister Mary. And we naïvely console ourselves that Jane Austen, whatever else she lacked, at least had Cassandra.

Apart from that very welcome interment, *Four Weddings and a Funeral* had something to be said for it: as a result of one typically embarrassing scene, an opportunist edition of 'ten Auden poems' climbed into the best-seller lists. This book was called *Tell Me the Truth About Love* and had a photograph of Hugh Grant on its cover (and Grant, incidentally, makes a very creditable Edward Ferrars in *Sense and Sensibility*). On Jane Austen, Auden was great but wrong:

> You could not shock her more than she shocks me;
> Beside her Joyce seems innocent as grass.
> It makes me most uncomfortable to see
> An English spinster of the middle-class
> Describe the amorous effects of 'brass',
> Reveal so frankly and with such sobriety
> The economic basis of society.

We of the 1990s would most certainly shock Jane Austen, with our vast array of slovenly and unexamined freedoms. Nonetheless, there is a suspicion of cant in Auden's elegant lines. 'Brass' – money, security – made Charlotte Lucas accept Mr Collins ('disgracing herself' with a prudential marriage), but it didn't make her love him. Elizabeth turned

---

* Writing five decades later, Anthony Trollope has the latitude to make the point more roundly. In *He Knew He Was Right*, Jemima Stanbury, a moneyed but now fairly elderly old maid, finds herself increasingly stirred and awakened to regret by the companionship of her lovelorn (and impoverished) niece, Dorothy. One night, bearing a candle, Jemima comes into Dorothy's bedroom, to rouse her with a magnanimous, life-solving promise. 'But what is it, aunt?' says Dorothy. And Jemima begins with the words, 'Kiss me, dearest.'

down Mr Collins; and, with so little endeavour at civility, she turned down Mr Darcy, too, with his ten thousand a year.

Writing about Gray's 'Elegy', William Empson said that the poem presents the condition of provincial oblivion as pathetic without putting you in a mood in which you would want to change it. But 'change' is the business of satire. Satire is militant irony. Irony is more long-suffering. It doesn't incite you to transform society; it strengthens you to tolerate it. Jane Austen was indeed an English spinster of the middle class. She died in unrelieved pain at the age of forty-one (and with the greatest 'last words' of all time: asked what she needed, she said, 'Nothing but death'). On the other hand, she has now survived for nearly two hundred years. Her lovers are platonic lovers, but they form a multitude.

New Yorker 1997

More Personal – 3

Christopher Hitchens*

'Spontaneous eloquence seems to me a miracle,' confessed Vladimir Nabokov in 1962. He took up the point more personally in his foreword to *Strong Opinions* (1973):

> ... I have never delivered to my audience one scrap of information not prepared in typescript beforehand ... My hemmings and hawings on the telephone cause long-distance callers to switch from their native English to pathetic French. At parties, if I attempt to entertain people with a good story, I have to go back to every other sentence for oral erasures and inserts ... [N]obody should ask me to submit to an interview ... It has been tried at least twice in the old days, and once a recording machine was present, and when the tape was rerun and I had finished laughing, I knew that never in my life would I repeat that sort of performance.

We sympathise. And most literary types, probably, would hope for inclusion somewhere or other on Nabokov's sliding scale: 'I think like a genius, I write like a distinguished author, and I speak like a child.'

Mr Hitchens isn't like that. *Christopher and His Kind* runs the title of one of Isherwood's famous memoirs. And yet *this* Christopher doesn't have a kind. Everyone is unique – but Christopher is preternatural. And it may even be that he exactly inverts the Nabokovian paradigm. He thinks like a child (that is to say, his judgments are far more instinctive and moral-visceral than they seem, and are animated by a child's eager apprehension of what feels just and true); he writes like a distinguished author; and he speaks like a genius.

* This piece was the foreword to *The Quotable Hitchens: From Alcohol to Zionism – The Very Best of Christopher Hitchens*, edited by Windsor Mann.

As a result, Christopher is one of the most terrifying dialecticians that the world has yet seen. Lenin used to boast that his objective, in debate, was not rebuttal and then refutation: it was the 'destruction' of his interlocutor. This isn't Christopher's policy – but it is his practice. Towards the very end of the last century, all our greatest chessplayers, including Gary Kasparov, began to succumb to a computer (named Deep Blue); I had the opportunity to ask two grandmasters to describe the Deep Blue experience, and they both said, 'It's like a wall coming at you.' In argument, Christopher is that wall. The prototype of Deep Blue was known as Deep Thought. And there's a case for calling Christopher Deep Speech. With his vast array of geohistorical references and precedents, he is almost googlelike; but Google (with, say, its ten million 'results' in 0.7 seconds) is something of an idiot savant, and Christopher's search engine is much more finely tuned. In debate, no matter what the motion, I would back him against Cicero, against Demosthenes.

Whereas mere Earthlings get by with a mess of expletives, subordinate clauses, and finely turned tautologies, Christopher talks not only in complete sentences but also in complete paragraphs. Similarly, although he mentions the phenomenon in these pages, he is an utter stranger to what Diderot called *l'esprit de l'escalier*: the spirit of the staircase. This phrase is sometimes translated as 'staircase wit' – far too limitingly, in my view, because *l'esprit de l'escalier* describes an entire subsection of one's intellectual and emotional being. The door to the debating hall, or to the contentious drinks party, or indeed to the little flat containing the focus of amatory desire, has just been firmly closed; and now the belated eureka shapes itself on your lips. These lost chances, these unexercised potencies of persuasion, can haunt you for a lifetime – particularly, of course, when the staircase was the one that might have led to the bedroom.

As a young man, Christopher was conspicuously unpredatory in the sexual sphere (while also being conspicuously pan-affectionate: 'I'll just make a brief pass at everyone,' he would typically and truthfully promise a mixed gathering of fourteen or fifteen people, 'and then I'll be on my way'). I can't say how it went, earlier on, with the boys; with the girls, though, Christopher was the one who needed to be persuaded. And I do know that in this area, if in absolutely no other, he was sometimes inveigled into submission.

The habit of saying the right thing at the right time tends to get relegated to the category of the pert riposte. But the put-down, the swift comeback, when quoted, gives a false sense of finality. *So-and-so, as quick as a flash, said so-and-so* – and that seems to be the end of it. Christopher's most memorable rejoinders, I have found, linger, and reverberate, and eventually combine, as chess moves combine ... One evening, close to forty years ago, I said, 'I know you despise all sports – but how about a game of chess?' Looking mildly puzzled and amused, he joined me over the sixty-four squares. Two things soon emerged. First, he showed no combative will, he offered no resistance (because this was *play*, you see, and *earnest* is all that really matters). Second, he showed an endearing disregard for common sense. This prompts a paradoxical thought.

There are many excellent commentators, in the US and the UK, who deploy far more rudimentary gumption than Christopher ever bothers with (we have a deservedly knighted columnist in London whom I always think of, with admiration, as Sir Common Sense). But it is hard to love common sense. And the salient fact about Christopher is that *he is loved*. What we love is fertile instability; what we love is the agitation of the unexpected. And Christopher always comes, as they say, from left field. He is not a plain speaker. He is not, I repeat, a plain man.

*

Over the years Christopher has spontaneously delivered many dozens of unforgettable lines. Here are four of them.

1. He was on TV for the second or third time in his life (if we exclude *University Challenge*), which takes us back to the mid-1970s and to Christopher's mid-twenties. He and I were already close friends (and colleagues at the *New Statesman*); but I remember thinking that nobody so matinée-telegenic had the right to be so exceptionally quick-tongued on the screen. At a certain point in the exchange, Christopher came out with one of his political poeticisms, an ornate but intelligible definition of (I think) national sovereignty. His host – a fair old bruiser in his own right – paused, frowned, and said with scepticism and with helpless sincerity,

'I can't understand a word you're saying.'

'I'm not in the least surprised,' said Christopher, and moved on.

The talk ran its course. But if this had been a frontier western, and not a chat show, the wounded man would have spent the rest of the segment leerily snapping the arrow in half and pushing its pointed end through his chest and out the other side.

2. Every novelist of his acquaintance is riveted by Christopher, not just *qua* friend but also *qua* novelist. I considered the retort I am about to quote (all four words of it) so epiphanically devastating that I put it in a novel – indeed, I put Christopher in a novel. *Mutatis mutandis* (and it is the novel itself that dictates the changes), Christopher 'is' Nicholas Shackleton in *The Pregnant Widow* – though it really does matter, in this case, what the meaning of 'is' is … The year was 1981. We were in a tiny Italian restaurant in West London, where we would soon be joined by our future first wives. Two elegant young men in waisted suits were unignorably and interminably fussing with the staff about rearranging the tables, to accommodate the large party they expected. It was an intensely class-conscious era (because the class system was dying); Christopher and I were candidly lower-middle bohemian, and the two young men were raffishly minor-gentry (they had the air of those who await, with epic stoicism, the deaths of elderly relatives). At length, one of them approached our table, and sank smoothly to his haunches, seeming to pout out through the fine strands of his fringe. The crouch, the fringe, the pout: these had clearly enjoyed many successes in the matter of bending others to his will. After a flirtatious pause he said,

'You're going to hate us for this.'

And Christopher said, 'We hate you already.'

3. In the summer of 1986, in Cape Cod, and during subsequent summers, I used to play a set of tennis every other day with the historian Robert Jay Lifton. I was reading, and then rereading, his latest and most celebrated book, *The Nazi Doctors*; so, on Monday, during changeovers, we would talk about 'Sterilisation and the Nazi Medical Vision'; on Wednesday, '"Wild Euthanasia": The Doctors Take Over'; on Friday, 'The Auschwitz Institution'; on Sunday, 'Killing with Syringes: Phenol Injections'; and so on. One afternoon, Christopher, whose family was staying with mine on Horseleech Pond, was due to show up at the court, after a heavy lunch in nearby Wellfleet, to be introduced to Bob (and to be driven back to the pond-front house). He arrived, much gratified by having come so far on foot: three or four miles – one of the greatest physical feats of his adult life. It was set point. Bob served, approached the net, and wrongfootingly dispatched my attempted pass. Now Bob was and is twenty-three years my senior; and the score was 6–0. I could, I suppose, plead preoccupation: that summer I was wondering (with eerie

detachment) whether I had it in me to write a novel that dealt with the Holocaust. Christopher knew about this, and he knew about my qualms.

Elatedly towelling himself down, Bob said, 'You know, there are so few areas of transcendence left to us. Sports. Sex. Art ...'

'Don't forget the miseries of others,' said Christopher. 'Don't forget the languid contemplation of the miseries of others.'

I did write that novel. And I still wonder whether Christopher's black, three-ply irony somehow emboldened me. What remains true, to this day, to this hour, is that of all subjects (including sex and art), the one we most obsessively return to is the Shoa, and its victims – those whom the wind of death has scattered.

4. In conclusion we move on to 1999, and by now Christopher and I have acquired new wives, and gained three additional children (making eight in all). It was mid-afternoon, in Long Island, and he and I hoped to indulge a dependable pleasure: we were in search of the most violent available film. In the end we approached a multiplex in Southampton (having been pitiably reduced to Wesley Snipes). I said,

'No one's recognised the Hitch for at least ten minutes.'

'Ten? *Twenty* minutes. Twenty-five. And the longer it goes on, the more pissed off I get. I keep thinking: What's the *matter* with them? What can they feel, what can they care, what can they know, if they fail to recognise the Hitch?'

An elderly American was sitting opposite the doors to the cinema, dressed in candy colours and awkwardly perched on a hydrant. With his trembling hands raised in an Italianate gesture, he said weakly,

'Do you love us? Or do you hate us?'

This old party was not referring to humanity, or to the West. He meant America and Americans. Christopher said,

'I beg your pardon?'

'Do you love us, or do you hate us?'

As Christopher pushed on through to the foyer, he said, not warmly, not coldly, but with perfect evenness,

'It depends on how you behave.'

*

Does it depend on how others behave? Or does it depend, at least in part, on the loves and hates of the Hitch?

Christopher is bored by the epithet *contrarian*, which has been trailing him around for a quarter of a century. What he is, in any case, is an autocontrarian: he seeks, not only the most difficult position, but the most difficult position for Christopher Hitchens. Hardly anyone agrees with him on Iraq (yet hardly anyone is keen to debate him on it). We think also of his support for Ralph Nader, his collusion with the impeachment process of the loathed Bill Clinton (who, in *The Quotable Hitchens*, occupies more space than any other subject), and his support for Bush–Cheney in 2004. Christopher often suffers for his isolations; this is widely sensed, and strongly contributes to his magnetism. He is in his own person the drama, as we watch the lithe contortions of a self-shackling Houdini. Could this be the crux of his charisma – that Christopher, ultimately, is locked in argument with the Hitch? Still, 'contrarian' is looking shopworn. And if there must be an epithet, or what the press likes to call a (single-word) 'narrative', then I can suggest a refinement: Christopher is one of nature's *rebels*. By which I mean that he has no automatic respect for anybody or anything.

The rebel is in fact a very rare type. In my whole life I have known only two others, both of them novelists (my father, up until the age of about forty-five; and my friend Will Self). This is the way to spot a rebel: they give no deference or even civility to their supposed superiors (that goes without saying); they also give no deference or even civility to their demonstrable inferiors. Thus Christopher, if need be, will be merciless to the prince, the president, and the pontiff; and, if need be, he will be merciless to the cabdriver ('Oh, you're not going our way. Well turn your light off, all right? Because it's fucking *sickening* the way you guys ply for trade'), to the publican ('You don't give change for the phone? Okay. I'm going to report you to the Camden *Consumer Council*'), and to the waiter ('Service is included, I see. But you're saying it's optional. Which? …What? Listen. If you're so smart, why are you dealing them off the arm in a dump like this?'). Christopher's everyday manners are beautiful (and wholly democratic); of course they are – because he knows that in manners begins morality. But each case is dealt with *exclusively on its merits*. This is the rebel's way.

It is for the most part an invigorating and even a beguiling disposition, and makes Mr Average, or even Mr Above Average (whom we had better start calling Joe Laptop), seem underevolved. Most of us shakily preside over a chaos of vestigial prejudices and pieties, of semi-subliminal inhibitions, taboos, and herd instincts, some of them ancient, some of them spryly contemporary (like moral relativism and the ardent xenophilia which, in Europe at least, always excludes Israelis). To speak and write without fear or favour (to hear no internal drumbeat): such voices are invaluable. On the other hand, as the rebel is well aware, compulsive insubordination risks the punishment of self-inflicted wounds.

*

Let us take an example from Christopher's essays on literature (which are underrepresented here, and impressive enough to deserve an appreciation of their own). In the last decade Christopher has written three raucously hostile reviews – of Saul Bellow's *Ravelstein* (2000), John Updike's *Terrorist* (2006), and Philip Roth's *Exit, Ghost* (2007). When I read them, I found myself muttering the piece of schoolmarm advice I have given Christopher in person, more than once: *Don't cheek your elders.* The point being that, in these cases, respect is mandatory, because it has been earned, over many books and many years. Does anyone think that Saul Bellow, then aged eighty-five, needed Christopher's half-dozen insistences that the Bellovian powers were on the wane (and in fact, read with respect, *Ravelstein* is an exquisite swansong, full of integrity, beauty, and dignity)? If you are a writer, then all the writers who have given you joy – as Christopher was given joy by *Augie March* and *Humboldt's Gift*, for example, and by *The Coup*, and by *Portnoy's Complaint* – are among your honorary parents; and Christopher's attacks were coldly unfilial. Here, disrespect becomes the vice that so insistently exercised Shakespeare: that of ingratitude. And all novelists know, with King Lear (who was thinking of his daughters), how sharper than a serpent's tooth it is to have a thankless reader.

Art is freedom; and in art, as in life, there is no freedom without law. The foundational literary principle is *decorum*, which means something like the opposite of its dictionary definition: 'behaviour in keeping with good taste and propriety' (i.e., submission to an ovine consensus). In literature, decorum means the concurrence of style and content – together with a third element which I can only vaguely express as *earning the right weight*. It doesn't matter what the style is, and it doesn't matter what the content is; but the two must concur. If the essay is something of a literary art, which it clearly is, then the same law obtains.

Here are some indecorous quotes from *The Quotable Hitchens*. 'Ronald Reagan is doing to the country what he can no longer do to his wife.' On the Chaucerian summoner-pardoner Jerry Falwell: 'If you gave Falwell an enema, he'd be buried in a matchbox.' On the political entrepreneur George Galloway: 'Unkind nature, which could have made a perfectly good butt out of his face, has spoiled the whole effect by taking an asshole and studding it with ill-brushed fangs.' The critic D.W. Harding wrote a famous essay called 'Regulated Hatred'. It was a study of Jane Austen. We grant that hatred is a stimulant; but it should not become an intoxicant.

The difficulty is seen at its starkest in Christopher's baffling weakness for puns. This doesn't much matter when the context is less than consequential (it merely grinds the reader to a temporary halt). But a pun can have no business in a serious proposition. Consider the following, from 2007: 'In the very recent past, we have seen the Church of Rome befouled by its complicity with the unpardonable sin of child rape, or, as it might be phrased in Latin form, "no child's behind left".' Thus the ending of the sentence visits a riotous indecorum on its beginning. The great grammarian and usage-watcher Henry Fowler attacked the 'assumption that puns are *per se* contemptible ... Puns are good, bad, or indifferent ...' Actually, Fowler is wrong. 'Puns are the lowest form of verbal facility,' Christopher elsewhere concedes. But puns are the result of an anti-facility: they offer disrespect to language, and all they manage to do is make *words* look stupid.

Now compare the above to the below – to the truly quotable Christopher. In his speech, it is the terse witticism that we remember; in his prose, what we thrill to is his magisterial expansiveness (the ideal anthology would run for several thousand pages, and would include whole chapters of his recent memoir, *Hitch-22*). The extracts that follow aren't jokes or jibes. They are more like crystallisations – insights that lead the reader to a recurring question: If this is so obviously true, and it is, why did we have to wait for Christopher to point it out to us?

- 'There is, especially in the American media, a deep belief that insincerity is better than no sincerity at all.'
- 'One reason to be a decided antiracist is the plain fact that "race" is a construct with no scientific validity. DNA can tell you who you are, but not what you are.'

- 'A melancholy lesson of advancing years is the realisation that you can't make old friends.'
- On gay marriage: 'This is an argument about the socialisation of homosexuality, not the homosexualisation of society. It demonstrates the spread of conservatism, not radicalism, among gays.'
- On Philip Larkin: 'The stubborn persistence of chauvinism in our life and letters is or ought to be the proper subject for critical study, not the occasion for displays of shock.'
- '[I]n America, your internationalism can and should be your patriotism.'
- 'It is only those who hope to *transform* human beings who end up by burning them, like the waste product of a failed experiment.'
- 'This has always been the central absurdity of "moral", as opposed to "political" censorship: If the stuff does indeed have a tendency to deprave and corrupt, why then the most depraved and corrupt person must be the censor who keeps a vigilant eye on it.'

And one could go on. Christopher's dictum – 'What can be asserted without evidence can be dismissed without evidence' – has already entered the language. And so, I predict, will this (coined too recently for inclusion here): 'A Holocaust denier is a Holocaust affirmer.' What justice, what finality. Like all Christopher's best things, it has the simultaneous force of a proof and a law.

*

'Is nothing sacred?' he asks. '*Of course not.*' And no Westerner, as Ronald Dworkin pointed out, 'has the right not to be offended'. We accept Christopher's errancies, his recklessnesses, because they are inseparable from his courage; and true valour, axiomatically, fails to recognise discretion. As the world knows, Christopher has recently made the passage from the land of the well to the land of the ill. One can say that he has done so without a visible flinch; and he has written about the process with unparalleled honesty and eloquence, and with the highest decorum. His many friends, and his innumerable admirers, have come to dread the tone of the 'living obituary'. But if the story has to end too early, then its coda will contain a triumph.

Christopher's personal devil is God, or rather organised religion, or rather the human 'desire to worship and obey'. He comprehensively understands that the desire to worship, and all the rest of it, is a direct reaction to the unmanageability of the idea of death. 'Religion', wrote Larkin:

> That vast moth-eaten musical brocade
> Created to pretend we never die ...

And there are other, unaffiliated intimations that the secular mind has now outgrown. 'Life is a great surprise,' observed Nabokov (b. 1899). 'I don't see why death should not be an even greater one.' Or Bellow (b. 1915), in the words of Artur Sammler:

> Is God only the gossip of the living? Then we watch these living speed like birds over the surface of a water, and one will dive or plunge but not come up again and never be seen any more ... But then we have no proof that there is no depth under the surface. We cannot even say that our knowledge of death is shallow. There is no knowledge.

Such thoughts still haunt us; but they no longer have the power to dilute the black ink of oblivion.

My dear Hitch: there has been much wild talk, among the believers, about your impending embrace of the sacred and the supernatural. This is of course insane. But I still hope to convert you, by sheer force of zealotry, to my own persuasion: agnosticism. In your seminal book, *God Is Not Great*, you put very little distance between the agnostic and the atheist; and what divides you and me (to quote Nabokov yet again) is a rut that any frog could straddle. 'The measure of an education,' you write elsewhere, 'is that you acquire some idea of the extent of your ignorance.' And that's all that 'agnosticism' really means: it is an acknowledgment of ignorance. Such a fractional shift (and I know you won't make it) would seem to me consonant with your character – with your acceptance of inconsistencies and contradictions, with your intellectual romanticism, and with your love of life, which I have come to regard as superior to my own.

The atheistic position merits an adjective that no one would dream of applying to you: it is lenten. And agnosticism, I respectfully suggest, is a slightly more logical and decorous response to our situation – to the indecipherable grandeur of what is now being (hesitantly) called the multiverse. The science of cosmology is an awesome construct, while remaining embarrassingly incomplete and approximate; and over the last thirty years it has garnered little but a series of humiliations. So when I hear a man declare himself an atheist, I sometimes think of the enterprising termite who, while continuing to go about his tasks, declares himself an individualist. It cannot be altogether frivolous or wishful to talk of a 'higher intelligence' – because the cosmos is itself a higher intelligence, in the simple sense that we do not and cannot understand it.

Anyway, we do know what is going to happen to you, and to everyone else who will ever live on this planet. Your corporeal existence, O Hitch, derives from the elements released by supernovae, by exploding stars. Stellar fire was your womb, and stellar fire will be your grave: a just course for one who has always blazed so very brightly. The parent star, that steady-state H-bomb we call the sun, will eventually turn from yellow dwarf to red giant, and will swell out to consume what is left of us, about six billion years from now.

Observer 2010

Twin Peaks – 3

Bellow: Avoiding the Void

The Life of Saul Bellow: To Fame and Fortune, 1915–1964
by Zachary Leader

When Saul Bellow emerged and solidified as an intellectual presence – in Chicago and New York during the 1940s – he seemed formidably, enviably, indeed inexcusably well equipped to flourish in the spheres of literature and love. 'Extremely handsome', according to one observer; 'stunning', 'beautiful', 'irresistible', according to others. After his first novel appeared, in 1944, Bellow got a call from MGM: although he was too soulful-looking for a male lead, they explained, he could prosper as the type 'who loses the girl to ... George Raft or Errol Flynn'. We may be sure that Bellow hardly listened. And it doesn't sound quite right for him, does it – aping a series of sexual inadequates (Ashley to Gable's Rhett?), in makeup and fancy dress, under the hot stare of the kliegs?

No, from the start Bellow radiated what Alfred Kazin called in his 1978 memoir, *New York Jew*, 'a sense of his destiny as a novelist that excited everyone around him'. Electrically sensitive to criticism, Bellow had a chip on his shoulder – but it was what one critic called 'the chip of self-confidence.' As Kazin wrote, 'He expected the world to come to him.' And it did. To quote from the opening sentence of Zachary Leader's magisterial biography, Bellow would go on to become 'the most decorated writer in American history'. He faced only one serious obstruction, and this vanished, as if at a snap of the fingers, on a certain day in 1949, when he was thirty-three and discovered 'what I had been born for'. As for women and love, on the other hand, he didn't get it right until 1986, when he was seventy-one.

To round out the panoply of the young Bellow's attractions, he had about him the glamour and gravitas of turbulent exoticism. When his family crossed the Atlantic from Russia (St Petersburg) to Canada (Lachine, then Montreal) in the early teens of the century, Saul was no more than a twinkle in his father's eye. Well, Abraham's eyes were capable of twinkling; far more typically, though, they blazed and seeped with frustration and rage. A versatile business flop, he struggled as a farmer, a wholesaler, a marriage broker, a junk dealer, and a bootlegger. 'His talent,' Saul would later write, 'was for failure.' Bellow Sr. eventually thrived (peddling fuel to bakeries), but he got angrier as he aged, and had fistfights in the street well into his sixties. The aggression was intelligible: Abraham knew what it was to wear the moral equivalent of the Star; Russian autocracy had condemned him to outlawry, imprisonment, ruin, and flight; later, too, he lost three sisters to the mechanised anti-Semitism of Nazi Germany.

In the end, Abraham was grateful to America (and even came to enjoy the novelty of paying his taxes), yet his assimilation was always fragmentary. 'Wright me,' he wrote to Saul, late in life: 'A Ledder. Still I am The Head of all of U.' And his wife, vague, frail, dreamy Liza, a figure of quiet pathos, simply didn't live long enough to adapt. As Leader records (and this is a typically luminous detail):

> A great treat for Liza was a movie matinée on the weekend. Bellow sometimes accompanied her and remembered a low rumbling in the theatre, that of dozens of child translators, himself included, whispering in Yiddish to their mothers.

Home life, then, was archaic, violent, loudmouthed and 'wholly Jewish'. A mixed blessing, you might say, but that's the kind of blessing that all writers hold most dear.

At the start of 1924, Abraham made his way to Chicago, and six months later the rest of the family was 'smuggled across the border by bootlegging associates', arriving on the Fourth of July in the capital of American 'hard-boileddom' (Bellow's epithet). And of all the 'reality instructors' who lined up to shape Saul's sensibility, the most dominant was that exemplary Chicagoan, Maury, the oldest of the brothers. Maury bestrides Bellow's fiction, making no fewer than five undisguised appearances.* 'You don't understand fuck-all,' Maury characteristically informs his bookish kid brother. 'You never will.' Originally a Mob bagman (and a skimmer), Maury married money and set about amassing a fortune in that hyperac-

---

* As Simon (*The Adventures of Augie March*), Shura (*Herzog*), Philip ('Him with His Foot in His Mouth'), Julius (*Humboldt's Gift*), and Albert ('Something to Remember Me By').

tively venal fringe between business and politics (one of the guests at his daughter's wedding was Jimmy Hoffa). As he saw it, all other concerns were mere snags in the engine of materialism.

'Enough of this old crap about being Jewish,' Maury used to say. In *Herzog* (1964), when the hero weeps at his father's funeral, the senior brother, Shura, snarls at him, 'Don't carry on like a goddamn immigrant.' Brazen American plenitude was what Maury championed and embodied – with his 'suburban dukedom', his 100 pairs of shoes and 300 suits. When Bellow won the Nobel, in 1976, Maury was at first affronted ('*I'm* really the smart one' was his attitude), then indifferent, despite a brief interest in the prize money – Was it tax-free? Could Saul stow it offshore? Yet Maury, a secret reader, harboured depth and convolution, and Bellow always believed that there was something tragic, something blind, headlong, and oblivion-seeking, in his drivenness. It was the revenge life takes on the man who knowingly chooses lucre over love.

*

And what about Bellow and love – the many affairs, the many marriages? Before we turn to them, we have to acknowledge a unique peculiarity of Bellow's art. When we say that this or that character is 'based on' or 'inspired by' this or that real-life original, we indulge in evasion. The characters are their originals, as we see from the family *froideurs*, the threatened lawsuits, the scandalised friends, and the embittered ex-wives. Leader deals with this crux immediately, in his introduction, and partly endorses the verdict of James Wood (one of Bellow's most sensitive critics), which invokes 'an awkward but undeniable utilitarianism ... The number of people hurt by Bellow is probably no more than can be counted on two hands, yet he has delighted and consoled and altered the lives of thousands of readers.' Bellow himself conceded that the question was 'diabolically complex'. But who in the end would wish things otherwise? That the characters come alive, or remain alive, on the page is not the result of artistic control so much as the sheer visionary affect of the prose. Bellow is sui generis and Promethean, a thief of the gods' fire: he is something like a supercharged plagiarist of Creation.

In his dealings with women he could be glacially passive, and he could be excitedly precipitate. 'Somewhere in every intellectual,' the brutal lawyer, Sandor, tells Herzog, 'is a dumb prick.' Bellow would have wholeheartedly agreed.

He got engaged to his first wife, Anita, in 1937; he was twenty-one. And the only surprise is that the relationship took so long to wind down – after fifteen years, twenty-two changes of address, and number-less infidelities. 'I have no intention,' he then wrote to his agent in 1955, 'of bouncing from divorce into marriage'. But that of course was exactly what he did, homing in, despite a fusillade of warning shots, on the naïve and volatile Sasha. Early on, a female friend noted that Bellow 'was the kind of man who thought he could change women ... And he couldn't. I mean, who can? You don't.' This is well said. But one surmises that the answer, if there is one, had more to do with literature than with life.

Happiness, noted Montherlant, writes white; it is invisible on the page. And the same is true of goodness. Anita was upstanding and altru-istic, and is therefore a pallid presence in the novels; Sasha, by contrast, would be mythologised, demonised, and immortalised in *Herzog* as the terrifying emasculatrix, Mady. The terms of divorce No. 2 were settled in 1961, and within a month he was married to the equally glossy and unpromising Susan. It seems that his creative unconscious was attracted to difficulty – to make his fiction write black. This time he did at least manage an interlude of what Leader calls 'strenuous womanising': he returned from a tour of Europe 'trailed by letters not only from Helen, Annie, Jara, and Alina' but also from Maryi, Hannah, Daniela, Maude, and Iline. As the first volume of *The Life* closes, Bellow is halfway through his matrimonial career; we know that there are two more divorces to go (Susan, Alexandra) before all is solved and salved with Janis, his true Platonic other. Hope triumphed over disappointment, and innocence triumphed over experience.

Something similar unfolded in the fiction. Again and again in his *Letters* (assembled in 2010), Bellow describes himself as a 'comic' novelist, and this feels just. But there was little sign of such a cheerful self-assessment, and such an outcome, in his 'prentice works' of the 1940s, *Dangling Man* and *The Victim*, which epitomise the sullen, cussed earnestness of the midcentury mood. His life-changing moment came with the con-ceptual birth of *The Adventures of Augie March* (1953) and took place, fit-tingly, in Paris – the world HQ of cerebral gloom. Bellow was in despair about his third novel, and with good reason: it was about two invalids in a hospital room. As he paced the streets one day Bellow watched the gutters being sluiced in 'sunny iridescence'. And it was a comprehensive epiphany: that was that. Marx, Trotsky, Sartre, *ennui, cafard, nausée,* alienation, existential woe, the Void, et cetera: all this he cancelled and cursed. From here on he would commit himself to the free-flowing, and to the childhood perceptions of his 'first heart' and his 'original eyes'. In short, he would trust his soul. And now the path was clear to the exuberantly meshuga glories of *Augie March, Henderson, Herzog,* and all the rest.

★

I knew Saul Bellow for two decades; I have known Professor Leader for three, and he is the author of a much-praised biography of my father, Kingsley Amis. So I may be disinterested, but I am not impartial. All the same, it is certain that I will not be alone in the expectation that *The Life of Saul Bellow* will prove definitive. Leader is respectful but unintimidated, balanced but never anodyne, and his literary criticism, like his prose, is unfailingly stylish and acute. The book is very learned and very long – the author happens to be a putter-in, not a leaver-out. But readers who enter into it will find a multitude of various fascinations: the gangland machine of Chicago, for instance; the tremors and prepercussions of the sexual revolution; Bellow's Romantic lineage (the affinities with Blake and Wordsworth); and the currents and commotions of the American cultural terrain, with its factions and rivalries, its questing energies, its stormy loyalties, and its stormier hatreds.

The really fit biography should duplicate and dramatise a process familiar to us all. You lose, let us say, a parent or a beloved mentor. Once the primary reactions, both universal and personal, begin to fade, you no longer see the reduced and simplified figure, compromised by time – and in Bellow's case encrusted with secondhand 'narratives', platitudes, and approximations. You begin to see the whole being, in all its freshness and quiddity. That is what happens here.

Right up to his death, in 1955, Abraham Bellow described Saul as a chronic worry to the family, the only son 'not working only writing'. Not working? He should tell that to Augie March (for Augie, it turns out, is the author of his *Adventures*):

All the while you thought you were going around idle terribly hard work was taking place. Hard, hard work, excavation and digging, mining, moling through tunnels, heaving, pushing, moving rock, working, working, working, working, working, panting, hauling, hoisting. And none of this work is seen from the outside. It's internally done. It happens because you are powerless and unable to get anywhere, to obtain justice or have requital, and therefore in yourself you labor, you wage and combat, settle scores, remember insults, fight, reply, deny, blab, denounce, triumph, outwit, overcome, vindicate, cry, persist, absolve, die and rise again. All by yourself! Where is everybody? Inside your breast and skin, the entire cast.

Vanity Fair 2015

Véra and Vladimir

Letters to Véra by Vladimir Nabokov

My sun, my soul, my song, my bird, my sweetheart, my pink sky, my sunny rainbow, my little music, my inexpressible delight, my softness, my tenderness, my lightness, my dear life, my dear eyes...

These endearments and salutations (backed up by a crowded menagerie of surrogates: Goosikins, Poochums, Tigercubkin, Puppykin) suggest a sky-filling adoration and, more than that, a helpless dependency. As early as Vladimir Nabokov's second letter to Véra Slonim, after a couple of months of chaste acquaintanceship, he lays it all before her:

> I cannot write a word without hearing how you will pronounce it
> – and can't recall a single trifle I've lived through without regret – so
> sharp! – that we haven't lived through it together ...You came into
> my life ... as one comes to a kingdom where all the rivers have been
> waiting for your reflection, all the roads, for your steps.

And so it goes on for over half a century, his ardour – at first sometimes skittishly insecure – gradually modulating into assurance and serenity. Warning: there is one seismic aberration (Paris, 1937), to which we will uneasily return.

Vladimir (rhymes with 'redeemer', he has said) was born in 1899, Véra in 1902. They met at a charity ball in Berlin in 1923, an occasion organised by the Russian émigré community – 400,000 strong, and notable for its cohesion, its material penury, and its intellectual wealth. Although very different in their origins (he was patrician-artistic, she professional middle-class and Jewish), they were fair representatives of their high-minded and unworldly colony. That party was a masquerade; and, throughout, Véra's mask stayed up.

He immediately had to go off to work on a farm in the South of France. As a devotee of his published verse (much of it confessional), she would have known that he had recently and tormentedly broken up with a girl he hoped to marry. Showing unusual forwardness, she wrote to him until he replied. 'I won't hide it,' begins his opening letter, where she is already ensconced as 'my strange joy, my tender night'. Once he was back in Berlin the romance proceeded, on his part at least, without a trace of inhibition. They were married in the spring of 1925.

One of Nabokov's most striking peculiarities was his near-pathological good cheer – he himself found it 'indecent'. Young writers tend to cherish their sensitivity, and thus their alienation, but the only source of angst Nabokov admitted to was 'the impossibility of assimilating, swallowing, all the beauty in the world'. Having a husband who was always so brimmingly full of fun might have involved a certain strain; still, the fact that Véra was not similarly blessed is just a reminder of the planetary norm. Indeed, their first long separation came in the spring and summer of 1926, when she decamped to a series of sanitariums in the Schwarzwald in the far southwest, suffering from weight loss, anxiety, and depression.

Véra was gone for seven weeks, and Vladimir wrote to her every day. Spanning more than a hundred pages, the interlude is one of the summits in the mountain range of this book. He endeavoured not only to raise her spirits (with puzzles, riddles, crosswords, which she almost invariably solved) but also to *love* her back to health – with punctual transfusions of his buoyant worship. Here one finds oneself submitting to the weird compulsion of the quotidian, because he tells her everything: about his writing, his tutoring, his tennis, his regular romps and swims in the Grunewald (for her the Black Forest, for him the Green); he tells her what he is reading, what he is eating (all his meals are itemised), what he is dreaming, even what he is wearing. Also, very casually, almost disdainfully (as befits the teenage millionaire he once was), he keeps noticing that they don't seem to have any money.

There was never any money, despite their frugality and thrift; they had to watch the pfennigs, then the centimes, then the nickels and dimes, all the way up to *Lolita* in the late 1950s – more than thirty years into their marriage. His first three novels, *Mary* (1926), *King, Queen, Knave* (1928) and *The Defence* (1929), were obvious masterpieces; he talked and read to ecstatic audiences in Berlin, Prague, Brussels, Paris, and London; everyone could tell he was a genius of outlandish size (Ivan Bunin, the first Russian Nobelist for literature, said soberly, 'This kid has snatched a

gun and done away with the whole older generation, myself included').
But there was never any money.

Their only child, Dmitri, arrived in 1934, and was rapturously received
(away from him Vladimir misses 'the circuits of a current of happiness
when he throws his arm across my shoulder'). It was no doubt a sense of
sharpened responsibility that got Nabokov out of the house and on the
road, in earnest. He trolled around Europe, juggling contacts and contracts,
writing reviews, reports, translations (some of them grimly technical) into
and out of Russian, English, and French. As late as the spring of 1939 he
was in London, lobbying and angling for an academic post in Leeds – or
possibly Sheffield. Nabokov in Yorkshire? This was among the multitude
of human possibilities wiped out by the Second World War.

Nabokov's father, Vladimir Sr., was a distinguished liberal statesman
(described with memorable bitterness in Trotsky's *History of the Russian
Revolution*); and he was semi-accidentally murdered by fascist thugs in
Berlin in 1922. For all this, you get the sense that his son regarded
political reality as a vulgar distraction, a series of what he called 'bloated
topicalities'. In Berlin the family sat through the passage of the Nuremberg
Laws in 1935 (unmentioned here). Véra and Vladimir had independently
fled the Bolsheviks; by 1936 he felt, with long-sublimated dread, that
Nazi Germany was no place for his Jewish wife and their 'half-breed'
child. To prepare for their escape to France, Nabokov journeyed to Paris
in early 1937 – and this is when it happened, the lapse, the shocking
solecism, or what Humbert described as the 'lethal delectation'. She was
an experienced handful named Irina Yurievna Guadanini.

The Vladimir-Irina entanglement has been public knowledge since
1986, and Stacy Schiff has a perceptive section on it in her biography
Véra (1999). But it is freshly and piercingly painful to follow the story
from the point of view, so to speak, of Nabokov's pen. That was a dreadful brew he cooked up for himself on the avenue de Versailles: mortal
fear for wife and son, a recklessly indiscreet affair, and a hideous attack
of psoriasis which, in coarse symbolism, bloodied his bed linen and his
underwear. And there is the great man, the great soul, queasily teasing
('Don't you dare be jealous'), sneering at all the 'vile rumors', and, in
general, mellifluously lying his head off. The old law has never struck me
with such power: people are original and distinctive in their virtues; in
their vices they are compromised, hackneyed, and stale. Here, there is a
vertiginous swerve in the direction of the ordinary.

And it didn't end there. In July, in Cannes, he confessed to Véra – confessed to what he felt was an authentic *amour fou* (mitigating the offence for us, perhaps, if not for her). Rather coolly, it seems, Véra told him to decide, to choose. Irina herself palely appeared at the seashore; but Vladimir had chosen, and it was over. 'You know, I have never *trusted* anyone as I trust you,' he had written to Véra in 1924: 'In everything enchanted there's an element of trust.' His confession and the Irina aftermath take place offstage. But in those Paris letters the corrosive side effects of the deception are everywhere apparent. Her sudden vague indecisiveness (about joining him); his querulous exasperation; a deficit in trust, and a deficit in enchantment.

The Nabokovs appeared to get over it more quickly than this reader expects to do. *Letters to Véra*, arranged and annotated with terrifying assiduity by Brian Boyd (the world's premier Nabokovian), is unavoidably bottom-heavy: 439 pages covering 1923–39; then, after a gap, a mere eighty pages (many of them airy) covering 1941–76. For the book to resemble a full record of their lives, the couple would have had to spend every other week apart. And they were now more or less inseparable. When he did travel without her, the daily rhythm of his correspondence immediately reasserts itself, and there is enough time and space for us to see that cloudless intimacy settle on them once again.

It is the prose itself that provides the permanent affirmation. The unresting responsiveness; the exquisite evocations of animals and of children (wholly unsinister, though the prototype of *Lolita*, *The Enchanter*, dates from 1939); the way that everyone he comes across is minutely individualised (a butler, a bureaucrat, a conductor on the Metro); the detailed visualisations of soirées and street scenes; the raw-nerved susceptibility to weather (he is the supreme poet of the skyscape); and underlying it all the lavishness, the freely offered gift, of his sublime energy.

New York Times Book Review 2015

Politics – 3

Politics – 3

On Jeremy Corbyn, Leader of Her Majesty's Opposition

When I was a ten-year-old resident of Princeton, New Jersey, I used to crouch by the radio on Saturday mornings to hear the children's songs, and I was always anxiously hoping for 'Carbon the Copy Cat.' You can find an intriguing rendition of 'Carbon' on YouTube by Tex Ritter, a vocalist who could impart a touch of gravitas and woe to the simplest chant or lullaby. The version I thrilled to, in 1959, was much smoother and jollier; whereas Tex was a Texan, the 'cover' was the work of an unnamed midwesterner, who pronounced Carbon 'Carbin' ('Wimbledin,' 'commitmint,' 'pregnint'). Is it any wonder, then, that I have been going around the place this summer singing 'Corbyn the Copy Cat'?

The comparison is far from airtight, I admit, but the example of the Copy Cat still has much to teach us. In the song, Carbon is a bloody fool of a feline who wants to join, or at least to imitate, animals from other species.

> Like a sheep he tried to baa (baa, baa)
> Like a bird he tried to chirp (chirp, chirp)
> Like a dog he tried to bark (bark, bark).
> He tried and tried the best he knew how.
> It always came out meow, meow, meow.

Jeremy Corbyn learnt to say meow early on in life (coached, at several removes, by a certain German economist); and it has never even occurred to him to try saying anything else.

We are exact contemporaries (born 1949, along with NATO); and for the lion's share of my twenties I found myself close to the epicentre of the Corbyn milieu. For I was on the staff of the *New*

Statesman – attending party conferences, drinking with parliamentary correspondents, and playing regular games of cricket and football against *Tribune* and other loose confederations of the left. There were Identikit Corbyns everywhere – right down to the ginger beard, the plump fountain pen in the top pocket, and the visible undervest, slightly discoloured in the family wash.

Weedy, nervy, and thrifty (you often saw a little folded purse full of humid small change), with an awkward-squad look about them (as if nursing a well-informed grievance), the Corbyns were in fact honest and good-hearted. Politically, they were the salt of the earth – 'those to whom,' at some stage and on some level, 'the miseries of the world / Are misery, and will not let them rest' (John Keats). What the exponents of the old left were like humanly depended – with mathematical precision – on how doctrinaire they were. You sought the company of Alan Watkins and Mary Holland, among many others; you avoided the company of Corin Redgrave and Kika Markham (as well as the more driven Corbyns).

All this was during the later 1970s – the apogee and swansong of the old left. Harold Wilson's short third term after the interregnum of Ted Heath; James Callaghan (1976–1979), and work-to-rule, the miners' strike (Arthur Scargill), the three-day week, plus a class war whose tremors you felt a dozen times a day; then came Margaret Thatcher (1979–1990). Everyone was old left. It was generally felt at the *Statesman* that the proletariat deserved to win, this time: now there would at last be moral redress.

My closest office colleagues were old left too, with variations. I agreed with James Fenton, pretty much, when he calmly stated: 'I want a government that is weak against the trade unions.' Julian Barnes clashed with a certain *Statesman* hard-liner when he revealed that he had once voted Liberal. That hard-liner was Christopher Hitchens. Throughout his polemical career Christopher maintained his peculiar blend of irony and granite. When he came up to the books and arts department, there would always be an exchange of taunts and teases. 'You want rule by yobs,' I used to tell him: 'Not just rule in their interests and in their name – but rule *by* yobs.' 'That's it,' he'd answer, with his equivocating smile: 'I live for the day when the berks are finally in the saddle.'

It is one of the most saliently endearing facts about Christopher – that he never, ever, stopped loving Trotsky. Everyone else was old left, too, though by then largely shorn of utopian romance. And everyone who looked in on the weekly editorial meetings, who dropped by with pieces entitled 'An End to Growth' and 'Whither the Closed Shop?,' was Jeremy Corbyn. Or were they? Corbyn himself wouldn't have joined us, as all the others did, in the pub or in the Bung Hole wine bar (he's tee-total), nor in the Italian café where we all lunched on the full English breakfast (he's vegetarian). Then, too, the bods who came to Great Turnstile were, once you got to know them, congenial types who, in addition, could put an argument together on paper, often with some panache. And Jeremy? After thirty-odd years as a safe-seat backbencher (Islington North), Corbyn is the fluky beneficiary of a drastic elevation. So it is time to take a serious look at his flaws.

★

First, he is undereducated. Which is one way of putting it. His schooling dried up when he was eighteen, at which point he had two E-grade A-levels to his name; he started a course at North London Polytechnic, true, where he immersed himself in trade-union studies, but dropped out after a year. And that was that. Corbyn says he enjoys 'reading and writing' (listing them, I thought, as if they were hobbies, like potholing and trainspotting); to my eyes, he doesn't have the eager aura of an autodidact. It is a fair guess that his briefcase, or his satchel, contains nothing but manifestos and position papers. In general, his intellectual CV gives an impression of slow-minded rigidity; and he seems essentially incurious about anything beyond his immediate sphere.

Second, he is humourless. Many journalists have remarked on this, usually in a tone of wry indulgence. In fact it is an extremely grave accusation, imputing as it does a want of elementary nous. To put it crassly, the humourless man is a joke – and a joke he will never get. When he was collared by a TV team and asked to say something about Tony Blair's wearily witty attacks on him, Corbyn straightened up and said he would respond only to 'substantive' questions. In his face there was not the slightest glint of amusement or defiance or spirit. And Blair's criticisms contained plenty that was 'substantive,' including the charge that everything Corbyn says, without exception, is pallidly thirdhand – his championship, for instance, of Clause 4 (on public ownership), which was first formulated in 1918. 'I don't do personal,' Corbyn has explained, shoring up one's surmise that he is 'modern' only in the up-to-date vulgarity of his syntax. When he found himself arguing for a United Kingdom where every house has a garden, Corbyn elaborated as follows: 'Anyone who wants to be a beekeeper should be a beekeeper.' Nobody with a sense of humour could possibly have said that.

Third, he has no grasp of the national character – an abysmal deficit for any politician, let alone a torchbearer. The idea of dismantling Trident looks set to gain a clear plurality on practical grounds; but his proposal to leave NATO ('a Cold War organisation'), and so paralyse the special relationship, causes only exasperated tedium in London and suspicious dismay in Washington. As for his proposal to scrap the army, last articulated in 2012: this would be a veritable spear through the British soul. It shows an indifference to both the past and the future. Philip Larkin spoke for the country, as he often did (it is both a strength and a weakness), in 'Homage to a Government' (1969):

> Next year we shall be living in a country
> That brought its soldiers home for lack of money.
> The statues will be standing in the same
> Tree-muffled squares, and look nearly the same.
> Our children will not know it's a different country.

The national character contains nationalism, naturally; and the British temper is above all gradualist. Enormous powers of suasion are needed to induce an electorate to waive what it values most, which is continuity.

Turning to Corbyn's foreign policies – well, here I'll deal only with the thing they call IT (international terrorism). When at last he managed to make himself clear about what he hoped would happen in the Middle East, Corbyn's vaunted 'friendship' with Hamas and Hezbollah became roughly intelligible. Far more damningly and tellingly, he often implied that July 7, 2005, was an act of revenge, a calibrated tit for tat, for the invasion of Iraq. We see here the dismally reflexive mental habit of seeking moral 'equivalence' at every opportunity; thus the glitteringly murderous theists of ISIS are indistinguishable from the coalition troops in Fallujah. And heed his Churchillian call for 'political compromise' with Abu Bakr al-Baghdadi and his genocidaires in Raqqa and Mosul.

★

Lavishly equipped with the demerits – the encysted dogmas – of the old left, Corbyn nonetheless gawkily embodies one of its noblest themes: the search for something a little bit better than what exists today: more equal, more gentle, more just.

If, as every commentator seems to agree, the current Corbyn is obviously unelectable, then in what direction will he be obliged to move? The recruitment of Seumas Milne (a far-left intellectual) as media manager changes nothing, though it does defer the prospect of a slicked-up, business-friendly Corbyn with a new suit and a new smile. That was always close to inconceivable. It is far easier to imagine a Labour party that devolves for now into a leftist equivalent of the American GOP: hopelessly retrograde, self-absorbed, self-pitying, and self-righteous, quite unembarrassed by its (years-long) tantrum, necessarily and increasingly hostile to democracy, and in any sane view undeserving of a single vote. Under him, the Labour Party is no longer Her Majesty's Opposition. There is no opposition; Labour is out of the game.

For all his charming insecurities, Carbon the Copy Cat boldly roamed the rural farmsteads, and showed an ardent interest in the exotic, the other – the mooing cows, the clucking hens, the quacking ducks. In contrast to the coal-black Carbon, Corbyn is a marmalade cat, homebound, perched like a tea cosy on the kitchen radiator, and contentedly wedded to the things he already knows.

The Sunday Times 2015

Postscript, August 2017. The penultimate paragraph above is something like a festival of false prophecies (these days Corbyn is even wearing a suit and tie). In the June 2017 general election, Corbyn successfully enlisted the angry millennials, who were in effect disinherited by their Brexiteer parents and grandparents; he also mobilised the nation's hatred of the politics of austerity. The result was the biggest lurch to Labour since Churchill vs. Attlee in 1945; and the opposition is now back in the game. Nevertheless, Corbyn's limitations persist: he has to some extent de-Marxified himself, but he is still intellectually narrow, still humourless, and still largely insensitive to the native character (and still tainted by anti-Semitism and softness on Islamism). In any case, can one ever fully forgive his weak-voiced torpor during the Brexit referendum (when he took a holiday in mid-campaign)? . . . An exponent of realpolitik, a cynical genius with a De Gaullean sense of historical pacing, might have played lukewarm on Europe in order to garner 'buyer's remorse' for the next electoral round. Partly to his credit, though, Corbyn is straighter than that; Europe is gone now anyway, and the pendulum of power seems to owe us a swing to the left.

President Trump Orates in Ohio[*]

In considering Donald Trump we should heed the Barry Manilow Law, as promulgated in the 1970s by Clive James. The law runs as follows: everyone you know thinks Barry Manilow is absolutely terrible, but everyone you don't know thinks he's great.

Trusting in the (alleged) wisdom of crowds, and hoping for an agreeable surprise, I traveled to Youngstown, Ohio, in midsummer – not to attend a Barry Manilow concert but to take my place at a rally held, or thrown (no entrance fee), by President Trump. The Covelli Centre had attained its full capacity: 7,900. And there I stood, surrounded by everyone I didn't know.

And there stood Donald Trump, fifty yards away, clapping his hands as he greeted the audience, and running through his repertoire of false smiles. False smiles are the only kind of smiles at his command, because whatever 'sense of humour' he might once have laid claim to has long since evaporated, together with its fraternal twin – balance of mind.

There are only three false smiles: the golf-pro smirk, revealing the golf-champ teeth; the one where he bites down on his sucked-in lower lip (this isn't a smile so much as an imitation of a regular guy); and, arguably the most dreadful of all, the flat sneer of Ozymandian hauteur

[*] This piece wasn't published until November 2017. As usual, under Trump, there were hourly bombshells to stay abreast of, most notably Trump's shameful response to the violence in Charlottesville; on that occasion he declined to condemn the murderous alt-right. Rather, Trump saw moral equivalence between the neo-Nazis and the ... who? The neo–Khmer Rouge? The version printed here dates from the second week in August, just before the exit of Steve Bannon.

that widens out almost from ear to ear, like a comic mask. The eyes, meanwhile, remain utterly unamused.

Yes, and Eric and Lara were there, and Rick Perry was there, and Anthony Scaramucci was there (judging by his outward form, the Mooch could be on the books of the same high-end gigolo agency that employs Don Jr.), and Melania was there. Trump's wife, Melania Knauss: *my* wife, a keen observer of body language, says there's no doubt at all that Melania hates Donald's guts. So maybe POTUS brings FLOTUS along to get a kiss and a hug and a feel of her hand, which, by now, is probably the extent of his wants. Some people (including me) believe that Trump's libido has been ridiculously overblown (not least by the germophobe himself, as self-publicist and locker-room braggart). All we know more or less for sure is that he has done it five times.

Even at $12,000 per suit or whatever it is, the tailor's art can do very little with the stubborn slab of DJT. Still, despite his mirthless beams and grins, he is clearly very happy at the Covelli Centre. Here he will get no 'mixed reviews,' as he does in the swamp and in the fake-news media. By watching Trump rallies on TV, the crowd has mastered a quartet of trisyllabic chants, which are BUILD THAT WALL, LOCK HER UP, and U-S-A; the fourth is WE LOVE TRUMP, as in WE LOVE TRUMP, WE LOVE TRUMP, WE LOVE TRUMP ...

His *strongly approve* numbers have recently plunged, from around 30 percent to around 20 percent. But they have risen again, thanks to his slanging match with Kim Jong-un. Trump's 'base' is said to be hovering at around 35 percent. So in Youngstown, let us say, we were seeing how the other third lives – and how it loves.

I'll return to the Covelli Centre. But first some more general observations.

★

Hillary Clinton has talked for years of 'a vast right-wing conspiracy.' This is a contradiction in terms – though not quite as absurd as Trump's reference to 'a global conspiracy' behind the Paris Accord (where the puppeteers were intent on swindling the United States). A 'conspiracy' is by definition 'secret.' Therefore any talk of a conspiracy that involves more than a handful of actors – or a single dedicated cadre – should be dismissed out of hand. This makes extra-obvious nonsense of the idea of a self-inflicted September 11, with its controlled-demolition crews and Tomahawk-missile operatives, among hundreds of others. Beyond a certain point, human nature being what it is, a secret will be a secret no longer.

The vast right-wing conspiracy does not exist. What does exist, as Joshua Green vigourously demonstrates in *Devil's Bargain: Steve Bannon, Donald Trump, and the Storming of the Presidency*, is a broadly dispersed and uncoordinated effort aimed without precision at an unevenly shared goal: defeating the globalist and multiculturalist Hillary Clinton and then (much, much later) promoting the nationalist and white-supremacist Donald Trump. The dramatis personae range from peddlers of anti-Hillary knickknacks (Clinton nutcrackers, bumper stickers saying LIFE'S A BITCH. DON'T VOTE FOR ONE) to a galère of ultra-rich and ultra-perverse donors (some of whom are also ultra-talented), backed up by a cast of clever quacks and charlatans – most notably Steve Bannon.

Take Robert Mercer. A self-made billionaire who collects machine guns and loves fancy dress, Mercer was gullible enough to promote the congressional candidacy of a certain Arthur Robinson, an Oregon 'research chemist' who, in his quest for the key to longevity, amassed 'thousands upon thousands of urine samples,' writes Green, 'which he froze in vials and stored in massive refrigerators.' Robinson lost, narrowly. After Trump's election, Mercer's middle daughter, the very committed Rebekah, pushed to have Robinson appointed as 'national science adviser.' That campaign failed too – and by a landslide, one would like to hope.

Gullible Mercer may be, but he was also sufficiently brilliant to revolutionise computer translation. In the early-middle 1990s this field was in the hands of linguists and grammarians. Mercer and his IBM colleague Peter Brown took an entirely different tack, 'relying on a tool called an "expectation maximisation logarithm"– a tool code breakers would use to find patterns.' The lexicographer scientists scoffed at Mercer's efforts, but 'statistical machine translation' worked – and for every language known to man. It is the basis of Google Translate.

Reading *Devil's Bargain*, you nurse the following suspicion: for every Bill and Melinda Gates there are, in the stratosphere of the 1 percent, a Robert and Rebekah Mercer, looking for trouble and looking for someone like Trump. None of this would've mattered much in the days before that judicial masterpiece, *Citizens United v. Federal Election Commission* (2010). Citizens United is a fringe Republican group of Clinton haters; its president is David Bossie, another busybody and nutter who was taken up by Bannon – and then by Trump, just as he began his 'birther' rampage.

We now go forward to mid-August 2016, with the election twelve weeks away. At this point Clinton's lead was close to double figures, and Trump was in the middle of what Douglas Brinkley memorably called his 'sick meltdown.' So Rebekah Mercer flew by helicopter to the East Hampton estate of Woody Johnson (owner of the New York Jets) for a face-to-face with the Republican nominee. Here is Joshua Green's version of what happened next:

> Her own family was into Trump for $3.4 million, more if you counted ancillary support such as *Breitbart*. The RNC, she told him, was days away from cutting him loose and turning its focus to saving the Republican majorities in the House and Senate.
>
> 'It's bad,' Trump admitted.
>
> 'No, it's not bad – it's over,' she shot back. 'Unless you make a change.'
>
> . . . Mercer told Trump that he needed to get rid of Paul Manafort, whose ill-conceived attempt to moderate him into someone acceptable to swing voters had plainly failed. Furthermore, Manafort's ties to pro-Kremlin autocrats was hurting Trump's campaign.
>
> 'Bring in Steve Bannon and Kellyanne Conway,' Mercer told him. 'I've talked to them; they'll do it.'

★

Bannon and Conway did it, and Trump did it, the American electorate did it, and the rest, embarrassingly, is history. Journalists are a rough-and-ready crowd; but how are *historians* going to address this tale? *Only an extraordinary concatenation of events*, they will no doubt begin, *could result in the ascendance of a figure so manifestly* . . . We blush for historians, we blush for history, and we blush for Clio, its muse. Discounting, for now, the unmeasurable contribution of James Comey, the man responsible for America's disgrace and disaster is Stephen Kevin Bannon.

If Christopher Hitchens were alive today, he would be the leading voice of the Resistance (along with Bernie Sanders). And I don't think Christopher, in this role, would waste much ammuniton on the barn door of Donald Trump; he would go straight for Bannon, who really is, or was, the 'great manipulator' showcased by *Time*. After a 'kaleidoscopic career' – naval officer, Goldman Sachs trader, earth-science researcher, Hollywood producer, online-gaming mogul, editor of *Breitbart News* – Bannon looked for a political instrument to help reify his 'vision.' At first he was drawn to Sarah Palin (which to some extent gives you the measure of the man); then he saw Trump.

Green characterises Bannon as 'a Falstaff in flipflops,' which is physically vivid but in all other respects inapt (in the bluster-and-cowardice department, you could as well call Trump a Falstaff in Brioni threads). Bannon is a recognizable type: the high-IQ cretin, or the Mensa moron. He is very smart and very energetic; what he lacks is even a trace of *moral* intelligence. And Falstaff had plenty of that: see his great satire on martial 'honour' ('He who died o' Wednesday. Doth he feel it?'). Although I'm familiar with the Bannon genus, I must admit that his brand of hip, gonzo nihilism strikes me as something quite new. 'When she comes into your life,' he said in unalloyed praise of Julia Hahn (one of his underling 'Valkyries'), 'shit gets fucked up.'

Despite his studied profanities, Bannon is intellectually pretentious, even grandiose. His supposedly all-consuming autodidacticism hasn't brought him close to full literacy ('Every morning President Trump tells Reince and I to . . .'); he is also a cerebral flibbertigibbet – Zen Buddhism, the writings of the French occultist René Guénon and the Italian racial theorist Julius Evola (the latter a Mussolini ally whose ideas gained currency in Nazi Germany). Similarly, his 'systematic study of the world's religions' hasn't shifted him from the Tridentine Catholicism of his origins.

The 'Tridentine' tag refers to the Latin Eucharistic liturgy used by popery from 1570 to 1964. Both dates are central to the Bannon calendar: the 1960s was when secular liberalism got out of hand (with its promiscuous dope-fueled iconoclasm); correspondingly, Bannon swooned over the policies mooted by Marion Maréchal-Le Pen (niece of Marine), saying that her programme was 'practically French medieval,' and adding, 'She's the future of France.' The Middle Ages lie ahead of us: that's Bannon. Also featured in this mess are the familiar platitudes about the "clash of civilizations" with Islam. It is not a clash of civilizations; it is a clash of one civilization against a mélange of religious gangsters (very many of them converts). Since September 11, murders committed by white-supremacist vigilantes have more or less kept pace with murders committed by Islamists (the figures are 106 and 119).

Clearly, Bannon is potentially a very dangerous figure: Trump's Cheney. This would be the surest way to marginalise the threat: put his face on every available magazine cover, and Trump would soon show him the door. But that, we now know, won't be necessary. Bannon skilfully maneuvered his vaudevillian dunce into the White House; lacking moral imagination, he didn't see, or didn't care, that as soon as he gained power Trump would be instantly corrupted and deranged by it, declaring himself to be 'my own strategist' (on top of being 'the greatest person in the world'), and would stop listening to anybody at all. Everywhere you look, now, Trump is being called 'stupid,' 'idiotic,' 'unhinged,' and 'crazy,' and Paul Krugman is not the only one plainly suggesting that Trump is in the early stages of senile dementia. Imagine his *second term* . . .

Let's be clear. The GOP's psychotic break began on election night in 2008 (and the Tea Party coalesced immediately after Obama's inauguration). *Horribile dictu*, but about one in three Americans cannot bear to see a black man in the White House. The hysterical blond who occupies it now is the direct consequence of that atavism. As for his tenure, this has always been the question, from day one: when would enough Republicans start putting *patrie* before party? As Steve Bannon might put it, 'How much shit can they eat?'

★

That night in Youngstown, early on, the president rhetorically asked, 'Is there anywhere more fun, more exciting, and *safer* than a Trump rally?' One of the three propositions was true – an astonishing veracity rate for Donald J ('Donald J,' incidentally, was an earlier trisyllabic chant, and one that handily rhymed with 'U-S-A'). I found this Trump rally inexpressibly tedious; it stimulated nothing but a leaden incredulity; but it *was* perfectly safe. There weren't any people dressed as storm troopers or Imperial Wizards. And during the warm-up, as the Pledge of Allegiance was solemnly intoned and everyone in the stadium got to their feet (most though not all placing a hand on the heart), I remained seated, up in the stands, and continued to write away in a highly suspicious Moleskine notebook. Nobody gave me a first glance, let alone a second.

During Trump's speech there were a few small-scale protests (inarticulate bawling) and the dissidents were quietly led to the exit. Trump has by no means lost his taste for vicarious violence (see his recent incitement to police brutality), but he greeted the ejections with a mild non-drollery and even made a mention of the First Amendment: there was no hot talk of stretchers and bloody noses. The other significant change in his MO concerns the beautiful wall on the southern border. Usually, when the chants of BUILD THAT WALL have at last died down, he asks, 'And who's going to pay for it?' while theatrically cocking an ear. Well, he doesn't anymore. Because the rejoinder, now, would not be the triumphalist 'MEXICO!' or '*THEY* ARE!' but the rather more muted 'AMERICA' or 'WE ARE' (and estimates go as high as $25 billion). Otherwise, Donald was a good boy, and never strayed from his teleprompter – neglecting to say, for example, that he was going to fire Jeff Sessions and replace him with someone who would fire Robert Mueller.

There were the standard untruths (Americans are among the most highly taxed people on earth) and some grotesque distortions (if insurance premiums in Alaska have risen 200 percent under the 'nightmare of Obamacare,' why did its senator cast one of the deciding votes against repeal?). Apart from that, though, if you tuned out the content, you would have to say that he seemed occasionally and fleetingly near-presidential. But what's a president doing at a rally after barely seven months in the White House?

He comes to these things, they say, for the validation. And he gets it. Validation, and a loyalty that is as wholly impervious to reality as the NRA. About a third of the billion or so guns on the planet (including all the armies') are in America: so that's about one each. Gun deaths average 93 per day. I reckon the trigger-and-bullet community would live with 930; but not with 9,300, which would slash the United States census by 25 percent in a single generation.

To lose his base, Trump would need to preside over something almost as cataclysmic. Turning the office held by George Washington, Abraham Lincoln, FDR, and LBJ into a morbidly obese cash cow hasn't done it. A financial crash (unlikely) could be scapegoated and wouldn't do it; a fresh sex scandal (barely conceivable) wouldn't do it. If the chemistry between the 'fat kid that's running North Korea' (in the words of John McCain) and the fat crock that's running America results in the vaporisation of, say, Los Angeles, and if this is followed by an arsenal-clearing response (with all its sequelae): *that* would do it. Trump is clearly praying for an excuse to wipe North Korea off the map, thereby winning the plaudits of a grateful planet. I hope he's listening when someone tells him the truth – that the United States would be a pariah for the rest of the century.

Trump's 35 percent is otherwise pretty sound. George W. Bush's base, as he told fellow diners at some million-dollar-a-plate fundraiser, consisted of the super-rich. What does Trump's base consist of?

*

Intel engineers did a rough calculation of what would happen had a 1971 Volkswagen Beetle improved at the same rate as microchips. . . . These are the numbers. Today, that Beetle would be able to go about three hundred thousand miles per hour. It would get two million miles per gallon of gas, and it would cost four cents. . . .

Thomas L. Friedman, *Thank You for Being Late*

The world is accelerating, and the Trump loyalists are idling in neutral, and in constant danger of slipping into reverse gear. Why and how does Trump give them hope? He gives them hope because – sotto voce – he is saying:

Elite media types tell you you're stupid and don't know anything. Well, look at me. I'm stupid too and I don't know anything either. I think Frederick Douglass [1817–1895] is still alive – and doing a great job, by the way. I think my hero and presidential model Andrew Jackson [1767–1845] was 'really angry' about the Civil War [1861–1865]. People don't realize, you know, the Civil War, if you think about it, why? My advisers tell me it was to do with slavery. Why could that one not have been worked out? You know what I say? 'Live and let live.' I came up with that phrase a couple of days ago. I thought it was good.

A guy who works for me, Steve Bannon, once said, 'You're a student of military history,' and when he came to mention it, I realized it was true.

Take Napoleon. Now you know Napoleon finished a little bit bad [he lost at least half a million troops in 1812]. *And his one problem was he didn't go to Russia that night − because he was screwing some broad in the City of Lights − and they froze to death* [Napoleon was in Russia for six months. Unencumbered by his army, he needed thirteen days to race back to Paris from Minsk]. *Maybe I should've said that Napoleon needed to start out for Russia that night. Because there was no Air France in those days. And he didn't have his own jet with* NAPOLEON *painted on it.*

The so-called media says you have no ideas. Like the Democrats. Now I'm a big military person [though a scrupulous noncombatant: what they call a chicken hawk], *and I've come up with two ideas that no one's ever thought of before. Number one, we should've taken the oil in Iraq, as a return on our investment. You just siphon it off through a tube, like stealing gasoline, but on a larger scale. Number two, we keep telling everybody what we're about to do, like with ISIS. So you lose the element of surprise! Why can't these huge modern armies just sneak up on the enemy? My two new ideas have gotten nowhere. Zero. And why? Bureaucracy, that's why. Well, all that stops right now, folks. And you'll finally get the leadership you deserve.*

The citified smart-asses say you live in a bubble. What's wrong with that? Bubbles are great. Me, I'm so out of it that I only see the little folder they hand me every morning, mostly stuff from Breitbart *and the* Drudge Report. *As far as I'm concerned my speech to the Boy Scouts met with universal acclaim. There was no 'mixed,' okay?*

To tell you the truth, I'm the least racist person there's ever been in the history of the world, and I say that with great surety. I just don't like Muslims, and I don't like Mexicans coming here and taking our jobs and living off our welfare. Plus I support − I spearhead − voter suppression. Look at that new committee I've formed about 'electoral integrity.' And you can't really do something like that without believing, deep down, as you do, my friends, that 'people of colour,' as the PC pointy-heads call them, shouldn't vote. Or shouldn't vote so often and in such huge numbers.

Steve Bannon said I was the greatest American orator since Brian William Jennings, whoever the hell he may be. But Steve was joking, right? This evening I talked on autocue, but anyone who's read my interviews knows fully well I can hardly brawl my way out of a five-word sentence. I'm like you. And we're the really smart ones.

All this. But yet I'm up there with the .01 percent. And you aren't − or not yet! It's true that I'm no longer the leader of the Free World. I unloaded that one on Angela Merkel, and I wish her lots of luck with it. But I'm still President of the United States of America. I'm the multibillionaire Commander in Chief. Okay?

So draw your own conclusions. . . I don't know why I even bother to say that. Because you already have.

★

When the young Bismarck left St. Petersburg after his four-year stint at the Prussian Embassy, he had the following verdict engraved on a ring: *La Russie, c'est le néant.* Sterile, sclerotic, and fatally introverted, the Tsarist autocracy was 'nothingness,' a vacuum, a void. Donald Trump is *le néant.* There's nothing there. No shame, no honour, no conscience, no knowledge, no curiosity, no decorum, no imagination, no wit, no grip, and no nous. Into this spotlessly empty vessel, certain Americans contrive to pour their anger, their resentments, their ambitions, and their hopes. How is it done?

★

The Trump transfusion, the way the utterly callous plutocrat gives heart to the stranded proletariat, was on lavish display in Youngstown. And it is a hauntingly desperate spectacle.

Some sensitive souls – Nabokov was among them – are repelled by circuses and zoos and other settings where animals are 'trained' by humans. What they find unwatchable is the insult visited on animal dignity. The audience in Youngstown was human, but the humans had surrendered their individuality to the crowd. So it is hard to say what kind of animal they had reduced themselves to. A millipedal hydra, perhaps – and the size of a leviathan. And at the direction of its tamer, this colossal beast performed its party tricks, its chants, its boos and hisses, its cheers and whoops; and for this it will be given no sugar lump.

The boos are elicited by references to Democrats, gun control, Obamacare, immigration ('We want them the hell out of our country! . . . We're sending them the hell back where they came from!'), and anything at all to do with political correctness; the whoops are elicited by references to law enforcement, the armed forces, the Second

358

Amendment, jobs, putting America first, defending our borders, family, fidelity, and faith in God.

★

The *Financial Times* columnist Janan Ganesh recently observed that impulsive, burn-your-boats populism is turning out to be a purely Anglo-American phenomenon (now watched with pity by the other developed nations). Plebiscitary frivolousness, Ganesh argued, is the result not of hardship but of relative ease – and decades of internal stability. France and Germany (though not Italy: think of Berlusconi) have been successfully inoculated by the experience of deep historical tragedy, and deep guilt (the Third Reich, Vichy), which still presides over their living memory. What 'nightmare,' apart from Obamacare, was the American working class struggling to awake from? Flat wages, a feeling of national ostracism, the dominance of elite expertise, and the shackles of political correctness.

No one ever *claims* to be politically correct, but every day we are being reminded how much we owe to that modest and no longer particularly erratic or repressive ideology. Its civilising effects have strengthened evolutionary progress, much to the benefit of women, minorities, and society as a whole, very much including heterosexual whites. In other words, the status quo wasn't the terminal carnage pictured by the yahoo with the microphone. The electorate nonetheless wanted change, and at any price. 'Donald Trump may give us nuclear war,' said a supporter, early on. 'But anything's better than Hillary.'

★

President Trump is not quite *le néant*. He is, for one thing, a truly gigantic category mistake – a category mistake made by the American people. When he said in mid-campaign that he could shoot somebody on Fifth Avenue without losing any votes, Trump subliminally blundered on a central truth. Because the electorate wasn't fully persuaded that he was 'real': he was real only in the sense that reality TV was real. Well, Trump is real now all right, and his sick meltdown is happening in the Oval Office.

Last November Steve Bannon somehow induced a plurality of citizens to vote in direct defiance of their own interests (as did Nigel Farage in the UK). It may be invidious to single out a particular constituency, but how can one avoid focusing on the huge 'minority' whose interests are already in shreds?

There were plenty of women in the Covelli Centre (some of them sitting under placards that read WOMEN FOR TRUMP); there were a few black and brown faces; there was even a black grandmother. Now that *Roe v. Wade* itself is under threat (from Justice Neil Gorsuch), and now that the attacks on Planned Parenthood, plus the notorious 'gag order,' are destroying female lives all over the world, I would like to address these closing words to the 53 percent of white women who, on November 8, 2016, voted not for a proactive feminist but for a relentlessly coarse and compulsive gynophobe. By making a considerable effort (all right, you're autonomous citizens and don't want your vote merely to reflect your gender), I can roughly understand how you felt then. But how do you feel now? And one additional question, which all freshly horrified Trumpists might care to answer: what on earth did you expect?

Esquire 2017

Index

All works are the author's unless otherwise stated.